a reader's guide to *William Faulkner*

Other Reader's Guides to Literature

a reader's guide to

William Faulkner

THE NOVELS

Edmond L. Volpe

SYRACUSE UNIVERSITY PRESS

First Syracuse University Press Edition 2003
03 04 05 06 07 08   6 5 4 3 2 1

Originally published in 1964 by Farrar, Straus and Giroux as *A Reader's Guide to William Faulkner*. Reprinted by arrangement with the author. Further copyright acknowledgement is made on page ix, which constitutes an extension of this copyright page.

The paper used in this publication meets the minimum requirements of American National Standard for Information Sciences—Permanence of Paper for Printed Library Materials, ANSI Z39.48–1984.∞™

Library of Congress Cataloging-in-Publication Data

Volpe, Edmond Loris.
   A reader's guide to William Faulkner : the novels / Edmond L. Volpe. — 1st Syracuse University Press ed.
     p. cm.
   Originally published: New York : Farrar, Straus, 1964.
   Includes bibliographical references (p.) and index.
   ISBN 0-8156-3001-8 (pbk. : alk. paper)
   1. Faulkner, William, 1897–1962—Criticism and interpretation— Handbooks, manuals, etc. 2. Faulkner, William, 1897–1962—Examinations— Study guides. I. Title.
PS3511.A86 Z983 2003
813'.52—dc21   2002032756

» » To my mother and to my wife

Contents

» » **PART III**: *Appendix, Notes and Bibliography*

Acknowledgments

Quotations from William Faulkner's *Soldiers' Pay* copyright © renewed 1954 and *Mosquitoes* copyright © renewed 1954 by William Faulkner are reprinted by permission of Liveright, Publishers, N.Y.; and by permission of Chatto & Windus Ltd., London. Quotations from William Faulkner's *Sartoris* copyright 1929, copyright © renewed 1956; *The Sound and the Fury* copyright 1929, copyright © renewed 1956; *As I Lay Dying* copyright 1930, copyright © renewed 1957; *Sanctuary* copyright 1931, copyright © renewed 1958; *Light in August* copyright 1932, copyright © renewed 1959; *Pylon* copyright 1935, copyright © renewed 1962; *The Unvanquished* copyright 1938; *The Wild Palms* copyright 1939; *The Hamlet* copyright 1940; *Go Down, Moses and Other Stories* copyright 1942; *Intruder in the Dust* copyright 1948; *Requiem for a Nun* copyright 1951; *A Fable* copyright 1954; *The Town* copyright © 1957; *The Mansion* copyright © 1959; *The Reivers* copyright © 1962 by William Faulkner and *Absalom, Absalom!* copyright 1936, copyright © renewed 1964 by Estelle Faulkner and Jill Faulkner Summers are reprinted by permission of Random House, Inc., N.Y., and by permission of Chatto & Windus Ltd. The map is from *The Portable Faulkner*, edited by Malcolm Cowley, copyright 1946 by the Viking Press, Inc. and reprinted by permission of the publisher.

Preface

For the many readers who have been simultaneously fascinated and baffled by William Faulkner's novels, a Guide needs no justification. Faulkner is a difficult artist, and a cooperative reading of his works can enhance the pleasure his art affords and deepen appreciation of it. My aim has been to provide a guideline through the complexities of technique and style to reveal the greatness of Faulkner's art and the scope and profundity of his personal vision of life.

The Guide is divided into three sections. In the Introduction, I have attempted—with full awareness of the perils of generalizing —to describe the dominant patterns in the fiction, by isolating Faulkner's major themes and by analyzing his narrative techniques and style. The second section offers individual interpretations of the nineteen novels, tracing the development of Faulkner's ideas. The Appendix contains detailed chronologies for difficult novels like *The Sound and the Fury*.

To readers unaccustomed to literary discussions, the analyses of the novels in Part II may seem more authoritative in tone and definitive than they are meant to be or could possibly be. In writing this book, I tried to address myself to the general reader as well as the scholar, and therefore I avoided critical arguments and references in the text. These, and the conflicting views of other critics, I relegated to chapter notes. Unfortunately, my manuscript was excessively long, and when faced with the choice of cutting notes or text, I sacrificed most of the notes.

To keep the work down to reasonable length, I also had to abandon my plan to treat the short stories. This omission, however, I do not consider too serious a loss to the Guide. As great as some of the short stories are, they do not appreciably add to our knowledge of Faulkner's techniques and ideas. To make the Guide as serviceable as possible, I have quoted from the most readily available editions of the novels.

Besides my indebtedness to many critics of Faulkner, I should like to acknowledge the assistance of my friends and colleagues—Arthur Zeiger, Leo Hamalian, Arthur Waldhorn, Frederick Karl, Theodore Gross, David Rudolph, Richard Goldstone, and Louis S. Pryor—who read and criticized various chapters of the manuscript. I am grateful for the confidence and patience of Cecil Hemley; and to the City College Research Fund I am indebted for grants which enabled me to visit Oxford, Mississippi and to devote a summer to completing the book. My wife Rose has provided continual encouragement besides practical and critical assistance, and my young daughters Rosalind and Lisa deserve recognition here, for adapting so cooperatively to a closed study door.

Edmond L. Volpe
The City College of the
City University of New York

List of genealogical tables

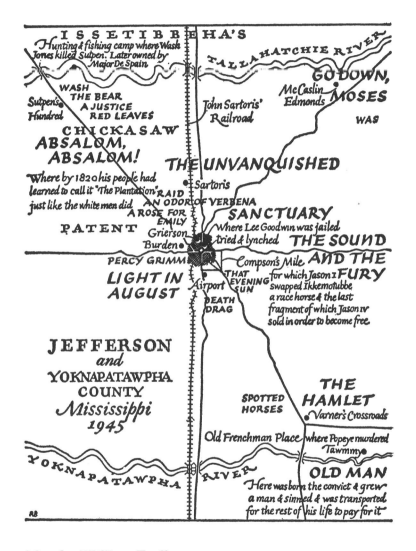

Map by William Faulkner

Introduction

1 / *Life and career*

Before 1950, William Faulkner wore the mantle of fame like Huck Finn a Fauntleroy suit. He granted few interviews and remained aloof from the literary world, living a life of relative seclusion in the small town of Oxford, Mississippi. Why Faulkner pursued fame and then rejected its honors is not clear—along with many other aspects of his personality and career—and will not be, until a definitive biography of this enigmatic man is written.

Many who knew him have described him as a shy man; others say that he was arrogant. He has been pictured as the prototype of the soft-spoken Southern gentleman, gentle, kind, and courteous. But he has also been reported as cold, a master of the withering rebuff. He frequently refused interviews with the comment that his private life was his own, and shied away from public appearances. He threw the producers of *Intruder in the Dust* into a panic when he decided not to attend the première of the movie, which was being held in Oxford. The film had been made in the town; the writer had cooperated with the director and the producers, but no one could persuade him to attend the opening. On the evening of the première, however, Faulkner was at the theater. Someone had thought to appeal to a matriarch of the family, an aunt in Memphis, who told her nephew that she wanted to attend and expected him to escort her.[1]

A similar panic was produced among his friends and relatives, it is said, when he decided not to travel to Sweden to receive the Nobel prize in 1950. He finally changed his mind because he wanted his daughter to see Paris. In the final year of his life, the author refused President Kennedy's invitation to a dinner at the White House for Nobel Prize winners. Faulkner was living in

FALKNER GENEALOGY

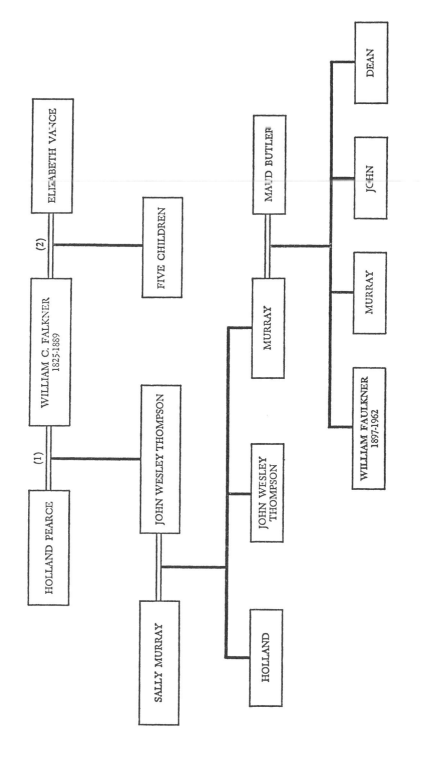

Virginia at the time, and the story is told that he declared a hundred miles too far to go for a meal.

Whether Faulkner was an arrogant man, or an individualist who preferred to do only what he wanted, or a shy man who was uncomfortable in the spotlight, or an artist who did not want his books to be effaced by his personal image as a man, or a combination of many things, it is at this point difficult to say. Perhaps he enjoyed the legends that his insistence upon privacy fostered. Certainly he did little to correct the many erroneous stories about his career that were printed. For many years, for instance, he was repeatedly said to have been wounded in action as a pilot during World War I. Actually, he joined the Royal Flying Corps because he was too short to qualify for the American and completed his flight training in Canada just as the war ended. He never went overseas, but he did sustain a minor leg injury. On Armistice day, so the story goes, he and a friend celebrated liquidly and were flying so high they crashed a training plane.

Many stories about him, some obviously true, concern his drinking. In 1955 he traveled to Japan as a cultural ambassador for the State Department and submitted to numerous interviews. In one he was asked if drinking were one of his hobbies. He replied, "I consider drinking a normal instinct, not a hobby. A normal and healthy instinct." [2] He is reputed to have arrived in Japan with his own cache of bourbon.

Faulkner's drinking habits and his desire for privacy indicate that there is much about the man that the limited biographical data available does not illuminate. Perhaps the personality of the artist should be an irrelevant factor in an interpretation of his works. My study of Faulkner's fiction, however, has convinced me that his work reflects not only his ancestry, experiences, and native region, but also his personal spiritual crises and struggles. To date, criticism necessarily has emphasized the historical, social, and moral aspects of the work, but when future biographers and scholars get the chance to interpret the life and the character of the man, many current interpretations may come to seem superficial. For one thing, we shall discover, I think, that his adolescence was the most troubled period of a spiritually and psychologically turbulent life. When we have that kind of biographical information, we shall be able to solve many of the puzzles of his fiction and see more clearly the overall pattern of his work. At the present time, what information is available does reveal how considerably Faulkner drew upon his own experiences for his fiction.

Perhaps the single most important fact about Faulkner is that he was born and bred in the South and lived there almost all his life. When he turned, in his third novel, *Sartoris*, to his proper subject—himself—he began that exploration of the Southern consciousness which produced the unique texture of his work. The novelist was three generations removed from the Falkner* who originally settled in Mississippi. The character and career of this great-grandfather and the novelist's birth three generations later in the twentieth century leave a strong imprint on the fiction.

This great-grandfather, Colonel William Cuthbert Falkner, pioneer, lawyer, soldier, railroad builder, politician, best-selling writer, was the kind of dynamic personality about whom legends develop. Soon after his birth in 1825 in Knox County, Tennessee, his family settled in Missouri. In 1839, at the age of fourteen, he went to join an uncle in Ripley, a north Mississippi town, making the trip alone and on foot. When he arrived, Falkner learned that his uncle, John Wesley Thompson, was in jail, in another county, charged with murder. At the jail in Pontotoc, William found his uncle studying law and preparing to serve as his own counsel. This trial was only the first of several murder trials that Falkner was to be personally involved in during his life. Thompson won acquittal, and returning to Ripley, put his nephew in school and began to practice law.

During his spare time, Falkner worked in the local jail. Within a few years, a sensational murder gave him the opportunity to display those qualities of courage, daring, enterprise, and intelligence that would make him one of the most important men in the region. An entire family was murdered by a man named McCannon. A posse captured him and a mob gathered to lynch the murderer. The nineteen-year-old Falkner helped save McCannon from the mob, and to show his gratitude, the murderer told Falkner the story of his life. Falkner quickly wrote and published the story as

* The novelist added the "u."

a booklet, and on the day of McCannon's execution sold several thousand copies, netting more than a thousand dollars.

During the Mexican War, Falkner joined a contingent of volunteers from Tippah County and was elected a first lieutenant. The war was over before the group arrived, but it did service as occupation troops. After this adventure, Falkner studied law with his uncle. In 1847, he married Holland Pearce, who bore him one son before her death. Two years after his marriage, Falkner became involved in a feud that cost two men their lives. One day, his friend Robert Hindman drew a pistol and fired it point-blank at Falkner's chest. Three times the pistol misfired before Falkner stabbed Hindman to death. Arrested and charged with murder, he pleaded self-defense and won an acquittal. He swore that he did not know what prompted his friend to assault him. One theory has it that Hindman wanted to join a club of which Falkner was a member. Though Falkner spoke in favor of his admission, someone reported to Hindman that Falkner had opposed his candidacy. At the trial, Hindman's brother spoke for the prosecution, and when Falkner left the courtroom, Thomas Hindman and several friends attacked him. In the fighting, Falkner killed a Hindman supporter. Once again he was arrested and charged with murder, again winning an acquittal. The feud did not end until Hindman finally left Ripley. During this period, Holland Pearce died, and Falkner married Elizabeth Vance, who bore him five children.

When Mississippi seceded from the Union, Falkner recruited a regiment and was elected its colonel. A small man (as his great-grandson was also), he was arrogant and irascible. After alienating enough men in his regiment to effect the election of another leader and his demotion to lieutenant-colonel, he left the outfit and returned to Ripley to recruit another.

At the end of the war, Falkner set about building a railroad from Ripley to Tennessee. A local banker, Richard J. Thurmond, was his partner in this venture. For nearly ten years the two men worked together; then they quarrelled and Falkner bought out his partner. During the twenty-five years that he lived after the war, the Colonel practiced law, bought a large plantation, and wrote several books, one of which, *The White Rose of Memphis,* became a national best-seller. In 1889 Colonel Falkner ran for the Mississippi legislature. His opponent in the contest was his former partner, Richard Thurmond. Falkner was elected but never held office. He was shot and killed by Thurmond. The Jackson, Mississippi *Clarion-Ledger* of November 14, 1889 described the event:

DEATH OF COL. W. C. FALKNER

A terrible tragedy was enacted at Ripley on Tuesday afternoon of last week—the widely and well-known Col. W. C. Falkner being the victim. Various and conflicting accounts have been published. A dispatch of the *Appeal* says:

At the time of the occurrence Col. Falkner was standing on the public square in Ripley, talking to his friend Thomas Rucker, about sawing some timber. Mr. J. H. Thurmond approached Falkner and without exchanging a word pulled a pistol and pointed it at Col. Falkner who exclaimed, "What do you mean, Dick? Don't shoot!" but Thurmond fired and Falkner fell.

After Dr. Carter, his son-in-law, wiped the blood from his face while he was still sitting on the pavement, he (Falkner) turned to Thurmond, who was near him, and said: "Dick, what did you do it for?" J. L. Walker, Elisha Bryant, Tom Rucker and John Smith were all present and saw what occurred. Mr. Rucker was so close to Col. Falkner that his face was powder burned by Thurmond's pistol. Col. Falkner had no weapon on his person, not even a pocket knife. The ball, .44-calibre, entered the mouth, ranged from the tongue, breaking the jaw bone, and lodged in the right side of the neck under the ear. Col. Falkner died at 11 o'clock.[3]

Thurmond was tried for murder and acquitted. Right after the trial he left the state and settled in North Carolina.

William Faulkner is descended from Colonel Falkner through John Wesley Thompson Falkner, the Colonel's first son and only child by Holland Pearce. John Wesley Thompson inherited his father's title and was known as the Young Colonel. He extended the railroad his father had built, became an Assistant U. S. Attorney, and president of the First National Bank of Oxford, the town in which he settled with his wife, Sally Murray. The couple had three children: a daughter named Holland, and two sons, John Wesley Thompson II, and Murray.

This youngest son, Murray, the father of the novelist, married an Oxford girl, Maud Butler, and set up housekeeping in New Albany, a town about thirty-five miles from Oxford. There, William, their first son, was born on September 25, 1897. Five years later, Murray and Maud Falkner moved to Oxford, settling in a house on South Lamar Street, not far from the house of the Young Colonel. The couple had three more children, all boys. Murray Falkner moved from job to job and ran a livery stable and then a hardware store before becoming business manager of the University of Mississippi in 1918.

Few details concerning Faulkner's early years are available. Apparently always indifferent to formal education, he read only what interested him. During his adolescent years he began to write poetry. At seventeen, he met Phil Stone, who, four years his senior, had degrees from Mississippi and Yale and was preparing to take law degrees at both universities. Stone had a passion for literature and became Faulkner's friend and literary mentor. A perceptive and honest critic, as his preface to Faulkner's first book of poetry indicates, he read the young poet's work and discussed it with him. By lending him books, he introduced Faulkner to the great poets and novelists.

When Faulkner returned to Oxford after the armistice in 1918, he joined his family in its new quarters on the campus of the University of Mississippi. He began to write for the school paper and magazines and enrolled as a special student. In 1919, *The New Republic* printed his poem, "L'Apres-Midi d'un Faune," and Faulkner began to play the role of literary eccentric. He became a topic of conversation among the townspeople and the student body by wandering aimlessly about the town, or staring at the courthouse and the statute of the Confederate soldier, or squatting to read near the magazine rack of Mack Reed's drugstore. For a time, he sported natty clothes and a walking stick. Such attire plus his refusal to settle down to a steady job earned him the title of "Count Nocount."

During 1920, he spent about six months in New York. Stark Young, the Mississippian who was becoming known in literary circles, put him up and arranged with Elizabeth Prall, the manager of Lord and Taylor's book department, to get him a job as a clerk in her department. Faulkner had probably gone to New York to establish himself in the art world, but when Phil Stone wrote that the postmastership at the University was available, he returned to Oxford. He became postmaster and in December of 1921 took the examination for a permanent postmastership. A little less than three years later, he resigned. As postmaster he was no great success. He apparently spent much of his time reading and writing, and complaints from students and faculty were frequent.

In December of 1924, Faulkner's first book, *The Marble Faun*, a collection of poems, was presented to the public. The book had few buyers and created no stir in the literary world. These poems, like most of Faulkner's poetry, deserved the cool response they received. They display a verbal facility and the penchant for sensuous imagery that distinguished Faulkner's later work, but they are derivative and amateurish. Stone suggested that Faulkner might achieve recognition via Europe as had Frost and Pound and Eliot. The friends traveled to New Orleans early in 1925 to find Faulkner a berth on a Europe-bound freighter. No openings were available and Stone returned to Oxford. Faulkner remained in New Orleans for six months, living in the Vieux Carré, the French Quarter frequented by artists and Bohemians. His short stay in New York now bore fruit. Elizabeth Prall had married Sherwood Anderson, and Faulkner met the author of *Winesburg, Ohio*. The two men liked each other and spent many hours together walking about the city and talking. Faulkner's short stay in New Orleans was a climactic period in his career. The city had become an artistic center, and through Anderson, Faulkner gained entry to the artist group. He met the editors of *The Double Dealer* who were encouraging young writers, and he contributed sixteen sketches and stories to the Sunday feature section of the *Times-Picayune*. He also met the artist William Spratling with whom he collaborated on a book, *Sherwood Anderson and Other Creoles* (1926).

During his few months in New Orleans, Faulkner began to write novels. He has said that knowing Anderson inspired him to become a novelist. The writer's routine of working mornings and spending the rest of the day with friends appealed to the twenty-seven-year-old literary aspirant. He spent his mornings writing, and within a short time had completed *Soldiers' Pay*.[4] It is said that Anderson came to Faulkner's room to find out why his friend had not been around the Quarter. When he discovered that a novel was keeping him occupied, he promised to recommend it to his publisher if he did not have to read it. Not long after completing *Soldiers' Pay*, Faulkner began work on *Mosquitoes*, in which he utilized some of the characters he came across during his sojourn in New Orleans.

The delayed trip to Europe finally came off in July of 1925. Faulkner landed in Genoa, roamed over northern Italy, and then went to Paris, where he settled for a while in the Latin Quarter near the Luxembourg gardens. By the end of December he was back in Oxford and he spent the following year working at various jobs in New Orleans.

In 1926, *Soldiers' Pay* was published. It received good notices but sold few copies. His book with Spratling, for which he wrote sketches of Vieux Carré inhabitants, cost him his friendship with Anderson. He parodied Anderson's style—far more gently than did Hemingway in *The Torrents of Spring*—and the older writer was offended. By the time *Mosquitoes* was published in 1927, Faulkner was back in Oxford. His second novel, too, was fairly well reviewed but sold few copies.

The year 1929 was important in the writer's life and career. Both *Sartoris* and *The Sound and the Fury* were published, and Faulkner married Estelle Oldham, whom he had known as a child. Though he had four books on the market and a fifth, *As I Lay Dying*, was to be published the following year, Faulkner was earning little money. Then his sixth, *Sanctuary*, published first in 1931 and reprinted in a Modern Library edition in 1932, was a financial success. The many stories rejected by editors and filed away by Phil Stone in his law cabinets were now sent back to the same magazines with a high price pencilled on the first page of the manuscript. Hollywood, too, sought his services, and money began to flow in. Faulkner's first major purchase was an old mansion, one of the finest in Oxford. It required many repairs and he went to Hollywood to work on the first of a number of scripts he was to do over the years whenever he needed money.

Though *Sanctuary* made him a national figure, it shocked his Oxford neighbors. And during the next thirty years of his life, most of whch he passed in the small town, he spent his leisure hours with only a few close friends and hunting companions. During the 1930's he indulged his passion for flying by buying an airplane, but he gave up flying when his youngest brother, Dean, was killed in a plane Faulkner had bought him. During these years, Faulkner also bought a farm some distance from town, which his brother John managed before he, too, began to write novels. On this farm lived Uncle Ned, the old Negro who had been with the Faulkner family for many years. In quarters behind the Oxford mansion lived another old Negro, Faulkner's childhood nurse, Aunt Caroline Barr, to whom he dedicated *Go Down, Moses.*

The Faulkners lost their first child soon after its birth; their second child, also a girl, they named Jill. The writer lived a quiet but productive life during the next decade, interrupting his writing schedule to join his hunting companions on trips into the woods. Aside from these expeditions, which were very important to him, as his fiction clearly shows, and an occasional trip to New York or Hollywood, he spent enough time at his desk to publish before the end of 1942, seven novels, two collections of short stories, and a book of poems.

Though two of the novels of this period, *Light in August* and *Absalom, Absalom!*, surely rank among the greatest novels in contemporary literature, by 1946 when Malcolm Cowley edited a Faulkner Viking Portable, most of Faulkner's books were out of print. Since 1946, Faulkner's reputation has soared nationally and internationally. In 1950, he was awarded the Nobel Prize for Literature.

There are few biographical details about these later and more public years that have any apparent bearing on Faulkner's fiction. During the decade of the 1950's, Faulkner began to spend more and more time away from Oxford. His daughter married and went to live in Charlottesville, the seat of the University of Virginia. Invited by the University to be writer in residence during the 1957-58 academic year, Faulkner settled in the town and was reported in 1959 to have purchased a house there. In his sessions with the students, he talked freely, though not always helpfully, about his work and ideas. His public appearances and public utterances became more frequent, and after the Supreme Court decision requiring

Integration of the schools, he became a spokesman for the South.

During the final few months of his life, he spoke in New York before the American Academy of Arts and Letters, and visited West Point, where he addressed the cadets and read from his final novel, *The Reivers*, which became, within a few days of publication, a national best-seller. He returned to Oxford in June, 1962. On the morning of July 6, the world learned that the writer was dead of a heart attack.

Droves of reporters descended upon the quiet small town, but there was little news to report. Only members of the family and a few close friends were invited to the private funeral services. As the small funeral cortege passed through the square that Faulkner memorialized, the townspeople paid their last respects to Oxford's world-renowned writer. William Faulkner's grave is not in the Falkner family plot. A hill separates the old section of the Oxford cemetery from the new, and at the base of the hill about a hundred feet from the road Faulkner lies beneath the Southern soil that he loved.

2/ *Character types and themes*

From 1926 to 1962, Faulkner published nineteen novels and more than seventy-five short stories. The setting of a majority of the stories and of all the novels, except *A Fable* and parts of *The Wild Palms*, is the American South. Fifteen novels and many of the stories are about people from a small region in northern Mississippi —Yoknapatawpha County, "William Faulkner, Sole Owner & Proprietor."

Early in his career, Faulkner began to write about a group of families living in or near a town he called Jefferson. His mythical town and county did not evolve gradually in his imagination and his fiction. He discovered it fully peopled and with a full array of family ghosts that kept him busy recording for several decades. Over the years he filled in details about the county, consciously working for continuity and unity in its history.

That history begins about 1800. The area from which the county will be formed belongs to a tribe of Chickasaw Indians led by Issetibbeha. The next chief is his son Moketubbe whose reign is short. Moketubbe's cousin, Ikkemotubbe, goes to New Orleans with the captain of a trading steamer. There, a Frenchman, the Chevalier Sœur Blonde de Vitry, introduces the Indian to the gamblers on the New Orleans river front as Du Homme, the Man. Ikkemotubbe likes the title, corrupted significantly to "Doom," and in 1808 he returns to his people and sets about getting the position to fit the title. He brings with him a potent white powder which, when administered to Moketubbe and his son, makes Doom the chief.

About this time, three white men settle in the area. A Frenchman, Louis Grenier, establishes a plantation on the banks of the Yoknapatawpha River.* To the northeast, near the Chickasaw village, Dr. Samuel Habersham, his eight-year-old son, and Alexander Holston settle. Holston serves as federal agent of the Chickasaw Agency before he opens an inn. Dr. Habersham's son grows up among the Indians and marries a granddaughter of Issetibbeha. When he is twenty-five he moves to Oklahoma with the dispossessed tribe. The Chickasaw matriarch, Mohataha, had made her cross on a document ceding to the United States the domain of her son Doom.

The descendants of these original settlers play no significant role in the development and future of the community. The real pioneers come into the area a short time later. By 1833, when Thomas Sutpen arrives, one of the earliest pioneers, Lucius Quintus Carothers McCaslin, has established a plantation and sired a legitimate white line of descent and an illegitimate mulatto line. In a horse race, Jason Lycurgus Compson has won from the Indians the square mile of land that will become the center of Jefferson. De-

---

* The name of Faulkner's county, according to Ward Miner, "is from two Chickasaw words—*Yocana* and *petopha*—meaning 'split land.'" *The World of William Faulkner* (New York, 1952), p. 69.

Spain and Stevens soon settle in the area, and John Sartoris arrives in 1837.

Named for a federal mail rider, the town of Jefferson grows rapidly in the next two decades. The pioneers are vigorous, ambitious men, and by the fateful year of 1861 they have created out of
the wilderness a thriving community that, in its social structure, is
a rough imitation of the plantation society of the Southeastern
states from which the pioneers emigrated. Jefferson is far west of
the main battle lines during the Civil War, but it is occupied and
its public buildings are burned.

Yoknapatawpha County covers an area of 2,400 square acres and
contains, according to Faulkner's count, 6,298 whites and 9,313
Negroes. Of these 15,000 inhabitants, Faulkner identifies by name
about six hundred. Approximately half of the identified inhabitants are white residents of Jefferson and the surrounding plantations; about a hundred are Negroes; and the rest are country people, most of whose farms are located around the hamlet called
Frenchman's Bend. The majority of Faulkner's important white
characters are members of a few country or pioneering families.
The names of the rural families are Ratliff, Varner, Snopes, Mc-
Callum, Bookwright, Armstid, Bundren, Quick, and Tull. Five
pioneers, Sartoris, Compson, Sutpen, McCaslin, and Stevens, sire
the elite families in the county. The important Negroes in the fiction, too, are members of a few families that serve the elite white
families.

In the Yoknapatawpha County fiction, the same characters
appear again and again, but the novels are not unified by an overall historical or social plan. Faulkner did not set out to present a
chronological history of the region, devoting different novels to
different historical periods. Neither did he attempt to present the
various social classes in a series of novels. Most of his major characters are, in fact, drawn from only three social levels: the aristocrats, the country people, and the Negroes. There are, in Jefferson,
intermediate social groups between the elite families and the Negroes, but these classes provide only background characters. An examination of the county novels and stories as a unit reveals that
Faulkner's cast of characters is actually much smaller than it appears at first.

» » The prototypes

The rural characters   Consider, for instance, the large cast of rural characters. Only a few are prominent in the fiction as a whole: V. K. Ratliff, Will Varner, and Flem and Mink Snopes are among the few who have important roles. *As I Lay Dying* is devoted to the Bundren family, but the Bundrens have no place in the rest of the fiction. The country people fit generally into one of two broad groups: the independent, morally upright, or the unscrupulous rubes who live by their wits. Ratliff, Bookwright, Quick, and Tull are of the first type. Flem Snopes and a majority of the characters sharing his surname belong to the second group. No matter to which group they belong, these rural characters possess a strong sense of individuality, a love of trading, a practicality and shrewdness, a penchant for tricks and jokes, and, frequently, a suppressed, easily detonated rage at the conditions of their tenant-farmer existence. Faulkner obviously admires the independence and strength of these people. He sympathizes with their hard life, and he enjoys them far more than he does his town characters. In fact, most of the humor in his fiction is sparked either by Negroes or by rural people. Perhaps the most admirable character in all Faulkner's fiction is the country-born-and-bred V. K. Ratliff. Straddling the country and the town, Ratliff combines the intelligence and sensitivity of the town-bred protagonists with the down-to-earth character of the country people.

The Negroes   Compared to the cast of country people, there is far less variety in Faulkner's major Negro characters or his elite-family characters. Most of the Negroes with important roles are variations on members of a single Negro family. Simon, the old servant in *Sartoris*, reappears as Roskus in *The Sound and the Fury*. Dilsey of that novel and Molly Beauchamp of *Go Down, Moses* are the same humane, self-sacrificing Mammy. Their daughters, whether Elnora, or Frony, or Paralee, are indistinguishable, all marrying men who go to France during World War I. Their grandsons Luster or Isom or Henry are identifiable one from the other only by their names. The Negro companion of the aristocratic white boy is named Ringo in *The Unvanquished* and Alex Sanders in

Intruder in the Dust, but their characters are almost identical. There are some major Negro characters, such as Nancy of *Requiem for a Nun* or Minnie of *Sanctuary*, who do not belong to the family group, but proportionate to the importance of the Negro in the fiction, the number of basic types with which Faulkner worked is very small. Even the unique Lucas Beauchamp of *Go Down, Moses* and *Intruder in the Dust* reappears in the final novel, *The Reivers*, as Uncle Ned. These chief Negro characters are delineated with skill and with respect for their individuality and character, but most of the other hundred or so Negroes are renditions of traditional Negro stereotypes.

The young protagonist Of great significance to an understanding of Faulkner's fiction is the similarity in background and character of the major figures belonging to the aristocratic families. Faulkner's typical protagonist is a young man. Bayard Sartoris III (*Sartoris*), Quentin Compson (*The Sound and the Fury*), Bayard Sartoris II (*The Unvanquished*), Ike McCaslin (*Go Down, Moses*), Charles Mallison (*Intruder in the Dust*, *The Town*, and *The Mansion*), and Lucius Priest (*The Reivers*), all share a similar family background and similar basic characteristics. Horace Benbow (*Sartoris* and *Sanctuary*) is only chronologically older than Quentin or Ike. And the kinship of Gavin Stevens, who appears as an adult in many novels, to these characters is apparent in *The Town*, where his young manhood is recounted.

That so many of the young protagonists are variations of a single prototype provides one of the unifying elements in Faulkner's work. Though Faulkner is too complex a writer to explain in terms of a single idea, much of his work can be understood by recognizing that at the center of the fiction is one crucial experience: the transition of a boy to manhood. In novel after novel he returns to the theme, and it is possible to trace the development of his ideas and the alterations of his moods and attitudes by examining the experiences of his young heroes.

Even for Faulkner's final hero, Lucius Priest of *The Reivers*, whose introduction to adult life is an amusing, sentimental odyssey, adolescence is a difficult period. And for the protagonists of the early novels, it is excruciatingly painful. The difficulties of these young men in approaching manhood can be traced to three major causes.

Born in the South just before the turn of the century, they are oriented during childhood toward the past, toward a mid-nineteenth-century world. Unfortunately for them, they come to maturity in the twentieth century. Secondly, like their literary contemporaries, the young heroes of Hemingway and Dos Passos, they are both idealists and puritans. Finally, they are intelligent, sensitive, and introspective. When these young men collide with the reality of twentieth-century existence, they are shocked, outraged, and confused.[5] Faulkner's novels combine the *Bildungsroman* and the family saga.[6] The young hero's simultaneous rebellion from the family traditions and his intense need for the security that the family provides produce much of the tension in the novels.

The forces that shape the archetypal boy hero's traumatic collision with modern life extend back to the Civil War. The family patriarch came into the Mississippi wilderness and in a few decades became an important and wealthy planter. The defeat of the South drastically altered the fortunes of his family. During the hardships of the Reconstruction Period, the family compensated for its vanished grandeur by keeping the past alive in memory and stories. In the family anecdotes, the pioneer who created and enjoyed the glorious period of the family's success became a legendary hero.

Each new generation provided the family bards a fresh audience for the old tales about the pioneer's character and adventures. Faulkner's hero is usually three (sometimes two) generations removed from the pioneer, and he is nurtured on stories of the family's former glory and of his bold, reckless, gallant great-grandfather. This legendary hero becomes the child's idol, his touchstone for judging himself and his own world.

But the pioneer belonged to a world that was obliterated at Appomattox. This nineteenth-century world, in Faulkner's Mississippi, was a unique combination of frontier society and a facsimile of the plantation society in the Southern coastal states. The pioneer emigrated from the Carolinas or Virginia because he was not born into the privileged wealthy class of that plantation society. He possessed courage, and ambition, and the strength to penetrate into the frontier wilderness and make his fortune. His ambition was to create for himself a replica of that aristocratic society from which he had been excluded by birth. He succeeded, but time and history were against him. During his own lifetime he watched the collapse of the world he had struggled to create.

This pioneer-ancestor dominates in the Faulkner county novels in the same way that the spirit of John Sartoris hovers as a palpable presence in *Sartoris*. Colonel Sartoris is the prototype of the pioneer characters in the fiction. Different aspects of his personality and his career receive emphasis when he is called Lucius Quintus Carothers McCaslin or Henry Sutpen, but all these characters are cast from the same mold. Interestingly enough, only when his name is not John Sartoris does the prototype escape the aura of legend. In *Sartoris* and in six of the seven episodes of *The Unvanquished*, he is the legendary hero. In the final episode of *The Unvanquished*, "An Odor of Verbena," he is portrayed realistically, but in the other novels concerned with the Sartoris family, those aspects of his career and personality that are critically examined when he is called Sutpen or McCaslin are glossed over. Elnora, for example, in *Sartoris* is a Negro. But in a short story, "There Was a Queen," she is, we learn, a mulatto, the daughter of John Sartoris by a Negro slave. In that same novel, Colonel Sartoris is depicted by his ardent admirer old Will Falls as a brave, gallant defender of the post-war South against the carpetbaggers and a heroic upholder of the principle of white supremacy. But in *Absalom, Absalom!* when he is renamed Sutpen (Elnora is renamed Clytie), his crime against the Negroes and the heritage of guilt that he passed down to his descendants is realistically assessed. In the stories about the McCaslin family, old Carothers McCaslin, the pioneer, is a shadowy figure; but one fact stands out boldly: he, too, had an illegitimate daughter by a Negro slave.

The young protagonist's idol during childhood is the legendary ancestor John Sartoris, but the ancestor with whom he must deal realistically as an adult is Henry Sutpen. Neither image can efface the other, and the young man, both enchanted and repelled by the past, suffers from the tension created by his antithetical feelings. It is the image of the Sartoris world, glamorized by family legends into a magnolia and moonlight Eden peopled by gallant men, and noble, pure women with beautiful manners and elevated moral standards, that the young protagonist brings out of boyhood and must use to assess himself, his family, and the reality of the twentieth-century world.

The comparatively simple society of the pioneer, in which class and social divisions are sharply drawn, in which a man is free to do what he wants and does it, in which social and moral questions have simple unequivocal answers, is the idealized image that haunts the young man when he finds himself trapped by the complications of modern society. His first impulse is to turn his back on the wasteland of the present and to withdraw into the security of his family. But in his own family history he discovers terrible crimes, and his immediate family is being rent apart by the same malaise from which he suffers. His desperate need for the security of family is symbolized by his fascination with the idea of incest and his horror of miscegenation.

The young boy's involvement with a glamorized past that never could or did exist does little to prepare him for maturity; and his difficulties are increased by his moral indoctrination. He is reared in Protestantism, which in Faulkner's South seems to be a mixture of Baptist, Methodist, and Calvinist theologies, adding up to a rigid moralism. His moral training is fused, of course, with the legendary past. His gallant ancestors are the guardians of morality. The chivalric code of the ante-bellum society, for instance, merges with his vision of women as morally pure and innocent creatures. The extent and importance of this merging is illustrated by the way the young hero usually recoils in horror when he discovers that girls of his own class indulge in sex, in contrast to his acceptance, with no trouble, of the sexuality of country women, or Negroes, or prostitutes.

» » The themes

The collision of Faulkner's intelligent, sensitive, and idealistic protagonist with the society of the twentieth century detonates the violence, sordidness and brutality of much of the fiction. The novels record the impact and explore its causes and its aftermath. Most of the major themes are directly related to this encounter. To isolate themes and discuss them apart from the novels tends to oversimplify them since Faulkner is characteristically ambivalent. But because some of the difficulties in reading this complicated writer might possibly be eased by such a presentation, I have chosen a few pivotal themes to present briefly what I consider to be the overall pattern of his fiction.

Modern society as a wasteland   The image of modern society as a wasteland pervades Faulkner's writing. The mechanized, industrialized society dehumanizes man by forcing him to cultivate false values and by encouraging atrophy of essential human virtues—courage, fortitude, honesty, and goodness. The man who has adapted to modern society is a kind of human cash register. He has lost his natural, "feeling" response to life; his religion is an empty formalism; he is incapable of love. Throughout Faulkner's fiction, twentieth-century society is seen as the enemy, encroaching upon the individual's integrity and strangling humanistic values.

Individualism   Individualism—the right of a man to live his own life—is one of Faulkner's central themes. Many of his stories and novels depict the numerous threats to individualism posed by modern society, by moral righteousness and moral rigidity, by taboos, and by traditions. Uncle Willy, the druggist, is hounded to his death by the moralists of Jefferson. Sam Fathers, a descendant of a Chickasaw Indian chief, must live as a Negro because he has Negro blood in his veins. The tragic plight of the Faulkner hero is that he is a prisoner of the past, of society, of social and moral taboos, and of his own introspective personality. He is so entrapped that his individuality, what Faulkner calls the central "I-Am" of his being, is practically obliterated.

The standard of individualism in the novels seems to be that of the nineteenth-century pioneer who epitomizes the free man, in control of his destiny as much as any human being can be—which is little enough in a universe governed by chance. None of the town characters, enmeshed in society, can hope to attain this freedom. The country people have some measure of independence, but the only true practitioners of individualism in Faulkner's twentieth-century world are the members of the McCallum family, and the McCallums, who live in the hills apart from society, are anachronisms. Theirs is a patriarchal society in which the family is the social unit. Virginius McCallum, the father, recognizes no mortal authority above his own. He and his sons live close to nature, occupying themselves with farming and hunting. In their masculine world, physical strength, courage, and skill in the woods are prime requisites. The McCallums will tolerate no encroachment upon their freedom. Any governmental regulation, they consider an unwarranted limitation of their rights as free men. Rather than permit the federal government to tell them what crops to grow during the depression years, they plant what they have always planted and let the produce rot in the field. Even the war-time draft is to them a limitation of freedom and an insult to their sense of responsibility. These are Faulkner's "Tall Men." * Why becomes clear in the contrast between these independent hill men with the great-grandsons of the pioneers.

Quentin Compson and Ike McCaslin, for instance, can never escape their heritage. As members of socially elite families, they are made aware from their earliest years of the role they are expected to assume in society. The entire county is aware of them as descendents of General Compson or old Carothers McCaslin. Ike is trained by his cousin Cass to take over management of the McCaslin plantation. When Ike decides to become a carpenter, he is not merely making a choice of career. He is refusing an inherited responsibility, and his decision becomes a symbolic repudiation of his past. Quentin Compson cannot forget that his ancestors included a general and a governor, and he is oppressed by the feeling that the physical and moral courage of the Compsons has deteriorated. Both young men, in short, are prisoners of the past.

Race relations Perhaps the plight of the young hero can best be exemplified by the besetting problem of race relations. For the pioneer-ancestor, race relations created few problems. To the twentieth-century descendant, however, the racial situation is a constant source of agitation. In the stories which describe, usually

* Faulkner titles one of his stories about the McCallums "The Tall Men."

with strong overtones of nostalgia, ante-bellum plantation life, the white man unquestioningly accepts his natural superiority to the Negro and his natural right to use him for his profit and pleasure. The plantation owner is generally presented as a benevolent master, and it is this tradition of kindly treatment of inferiors to which the aristocratic families such as the Sartorises adhere, long after the slaves are free men. The Sartoris and Compson Negroes accept their position as inferiors and their relations with their white masters are affectionate and placid.

But the slave holder's great-grandson cannot escape the tensions of race relations in the modern South. Several of Faulkner's boy heroes grow up with Negro companions of their own age, sleep in the same bed with them, and eat the same food at the same table. The white boy knows his companion as a fellow human being. As both grow up, however, they are indoctrinated into the traditional code that governs race relations. And one day, as Faulkner describes it in "The Fire and the Hearth," an episode in *Go Down, Moses*, the white boy suddenly becomes aware of his heritage. He refuses to sleep with his companion. Immediately he regrets what he has done, but the Negro boy has already assumed the mask of Sambo. An impenetrable barrier has been raised between them. From then on their relations are in accord with the Southern code.

The white boy is as much a prisoner of the taboo as the Negro; his response to another human being cannot be natural. The boy knows that the Negro is not his inferior, but to defy that code is to alienate himself from his family, his society, and his heritage. Faulkner's hero is also deeply troubled by the guilt which his ancestors incurred in enslaving a people, a guilt which is equally his own. Ike McCaslin tries to expiate the crime of his ancestor and his society. In his justification of his action, he declares the Negro better than the white because the Negro has no heavy heritage of guilt. But even as he makes the declaration, Ike feels he is guilty of heresy. In the very process of repudiating that tradition, Ike cannot free himself from the past.

The prisoner of society   The racial code, to which these young Southerners are emotionally bound by their early indoctrination, is only one of their many chains. Faulkner presents social man as the end-product of a process of psychological conditioning that practically eliminates his chance of responding naturally to the experiences of his existence. His feelings, his thoughts, his actions are determined by his relations to his parents and his society. Many of Faulkner's characters are victims of their religious background. These characters are unable to respond to God as Ike McCaslin responds to the Omnipotent Force he senses in the woods. Ike undergoes a true religious experience by opening his heart to God. But to achieve this confrontation, Ike has to strip himself of his accumulated social heritage. It is that heritage of codes and concepts which prohibits a feeling response to life. The view of many Faulkner characters, that life is nothing more than a preparation for a blissful after-life to be achieved by adhering rigidly to an established code of conduct, is a view that is imposed upon them during childhood. Their response to any experience is conditioned by the code. Alienated from the reality of immediate experience, they become, in Faulkner's word, "ghosts."

For example, in the sixteenth century, John Calvin decided that if God was omniscient, He obviously knew which of His creatures were eternally damned and which eternally saved. A man could not alter his immortal destiny but he could prove that he was among the elect by obeying a prescribed pattern of conduct. A child indoctrinated with such a concept has little chance of deciding for himself whether the concept has validity. Before he matures sufficiently to challenge the concept, his emotional responses have been affected. If he does rebel, he is torn and twisted by his rebellion because he is so deeply involved emotionally with the concept. And the real tragedy is that he dissipates his energy and his life struggling with a concept, an abstraction.

Modern man's separation from his God by abstractions is typical of his entire existence. He is involved with shadows, symbols, rather than reality. The original pioneers in Yoknapatawpha County have to struggle for their very survival. If someone threatens their security, they have to defend themselves. When they organize their community, Faulkner tells us in *Requiem for a Nun*, their first communal project is to build a jail. The jail symbolizes their desire to delegate the responsibility of their individual safety to the community. Next, they adopt certain laws to protect each man's rights. Their second building is the courthouse, a symbol of justice. With the establishment of the judicial process, the citizen no longer has to struggle to guarantee his physical safety.

The pioneer's children and grandchildren are protected by laws, which are words, abstractions. These descendants are not only protected, however; they are subject to these laws. If they or their property are harmed, they deal with the criminal through the courts, and in the courts they are involved with laws and procedures—words. This same process of alienating modern man from real existence and involving him with abstract symbols is apparent on another level of living. The pioneer grew his own food and built his own shelter. But as the community developed into a society, the citizen did not provide these basic necessities himself. He worked for money, a symbol, to pay others to farm and to build. Soon the symbol became important in itself, an emblem not of tangible things like food and shelter but of such intangibles as status. Thus, the abstractions and symbols which came into being as man's servant become his master.

The power of symbols, of words, over the mind and life of man is illustrated by the basic experience of love. A young person can form by reading or simply by listening to adults a conception of romantic love. Without ever having experienced the emotion, he knows exactly the way he should and will feel when he falls in love. His reactions to the real experience are to a great extent already determined by this process of verbal conditioning. Often, as Faulkner shows in several stories, the gap between the idea of love and the real experience is so great that the result is intense disillusionment. This important theme of the gap between words and reality is succinctly expressed by Addie Bundren in *As I Lay Dying:*

. . . I learned that words are no good; that words don't ever fit even what they are trying to say at. . . . I would think how words go straight up in a thin line, quick and harmless, and how terribly doing goes along the earth, clinging to it, so that after a while the two lines are too far apart for the same person to straddle from one to the other; and that sin and love and fear are just sounds that people who never sinned nor loved nor feared have for what they never had and cannot have until they forget the words. (463, 465)[7]

The whole process of social conditioning is achieved, to a great extent, through words. It is through language that the past is transmitted to the boy hero. In this process it is transformed and idealized. The figures from that past are shadows, their actions, shadows; but this past that exists only in words exerts a tremendous influence on the feelings, thought, and actions—the personality of Faulkner's elite characters. Throughout their lives the past conditions their responses to immediate and real experience.

The primitive man   Against this imprisoned, confused, and fragmented social man, Faulkner sets an antithesis, primitive man. And against the concept-ridden, complex world of society, he sets the natural world. Like the pioneers and the young protagonists, the primitives are variations of a prototype. Primitives, such as Lena Grove of *Light in August*, Sam Fathers of *Go Down, Moses*, the tall convict of *The Wild Palms*, all are simple non-intellectual people who have somehow escaped social conditioning. They do not bring any preconceptions to their experience and are therefore free to respond naturally. They do not resist the conditions in which they find themselves, but accept them and make the best adjustment they can. They are open to experience; they are spontaneous and natural. Because man is a part of the natural world, his natural or unconditioned responses are in harmony with nature.

Social man, alienated from his own being and from the world of nature, is often not free to respond naturally to experience. He constantly attempts to understand life, to find an explanation for death. He resists the idea of death with a variety of concepts that are designed to rationalize it away. He wants life to be logical and explicable. Because he places so much faith in a rational view of existence and because his explanations fail ultimately to explain life, social man is subject to increasing disillusionment and finally to despair. A cerebral approach to life can only lead to a recognition of the ultimate absurdity of existence. It is from this point of view, as we shall see, that Faulkner's earlier, greater novels were written.

The primitive, natural man does not attempt to interpret life, to explain away death. He accepts the life-and-death pattern of existence unquestioningly, and through this acceptance attains an enviable strength and peace. Faulkner's view of nature is not Wordsworthian, however. The pattern of existence is brutal. The strong feed upon the weak; animals must continually struggle to survive. But the life-death cycle, the spring and the winter of the earth, the birth and the death of the animals, is reality in Faulkner's world. Man, by turning his face away from reality, by alienating himself from truth with his attempts to explain the inexplicable, becomes weak and cowardly, confused and ineffectual. His body anchors him to the life-death cycle, but his mind separates him from it, and he becomes fragmented. If modern man could sweep aside his accumulated heritage and expose his natural being he might discover his true identity and recognize his innate capacity to accept and endure.

In *The Sound and the Fury*, in which despair is the dominant mood, only the Negro Dilsey provides a measure of hope. Faulkner's choice of a Negro to dramatize hope is explained in *Go Down, Moses*. The Negro is close to his sources in the natural world. Only a few generations removed from the jungle, his accumulated social heritage has not yet conditioned his responses, choked off his natural feelings. In "The Old People" Cass Edmonds tells his cousin Ike that the blood of Sam Fathers, part Negro, part Indian, and part white "on both sides, except the little white part, knew things that had been tamed out of our blood so long ago that we have not only forgotten them, we have to live together in herds to protect ourselves from our own sources." (167)

In his first novel, *Soldiers' Pay*, Faulkner describes a Negro religious service. Two white men, standing outside the shabby church, listen to the singing Negroes. Within the church is "a soft glow of kerosene serving only to make the darkness and the heat thicker, making thicker the imminence of sex after harsh labor along the mooned land; and from it welled the crooning submerged passion of the dark race. It was nothing, it was everything; then it swelled to an ecstasy, taking the white man's words as readily as it took his remote God and made a personal Father of Him. Feed Thy Sheep, O Jesus. All the longing of mankind for a Oneness with Something, somewhere." (221)

In "The Old People," and "The Bear," Faulkner's young hero Ike goes through a process of indoctrination that serves gradually to bring him back beyond his heritage until he is as free as the old people, pristine men. Only then can he feel in the woods a Oneness with the Omnipotent Force of nature.

Below the layers of social encrustation, there is in every human being the natural man, just as in every man there are those potentials for love and self-sacrifice that are embodied in the Christ myth. In his primitive characters, Faulkner dramatizes this buried natural man. In such people, the innate human virtues—honor and pride and pity and justice and courage—can operate freely. These primitive characters are living proof that, despite the injustice, pain, and brutality of life, inflicted by God and man, man can and will survive.

Affirmation is an integral aspect of Faulkner's work, though muted in the earlier novels. The natural man exists in every human being, but society encroaches constantly upon the woods, and social man smothers the natural within himself. Nature and society are inimical, and if man can, in his heart, accept the inexplicable conditions of existence and find peace, he cannot, if he is an intelligent being, ignore his mind, which demands explanations and can find none. In the later novels, the note of affirmation is stronger, the mood is mellower, but the tensions of the earlier works are still present.

3 / Narrative structure and techniques

Faulkner's greatness as an artist is due to a great extent to what might be called his stereoscopic vision, his ability to deal with the specific and the universal simultaneously, to make the real symbolic without sacrificing reality. He is unquestionably the greatest of the American regional writers. His fiction is as Southern as bourbon whiskey. Southern history, climate, geography, natural life, society, customs, traditions, ideologies, living conditions, speech patterns—everything that particularizes the American South and its inhabitants is rendered realistically in his writing. But he is far more than a regional writer, and the breadth of his achievement is due, in large measure, to his narrative structure, narrative techniques, and his style.

Certain important characteristics of Faulkner's talent are more apparent in his short stories than in his novels. For one thing, reading through the *Collected Stories* makes us realize that he is a born storyteller, that he loves to tell stories, and that he has a passionate, almost obsessive desire to understand his fellow human beings. He is fascinated by people, continually amazed, shocked, horrified, and amused by their antics. He is, in fact, a gossip, a gossip elevated by genius to the stature of an artist. Faulkner lacks the self-righteousness and malice that motivate the gossip, but he shares the gossip's passion for the skeleton in the family closet. He writes about the bizarre and the unpleasant: the sexual escapades of members of the town's leading families, the old woman of good family who lives in isolation, who refuses to pay taxes and who is suspected of having murdered her suitor, the local druggist who is a narcotics addict, the frustrated old maid who suddenly accuses a Negro of raping her, the incredible antics of the country folk, the machinations of the avaricious and diabolically shrewd rube who ends up as president of the First National Bank.

Faulkner is this kind of local tale-teller; a great many of his short stories are little more than anecdotes. Often he created great stories, but often too he wrote for the slick magazines. In most of his short stories, Faulkner's talent is obvious. He had a sensitive ear for local speech patterns; he could deftly create character, atmosphere, and settings. But most of the stories lack the technical ingenuity, the evocative style, the profound themes and broad vision that make many of the novels great works of art.

Paradoxically, Faulkner is primarily a short story writer. He was able to fulfill his artistic potential only in the novel form, although his talent was not for the long narrative.[8] The majority of his novels are either thematic expansions of narratives little longer than short stories or they are fusions of short stories. *The Sound and the Fury* began as a short story, and in terms of narrative action is little more than that. *Light in August* combines three separate tales. *The Wild Palms* contains two separate short novels connected only by thematic relationship. *Sartoris*, if stripped of its many tales of the past which are related or recalled by the various characters, would be a very short book about a returning veteran who finally gets himself killed. Both *The Unvanquished* and *Go Down, Moses* have seven chapters, and in both novels, six of the seven sections were originally published as separate stories. The three novels dealing with the Snopes family are made up of short stories, many of which were published apart from the novels. An entire long section of *A Fable* was presented separately as "Notes on a Horsethief." The only two books whose basic plots are sufficiently developed for novel length are *Intruder in the Dust* and *The Reivers*, both popular rather than literary successes.

In structuring his novels, Faulkner often achieved thematic unity by grouping stories which were concerned with the same family. To the title *Go Down, Moses* in the original edition, Faulkner added the phrase "And Other Stories." In the next edition, he decided to drop that phrase; for, in comparison, for instance, to *Knight's Gambit*, which is a collection of detective stories united only by the presence of Gavin Stevens in each, *Go Down, Moses* is a unified novel. It concerns the McCaslin family in several generations, from the 1850's to about the fourth decade of the twentieth century. In this novel, the stories are not placed in chronological order. The first takes place about 1855, the second and third are set in 1940, the fourth and fifth jump back to the 1880's, and the sixth and seventh are again in 1940. By fragmenting chronological time, juxtaposing stories of the past with stories of the present, Faulkner reveals the effect of the past on the present. Events of the past determine what occurs in the present. No act, no thought is isolated in time. By deliberately breaking up the chronology of his narrative, Faulkner also dramatizes his recognition that though the human body must exist in chronological time, the mind does not function within the barriers imposed on the body. The mind fuses past, present, and future. Because we think beyond clock-measured time and because what we do today is shaped by what happened yesterday, "Yesterday today and tomorrow are Is: Indivisible: One." [9]

By juxtaposing stories of the past and present, Faulkner also expands the significance of what occurs in the present. Against the backdrop of extended time, the specific history of the McCaslin family comes to reflect the moral history of the South. But the themes of moral transgression and inherited guilt transcend, as they do in the drama of Aeschylus, historical time and geographical location. Thus, though each story in *Go Down, Moses* has its own plot and theme, when united with the other stories in the novel, it becomes a unit in an inclusive narrative with a broader and more universal theme.

The use of this type of montage structuring allows Faulkner to combine the techniques of twentieth-century realism with the techniques of nineteenth-century American metaphysical novelists like Hawthorne and Melville. Faulkner's characters are products of a particular society at a particular moment in history. The tensions, drives and needs of a character such as Quentin Compson, for instance, are those of a young man born of Jason and Caroline Compson in Jefferson, Mississippi about 1890. Quentin's problems in *The Sound and the Fury* are rooted in his childhood experiences. His mother and father, his relationship to them, the society of Jefferson with its stratified class structure, its tradition of plantation aristocracy, all contribute to his suicide. Quentin is individualized, and yet partly because of the structure of *The Sound and the Fury*, his is a story within a larger story that describes what is, in some degree, the terrible fate of modern man. In the same way, Ike McCaslin's repudiation of his heritage in "The Bear" is the act of a young man whose experience and background are unique. He is the child of parents who marry when they are old, the grandson of a man who could treat his own mulatto daughter as a sexual implement, and the spiritual son of Sam Fathers who provides the paternal guidance the fatherless boy needs. But, again, partly due to the narrative structure of *Go Down, Moses*, Ike's story mirrors a universal moral problem.

A Faulkner novel is structured to tell a story and at the same time to explore the social, historical, and moral significance of that story. Present action, for example, in *Light in August*, extends over a period of one week. Joanna Burden has been murdered and her house set on fire. The murderer escapes, is hunted down and lynched when he is declared to have Negro blood. That is the story that provides forward narrative action in this long novel. Why Joanna was murdered, what specific psychological and social forces culminated in this act of violence and what forces produced the lynching are explored in the subsidiary stories erected upon the action taking place in the present. The manner in which Faulkner weaves his various stories together and structures his scenes gives to his novels their broad thematic significance. Each of the stories is interesting and meaningful by itself, but when set as complements or contrasts to one another, they create a suprastory with a universal theme.

In his greatest novels, Faulkner's architectonic sense operated to unite the various stories thematically. Considering the incredible complexity and difficulty of such narrative structuring, he was frequently successful. But there are novels in which he lost control and either added stories that contributed nothing through tone or meaning to the overall theme or he failed to establish their thematic relationship. In *The Town* and *The Mansion*, for example, he seems to have been so caught up with the idea of unifying all his county novels that he spent an inordinate amount of space retelling stories included in previous novels that have little discernible relevance to narrative, tone, or theme.

In comparison with novels written in more traditional form, a Faulkner novel places a considerable burden upon the reader. The novel's real theme is not always explicit. The reader of *Light in August* must recognize that the story of Lena Grove, which is a minor story that opens and closes the novel, is included for a thematic purpose. And he must sensitively respond, as if listening to a symphony, to the contrasting or complementary motifs of the various scenes and stories. Faulkner was perfectly capable of writing a simple straightforward story; the vague references, ambiguities, avoidance of transitions, withholding of vital information are always deliberate. Faulkner's techniques may sometimes exasperate, but they are effective in compelling the reader to join in the writer's search for truth.

The effects achieved with this type of structuring are complemented and extended by Faulkner's other techniques of narration. He frequently uses third-person narration, as in *Sartoris* and *Light in August*. Third-person narration provides an author a great deal of freedom in the development of his story. The omniscient author shifts from one character to another informing us what each one is thinking. A refinement in story-telling is to limit the point of view, that is, to view all the action through the eyes and mind of one character. This method of narration brings us closer to the reality of consciousness. In life, we can only know what other people do and what they say. What they are thinking, what internal forces motivate them, we must deduce from the evidence of their words and deeds. When an author arbitrarily decides to tell his story through the mind of one character, he is deliberately limiting his own narrative freedom. The character whose mind represents the central consciousnesss must be present in all the scenes, or he must be the recipient of information about an incident that occurred when he was not present—if the author needs that scene in his story.

Despite the limitations and difficulties this technique poses for the story-teller, it offers the novelist an opportunity for realistic analysis of the way the mind works. If his major interest is in the inner world of his characters, he can pay comparatively little attention to external events. As a result we usually do not witness the events themselves but the way they are registered in a particular mind. Faulkner adopted this technique and developed his own variations of it. Three of the four sections of *The Sound and the Fury* are adaptations of the interior monologue technique. *As I Lay Dying* introduces another variant of the method by telling the story of a burial journey exclusively by means of the monologues of fourteen characters.

However, though he used the interior monologue effectively in these two early novels, Faulkner ultimately abandoned it in favor of telling his stories through narrators. A character, either one involved directly in the action, or a witness, or hearer of it, tells the story, and the author himself is not heard from. This narrative technique parallels and complements the narrative structuring which tells stories within stories. For instance, if the narrator, as is often the case, is an adolescent, the reactions of the adolescent to the incident he is recounting constitute another story and expand the significance of the central tale. With this technique, Faulkner is also able to dramatize his concept of time. When the boy recounts events from a time long before he was born, we are made aware that these events are as much a part of his personality as his own childhood past that in his mind past and present are one.

An extension of this technique is the use of multiple narrators. In *Absalom, Absalom!*, Rosa Coldfield tells what she knows about the central character of the novel, Thomas Sutpen. Her view of him is colored by her own experiences and her personality. We therefore learn about Sutpen and, at the same time, about the effect he had upon Rosa. She is only one of four narrators in the novel. And each narrator provides a different perspective for viewing Sutpen's story, depending upon his own degree of involvement in the story, his own predilections, his own psychological make-up. None of the four narrators can be considered the voice of the author. The reader, therefore, cannot accept any account as authoritative. The effect of this removal of the author from the story is a dramatization of Faulkner's view of reality. In reading *Absalom, Absalom!*, for instance, we are presented with certain facts: Henry Sutpen murders Charles Bon. The mind can register this as fact, but as soon as it seeks motive, attempts to understand the Why of the murder, it enters the realm of speculation.[10] In this realm there can be no certainty. The mind, however, seeks truth, but the conclusions that one mind reaches will differ from the conclusions of another. *The Town* provides another illustration. One of the narrators of the novel, Gavin Stevens, wonders about Flem's motive in closing Montgomery Snope's pornography show. His speculations reveal more about Gavin than they do about Flem. Then Ratliff speculates. He is more practical than Gavin, so his view is quite different.

Because the author does not enter these novels, we, as readers, must join the game of speculation by examining the thoughts of the narrators. Our conclusions will probably be affected by our own experiences and personalities. Two interesting effects are achieved with this type of narration. First, Faulkner skillfully explores what the mind does with the information concerning external events brought to it by the senses and thereby explores the nature of reality. Second, by involving the reader in this process of philosophical speculation and investigation, Faulkner broadens the meaning of his story. The reader is forced to contribute his own meaning, to join in the search for truth in these epistemological novels.

Another important means by which Faulkner reveals the universal in the specific is symbolism. Faulkner's symbols can be divided into two types: narrative symbols and thematic symbols. A narrative symbol is used to develop the individual scene or story within the novel. Honeysuckle, in Quentin's section of *The Sound and the Fury*, symbolizes the complex relations of Quentin and his sister, the memory of which Quentin has attempted to bury below the level of consciousness. Symbols such as this are frequently used by Faulkner to represent the unformulated needs, the unconscious drives of the characters. In "An Odor of Verbena" the flower is used as a tangible representation of the traditional concepts and mode of action which the young hero is opposing when he refuses to avenge the murder of his father. A thematic symbol develops and furthers the theme of the entire novel rather than that of the narrative unit, in which it occurs. In a Faulkner novel, with its montage structure and its supra-story, an incident or even a character can become a thematic symbol. In *The Sound and the Fury*, the image of the idiot, Benjy, holding a narcissus, serves as a thematic symbol. Against the background of the whole novel, the idiot symbolizes modern man, inarticulate in a man-centered world without love or moral values. Joe Christmas, in *Light in August*, believes he has Negro blood. As a putative mulatto he fits neither into the white world nor the Negro world. Within the framework of the entire novel, Joe is a symbol of the tensions that afflict modern man. Though these characters and scenes are presented in realistic detail and are not immediately apparent as symbols, as Faulkner widens the angle of vision, the situations and characters become symbolic.

To broaden the perspective of his novels, Faulkner frequently employs mythological allusions. In *The Hamlet* the battle of the local swains over Eula Varner is ironically compared to the Trojan

War. In *The Town,* Eula is compared to Semiramis, Lilith, Eve, and Helen to give her the stature of the mythical temptress and the earth goddess. In these novels, Eula is an incarnation of sex, elevated to mythological proportions because she embodies a single attribute of the human being. The presence of such a myth-like character among the complex, more realistically portrayed characters like Gavin Stevens amplifies the significance of the stories.

Faulkner also uses Biblical allusions to give depth and universality to his fiction. Temple and Gowan Stevens re-enact the garden of Eden myth in *Requiem for a Nun.* Faulkner's use of the New Testament throughout his work to broaden perspective culminates in *A Fable,* in which he retells the Christ story. In book after book, the Christ story, which in an early sketch he called "a fairy tale that has conquered the whole Western earth," is utilized, often ironically, to provide a broad framework for his novels.[11] A number of characters, for example, are thirty-three years old, like Christ, when they are killed. Present action in *The Sound and the Fury* occurs during Easter Friday, Saturday, and Sunday.

By employing these devices—myth, symbol, various narrative techniques and narrative structure—Faulkner transforms Yoknapatawpha County into a microcosm of the world.

4 / Style

For the uninitiated reader, the difficulties of structure and narrative technique are compounded by Faulkner's style. Yet the brilliant effects of the great novels are due, to a great extent, to style, which is also employed to broaden perspective. An analysis of the style may help to alleviate some of the difficulties in reading such works as *Absalom, Absalom!* and also demonstrate how Faulkner's style is one of his greatest achievements.

One of the fascinating discoveries one makes in a study of Faulkner's rhetoric is that despite his reputation for prolixity and complexity, Faulkner could and frequently did write simple, clear prose in which concrete nouns and strong verbs dominate the short sentences. In "The Bear" occurs the following:*

He went back to the wagon. He realised then how far they had run. It was already afternoon when he put the mules into the traces and tied the horse's lead-rope to the tail-gate. He reached Coon bridge at dusk. The skiff was already there. (244)

Typical of much of the style in *Light in August* is this passage from the opening chapter:

The wagon mounts the hill toward her. She passed it about a mile back down the road. It was standing beside the road, the mules asleep in the traces and their heads pointed in the direction in which she walked. She saw it and she saw the two men squatting beside a barn beyond the fence. (6-7)

The "she" in this passage is the simple Lena Grove. Her character, however, does not determine the style. In chapter twelve, which concerns the complex relations of Joe Christmas and Joanna Burden, the prose is also simple.

The sewer ran only by night. The days were the same as they had ever been. He went to work at half past six in the morning. He would leave the cabin without looking toward the house at all. (224)

Obviously, such passages could not have provoked the charge of one critic that Faulkner's prose is "perhaps the most elaborate, intermittently incoherent and ungrammatical, thunderous, polyphonic rhetoric in all American writing." [12] What probably did was a passage such as the following from *Absalom, Absalom!*, where Rosa Coldfield is the speaker. Charles Bon is dead and Rosa runs up the stairs to the room in which his body lies. She meets Charles's fiancée. Judith is cold and calm. Rosa describes her own reaction:

* See footnote 7 for the editions of the novels used for page references in this study of style.

That's what I found. Perhaps it's what I expected, knew (even at nine-teen knew, I would say if it were not for my nineteen, my own par-ticular kind of nineteen years) that I should find. Perhaps I couldn't even have wanted more than that, couldn't have accepted less, who even at nineteen must have known that living is one constant and perpetual instant when the arras-veil before what-is-to-be hangs docile and even glad to the lightest naked thrust if we had dared, were brave enough (not wise enough: no wisdom needed here) to make the rend-ing gash. Or perhaps it is no lack of courage either: not cowardice which will not face that sickness somewhere at the prime foundation of this factual scheme from which the prisoner soul, miasmal-distillant, wroils ever upward sunward, tugs its tenuous prisoner arteries and veins and prisoning in its turn that spark, that dream which, as the globy and complete instant of its freedom mirrors and repeats (repeats? creates, reduces to a fragile evanescent iridescent sphere) all of space and time and massy earth, relicts the seething and anonymous miasmal mass which in all the years of time has taught itself no boon of death but only how to recreate, renew; and dies, is gone, vanished: nothing —but is that true wisdom which can comprehend that there is a might-have-been which is more true than truth, from which the dreamer, waking, says not 'Did I but dream?' but rather says, indicts high heaven's very self with: 'Why did I wake since waking I shall never sleep again?' (142-3)

This kind of prose has exasperated many readers and critics, pro-voking an explosion of adjectives, both laudatory and derogatory: *ambiguous, over-elaborate, surrealistic, romantic, precious, lyrical, incantatory, turgid, baroque, archaic, compulsive, hypnotic, lush, bizarre, picturesque, garrulous, eccentric.*

To the neophyte Faulkner reader, the prose may seem a con-tinual flow of words that obscures the story action rather than de-veloping it. The difficulties should not be minimized. The dic-tion, the syntax, seem designed to obfuscate, not communicate. Faulkner sometimes deliberately withholds important details, and the narrators frequently refer to people or events that the reader will not learn about until much later, making the style seem even more opaque than it actually is. And the long sentences are difficult to follow, with clauses that proliferate, developing not from the main subject or verb of the sentence, but growing out of preceding clauses. As a result, the main thought is often lost in the mass of amplifying or qualifying ideas. Antecedents of personal pronouns are frequently not clear. Faulkner's style does not provide relaxing reading, but forces the reader to participate in the search for understanding and truth.

» » Oratorical prose

Had Faulkner been a U. S. senator, his speeches would have been squarely in the tradition of Southern oratory. Some of his sentences sound almost like selected passages from a filibuster. Rather than run the risk of interruption and lose the floor, he does not pause; he rolls on, using all the rhetorical devices of the speechmaker: colorful, grandiloquent and emotive words, repetition, parallel structure, a series of negative clauses preceding a positive, delayed climax. The following example from *Intruder in the Dust* is typical:

. . . and now he seemed to see his whole native land, his home—the dirt, the earth which had bred his bones and those of his fathers for six generations and was still shaping him into not just a man but a specific man, not with just a man's passions and aspirations and beliefs but the specific passions and hopes and convictions and ways of thinking and acting of a specific kind and even race: and even more: even among a kind and race specific and unique . . . . (151)

The sentence goes on for two more pages. Faulkner is usually not so clearly oratorical, but the passage reveals the vocal quality in his style. Many of his stories and novels are actually oral narrations: in *Absalom, Absalom!* the narrators Miss Rosa and Mr. Compson are talking to Quentin, and Quentin and Shreve, the other narrators, talk to each other. In the famous fourth section of "The Bear" Ike McCaslin explains to his cousin his reasons for giving up his inheritance. And in the final novel, *The Reivers*, the protagonist is describing his boyhood adventure to his grandchildren. Faulkner seems often to write as if he were listening to a voice and setting down what he hears. Sometimes, as in the preceding quotation, it is the voice of the stereotyped Southern colonel. Often, it is the soft, musing voice of one who narrates what he can hardly believe. In other stories, the voice is outraged and incredulous. Not infrequently, the prose sounds like a recording of a compulsive talker.

One of the achievements of this talk-prose is its communication of feeling and attitude. Miss Rosa's bitterness and sense of outrage, Quentin's incredulity and bewilderment establish the tone of their narrations and help to create the atmosphere of *Absalom*.

» » Syntax and diction

The vocal quality of the style also explains, to some extent, the complexity of the syntax. In talk, the sentence as a unit of thought complete in itself is far less important than it is in writing. Much conversation would defy conventional syntactical analysis. Units of the thought are connected by *and* or *but* or *which* or *because* in a continual flow of words. Faulkner's long sentences have this quality. They are not, however, so casual. He makes use of the rhetorical devices of oratory, building his sentences with parallel units. A series of nouns, or verbals, or phrases, or clauses with their modifiers are set in parallel construction:

It was the summer after that first Christmas that Henry brought him home, the summer following the two days of that June vacation which he spent at Sutpen's Hundred before he rode on to the river to take the steamboat home, that summer after my aunt left and papa had to go away on business and I was sent to Ellen . . . to stay. . . . (*Absalom*, 145)

The sentence is structured on the predicate noun *summer*. Repeated three times, each *summer* has modifiers. The first two sets of modifiers are in turn modified: the first *summer* is modified by the prepositional phrase *after that first Christmas* and the noun *Christmas* is modified by the *that* clause.

One of Faulkner's favored constructions is a series of parallel verbals:

But not drifting, these: paddling: because this was upstream, bearing not volitionless into the unknown mystery and authority, but establishing in the wilderness a point for men to rally to in conscience and free will, scanning, watching the dense inscrutable banks. . . . (*Requiem for a Nun*, 236)

The influence of traditional rhetorical devices is obvious too in the balancing of negatives against positives:

But the lock was gone; nor did it take the settlement long to realize that it was not the escaped bandits and the aborted reward, but the lock, and not a simple situation which faced them, but a problem which threatened. . . . (*Requiem*, 187)

Faulkner's passion for exactness and his almost compulsive need to make words convey not only the image or thought in his mind but the related feelings or mood also contributed to the complexity of his style. When words do not exist, he does not hesitate to create them by joining two words into one—*fecundmellow, Allknowledgeable*—or compounding with a hyphen—*pollen-wroiled, miasmal-distillant*. Often he ignores the dictionary meaning of a word for its connotative effect: ". . . it looked like an aged or sick wild beast, crawled terrifically there to drink in the act of dying." *Terrifically* in this sentence conveys feeling rather than meaning.

Adjectives, compounded or in series, swell his sentences.

A month after that Varner bought a new runabout buggy with bright red wheels and a fringed parasol top, which, the fat white horse and the big roan in new brass-studded harness and the wheels glinting in vermilion and spokeless blurs, swept all day long along back country roads and lanes while Varner and Snopes sat side by side in outrageous paradox above a spurting cloud of light dust, in a speeding aura of constant and invincible excursion. (*The Hamlet*, 90-1)

Nearly every one of the common nouns in this sentence has at least one adjective to modify it. Faulkner's power of observation was remarkably acute and he often appears to have been impelled to include in his descriptions all the minute details his memory recorded. Sometimes he can create a sharp image with a few words—"yellow slashes of mote-palpitant sunlight"—but more frequently he requires qualifying phrases and even clauses:

The path (it was neither road nor lane: just two parallel barely discernible tracks where wagon wheels had run, almost obliterated by
this year's grass and weeds) went up to the sagging and stepless porch
of the perfectly blank house. . . . (*The Hamlet*, 19)

By compounding adjectives or amassing them, Faulkner expresses nuances of thought and feeling. Adjectives, for example,
are often contradictory: "the expression of fatalistic and amazed
determination." *Fatalistic* conveys grim inevitability; *amazed*
would seem to deny inevitability. Compounded, the words capture the tension of the facial expression.

In the same way that Faulkner uses single adjectives, he uses series
of qualifying or amplifying phrases and clauses. A noun, as in the
following, is followed by adjectives and amplifying clauses:

. . . the fragile wisp of a man ageless, hairless and toothless, who
looked too frail even to approach a horse, let alone ride one six hundred miles every two weeks, yet who did so, and not only that but
had wind enough left not only to announce and precede but even
follow his passing with the jeering musical triumph of the horn:—a
contempt for possible—probable—despoilers matched only by that for
the official dross of which he might be despoiled, and which agreed to
remain in civilized bounds only so long as the despoilers had the taste
to refrain). . . . (*Requiem*, 187)

This entire description modifying the noun *man* is a parentheti-
cal element within a parenthesis. The entire parenthesis covers
twelve lines and separates the subject and the verb of the main
sentence. Such an accumulation of descriptive material though ad-
mittedly not easy to follow gives depth and background simultaneously with the development of the story action.

The characteristic quality of a Faulkner sentence is, in part,
due to his placing modifying elements after the noun. By inverting
the usual order, he can keep adding modifier after modifier:

. . . and always the rider, Pettigrew, ubiquitous, everywhere, not helping search himself and never in anyone's way, but always present, inscrutable, saturnine, missing nothing. . . . (*Requiem*, 188)

Frequently, Faulkner's quest for exactness is apparent in the sentence structure: ". . . she could write her name, or anyway make something with a pen or pencil which was agreed to be, or at least accepted to be, a valid signature. . . ." (*Requiem*, 189)

Not only with adjectives, but also with nouns and verbs is Faulkner's invention free-wheeling. Many sentences are developed on a parallel series of appositive nouns, or a series of nouns: "his plantation: his manor, his kitchens and stables and kennels and slave quarters and gardens and promenades and fields. . . ." (*Requiem*, 196). Verbs, too are compounded or massed: "So it was solved, done, finished, ended."

The words flow in torrents not only because Faulkner sought exactness and completeness but also because he had the poet's love of words, a passion for the sound of them, their cumulative power and force. He was, as one critic called him, a "verbal voluptuary." [13] He had a lust for language, and especially for words derived from the Latin. The large number of words ending in *ant* or *able* give his prose a lush quality: *repudiant, scintillant, abnegant, suspirant, palpitant, uninferant, vociferant, intractable, implacable, imponderable, immutable, inviolable*. As a result, Faulkner occasionally sounds stilted, like a self-educated man proudly using the esoteric synonym in place of the one in common usage.

Faulkner's temperament was romantic and he seems to have responded intensely to the romantic poets. The lyricism integral to his style swells to a crescendo when flowers or trees, sky or earth, are his subject:

Now he watches the recurrence of that which he discovered for the first time three days ago: that dawn, light, is not decanted onto earth from the sky, but instead is from the earth itself suspired. Roofed by the woven canopy of blind annealing grass-roots and the roots of trees, dark in the blind dark of time's silt and rich refuse—the constant and unslumbering anonymous worm-glut and the inextricable known bones —Troy's Helen and the nymphs and the snoring mitred bishops, the saviors and the victims and the kings—it wakes, up-seeping, attritive in uncountable creeping channels: first, root; then frond by frond, from whose escaping tips like gas it rises and disseminates and stains the sleep-fast earth with drowsy insect-murmur; then, still upward-seeking, creeps the knitted bark of trunk and limb where, suddenly louder leaf by leaf and dispersive in diffusive sudden speed, melodious with the winged and jeweled throats, it upward bursts and fills night's globed negation with jonquil thunder. (*The Hamlet*, 184)

The passage comes from that section of *The Hamlet* describing the idiot boy's love affair with a cow, and in context, the excessive lyricism contributes to the ironic tone of the idyll about perversion. Though the excesses of this passage are deliberate, there are many passages whose excesses are obviously not intentional. Faulkner had a strong sentimental streak that could and often did, in his short stories particularly, get out of control. One sample should suffice: at the end of the novel about the Sartoris family he writes, in all seriousness, about the family name: "For there is death in the sound of it, and a glamorous fatality, like silver pennons downrushing at sunset, or a dying fall of horns along the road to Roncevaux." (*Sartoris*, 317)

Faulkner's romanticism is apparent also in the importance of nature in his fiction. Many of his finest images and symbols are drawn from nature; animals are the subject of many passages and stories, and many lines of description are devoted to natural settings. He was very sensitive to the sounds and smells of nature and to the shifting patterns of color and light.

Water chuckled and murmured beneath the bridge, invisible in the twilight, its murmur burdened with the voice of cricket and frog. Above the willows that marked the course of the stream gnats still spun and whirled, four bull bats appeared from nowhere in long swoops, in mid swoop vanished, then appeared again swooping against the serene sky, silent as drops of water on a window-pane; swift and noiseless and intent as though their wings were feathered with twilight and with silence. (*Sartoris*, 135)

Faulkner's ear was also sensitively attuned to the syntax and diction and tone of speech. He reproduced with fidelity the dialects of his Mississippi characters. Without excessive violation of standard spelling he captured the slow drawl of the Southern Negro, the tone of the redneck's speech pattern, and the more refined tones and diction of the educated townspeople. When he uses narrators, he has them speak in their own language. The uneducated country boy who narrates the story "Shingles for the Lord" begins:

Pap got up a good hour before daylight and caught the mule and rid down to Killegrews' to borrow the froe and maul. He ought to been back with it in forty minutes. But the sun had rose and I had done milked and fed and was eating my breakfast when he got back, with the mule not only in a lather but right on the edge of the thumps too. (*Collected Stories*, 27)

When he uses several narrators as he does in *The Town*, the tone and style shift to fit the character of the narrator. V. K. Ratliff is country-born, and in his section the imagery and speech patterns reflect his background: "And Lawyer Stevens setting there calm and still, with his face still white and still as paper. And maybe he hadn't learned how to fight yet neither." (86) In contrast, Gavin Stevens is highly educated and introspective: "No: that's wrong. It's because you dont dare to hope, you are afraid to hope. Not afraid of the extent of hope of which you are capable, but that you—the frail web of bone and flesh snaring that fragile temeritous boundless aspirant sleepless with dream and hope—cannot match it. . . ." (88) Faulkner's ability to shift style with such ease and effectiveness indicates that he cultivated what we think of as typical Faulknerian prose.

Perhaps Faulkner himself best described the achievement of his style when, speaking of himself and Thomas Wolfe, he declared: "We tried to crowd and cram everything, all experience, into each paragraph, to get the whole complete nuance of the moment's experience, of all the recaptured light rays, into each paragraph." [14]

The Novels

Soldiers' Pay

Faulkner's first novel (1926) is, in many ways, a lost-generation novel, a period piece, reflecting the literary climate of the post-World War I era; but it is also a fascinating revelation of genius finding itself. *Soldiers' Pay* is weakest when it is furthest from the themes and techniques that characterize Faulkner's great works, strongest when it clearly anticipates them.

An erratic novel, it contains many over-written, over-poetic, and awkward passages; yet, there is some admirably lyric prose and a number of scenes and characterizations which are excellent. The first chapter, for instance, is amateurish, the final chapter beautifully written. The weakest portions of the book are imitative, offering the fare of many post-World War I novels: the disillusioned soldiers returning to a society from which they feel alienated, the veterans' feeling of rootlessness, their awareness of the hypocrisy of the civilians, their bitterness toward the women they left behind. The novel also is weak when Faulkner employs the then-popular sophisticated dialogue. Not until he completed his second book was Faulkner to realize that such dialogue was not his forte.

Just as it is apparent in *Soldiers' Pay* what Faulkner could not do well, so there are also indications of his own special talents. The touch of the grotesque in the portrait of Januarius Jones foreshadows the comedy typical of *As I Lay Dying* or *The Hamlet*. Irony of situation, an effective technique in many novels, is achieved here in the scene in which the widow of Lieutenant Powers meets the mother of Dewey Burney, the boy who, in a moment of hysteria at the front, had killed the Lieutenant. The novel also contains Faulkner's technique of interlocking individual stories, his penchant for mythology and mythological allusions, his love of nature imagery and his tendency to speculate about the difference between the nature of the female and the male.

Most important, *Soldiers' Pay* sounds a basic theme of many of the later works: the absurdity of the human condition and modern man's inability to cope with existence. Though the milieu and situation are different, the malaise of the Sartorises and the Compsons afflicts the characters of *Soldiers' Pay*: they are rootless, confused, and insecure; they are alienated from the world of nature; their religion is form without meaning, their lives motion without meaning. This first novel, however, does not sound quite the note of despair characteristic of those that follow in the next few years; the tone here is sophisticated disillusionment. The disillusionment is undoubtedly sincere, but, for the most part, its expression rings false. It is both too self-conscious and too literary. Faulkner has not yet found his own voice, and the echoes of Housman and Swinburne and other poets Faulkner liked are intrusive.

The novel is divided into nine chapters, each of which contains a varying number of sections indicated by Roman numerals. These divisions permit Faulkner to shift from one character to another without transitions. Spaced throughout the book are a series of love letters from Julian Lowe to Margaret Powers which provide a clue to the unifying theme of the novel. Julian, whose dream of being a flying hero is frustrated by the armistice, mistakes his adolescent attraction to an older woman for love. Though he becomes involved with girls his own age, he continues to declare his undying love for Margaret. Julian is silly and superficial, but his letters express the feeling shared by all the characters in the story. Each longs for something beyond reach; each is engaged in the pursuit of the unattainable; each fastens upon some immediate, specific goal. What these characters really seek they do not even realize. That is their tragedy. Typical of their society and time, they are incapable of recognizing their need for a "Oneness with Something, somewhere." (221)* They can only sense the void in their existence.

The novel's center is Donald Mahon, a living corpse. Dreadfully

---

* Signet Edition, New American Library.

scarred and nearly blind, cut off from everything in his past by a loss of memory, he exists only physically in the present. In centering his drama upon Mahon, Faulkner hit upon a technique that he was to develop skillfully in his future novels. The return of the wounded veteran initiates a series of concentric actions and reactions that extend outward from the people immediately surrounding Mahon to the entire town of Charlestown. The technique permitted Faulkner to examine in depth a group of individuals and their society. The action of the novel covers less than two months, beginning in early April and ending sometime in May. What little action occurs revolves about the marriage of Donald. Cecily, to whom he was engaged before the war, refuses to marry him, gives herself to George Farr to defy her father, decides to marry Donald because she fears Jones will blackmail her, and then runs off and marries George. Margaret Powers marries the dying veteran. After Mahon's death she refuses to marry Joe Gilligan and leaves town. What happens, as in most of Faulkner's work, is far less important than the reasons why.

Margaret Powers, for instance, sees the semi-conscious Donald Mahon on the train and decides to help Joe Gilligan bring him home. Why she feels compelled to assume such a burden and what her reasons disclose about her and about her world are gradually revealed throughout the novel. To her view, she and Dick Powers "had taken advantage of a universal hysteria for the purpose of getting of each other a brief ecstasy." (26) They married three days before Dick was scheduled to sail for France. Both were aware that they were not in love, and they agreed that each should pursue his own pleasures while Dick was away. Faulkner's probing of Margaret's psychological state is deft and skillful. She was tricked by "a wanton Fate: a joke amusing to no one." (26) For a few days after her husband's departure, Margaret was lonely; then she returned to the Red Cross canteen where she was a hostess. Her loneliness revived temporarily when she received his first letters. When she decided in all honesty that the relationship had nothing to justify it and should be terminated, she wrote to her husband announcing her decision. Before he could receive her letter, he was dead.

When Margaret meets Donald Mahon on the train, she is in a

state of emotional sterility. She does not regret that she wrote such a letter to a man a few hours away from death. Her feeling is a kind of frustration, as if she were suspended in an unresolved state of emotion. Had her husband received her letter and then died, the relationship would have been terminated, the separation between them completed not by death but by her letter. Her decision to sever the marriage bond was inspired by the single unequivocal feeling she knew during her three day marriage to Powers. In Margaret's thoughts about her husband her ambivalent feelings are exposed. She remembers him as beautiful but ugly. He was physically attractive to her; she desired him, but sex was a violation which she recalls as the ugliness of the naked male body; she also recalls a sense of relief that he was not able to hold her: her body flushed her free. He was her lover whom she did not love: "Dear dead Dick." (32) When her letter fails to reach Powers, her emotions are frozen. She cannot love another; she can feel her sexuality, but she cannot know desire. The one emotion she is capable of is pity. Her marriage to Donald Mahon unites two of the living dead, both victims of "rotten luck."

Mahon, too, is in a state of suspension, hanging between death and life, waiting, as the doctor says, to finish something: "Something he has begun, but has not completed, something he has carried from his former life that he does not remember consciously." (107) Just before he dies, Donald recalls the day he was wounded and he completes the process of dying which was suspended for over a year. Each character in the novel is like the "bold lover" on Keats's Grecian urn, who, though ever in pursuit, can never kiss. Even a minor character like Robert Saunders is frustrated in his desire to see Donald's horribly scarred face. Joe Gilligan, deeply in love with Margaret, as close to her as any human being can be, admired and respected by her, cannot possess her. His parting with her—she on the observation platform of the departing train, he running wildly and desperately after her—is an image that captures, like Keats's poem, man's pursuit of the unattainable but without the compensatory idea that the arrested state defies the evanescence of time and life.

The war, for those it touched, destroyed the screen which, like the hospital screen set between the dying man and his fellows, men set up in their minds to block out the horrors of mortality. Those in *Soldiers' Pay* whom the war has scarred recognize their plight: Joe Gilligan curses the conditions of existence, Margaret acknowledges a wanton Fate. The civilians, however, ignore reality. But their condition is identical: they, too, are lost and rootless; their life is meaningless, and they seek vainly for something that will provide meaning. The major difference between civilians like Januarius Jones and veterans like Joe Gilligan is that Jones ignores the realities of life and death which Joe Gilligan faces.

Among the group of civilians, Cecily Saunders is the least contemplative and the most obviously involved in meaningless motion. Cecily is an excellent rendition of the much-described flapper of the period. Into her portrait, Faulkner pours all his venom for the superficiality and shallowness that he sees in society. The thought of childbearing is repulsive to Cecily. She is a flirt with a supple boy-body. She plays at sex but lacks sensuality. She is the idol of a generation of hollow men whose ideal female is an epicene creature—asexual, superficial, selfish, and silly. Cecily's life is a game of flirtation; anything more serious bores her and throws her off balance. The return of her fiancé plunges her into a situation far beyond her depth. The idea of being engaged to an aviator and a wounded war hero is fascinating, but she cannot stand being in the presence of a sick, scarred man. When her father insists that she help Donald recover by spending some time with him, she gives herself sexually to George Farr, the boy her father has forbidden her to see. In this act of defiance, Cecily is still playing at sex, using it as a means of expressing her rebellion.

The sexual experience, however, repels her. It brings her too close to reality. George Farr can no longer be a playmate, and deliberately ignoring him, she flirts with others. Her fear that Jones will expose her affair with George drives her hysterically to the dying Mahon. And when her parents prevent her marriage to Donald, she flees to George. She treats her marriage to him as lightly as she treats sex. Cecily is woman detached from femaleness: she is not "for maternity, not even for love: a thing for the eye and the mind." (156) She hates the idea of having a baby, "blurring her slim epicenity, blurring her body with pain." (99) Cecily wants only to flirt and play, but her own superficiality traps her into marriage.

George Farr, madly in love with Cecily and tormented by jealousy, is a figure of frustrated longing, stealing glimpses of Cecily walking through town or dancing with other men. George seeks refuge from his despair in cheap alcohol. And finally when Cecily marries him, George receives nothing; he cannot possess her love. On the station platform, when he and his bride return to town, Cecily weeps in her father's arms and George stands behind "morose and thunderous . . . Ignored." (212)

Emmy, too, iterates the theme of frustration and despair. She yearns for that momentary experience in the past when Donald made love to her and gave meaning to her drab existence. When Donald returns and fails to recognize her, Emmy's dream is shattered. Without her dream she has nothing, so she separates the Donald of the present from the Donald whom she remembers in the moonlight beside the lake. The death of Donald strips her life of meaning. Passive and indifferent, she lets Jones take her body on the day of Donald's funeral. That evening she returns to the lake and sitting on the wet earth, looks at the moon shining through the trees. "A dog saw it also and bayed: a mellow, long sound that slid immaculately down a hill of silence, yet at the same time seemed to linger about her like a rumor of a far despair . . . the dog bayed again, hopeless and sorrowful, dying, dying away. . . . After a while she rose slowly, feeling her damp clothes, thinking of the long walk home. To-morrow was washday." (208)

Emmy pursuing her phantom dream is pursued in turn by Januarius Jones, the strangest character in the novel—half real, half symbol. Jones has no past. He is an orphan, "becoming Jones alphabetically, January through a conjunction of calendar and biology." (40) His yellow eyes, likened constantly to the eyes of a goat, his baggy tweeds and his pipe evoke an image of Pan, the pagan deity that Christianity buried. Faulkner's juxtaposition in the novel of the Pan image with Parson Mahon whose God is Circumstance produces the antiphonal cry of the modern world: "Pan is dead and so is God." Although a Latin scholar, Jones finds no meaning in the past. Sensuality, "eating and sleeping and procreating" is life, and Jones frantically pursues sensation. (42) Indifference deflates him, but reaction of any kind to his advances stimulates him. Emmy's hatred, her violent repulsion of his proposals make her so attractive to him that his desire to possess her becomes an obsession. Jones is motion for the sake of motion. As with Cecily, on a coarser level, sex play rather than sexual fulfillment is his goal. He knows, for instance, that Cecily is shallow and epicene: she inspires in him "a chaste Platonic nympholepsy . . . shaping an insincere, fleeting articulation of damp clay to an old imperishable desire, building himself a papier mâché Virgin. . . ." (156) Jones even proposes marriage to Cecily, wanting to hold on to the sensation she stirs in him. With this dream of the papier mâché Virgin, Jones also pursues the unattainable. Faulkner's presentation of Jones shifts from the comic to the serious to the symbolic in a rather confusing manner, but it does serve to create an image of a rootless, aimless, decadent generation pursuing sensation and empty dreams to escape boredom. In Jones's final scene, Gilligan prevents him from climbing to Emmy's bedroom window, and Jones walks through the evening quoting Omar Khayyam, wishing he had a girl. He leans upon a fence and emits "a sigh of pure ennui." (218)

In the first scene in which he appears, Jones discusses religion with Parson Mahon. In the background of the garden is the Parson's church with its spire. Jones, "caught in the spire's illusion of slow ruin," opens the conversation: " 'Watch it fall, sir.' " (40) The rector invites him into the garden and they lie on the grass to gaze at the spire. The scene is filled with irony. Jones's face is "a round mirror before which fauns and nymphs might have wantoned when the world was young." Referring to the spire, "a prayer imperishable in bronze," the rector declares: "it is by such as this that man may approach nearest to God . . . He stared unblinking into the sun-filled sky: drowned in his eyes was a despair long since grown cool and quiet." (41)

Never once through the ordeal of watching his son die, does Parson Mahon find comfort in his religion. He deludes himself with the thought that Donald will recover, but his knowledge is entoned in the suppressed refrain, "This was Donald, my son. He is dead." Despair is the rector's companion, his garden his comfort.

"God is Circumstance," he tells Gilligan, and to Jones he says, " 'As I grow older, Mr. Jones, I become more firmly convinced that we learn scarcely anything as we go through this world, and that we learn nothing whatever which can ever help us or be of any particular benefit to us, even.' " (48-9) Seeking in his garden what he cannot find in his faith, Doctor Mahon is a pathetic figure of quiet despair. In the final scene of the novel, Joe Gilligan and the pastor walk in the darkening evening. They stop near a Negro church and listen to the singing. And as they listen, the shabby Negro church becomes "beautiful with mellow longing, passionate and sad." The Negro, primitive and unsophisticated, expresses in his singing the longing which the white man, sophisticated and cut off from his roots in the world of nature, cannot even identify. The germ of the final chapter of *The Sound and the Fury* is in this finale of Faulkner's first novel, just as the small town of Charlestown, centered about the courthouse and the statue of the confederate soldier is the genesis of Jefferson.

But more significantly, the picture of the contemporary world and of its inhabitants in this first novel is the image of that world throughout Faulkner's fiction. *Soldiers' Pay*, though set in the South, does not deal, as do the novels to come, with typically Southern problems; but it does embody their central vision of modern man as confused and lost, aware of a void in his existence without realizing what he is missing.

Mosquitoes

Faulkner's second novel, published in 1927, must be consigned to the overcrowded literary limbo of interesting failures. It has many weaknesses, but its most glaring fault is lack of artistic control. The young writer seems unsure of the type of novel he wants to write. He is groping his way toward his future method of thematic structure, but he has not yet learned to control his episodes and characters to dramatize theme. He apparently sets out to write an Aldous Huxley type "novel of ideas," and finds the genre not quite suited to his aims. The first "conversation" in the novel is filled with general observations about society; most of the others are more closely related to his major theme, art.

He also tries his hand at writing burlesque. In his future work, he uses comedy effectively to create tone and develop theme, but in this early work, only a small part of his comedy is integrated. Major Ayers, for example, the gullible Englishman who knows nothing about America and Americans, is obviously introduced to justify comments about American society. He turns into a sounding board for Dawson Fairchild's tall tales about Al Jackson. These tales are amusing and delightful, but they have little relevance to the rest of the novel. Pete's obsession with his straw hat is humorous and so is Talliaferro's absorption with seduction. As the novel progresses, Talliaferro's passion becomes meaningful; Pete's unwillingness to put his hat down remains pure burlesque.

The confusion produced by the uncontrolled mixture of comedy and serious theme is most obvious in the character of Mrs. Maurier. Many of the comedy scenes revolve about the older woman's reactions to violations of decorum and propriety. Too early in the book, however, Faulkner reveals the silly woman as a pitiable person; as a consequence, the humor at her expense is in bad taste, like joking about a cripple.

Faulkner's uncertainty of artistic purpose is apparent in other characters as well, for he vacillates between caricature and characterization. At times, Mrs. Maurier and Ernest Talliaferro are presented through the eyes of a caricaturist; at others, through the eyes of a sympathetic observer of human frailty. Partly for this reason, Faulkner fails to bring his characters to life. He often characterizes with labels. Three times within three hundred words, Mrs. Maurier's expression registers "infantile astonishment." David, the steward, is so often described as looking at the girl Pat with "a dumb and utter longing" that his suffering becomes, unintentionally, comical. Gordon invariably looms above the others with "his hawk face raised to the sky."

Stylistically, too, the book is inconsistent and irritating. Simple, straightforward narration gives way to imagistic interior monologue. One section of the epilogue is surrealistic. There are too many passages of lush poetic prose, such as the epigraph's "But now, as August like a languorous replete bird winged slowly through the pale summer toward the moon of decay and death. . . ." There are also many stylistic crudities, such as "Mrs Wiseman washed and bound Jenny's hand, interestingly. . . ." (167)*

Despite all these weaknesses, the novel is interesting because Faulkner is dealing with a serious theme and attempting a difficult technical innovation.

In *Mosquitoes*, Faulkner defines his artistic credo. He acknowledges his debt to Sherwood Anderson and declares his artistic independence of the older writer. In the ninth section of the final chapter, Dawson Fairchild, who is probably modeled upon Anderson, understands and articulates the credo. The scene is set in the Vieux Carré of New Orleans. Dawson is drunk and wanders through the Quarter with two friends, both of them his critics: Julius Kauffmann, explicitly; Gordon, the sculptor, implicitly. In this surrealistic scene, the triumvirate is fused into a single consciousness and a single voice. The novel reaches its climax in this Joycean epiphany, which is an illumination of the meaning of art. The fusion of the three characters clarifies the theme Faulkner was confusingly trying to develop. Each of the characters represents one aspect of Faulkner's image of the artist.

Julius Kauffmann is seldom identified except as the "Semitic man," which emphasizes his alienation from the Protestant midwestern small town culture that the novelist Dawson Fairchild embodies. Julius is not a creator but a perceptive observer of society and people, and he has critical objectivity. He and his sister, Mrs. Eva Wiseman, continually criticize their friend Dawson and his work. Most of their criticism is applicable to the work of Sherwood Anderson. Julius tells Dawson that he is " 'Corn belt . . . Indiana talking. You people up there are born with the booster complex.' " (44) Eva declares: " 'And there's the seat of your bewilderment,

* Dell Edition.

Dawson—your belief that the function of creating art depends on geography.' " Her brother elaborates the point:

"Clinging spiritually to one little spot of the earth's surface, so much of his labor is performed for him. Details of dress and habit and speech which entail no hardship in the assimilation and which, piled one on another, become quite as imposing as any single startling stroke of originality, as trivialities in quantities will." (151)

Such criticism of Anderson in a novel by the future creator of Yoknapatawpha County seems at first unwarranted. But the real object of the criticism becomes clear later when Julius chastises Dawson for believing he should restrict his talent to " 'delineating things which his conscious mind assures him are American reactions.' " (200) He advises the novelist to let himself go. If he were to describe " 'in a manner that even translation cannot injure (as Balzac did) American life as American life is, it will become eternal and timeless despite him.' " Julius's concluding statement is particularly pertinent to Faulkner's own work and his artistic aims:

"Life everywhere is the same, you know. Manners of living it may be different—are they not different between adjoining villages? family names, profits on a single field or orchard, work influences—but man's old compulsions, duty and inclination: the axis and the circumference of his squirrel cage, they do not change." (201)

The conflict between duty and inclination is the source of many of Faulkner's themes. And his narrative and stylistic techniques were developed, as we have seen, to encompass the universal within the particular. Though Julius concedes that Dawson is a good writer, he excludes him from the category of artists: " '. . . you are not an artist. There is somewhere within you a bewildered stenographer with a gift for people, but outwardly you might be anything. You are an artist only when you are telling about people. . . .' " (43) Both Julius and Dawson identify Gordon as the true artist.

What makes Gordon an artist and Dawson a stenographer? Faulkner emphasizes two qualities in Gordon. He is too absorbed in feeling and experiencing life to be a detached observer of it; and secondly, his vision penetrates the surface of existence and focuses upon the eternal and timeless. Dawson's limited perception is symbolized by his failure to penetrate the mask of silliness that Mrs. Maurier wears. Gordon immediately perceives the tragic woman beneath the mask. Dawson, standing before the bust Gordon has made of the woman, is shocked by his own obtuseness: " 'I've known her for a year, and Gordon comes along after four days— Well, I'll be damned.' " (266)

Gordon towers above the other mortals and stares into the sky. "Heard melodies are sweet / but those unheard are sweeter," wrote Keats in his "Ode on a Grecian Urn," the poem which seems to have inspired Faulkner and provided some of his images for his surrealistic epiphany. Gordon's heart is attuned to both melodies. His statue of the young girl is a "silent form" that "dost tease us out of thought / As doth eternity." The torso is no particular girl: it is the timeless spirit of youth. Gordon feels the pulsations of "the dark and simple heart of things." (281)

Dawson with his talent for people, Julius with his critical intelligence, and Gordon with his vision of essence merge into one artist in the climax of the novel. In that scene, the three men, who have been drinking heavily, wander through the streets. The interspersed story of the beggar lying at the gates of the former convent reveals the artist's participation in what Faulkner calls the "hackneyed accidents which made up this world—love and life and death and sex and sorrow." (281) The number three predominates. Julius's refrain, "I love three things" is paralleled by the three meandering men, the three rats crawling over the beggar sniffing his intimate parts and by the successive groups of three priests that come upon the body. The images of decay and death are united with the image of unheard melodies:

. . . *silence comes slow as a procession of nuns with breathing blent. Above the hushing walls, a thing wild and passionate, remote and sad; shrill as pipes, and yet unheard. Beneath it, soundless shapes amid which, vaguely, a maiden in an ungirdled robe and with a thin bright chain between her ankles, and a sound of far lamenting.* (278-9)

These images merge with those of sexual desire as Gordon asks the Semitic man for money to go to a brothel.

The wind rushes on, becoming filled with leaping figures antic as flames, and a sound of pipes fiery cold carves the world darkly out of space. The centaurs' hooves clash, storming; shrill voices ride the storm like gusty birds, wild and passionate and sad. (280)

Julius and Dawson see the sculptor enter a door and "lift a woman from the shadow and raise her against the mad stars, smothering her squeal against his tall kiss. *Then voices and sounds, shadows and echoes change from swirling, becoming the headless, armless, legless torso of a girl, motionless and virginal and passionately eternal before the shadows and echoes whirl away.*" (280)

Out of the felt and experienced reality of sorrow and suffering and passion the artist creates timeless beauty. Dawson, for the first time, understands the artist's total immersion in life. Leaning against a wall, staring into the sky as Gordon so often does, and "listening to the dark and measured beating of the heart of things," Dawson articulates a credo, which the other novels show to be Faulkner's own:

"That's what it is. Genius . . . People confuse it so, you see. They have got it now to where it signifies only an active state of the mind in which a picture is painted or a poem is written. When it is not that at all. It is that Passion Week of the heart, that instant of timeless beatitude which some never know, which some, I suppose, gain at will, which others gain through an outside agency like alcohol, like tonight —that passive state of the heart with which the mind, the brain, has nothing to do at all, in which the hackneyed accidents which make up this world—love and life and death and sex and sorrow—brought together by chance in perfect proportions, take on a kind of splendid and timeless beauty." (280-1)

Several ideas in this statement deserve emphasis. The mind has no major role in the creation of Art. Art is not a commentary on life, an interpretation or analysis of it. The mind works with abstractions, ideas and words. Art transcribes felt reality. The Passion Week culminates in resurrection, a transcendence of the temporal. Gordon works directly from felt experience and his statue becomes "the unravished bride of quietness, the foster child of silence and slow time." Art is not idea made concrete but the "form solidity color" of actual life.

This definition of art clarifies Faulkner's intention in *Mosquitoes*. He tried and failed to create Gordon's rendering of the spirit of youth. Aside from his lack of artistic control, he failed because he was not able to sustain his equation of the artistic spirit with the spirit of youth. On several levels, however, the two are merged successfully. Gordon's absorption in the "dark and simple heart of things" is reflected in the unthinking absorption of the young people in immediate experience. In contrast, the older characters pursue phantoms of their lost youth. As Dawson expresses it:

"When youth goes out of you, you get out of it. Out of life, I mean. Up to that time you just live; after that, you are aware of living and living becomes a conscious process. Like thinking does in time, you know. You become conscious of thinking, and then you start right off to think in words. And first thing you know, you don't have thoughts in your mind at all: you just have words in it." (190)

Though he is thirty-six, Gordon, the true artist, remains in life. The other adults are too conscious. They react to ideas and words, not to experience. Gordon, breaking away from one of the many conversations about art and life, thinks: "Talk, talk, talk: the utter and heartbreaking stupidity of words. It seemed endless, as though it might go on forever. Ideas, thoughts, became mere sounds to be bandied about until they were dead." (153)

The people Faulkner brings together aboard Mrs. Maurier's yacht, the *Nausikaa*, form two groups, the young and the old. In one scene, four young people, Pat, Ted, Jenny, and Pete, stand together. "So flagrantly young they were that it served as a barrier between them and the others." (197) Faulkner's efforts in the novel are devoted to showing these young people "just being." Mrs. Maurier's nephew Ted, whom Pat, his sister, calls Josh, concentrates so completely on carving his double-barreled pipe that no thought violates his mind. Ted, whom we are told is going to Yale, seems a sad candidate for any college. Nothing much can be said about Pete except that he just exists. With the young girls, Faulkner does a better job of characterization. He provides enough action to dramatize Jenny's "soft placidity, her sheer passive appeal to the senses." (85) And he comes close to making Pat the living model of Gordon's statue of youth. As Gordon swings Pat from the tender to the deck of the yacht and holds her momentarily suspended against the sunset, "her taut simple body, almost breastless and with the fleeting hips of a boy, was an ecstasy in golden marble, and in her face the passionate ecstacy of a child." (68)

At eighteen, Pat retains the curiosity and innocence of a child. She delights in the sensations her body provides when she walks naked in the foggy dawn or when she moves through the water. She has no patience with pretense and cuts through the words and shams of the adults with a bluntness that would be cruel if it were not so guileless. Ernest Talliaferro freezes in horror when she calls him by his real name, Tarver. He has assumed a foreign name and an accent to match the name, and he wonders, "Were children really like dogs? Could they penetrate one's concealment, know one instinctively?" (27)

Pat and the other young people follow their inclination. Having quarreled with Pete, Jenny gets bored, seeks diversion in petting with Ted, and even lures Mr. Talliaferro to a secluded spot. But Jenny's inclination does not go beyond flirtation. Faulkner presents young people here as innocent, apparently desiring to demolish the myth that the girls of the 1920's were wild and immoral.

In one of their discussions, Julius and Dawson make the point that youth always reflects the values of the preceding generation. Despite the freedom of the modern girl and her flippant attitude, she is as innocent as her mother and grandmother. Some of the most awkward and least integrated scenes in the novel are designed, apparently, to illustrate this observation. In one, Pat for no apparent reason goes into the cabin Jenny shares with Eva Wiseman. Jenny is preparing for bed, and Pat lies on Eva's bunk and watches the other girl take off her clothes. Naked, Jenny lies beside Pat. After some conversation, Pat strokes Jenny's bare flank, murmuring, " 'I like flesh . . . Warm and smooth. Wish I'd lived in Rome . . . oiled gladiators . . .'" (121)

Throughout much of the book Faulkner crudely introduces sex, as it dramatizing the principle enunciated in one of the conversations—to the effect that sexual titillation is what makes art attractive to most people. The very scenes intended to show sexual innocence are full of irrelevant suggestiveness. In the same cabin scene, for instance, Pat suddenly asks Jenny if she is a virgin. Jenny immediately answers, " 'Of course I am,' " and then is chagrined to have been caught off guard. (121) When she throws the question back to her companion, Pat's answer is the same and she too is annoyed at the admission which violates the image of herself as modern.

Pat's relationship with David, the steward, though innocent, is also charged with sexual overtones. Pat insists that David, who has no bathing suit, swim in his underwear. She swims naked at dawn and climbs out of the water with David staring at her. In the swamp she takes off her dress, and at the end of their adventure, she naïvely tells him she is sorry: " 'What can I do about it? Tell me: I'll do it. Anything, just anything.' " (175) In this relationship with David, Pat is a child. She finds in the steward a playmate, one who will swim with her and tell her stories about faraway lands. For her, their escapade is a childish lark that suddenly becomes too real, too adult. The mosquitoes turn the game into a nightmare.

In his epigraph, Faulkner describes mosquitoes in two seasons: "In spring, the sweet young spring, decked out with little green, necklaced, braceleted with the song of idiotic birds," the mosquitoes "were little and young and trusting," but in August which is like a replete bird winging toward "the moon of decay and death," the mosquitoes are "ubiquitous as undertakers." The mosquitoes symbol is not well integrated into the novel, but it clearly is the threat of maturity and passing time. The mosquitoes are like the words of the adults who have gone past the springtime of their lives and exist in the realm of words rather than just being.

In his handling of adult characters in *Mosquitoes* Faulkner displays less thematic control than in depicting the young people. All the adults experience "the old thin sorrow" that Fairchild knows as he reads David's letter of resignation, remembering "youth, thinking of age and slackening flesh like an old thin sorrow everywhere in the world." (195) All of the adults futilely try to fill a void within themselves. Talliaferro's illusion is that there is a trick, a magic word that will make him the romantic seducer of women. At the end of the novel his humiliation by Jenny in the dance hall leaves him "feeling empty and a little tired and hearing his grumbling skeleton." Engaged to be married to Mrs. Maurier, Talliaferro has a final fling at seduction: "a final flare of freedom and youth had surged in him like a dying flame." (286) He fails, but knows only momentary despair. Within a short time, he is certain that he has at last discovered the correct technique, found the magic word that will conquer women.

Mrs. Maurier, whose youth was sacrificed in a marriage to a man too old for her, fills her empty years by patronizing artists. Dorothy Jamieson knows that she cannot keep a man, but she works desperately and vainly to deny what she knows is true. It is difficult to know whether Mrs. Eva Wiseman indulges a secret desire when she fondles and kisses the placid Jenny, or if she simply touches the tangible spirit of her lost youth. For all the adults, living has become a process of compensating for their ebbing youth.

The correspondence between youth's unconscious absorption in "just being" and the artist's immersion in experience is rather tenuous, but Faulkner's attempt to dramatize his definition of art in his story is obvious. Art is, as Fairchild declares, " 'getting into life, getting into it and wrapping it around you, becoming a part of it. Women can do it without art—old biology takes care of that.' " (264) The verbal artist, the writer, must beware of the sterility of words: " 'You begin to substitute words for things and deeds . . . and pretty soon the thing or the deed becomes just a kind of shadow of a certain sound you make by shaping your mouth a certain way.' " (173)

But the true artist, as Faulkner sees him, is wrapped up in the actuality of life, and his art is reality with form, solidity, and color. Faulkner later developed many of the germinal ideas he introduces in this novel. His primitive characters, for instance, will "just be" as the young people in this early work are. Women, throughout his work, have the advantage of biology and remain closer to nature than the men. And Faulkner would, within a short time, create art that shaped "the hackneyed accidents" of this world into a work of "splendid and timeless beauty." But *Mosquitoes* itself is not such a work; it is, in fact, a good example of what Faulkner condemns—too much talk and too little art.

Sartoris

Published in 1929, though probably written a year or so earlier, *Sartoris* is the first of the county novels. In this book, Faulkner begins to draw upon his own past, experiences, and feelings to create the world that he will explore throughout his career. Many of the characters, character types, major themes, and situations of Faulkner's later fiction have their genesis in *Sartoris*. For example, Grandfather Sartoris, resisting the advent of the automobile, will reappear as Grandfather Priest in the final family novel, *The Reivers*. Aunt Jenny's quick response to the lure of the motorcar is paralleled by Grandmother Priest's in the novel published thirty-three years later. The advent of the machine is a key symbol in Faulkner's fiction, which records the clash of the twentieth-century world with that of the nineteenth, and the devastating effect of that collision upon those young people who lived through the transitional struggle.

More clearly, perhaps, than in the future novels the two worlds and their representatives are identified. *Sartoris* has two protagonists: Colonel John Sartoris (1823-1876) and his great-grandson Bayard (1893-1920). Present time in this novel, as in many of the others, is the second decade of the twentieth century. Colonel John has been dead for close to a half-century, but he looms as a "palpable presence" in the lives of his descendants. He and his era have been transformed into legend by family storytellers such as

SARTORIS GENEALOGY

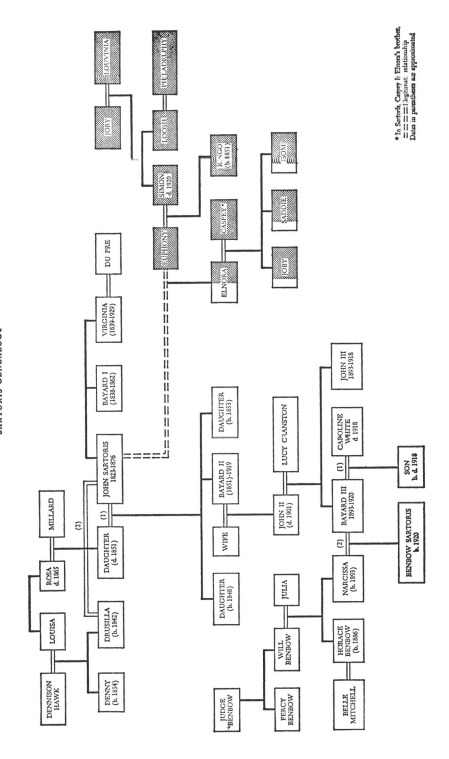

* In Sartoris, Caspey is Elnora's brother.
═ ═ ═ ═ = Illegitimate relationship
Dates in parentheses = approximated

Aunt Jenny, whose tales over the years "grew richer and richer, taking on a mellow splendor like wine. . . ." (33)*

The grandchildren and great-grandchildren of the Civil War veterans are nursed on these legends. The ante-bellum era and its heroes, transfigured and glorified, become as influential in the development of their personalities and attitudes as their own parents. The legendary nineteenth-century ante-bellum South, its manners and morals, its values and beliefs, represent to them the golden age, the apex of human glory and life, the garden of Eden from which man was driven. Faulkner examined this legend critically and recognized its distortions and its crippling effect upon its inheritors; but as one of its inheritors, he could never dismiss the childhood feelings it engendered.

In *Sartoris*, the past is presented both as a lost Eden, and as a psychological crippler. Written from the point of view of one who has achieved maturity in the modern world, the novel depicts a decline in character and a deterioration of moral and social values from the lengendary high standards of the Colonel and his society. But it also reveals the oppressive burden of the legend. The Colonel's twentieth-century descendants are the victims of a tug-of-war between the legend of the past and the reality of the present. The opposed forces maim or destroy them. Bayard Sartoris is the first in a long series of tortured victims.

His great-grandfather, Colonel John, is like the "creatures of that prehistoric day that were too grandly conceived and executed either to exist very long or to vanish utterly when dead from an earth shaped and furnished for punier things." (28) But "by losing the frustration of his own flesh he could now stiffen and shape that which sprang from him into the fatal semblance of his dream." (44) The Colonel's dream belongs to a world that history obliterated; his descendants' attempt to retain even the semblance of that dream is fatal.

The legendary world of John Sartoris is the stereotyped society of the Southern sentimental novel. The men are swashbuckling, sabre-carrying soldiers and gentlemen. They are brave and reckless, gallant and courteous toward their women, whose honor they will defend with their lives. These heroes live in great manor houses

* Signet Edition.

and own large plantations worked by Negro slaves who are, of course, treated as members of the family. The women are invariably innocent and pure. When this magnolia-blossom and moonlight version of the Carolinas is transferred to Mississippi, there is an additional element in the legend. The plantation owner is a pioneer who came into virgin territory and created his own replica of the Eastern society. Thus the stereotyped Southern Colonel is superimposed upon a strong, ambitious man who pits himself against the wilderness, maintaining the vigor and power of the settler. The society of Colonel Sartoris is virile and patriarchal, shaped by pioneers who are dreamers as well as men of action. On his stone pedestal in the Sartoris burial ground, the Colonel towers above the headstones of his descendants, his "back to the world and his carven eyes gazing out across the valley where his railroad ran, and the blue changeless hills beyond, and beyond that, the ramparts of infinity itself." (313)

Sartoris is the prototype of men like Thomas Sutpen in *Absalom, Absalom!* who formulate grand designs and blindly devote themselves to realizing them. This tendency of the human intellect to create and then be enslaved by an abstract concept (which Faulkner associates mainly with the male) is often expressed in bombast and rhetoric. Colonel Sartoris, to a great extent, fuses word and deed, but his descendants will substitute word for deed, thereby detaching themselves dangerously from reality.

In twentieth-century Jefferson, the vital power of the legend is reflected in the social structure of the town. No matter what their present economic circumstances are, the families of the early pioneers and plantation owners continue to be the aristocracy. The Sartorises, as the Negro Simon declares, are "quality." And their manner of living follows the customs prescribed by the legend. Grandfather Bayard is known as the Young Colonel. The unearned title is an inheritance from Colonel John, his father. The Young Colonel's routine, like his title, is inherited. On roads over which automobiles owned by "white trash" are driven, Old Bayard rides in a horse-drawn carriage. Each morning, the old Negro, Simon, dressed in linen-duster and top hat, drives him the four miles from the plantation house to the bank in Jefferson. Each afternoon, Simon, sitting erect and smart in the carriage, salutes as Old Bayard climbs in for the return trip. At home, the banker changes into riding habit. His horse, saddled and readied by the Negroes, awaits him for a canter. The land over which the Young Colonel rides, however, is no longer cultivated by slaves; it has been divided into small units and is farmed by sharecroppers. The manor house which the Colonel rebuilt after the war is no longer the scene of grand balls and receptions. The front parlor is seldom opened except for cleaning. The house and the grounds are cared for by a single small family of Negro servants. When he is not driving, Simon doubles as butler and general handyman. His daughter Elnora works in the kitchen, his son Caspey and grandson Isom tend the garden and the stable.

Even these vestiges of past glory are nearly extinct. Caspey returns from service in France and objects, at least temporarily, to his feudal role. And when the Young Colonel's grandson, Bayard, returns from World War I and buys a car, Old Bayard, after a short-lived resistance, gives up his carriage and is driven to and from the bank in the car. Superseded by a machine, Simon laments the corruption of manners and custom among "quality folk."

As time passes, the barriers between social classes begin to disappear. The Mitchell house in Jefferson had been built and occupied by a peasant from Frenchman's Bend, who did not reside there long because he felt out of place. Now, however, Flem Snopes has not only moved into town with his wife and her child, but he has risen to be vice president of the Sartoris bank. The Snopes invasion has begun. "The older residents from their Jeffersonian houses and genteel stores and offices, looked on with amusement at first. But this has long since become something like consternation." (158) Flem's relative, Byron, who works in the Sartoris bank, both dares to desire a daughter of the aristocracy and dreams of possessing her. And the aristocrat, Narcissa Benbow, secretly enjoys the vulgar, anonymous letters Byron sends her.

Narcissa reveals a weakening of the moral fiber in the Southern woman. The standard of the past is represented by Aunt Jenny Du Pre, Colonel Sartoris's widowed sister, a woman of strong character, able to accept without flinching the many tragedies that befall her; Narcissa, by contrast, is weak and afraid of life. In Faulkner's image, she walls herself into a serene small garden. Her own sexual desires are a threat to her serenity. Nevertheless, despite her fear of men, Narcissa, as a female, is fundamentally more stable than the male. The tendency toward abstraction, which removes the human being from his own nature and the natural world is, in Faulkner's view, tempered in the female by biology. As childbearer and mother, the female has strong instincts related to reproduction of the species. Attached more firmly than the male to the forces operative in nature, the female is less liable to be absorbed by concepts that have no connection with reality. Narcissa is transformed by motherhood into a strong, stable force, determined to protect her child from the Sartoris malaise.

The young men of the twentieth century, Bayard Sartoris and Horace Benbow, reveal a weakening of the masculine character after three generations, and are isolated from the natural world by their submission to abstract concepts of honor or tradition or beauty. The only peace Bayard experiences when he returns to Jefferson is during the period that he works on the farm.

For a time the earth held him in a hiatus that might have been called contentment. He was up at sunrise, planting things in the ground and watching them grow and tending them . . . and went to bed with grateful muscles and with the sober rhythms of the earth in his body and so to sleep . . . Without being aware of the progress of it he had become submerged in a monotony of days, had been snared by a rhythm of activities repeated and repeated until his muscles grew so familiar with them as to get his body through the days without assistance from him at all. He had been so neatly tricked by earth, that ancient Delilah, that he was not aware that his locks were shorn. . . . (181-2)

In *Sartoris*, then, Faulkner began to develop the themes that occur in his later work—the deterioration from the past, the clash of past and present, the alienation of man from nature. But he does not, in *Sartoris*, encompass the general in the specific, express in the torment of his protagonist the torment of modern man. Bayard's trouble is personal and limited, and the despair expressed in the descriptive passages about his mental and spiritual condition seems disproportionate and imposed from without. For example, when Bayard is released by the approach of summer from the absorbing routine of farm work, Faulkner describes him as "coming dazed out of sleep, out of the warm, sunny valleys where people lived into a region where cold peaks of savage despair stood bleakly above the lost valleys, among black and savage stars." (183) Neither Bayard's personality nor his situation can dramatically support such an expression of cosmic despair.

The source of Bayard's torment is an oppressive feeling of guilt for having betrayed his heritage. This alienation from the masculine tradition of Colonel Sartoris is developed on two levels through the complementary stories of Bayard and Horace Benbow and by juxtaposition with the other stories which compose the novel. Story action is provided by the pivotal story of young Bayard. He returns from the war in 1919, buys a car that he races recklessly around the countryside, splits his head riding a wild horse, overturns his car and breaks some ribs, marries Narcissa Benbow and makes her pregnant, runs off to the hills and then California after a near-accident in the car results in his grandfather's fatal heart attack, and finally gets himself killed flying a crack-pot inventor's experimental plane.

Around this pivotal story, Faulkner weaves a number of thematically related stories. Some of these, such as Simon's use of the church funds to subsidize Meloney, and his release from his predicament by Old Bayard, who repays the money, serve to establish the background of a tradition-bound society. Other stories, told by Aunt Jenny about her brother Bayard's fatal adventure and by Will Falls about Colonel John, explain young Bayard's violent pursuit of death.

All these tales about the first generation Sartorises have a common theme of reckless courage. Bayard I, Aunt Jenny's brother, gaily and foolishly rode into the enemy commissary tent to capture anchovies; Colonel John courageously penetrated the Yankee lines with his band of irregulars; he remained calm and cool while the Yankee patrol approached his house seeking him, and he glamorously effected his escape; he walked into the hotel room where the two carpetbaggers awaited him with drawn pistols, and emerged to apologize calmly and gallantly to the hotel keeper, Mrs. Winterbottom, for having been obliged to kill them and bloody up her hotel.

These anecdotes of cold courage are paralleled by the story of young Bayard's twin, John, who, wounded, steps from his falling plane, smiles and, thumbing his nose at his twin, falls to his death. John was the only person whom Bayard really loved. But the tension and torment that Bayard must express in violence is not caused by the anguish of loss; it has its source in guilt. Bayard fears dying.[1] And his fear is a betrayal of his family's attitude toward death. In the night as he relives John's death, his body does not stiffen with horror but with terror:

Then, momentarily, the world was laid away and he was a trapped beast in the high blue, mad for life, trapped in the very cunning fabric that had betrayed him who had dared chance too much, and he thought again if, when the bullet found you, you could only crash upward, burst; anything but earth. Not death, no: it was the crash you had to live through so many times before you struck that filled your throat with vomit. (181-2)

In Horace Benbow is dramatized another level of alienation from the masculine tradition. Idealistic, sensitive, intelligent, romantic, Horace is no man of action. During the war, he serves as a noncombatant in the YMCA unit. A dreamer, he lives in a fantasy world of words and poetic images, where his "wild, fantastic futility" can voyage "in lonely regions of its own beyond the moon, about meadows nailed with firmamented stars to the ultimate roof of things, where unicorns filled the neighing air with galloping, or grazed or lay supine in golden-hoofed repose." (162) Trained as a lawyer, Horace dreams of capturing the beauty of Keats's urn in blown glass.

In Horace that tendency of the intellect to substitute word for deed reaches its extreme. Colonel Sartoris turned dream into reality, but Horace, with "his air of fine and delicate futility" merely talks and dreams. (149) The loss of masculine power in Horace is symbolized by his submission to women. The female tends to envelop the male unless he fights himself free. Even Aunt Jenny protects and mothers the males in her family as much as she can. The Sartoris males resist, but Horace actively seeks absorption in the tranquillity and serenity of his sister's affection. Narcissa, seven years his junior, replaced the invalid mother who died when Horace was fourteen; and when he returns from France "his spirit slipped, like a swimmer into a tideless sea, into the serene constancy of her affection again." (160) The water-womb image is also used to describe Horace's submission to Belle Mitchell. Though he realizes that Belle is a calculating woman, he does nothing to prevent her from "enveloping him like a rich and fatal drug, like a motionless and cloying sea in which he watched himself drown." (223)

In this trio of young men, only John wears the mantle of the Colonel naturally and easily; but he is not, as was his great-grandfather, a vigorous entrepreneur, a potential force in the community. His gay recklessness, his wild escapades, his indifference to danger alone are emphasized in the memories of those who survive him. Narcissa and the MacCallums* remember John as vitally responsive to life, seeking experience with joyful abandon. In contrast, his twin Bayard, pursued by the furies of fear and guilt, escapes from life: his violence is not motivated by a desire to touch the horizons of experience; it is self-destructive. And Horace, too, is isolated from life, immured as he is in his abstract fantasies. The difference between John and the other two young men is similar to the difference between the artist and the pseudo-artist whom Faulkner describes in *Mosquitoes*. The artist gets into life, wraps it around him, becomes part of it. In this sense, John, as Horace notes, is a poet.

Faulkner's characterization of Horace is far more successful than his portrayal of Bayard. The brooding sensitivity attributed to Bayard is not consistent with his crude, cold egoism; and the fear of dying which absorbs his thoughts seems out of line with his career. As a boy and young man he shared all of John's wild escapades. During the war, he was wounded in the stomach by a tracer bullet and was returned to the United States where he taught in a flying school. Then he voluntarily returned to the battle front to fly with his brother. It might be argued that until he sees his twin die, Bayard has no fear of dying. But if the experience is so traumatic, then he displays real courage in seeking out the German ace who downed John. Certainly, nothing in his career be-

---

* Faulkner's spelling of this family name is inconsistent. In this novel it is *MacCallum*; in "The Tall Men" it is *McCallum*.

fore or after the death of his brother accounts for the sense of guilt that plagues him. In *The Mansion*, one of the characters suggests that Bayard knew the fleeting thought that, as a twin, he had a double chance of remaining alive, and that when his brother was killed he assumed the guilt for John's death. The explanation is interesting in focusing attention upon Bayard's fear of dying and his sense of guilt, but it does not explain why his torment drives him to violence that is a continual testing of his courage. If, however, a man with Horace's sensibilities and wartime record were a Sartoris, the oppressive guilt produced by alienation from the tradition would be convincing. In these two characters, Faulkner seems to have dramatized his own feeling of alienation from the tradition of his great-grandfather.

Faulkner's failure to bring his main character to life is a serious flaw in the novel. Another defect is the intrusion of a mawkish and sentimental note in the glamorous fatality Faulkner attributes to the Sartoris family. The facts we are given about the Sartorises hardly warrant the romanticism. The Young Colonel leads a peaceful small-town existence and dies at an advanced age of a heart ailment. If one is going to view the death of one's ancestors as proof of glamorous fatality, then every family has death in the sound of its name. The father of the twins, John and Bayard, dies of yellow fever, and the Colonel himself, though a romantic and adventurous figure, comes through five years of war without a wound and with no feeling that he is doomed. He has sufficient vigor and vitality after the Civil War to rebuild his plantation house and recoup his fortunes. The Colonel is only in his early fifties when he is killed, but even in his death he is hardly a victim of doom. He chooses deliberately and consciously to go without his weapons on the day Redlaw kills him.*

Aside from these weaknesses, and Faulkner's failure to capture the general in the specific, *Sartoris* is a rich and interesting novel. Many characterizations—Aunt Jenny and Simon, Narcissa and Horace—are well done, and such minor characters as Byron Snopes, Will Falls, Doc Peabody, the members of the MacCallum family are masterfully created. Most of the scenes are successful. Although a few of the tales included are irrelevant to the main

---

* "Redlaw" becomes "Redmond" in *The Unvanquished*.

theme, the novel has a kind of structural unity. Perhaps of most importance, Faulkner has begun to use the novel form poetically, to communicate mood. *Sartoris* is significant as a threshhold novel. In It, Faulkner develops the techniques and themes and expresses the mood of existential despair that generate the masterpieces of the next few years.

The Unvanquished

The Unvanquished (1938) * has received little recognition as a serious work and as a novel.[1] Most critics have dismissed it as a collection of short stories, though its seven stories have far more structural unity than the stories in *The Hamlet* or *Go Down, Moses,* which are generally accorded the status of novels. All the stories in *The Unvanquished* have the same central character and narrator, Bayard Sartoris (Old Bayard of *Sartoris*), and each of the stories constitutes an episode in the transition of Bayard from childhood to manhood.

To declare that *The Unvanquished* is a serious novel is not, by any means, to insist that it has great literary merit. Five of the seven stories were originally published in the *Saturday Evening Post,* and Faulkner's revisions did little to improve the slick plots, the grating sentimentality, the stereotyped characters, and the stock situations. Stylistically, the book is erratic. Some of the scenes are among the worst Faulkner ever wrote; others, such as the mesmerized flow of Negroes to the river, are among the best.

Despite the commercial slickness of the majority of these stories,

* I have chosen to discuss this novel out of chronological sequence not only because it concerns the Sartoris family and therefore forms a unit with *Sartoris* but also because it clarifies Faulkner's attitude toward the past, and thereby contributes to our appreciation of difficult novels such as *The Sound and the Fury* and *Absalom, Absalom!*

they deal effectively with a serious theme: the heritage of the past. In no other novel does Faulkner deal with the Southern heritage so forthrightly. The protagonist's progression from a wide-eyed romantic child to a realistic adult critic of the tradition is a manifestation of the simultaneous enchantment and disenchantment with the past characteristic of all Faulkner's novels. In this novel, the legend is evaluated.

Though "present time" in *The Unvanquished* is the Civil War and post-War period, the era is dealt with as the past. The narrator, Bayard Sartoris, is recalling events that took place many years before. The narrator's temporal distance from the incidents he describes, emphasized by occasional interjections, establishes perspective. Bayard comments about his childish response to the odor of his father's clothes: "which I believed was the smell of powder and glory, the elected victorious but know better now: know now to have been only the will to endure. . . ." (11)* Bayard recalls only those events which his consciousness registers at the time the events took place. Thus Faulkner is able to present the past in successive episodes through the mind of a twelve, then thirteen, fourteen, and fifteen-year-old boy, and finally of a twenty-four-year-old man. The stories trace the gradual intrusion of reality upon the boy's consciousness. A passage from the first story and one from the last illustrate the technique and the theme. In "Ambuscade," Colonel John Sartoris seems a story-book hero to his twelve-year-old son: "He was not big; it was just the things he did, that we knew he was doing . . . that made him seem big to us." (10) At twenty-four, Bayard sees clearly his father's "violent and ruthless dictatorialness and will to dominate." (142) And he perceives in his father's "intolerant eyes . . . that transparent film which the eyes of carnivorous animals have and from behind which they look at a world which no ruminant ever sees, perhaps dares to see, which I have seen before on the eyes of men who have killed too much, who have killed so much that never again as long as they live will they ever be alone." (146)

At twelve, Bayard sees the Civil War as a gigantic display of Southern heroism and gallantry. In the opening scenes of the novel, he and his Negro friend Ringo play at war. Laboriously, they con-

* Signet Edition.

struct a mud Vicksburg and take turns being General Pemberton and General Grant. Ringo's uncle, Loosh, suddenly interrupts their game. Bayard notes that the Negro's eyes seem strange and that his wife's voice sounds curious, but he cannot comprehend Loosh's intense excitement at the advance of the Yankee troops into Mississippi. The Negro's attitude and his words register in the child's mind simply as an inexplicable interruption of their game.

The year in this first episode is 1863. On January 1, Lincoln issues the Emancipation Proclamation. On July 4, Pemberton surrenders Vicksburg to Grant. To the north of the Sartoris plantation, Corinth falls, and the Yankees sweep over Mississippi. Around the twelve-year-old, the old order is crumbling, but he cannot understand the significance of the events his consciousness registers. The Colonel arrives and the two boys await impatiently for evening and the stories of battle and glory. The Colonel's abstracted air and his dismissal of the boys to bed surprise and disappoint them, but they cannot keep awake as they watch from the top of the stairs the preparations to bury the family silver. The activities of the adults are mysterious and exciting and only faintly ominous. Reality impinges hazily upon the child's world, and the next day Bayard cannot decide if he dreamed or heard his father warn Granny to watch Loosh.

The finale of this story is slick and offensively coy, but thematically it is appropriate. The boys shoot at the Yankees and then hide beneath the spread skirts of Granny. They are frightened, but war remains an exciting game in which only a horse gets hurt. The enemy enters into the spirit of the game: the Yankee officer is kindly and indulgent. And once the excitement dies down, the security of routine life is re-established as Granny forces the boys to observe the ritual of washing out their mouths for swearing.

In the second episode, "Retreat," Bayard and Ringo are thirteen. John Sartoris, with his band of irregulars, has been harassing the enemy troops. Loosh's growing excitement brings about Rosa Millard's decision to leave the plantation rather than expose the Colonel's family to possible retribution. Her attitude toward Loosh on the evening before they leave impresses Bayard, but he still does not understand why Loosh is acting so strangely, and why Granny insists that the chest of silver be brought to her room. He does, however, take a bit of Sartoris soil with him when they leave. His meeting with Uncle Buck McCaslin in Jefferson forces him to recognize his social role as the son of Colonel Sartoris. But he and Ringo are children, and when they encounter the Yankees on the road they thoughtlessly leave Granny and ride off after the mules that the enemy steals. Their escapade with Colonel John gives them a taste of the war they have been playing at in their games. The reality turns out to be just as they imagined it—glamorous and thrilling. Colonel John fools the Yankees into thinking they are surrounded. The surrender is quick and no one is hurt. The prisoners are stripped of their possessions and clothing, and permitted to escape during the night as their amused captors look on. The Colonel lives up to the image of romantic hero that Bayard has created, and in the final scenes of the story, the boy recalls vividly and in detail the exciting escape his father makes when the Yankees approach the plantation. He barely mentions the burning of the Sartoris house.

These first two stories present the Civil War as the legend of heroism and glory that is the heritage of the Southern child. In the third episode, "Raid," however, the reality of the Southern tragedy pierces the legend as Bayard, now fourteen, begins to comprehend. On the trip to Hawkhurst in Alabama, Bayard and Ringo boyishly contemplate seeing the railroad. Bayard had visited Hawkhurst once and his experience is one of the few that the two boys have not shared. Ringo eagerly anticipates the opportunity to catch up with his friend. Absorbed though he is by this childish rivalry, Bayard notes the cruel scars the war has left upon the land they travel through. His awareness of the widespread destruction reaches its climax when he sees the railroad tracks at Hawkhurst, torn from the ground and twisted around a tree. He is now ready to understand the symbolic significance of Drusilla's story about the defiant and proud Confederate locomotive racing for the last time along the tracks with the Yankee engine in pursuit. And he does not miss the irony of Drusilla's bitter speech about how dull and stupid life was before the fathers and fiancés went off to war to be killed. Bayard is now capable of understanding

Loosh's strange excitement and of sensing the tragedy of the chanting hypnotized Negroes moving blindly toward a freedom they long for but do not understand.

Notable in "Raid" and in the other episodes of the novel is the absence of bias. In no scene are the Yankees depicted as cruel invaders, and the Negroes are handled with compassion and understanding. Ringo, a Negro who remains faithful to the old order, is not accorded more sympathy than Loosh, who seeks freedom. Granny Millard treats Loosh and the Negroes they meet along the road as foolish and misguided children, but when she asks Loosh what right he had to tell the Yankees where the Sartoris family silver was buried, she can offer no reply to his poignant response:

"You ax me that? . . . Where John Sartoris? Whyn't he come and ax me that? Let God ax John Sartoris who the man name that give me to him. Let the man that buried me in the black dark ax that of the man what dug me free." (50)

Ringo enters manhood in this third episode, which is the best of the first six stories. On the trip to Hawkhurst, Granny will not permit either boy to drive the mules she has been forced to "borrow." After they leave the Yankee camp with the twelve chests of silver, the sixty mules and the column of Negroes, Ringo takes the reins and responds to the Yankee lieutenant who asks them how many of the one-hundred-and-ten requisitioned mules they lack. The fourteen-year-old Negro boy, whom the Colonel said was more intelligent than Bayard, begins his activities as Granny's partner. The superiority of Ringo is dramatized in the story that follows, "Riposte in Tertio." It is Ringo who understands the character of Ab Snopes whom Granny is forced to deal with, and it is Ringo who first realizes that Ab has sold them out. Several incidents reveal the significance of the Negro's assumption of leadership over Bayard. Distrusting and disliking Ab Snopes, Ringo does not call him "Mister," a violation of the code governing the relations of white and Negro. Granny insists, however, that Ringo use the correct form. In the church scene, Ringo, who has kept Granny's accounts in the ledger and reads out the names of the people whom Mrs. Millard has helped with loans of money and mules, cannot sit with Granny and the white people. He must stay in the gallery reserved for the former slaves.

Despite the drastic alteration of social and economic conditions that the war has brought about, the ante-bellum code continues in force. The war permits Ringo to utilize his natural intelligence and display his superiority to the white boy, and Faulkner dramatizes the disparity between the code, based upon the assumption of Negro inferiority, and reality. Rosa Millard has worked with Ringo; she trusts and respects him; but she adheres rigidly to the old forms though the assumption upon which they are based is manifestly false.

In this church scene, Rosa's actions are ritualistic, her manners stylized. The old customs, which have lost their meaning, are already hardening into forms. Mrs. Millard lives in a cabin no better than the dwellings of the people she is regally patronizing, but her manners are those of a matriarch doling out alms to the peasants.

In the same way that the Civil War destroyed the economic foundations—the slave system, the plantations—upon which the social hierarchy was erected, it also lowered the moral barriers between the aristocrats like Miss Rosa and the entrepreneurs like Ab Snopes. Rosa's war-time activities, though morally questionable, do not actually dramatize a weakening of the aristocracy's moral integrity, for Mrs. Millard gives to the poor what she takes from the enemy. While there is a widening gap between the morality she practices and the morality she teaches Bayard and Ringo, her actions are necessary under the circumstances. In the first two stories, Faulkner underscores the breach between the romanticized vision of the child and the reality; in the next two stories, he reveals the widening breach between the older social and religious forms and the new realities that the war creates.

It takes the shock of his grandmother's brutal death to thrust Bayard over the threshhold of maturity. "Vendee" is a somber, bitter tale. The sunlight that bathed the four preceding episodes is gone. A steady rain begins to fall on the freshly dug grave of Rosa Millard and continues to fall through the long weeks of the vendetta. Bayard's relentless determination to avenge the murder of his grandmother is not, however, simply a ritualistic observance of the traditional code. Nothing in the story suggests a blind adherence to a formal code. Bayard's pursuit is motivated by deep personal grief, by anger, and by shock; but it is also a declaration of war against the scavengers of the post war South. Crumby is a Southerner, plundering his own defeated land and people. During the Yankee occupation, women and children were safe; now the Grumbys terrorize the defenseless widows and orphans. The brutality of Bayard's vengeance—pegging Grumby's body to the compress door and cutting off the hand that murdered Granny—is commensurate with Grumby's crime, and it serves as a warning to all the Grumbys plaguing the defeated confederacy. Significantly, Grumby's gang leaves for Texas. The events of the preceding three years have swept away Bayard's romanticism, and at fifteen he is grimly realistic. Thus in the next story, "Skirmish at Sartoris," though he is still only fifteen, he is acutely aware of what is happening in the post-war South.

Though handled lightly, this story is a perceptive analysis of the genesis of those attitudes that will plague Southerners for generations to come. Aunt Louisa, Mrs. Habersham, and the other women blindly adhere to customs, manners, and attitudes that have no relation to post-war conditions. Though they live in hovels, they act as if they presided over mansions, as if the Civil War has not occurred, as if the South has not been devastated. They cannot and will not adapt to the changed conditions. Drusilla, during the fighting, abandoned the traditional role of the Southern woman: she cut her hair short, and dressed and fought as a man. She now works side by side with John Sartoris to rebuild the plantation, but the older women will not permit her to act as if the old South were dead and a new South must be created. These matriarchs, whom Faulkner consistently depicts as the curators and transmitters of the old traditions, will continue to impose upon future generations the empty and meaningless forms that will, within several generations, isolate the Southerner from twentieth-century reality and sap his individuality.

In this story, too, Bayard recounts the genesis, as Faulkner sees it, of the post-war racial problem. The carpetbaggers and avid reconstructionists cause the tensions that create the adamant segregationists of the future. At the beginning of the story, it is implied that the Southern men might have been able to adjust to altered conditions and resolve the racial problems if the reconstructionists had not interfered. Bayard describes the men and women as drawn up in a battle line against each other "for the reason that the men had given in and admitted that they belonged to the United States but the women had never surrendered." (119) Bayard records hearing his father say, " 'We were promised Federal troops; Lincoln himself promised to send us troops. Then things will be all right.' " About this statement, Bayard comments, "That, from a man who had commanded a regiment for four years with the avowed purpose of driving Federal troops from the country. Now it was as though we had not surrendered at all, we had joined forces with the men who had been our enemies against a new foe whose means we could not always fathom but whose aim we could always dread." (125-6)

By putting up Negro candidates for elected offices, the reconstructionists, in effect, strip the whites of all control over their local governments, placing it in the hands of Negroes totally unprepared to assume such responsibility. Uncle Cash, who was a carriage driver before he ran off to join the Yankees, is the candidate for town marshal. When all attempts fail to persuade the reconstructionists that their tactics are wrong and intolerable, Sartoris and the other white men resort to violence. The two Burdens are shot and killed by Sartoris, and the ballot box is carried off to the Sartoris plantation by Drusilla. The Negro is effectively disenfranchised as George Wyatt hands out the marked ballots to the assembled white men. The lawless pattern of the future has been established. The modern South is born.

Within a few years, the ante-bellum codes and social forms and attitudes harden into an iron mold that threatens individuality and integrity. In the final and best episode of the novel, "An Odor of Verbena," Bayard must break from the tradition to preserve his integrity. As the son of John Sartoris, he is expected to avenge the murder of his father. Faulkner powerfully expresses the binding force of the tradition by giving his story the framework of Greek tragedy. Bayard becomes Orestes, and Drusilla becomes Electra. The scenes and the conversations are stylized, and the action and thought are mannered as if prescribed by ancient and inviolable ritual. The year is 1876, only eleven years after the end of the war, but the patterns are already rigid. Bayard's experiences have made him aware of what has taken place in the South. His conflict is precisely and simply stated in the opening scenes of the chapter when Bayard decides not to tell Professor Wilkins that he intends to defy the code of vengeance. He muses that the professor is "too old to have to stick to principle in the face of blood and raising and background." (137) That is for Bayard, at twenty-four, to do. Long before Ringo arrives to inform him that his father has been murdered, Bayard has decided what he would do when the long awaited knock on the door sounded. On the ride to Jefferson, Bayard imagines Drusilla awaiting him on the steps of the rebuilt mansion, the pistols in her outstretched hand, the sprig of verbena, her symbol of courage, in her hair. He pictures her as "the Greek amphora priestess of a succinct and formal violence." (139)

Faulkner uses flashbacks to dramatize Bayard's reasons for breaking with tradition. The young man recalls two scenes in which he walked with Drusilla in the garden. The first scene takes place four years earlier, when Bayard is twenty. At that time, the Colonel and Drusilla have been married four years. The mansion which Drusilla describes as the aura of her husband's dreams has been rebuilt, and the Colonel has started his railroad venture with Redmond as partner. Bayard walks with his father's wife shortly after he has seen his father clean and reload the derringer with which he has killed a country man, "almost a neighbor . . . who had been in the first infantry regiment when it voted Father out of command; and we never to know if the man actually intended to rob Father or not because Father had shot too quick." (140) Bayard has also witnessed the dead man's wife walk into the house and fling the money John Sartoris sent her into the Colonel's face.

In the garden colloquy, Drusilla argues that Father's dream is worth all the killing and the pain. His is not, she declares, simply a dream of personal success like Thomas Sutpen's, because the Colonel is " 'thinking of this whole country which he is trying to raise by its bootstraps.' " Bayard replies that it will do the people Father is trying to help little good if they are dead by the hand of their benefactor. Drusilla insists that to make dreams a reality, killing is necessary. She cites the murder of the two Burdens. Bayard, who records that event without comment in "Skirmish at Sartoris," now answers: " 'They were men. Human beings.' " (141)

The moral issue is clearly defined when Drusilla declares: " '. . . if it's a good dream, it's worth it. There are not many dreams in the world, but there are a lot of human lives. And one human life or two dozen—' " (141) For Bayard, no dream, no abstract design, is worth a single human life.

The second garden scene takes place four years later, a few weeks before Redmond kills Sartoris. Bayard has followed his father's political campaign against Redmond for the state legislature, and he knows that his father has needlessly taunted his opponent whom he drove out of their partnership and whom everyone knows he will defeat in the election campaign. The townspeople, represented by George Wyatt, realize that Sartoris is badgering his opponent excessively. Wyatt tells Bayard: " '. . . he ought to let Redmond alone. I know what's wrong: he's had to kill too many folks.' " (143)

Walking in the garden, Drusilla tells Bayard that there are worse things than killing or being killed. " 'Sometimes I think the finest thing that can happen to a man is to love something, a woman preferably, well, hard hard hard, then to die young because he believed what he could not help but believe and was what he could not (could not? would not) help but be.' " (143)

Drusilla is a personification of the forces that Bayard must defy; to retain his integrity and individuality he must uphold his belief in the sanctity of the human being. The power of the forces he opposes with principle is symbolized in the scene where Drusilla makes him kiss her. The pull of blood, environment, and tradition is cleverly equated with the powerful sexual response of a young man to a beautiful older woman. By walking unarmed into Redmond's office, Bayard courageously declares that the traditional code is outmoded. As George Wyatt admiringly acknowledges, " 'Well by God . . . Maybe you're right, maybe there has been enough killing in your family. . . .' " (158) Of more importance, Bayard passes moral judgment upon his father and the tradition. Sartoris goaded Redmond to the point where he had to murder or face himself as a coward. Like Thomas Sutpen in *Absalom, Absalom!*, Sartoris is consumed by his dream and becomes indifferent to the integrity of others. Bayard's moral criticism of the past will be more precisely articulated by Ike McCaslin in the fourth section of "The Bear."

Faulkner's own critical attitude towards the tradition needs emphasis because it refutes George Marion O'Donnell's still slavishly accepted thesis that Faulkner equated traditional morality with the Sartorises.[2] Faulkner made no such simple equation. Certainly, he created around the Sartoris family an aura of romanticism that he could not and probably did not want to shake off. Almost invariably, he invoked the romantic legend by viewing it through the mind of a boy-narrator, but he was clearly aware that these legendary figures, whom he cherished and admired, did not share his own moral position. It is clear in Faulkner's novels that the author was aware that the moral heritage the Sartorises transmitted to their heirs was a terrible and oppressive burden.

The combination of romanticism and realistic criticism of the past in *The Unvanquished* thus characterizes Faulkner's own relation to his heritage. His mature appraisal of the past did not correspond to his boyhood feelings, but one did not negate the other; in this book and in many other stories he expressed both attitudes simultaneously. Unfortunately, whenever Faulkner attempted to render the past as it probably existed in his boyhood imagination, he tended to resort to melodrama and sentimentality. When he dealt with the past critically, as he docs in *Absalom, Absalom!* he recreated that past effectively and powerfully. Artistically, the stories such as "An Odor of Verbena," which reveal the emptiness of the traditional forms, are far superior to such stories as "My Grandmother Millard," which sentimentalize the chivalric tradition.

The Unvanquished is a serious assessment of the Southern legend, and a declaration of moral—if not social and emotional —independence from the past. With its ritualistic atmosphere, its use of the ancient Greek myth, "An Odor of Verbena" expresses tangibly the heavy imprisonment of the individual by the past. It is significant, I think, that both Bayard and Ike McCaslin, the only two of Faulkner's young protagonists to defy the tradition, grow up in the nineteenth century. They are still close enough to the real past to have something to strike out against. The twentieth-century protagonists of the early novels are held in suspension by a past that has no reality for them and by a present whose reality they reject. Not even through defiance can they achieve identity as does Bayard. After a few decades have passed, they have nothing sufficiently tangible to rebel against.

The Sound and the Fury

The Sound and the Fury (1929), Faulkner said, began as a short story about Caddy Compson. Though the novel expands her story into the story of the Compson family, Caddy remains the focal center. The first three sections present, through the minds of her brothers, Caddy's tragic history and its effects upon their own lives. By means of the interior monologue technique in these sections, the past and the present are juxtaposed, the effects related to the cause. This method, used in three of the four sections, is confusing to the uninitiated reader, and it might be helpful to begin the analysis of the novel with a study of its technique.

» » Narrative technique: Section I

The first section is set in the mind of a thirty-three-year-old idiot, Benjy, the youngest of the four Compson children. By choosing to tell his story through the mind of an idiot, Faulkner imposed rigid limitations upon himself. Benjy cannot talk; he can communicate his feelings only by howling, moaning, or remaining placid. He reacts to sensual stimuli; otherwise, the activity of his brain is limited to memory. He is incapable of making judgments, of un-

COMPSON GENEALOGY.

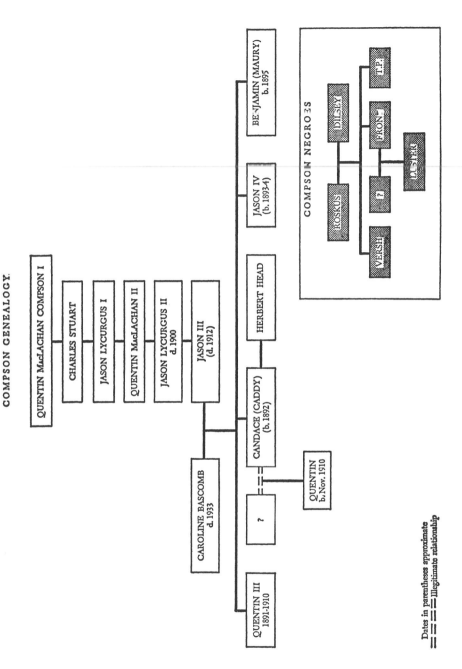

QUENTIN McLACHAN COMPSON I

CHARLES STUART

JASON LYCURGUS I

QUENTIN McLACHAN II

JASON LYCURGUS II
d. 1900

JASON III
(d. 1912)

BENJAMIN (MAURY)
b. 1895

JASON IV
(b. 1893-4)

HERBERT HEAD

CAROLINE BASCOMB
d. 1933

CANDACE (CADDY)
(b. 1892)

QUENTIN
b. Nov. 1910

?

QUENTIN III
1891-1910

COMPSON NEGROES

ROSKUS

DILSEY

T.P.

FRONY

LUSTER

VERSH

?

Dates in parentheses approximate
= = = = Illegitimate relationship

derstanding relationships between ideas or events. At thirty-three, he has not learned that fire burns. He places his hand on the hot stove, but makes no association between the pain in his hand and the heat created by the fire. Benjy also is devoid of a time sense, making no differentiation between the past and the present. A remembered event is as real to him as an occurrence in the present.

Faulkner is extraordinarily successful in creating the illusion of an idiot mind. One of the reasons for his success is that he did not use the usual devices of the stream-of-consciousness technique to establish transitions between thoughts (such devices are used in Quentin's section); for Benjy, Faulkner skillfully gives the reader external physical clues to indicate a transition in thought. Sometimes a shift from the present to the past, or from one remembered scene to another, is indicated in the text by a change in type face. But frequently in a long "recalled" scene that begins in italics, Faulkner reverts after a few lines to Roman type. Thus, though the type shift offers a clue to a transition in Benjy's thoughts, it is not always a reliable guide. Another clue to a shift in scene and to the chronology of events in the story is provided by Benjy's Negro companions. Three Negroes serve as his caretakers: Versh, T.P., and Luster. In almost every scene set in the present (April 7, 1928), the name of Luster appears. Scenes from the past are readily identifiable by the presence of Versh or T.P. The Negroes also indicate the approximate time that an event occurs. When Benjy is a child, he is cared for by Versh; when the idiot is about eleven, T.P. takes over the role of caretaker.

After a few pages, the reader can begin to recognize that a shift in scene has occurred, but he may still be puzzled by the fragmentation of the scenes. Benjy relives fifteen events from the past. Many of these events are presented in short fragments, each of which is a unit in a sequence. Benjy's mind works slowly and ploddingly, and because he actually relives the event, all his remembered scenes are developed in chronological sequence. When Benjy's memory is stimulated, and the stimulus is associated with an episode of the remembered event out of its chronological sequence, Benjy usually returns to the beginning of the scene and moves through it as it actually occurred. The first scene from the past in the novel, for example, is that of December 23rd. Getting

caught on a nail as he goes through a hole in the fence with Luster stimulates Benjy to relive the day a quarter-century earlier
when he and Caddy were delivering a message from Uncle Maury
to Mrs. Patterson. On that day, Benjy snagged his clothing returning from the Patterson house. After recalling this fragment of the
event, Benjy's memory shifts to the beginning of the sequence
when he is in the house and wants to go out to the gate to meet
Caddy.

A number of the events that Benjy recalls are presented in
closely spaced fragments, but other events are broken up into episodes scattered throughout Benjy's section of the novel. Recognition of the relationship between fragments is possible through
clues Faulkner provides. The presence of certain characters in certain settings is a clue, but more important is the repetition of key
words. T.P.'s drunken "whooey," his mention of "sasprilluh," for
instance, immediately identify the fragment as an episode in Caddy's wedding scene.*

Benjy is incapable of association of ideas; therefore, his memory
is stimulated by a physical sensation—a sound, or a motion, or the
sight of an object either in the present or in a scene being relived.
Sitting with his feet in the water of the creek as Luster searches for
a lost quarter duplicates the sensation Benjy experienced in 1898,
and he begins to relive the events of the day that his grandmother,
Damuddy, died. Once he begins to relive a scene, Benjy can be dis-
tracted momentarily by something that arrests his attention in the
present, such as Luster saying or doing something to him. But he
usually continues with a remembered scene unless he is diverted
by another memory or unless his attention is arrested by an occurrence in the present.

Because his mind registers no distinction between the present
and the past, Benjy's awareness of detail is the same for the past as
for the present. Each of the recalled scenes has emotional significance for him, and his memory has retained every detail, including
conversations and statements, such as his father's "*Et Ego in Ar-*

* See the Appendix, pp. 353-365, for a chronological listing of the fifteen remembered scenes, for a description of each of these scenes with the fragments
unified, for the clues to the identification of the fragments, and for a paginated
guide to the identification of each fragment.

cadia," which he could not possibly understand. Though some critics have questioned the validity of such total recall by an idiot, the overall impression created by Section I is that we are in the mind of an idiot.

The limitations imposed by Benjy's mind upon the narrative technique actually make Section I—once certain devices are recognized—easier to understand than Quentin's section, which is filled with allusions, images, symbols, and thought associations. Every line in Benjy's section (except one or two "Caddy smelled like trees") can be identified either as part of one of the fifteen scenes recalled by him, or as part of the action in the present. Some of the remembered scenes are long—Damuddy's death scene has eighteen fragments scattered throughout the section; the scene where Benjy's name is changed has twenty separate fragments—but most of the scenes are short, with the segments roughly contiguous.

Identifying scenes and fragments does not in itself, of course, make Benjy's book meaningful. Faulkner demands of his reader a great deal of active participation in the creative process. He has chosen certain scenes for Benjy to remember, and he presents these without interpretive comment. The reader must determine the relevance of the various scenes and recognize that the juxtaposition of certain scenes—Caddy in the swing and her daughter Quentin in the swing—is significant. Faulkner uses many images and symbols which the attentive reader must recognize and react to. But it is precisely the quality and intensity of reader participation that Faulkner requires which makes *The Sound and the Fury* a reading experience of the highest order.

» » Narrative technique: Section II

In Quentin's section, the interior monologue technique poses different problems. Quentin is intelligent, his mind moves rapidly from one thought to another—ideas, allusions, memories flash across his consciousness. Thoughts and memories are frequently fused: "shot his voice through the," "by the nose seen." He thinks in abstractions and symbols. But because Quentin's is an obsessed mind all his thoughts, images, allusions, memories, and reactions to immediate stimuli are related to his obsession. When he awakens on the morning of June 2, 1910, Quentin's psychological illness has just about run its course. He knows that this is to be the final day of his life. He has made his decision to commit suicide, and not once throughout the entire day does he betray any sign of indecision. The image of his body in the water recurs constantly as an image of longed-for peace. At about eight-thirty in the morning, less than an hour after he has awakened, Quentin mails his trunk key to his father. Throughout the day, Quentin's thoughts are focused on the events and relationships that fostered his inflexible determination to kill himself.

The first impression created by the opening pages of Section II is that the thoughts flashing through Quentin's mind have no connection with each other, but one discovers that they are all related. For example, as he stands at his dormitory window listening to the eight o'clock chimes and staring at the sparrow on the ledge, the lingering sounds of the last chime are associated in his mind with the dying light rays of time connecting the past and the present through Jesus. The thought of Jesus suggests St. Francis, who called death "little sister." Death and sister are associated with hell and punishment for incest, the incest Quentin did not commit but which he nevertheless confessed to his father. The memory of this confession forces to the surface the thought he is fighting to keep below the level of consciousness—his sister's affair with Dalton Ames.

The relationship of these fused thoughts is, of course, not immediately apparent, but gradually, as Quentin becomes involved in the events of his final day, the memories he is trying to avoid surge into his consciousness, and the fragmentary allusions are clarified and their relationship established. Not only do all of Quentin's memories and allusions reflect his anguish, but everything that occurs to him in the present becomes associated with it. Because Spoade, a Harvard senior, joked about Quentin's chivalric attitude toward women, Spoade is automatically associated with Caddy's seducer, Dalton Ames. Whenever he thinks of Harvard, Quentin is led to the memory of Caddy's wedding because Herbert Head, whom she marries, attended Harvard.

Such associations from the present stimulate Quentin's memories, and gradually the sequence of events that have driven him to suicide is unfolded. Unlike Benjy, Quentin constantly makes judgments, establishes relationships, derives significance from remembered scenes and from the situations he becomes involved in as he wanders about during his final day. Quentin's intelligent and anguished mind poses a problem for the reader. The significance of these memories for Quentin is not necessarily their real significance. If Quentin is not mad, he is on the border of madness, and the reader must therefore set Quentin's reflections into their proper perspective.

» » Narrative technique: Sections III and IV

Of the three sections, the third, Jason's, is the simplest. Jason is by no means a balanced individual, but his thought-pattern is logical. Also, because he is ignorant, superficial, and egotistical, his thoughts are easy to follow. He is prejudiced and his mind is filled with tags and clichés: once a bitch always a bitch; just like a woman; Negroes are all worthless and lazy; Jews are fine as individuals but. . . . In contrast to Quentin, Jason has tried to cut himself off from the past. The few scenes he recalls are registered in his mind in the present: "she says, I says." His thought-flow, for the most part, records his reactions to the events of the present, April 6, 1928. Because Jason's thoughts are easy to follow, a reader may tend to accept Jason's reflections at face value. But this Compson is no objective reporter. His thinking is biased, perhaps even more biased than Quentin's.

Book IV, Dilsey's section, provides a conclusion and a thematic counterpoint to the preceding books. It is written in traditional third-person narration without any attempt to render a single point of view. Most of the narration centers about Dilsey, but Faulkner also uses Dilsey to give an account of the final events in the Compson story.

» » The ordering of the sections

Each of the four sections is dated. If they were arranged in chronological order, Quentin's (II), dated June 2, 1910 would come first, followed by Jason's (III), then Benjy's (I), and finally Dilsey's (IV); the last three are dated April 6, 7, 8, 1928 respectively. Much critical energy has been expended on defenses and attacks of the arrangement that Faulkner chose for the sections. Some have argued, with justification, that if Jason's section preceded Benjy's the reader would have less difficulty following the story. But, as Jean-Paul Sartre has noted, when a reader attempts to set the scenes in each section into chronological order, he discovers that he has constructed a different novel; the same is true if the ordering of the sections is altered.[1] The most common justification offered for the book's order is that Benjy's section contains all the scenes and themes that are developed in the following books. The Damuddy death scene, which absorbs so much of Benjy's section, is referred to only twice, and briefly, in Quentin's. The long name-change scene of the first book occurs only once in Quentin's recollections, though the change of name is alluded to constantly. The only scene that Books I and III have in common is the funeral of Mr. Compson. Jason's description of the scene is in no way dependent upon the information presented in Benjy's section. The thoughts of the three brothers have many references in common, but the scenes that Benjy recalls are hardly essential to an understanding of the following sections.

Structurally, the arrangement is justified. As the novel stands, the sections are in their chronological order. *The Sound and the Fury* is not the story of Benjy, Jason, Miss Quentin, and Dilsey, on the Easter Days of 1928. It is the story of the Compson family, a story that extends from 1898 through the flight of Caddy's daughter, Quentin, from the Compson house in 1928. In Section I, Benjy's recollections present the essential details of the early childhood and adolescence of the Compson children. Quentin's thoughts seldom touch upon these early scenes; they are centered upon the events of the summer of 1909. In the third section, Jason recalls briefly only one incident before the funeral of Mr. Compson in 1912: the time Mrs. Compson mourned because Caddy kissed a boy. The final section is set entirely in 1928. The four sections tell the story of the Compson family and the arrangement of the books is therefore chronological, logical, and unalterable. In a Faulkner novel, structure and theme are inseparable.

» » The theme

The Sound and the Fury has occasioned wide critical interest. Interpretations have ranged from Sartre's declaration that it is a metaphysical novel concerned with time to Irving Howe's conclusion that it is a social novel depicting the deterioration of a family and of the American South. The scope of the book is so broad that, like a Shakespearean play, it can sustain any number of specialized interpretations. One basic fact that most of these interpretations touch upon is that the novel dramatizes a deterioration from the past to the present. A tragic sense of loss is so predominant and pervasive in each section and in almost every scene, that it can be considered the basic theme of the novel—a theme similar to that of Eliot's "The Waste Land." [2]

A superficial comparison of the two works can help to illuminate certain important elements in Faulkner's novel. Both Eliot and Faulkner present modern man as a self-centered being in a society where commercial values have replaced humanistic values. Both writers use the past to reveal, by contrast, the sterility of the present. In their handling of the past, however, they differ vastly. Eliot uses specific historical or literary contrasts to evoke specific values: the meaningful rituals of primitive society in comparison to the meaningless rituals of modern society; the sacrificial love of Cleopatra in contrast to the sterile love of modern woman. Faulkner's handling of the past is far less specific. Several critics have said that the values Faulkner upholds in *The Sound and the Fury* are those of the ante-bellum society of the South. A careful study of the novel, however, reveals few specific values assigned to that period from the past. The vague notions that Quentin holds about plantation society are clearly established as romantic and adolescent. Despite the paucity of specific contrast in values, Quentin's section does evoke a feeling about the past that serves to make the present appear a waste land, but the past that Faulkner uses to set off the present in the novel is not the past of an earlier society or historical period, but the immediate past—the world of childhood, innocent and idealistic. Quentin is separated by two generations from the ante-bellum society. The values he associates with that society are transmitted to him by his father. Exactly how these are communicated to him is not indicated in this novel, but if the evidence of Faulkner's other work is relevant here, then it is through stories about his ancestors, their heroic exploits, their virtuous, aristocratic way of life. Such stories, as Faulkner shows in *Sartoris* and other works, are embroidered by the storytellers into glorious golden legends. They provide the child with a particular vision of the world, with codes he is to maintain, virtues he is to practice, reflecting the storyteller's own ideal of the way life should be. The child cannot discern in the stories where reality ends and legend begins, and he makes these stories a part of his own vision of life. It is therefore Quentin's feelings about the ante-bellum society rather than the actual values of that society that lead him to reject the present. In Faulkner's novel, the idealized childhood feeling about the past serves the same purpose as does the historical and literary past in Eliot's poem.

By juxtaposing the childhood of the Compson brothers with their present existence, Faulkner develops the theme of deterioration and loss. And by working many variations on his theme, he extends the meaning of his story far beyond the individual lives of the Compsons. It encompasses the degeneration of a family and of a society, becoming like Eliot's poem a revelation of the spiritual state of modern man.

This cursory comparison with "The Waste Land" can serve to point up another characteristic of the novel—its similarity to poetry. Like a poet, Faulkner is communicating primarily on an emotional level. His techniques, interior monologues, symbols, images, allusions, his structural devices, all contribute to the creation and communication of feeling. A specific device will illustrate the point. Faulkner's dating three of the four sections to correspond with the Easter season is obviously designed to evoke associations for the reader with the story of Jesus and the story of the Resurrection, and thereby provide an ironic contrast to the loveless, dying world of the Compsons. In the final section, Dilsey's response to the Easter sermon is used by Faulkner to communicate the feeling, without ever stating the idea, that human compassion is what modern man has lost and what he must recover to achieve regeneration.

It should be remembered that a detailed analysis of *The Sound and the Fury* can explain the significance of scenes and symbols, but the scenes and symbols in this novel are not so much intellectually meaningful as they are emotionally evocative. An interpreter, therefore, can strive to reveal the relationship of the parts to the whole, but he cannot hope to convey the full resonance of the scenes and symbols.

» » Two moods in the novel

Two literary works, alluded to by Faulkner in his novel, can serve to focus attention upon two dominant moods in *The Sound and the Fury*. The first, of course, is the passage from *Macbeth*, Act V, Scene V, from which the title is derived:

> To-morrow, and to-morrow, and to-morrow,
> Creeps in this petty pace from day to day,
> To the last syllable of recorded time;
> And all our yesterdays have lighted fools
> The way to dusty death. Out, out, brief candle!
> Life's but a walking shadow, a poor player
> That struts and frets his hour upon the stage,
> And then is heard no more. It is a tale
> Told by an idiot, full of sound and fury,
> Signifying nothing.

The despair and nihilism conveyed by this passage is the dominant mood of Faulkner's novel, offset only by the muted, antithetical mood created through the role of Dilsey in the final section. This second mood is conveyed in the hymn of St. Francis, "Canticle of the Sun," the poem from which the allusion "little sister death" in Quentin's section is taken. The canticle, as Matthew Arnold wrote, "artless in language, irregular in rhythm . . .

matches the childlike genius that produced it, and the simple natures that loved and repeated it." *

"O most high, almighty, good Lord God, to thee belong praise, glory, honour, and all blessing!

"Praised be my Lord God with all his creatures; and specially our brother the sun, who brings us the day, and who brings us the light; fair is he, and shining with a very great splendour: O Lord, he signifies to us thee!

"Praised be my Lord for our sister the moon, and for the stars, the which he has set clear and lovely in heaven.

"Praised be my Lord for our brother the wind, and for air and cloud, calms and all weather, by the which thou upholdest in life all creatures.

"Praised be my Lord for our sister water, who is very serviceable unto us, and humble, and precious, and clean.

"Praised be my Lord for our brother fire, through whom thou givest us light in the darkness; and he is bright, and pleasant, and very mighty, and strong.

"Praised be my Lord for our mother the earth, the which doth sustain us and keep us, and bringeth forth divers fruits, and flowers of many colours, and grass.

"Praised be my Lord for all those who pardon one another for his love's sake, and who endure weakness and tribulation; blessed are they who peaceably shall endure, for thou, O most Highest, shall give them a crown!

"Praised be my Lord for our sister, the death of the body, from whom no man escapeth. Woe to him who dieth in mortal sin! Blessed are they who are found walking by thy most holy will, for the second death shall have no power to do them harm.

"Praise ye, and bless ye the Lord, and give thanks unto him, and serve him with great humility."

The simplicity of the faith that finds expression in this poem is similar to the mood evoked by the Easter sermon in the final section of the novel, and Dilsey certainly belongs with those "who pardon one another for his love's sake, and who endure weakness and tribulation." In the words of St. Francis and of Faulkner, "they . . . shall endure."

* Translated by Matthew Arnold for his essay "Pagan and Medieval Religious Sentiment," which is included in *Essays in Criticism*, First Series.

» » Caddy's story

The nihilistic mood of the first three sections of the novel is created to a great extent by the reactions of the Compson brothers to the intrusion of reality upon their childhood world. Caddy's sexual maturity initiates that intrusion for Benjy and for Quentin, and the results of her maturation affect Jason's ambitions and dreams. Caddy's own encounter with reality and the way she reacts to it is therefore the focal point of the novel.

Only one Compson is capable of giving herself to love and to life—Caddy. Everyone else is completely self-absorbed. Caddy is the only vibrant, warm, and loving person in the family. In adolescence, she responds to love and to life; later her natural response is twisted into something corrupt by her family. Driven by the sense of guilt they foster in her, she becomes promiscuous.

During her early adolescence, Caddy begins to attract boys and to react to them. At fourteen, she becomes interested in clothing, dresses herself up prettily and uses a bit of perfume. At fifteen she is at the kissing stage. Her behavior is normal and innocent, but Benjy, Quentin, and her mother react violently to these signs of maturity. Caddy is seventeen when she gives herself to Dalton Ames. She is passionately in love with him. As far as can be ascertained, he seems to return her love. He appears concerned for her in his meeting with Quentin, and shows himself in that encounter courageous, strong, and kind, treating Quentin with gentleness and understanding. We cannot be certain from the information provided, but it is possible that Dalton does not coldly and cruelly desert Caddy. Suspecting that Quentin planned to meet Dalton, Caddy follows her brother. When she hears the pistol shot and rushes toward the bridge, she meets Dalton, who is leaving. Almost hysterical with fear for her brother's safety, she tells her lover that she never wants to see him again. Finding Quentin safe, she tries to pull free from her brother to run after Dalton to apologize; Quentin, however, holds her. We hear nothing more about Dalton's presence in the town after this scene; he may have left town immediately, and Caddy may never have had the chance to explain. Her anguish over her loss of Dalton is compounded by her mother's lamentations and her own sense of guilt about Benjy and Quentin. She loves her brothers; she has, in fact, provided them the female love and tenderness that their mother could not give them. She understands Quentin's feelings far more clearly than he does himself. Her compassion for him is great enough to be self-sacrificial. She does not object to his proposal of a death-pact. She is too vitally alive, however, to help him plunge the knife into her throat. And later, though she is in love with Dalton, she is willing to commit incest if the act will bring Quentin release from his anguish. Caddy's love for her brother is not essentially incestuous; her offer of herself is an act of abnegation, motivated by a love that is almost maternal. Caddy's dilemma is that she must sacrifice her own response to life if she is to keep her brothers happy; but she is too passionate, too vibrantly alive, too vital to immolate herself.

Her loss of virginity produces a neurotic furor in the family. On orders from Mrs. Compson, Jason spies on his sister. Her mother's self-pitying lamentations turn Caddy's love for Dalton into something evil. Quentin's desperate death-plea borders on madness, and Benjy's howl tears at Caddy's heart. Mrs. Compson carries Caddy off to French Lick to find her a husband, an action that distorts Caddy's love by emphasizing its sinfulness. Between her affair with Dalton Ames and her marriage to Herbert Head nine months later, Caddy does become promiscuous. Her statements to Quentin on the eve of her marriage reveal how deeply the reactions of her family have affected her. She has apparently been punishing herself by taking lovers: *"There was something terrible in me sometimes at night I could see it grinning at me I could see it through them grinning at me through their faces. . . ."* (131)* She is two months pregnant by an unknown lover when she marries Herbert, whom she does not love. Certainly one of the reasons that she marries is to save her family from disgrace. She is a tortured young woman when, about to marry, she begs Quentin to care for Benjy and her father. Her sense of guilt about them is an unusual display of concern for others in a household like the Compsons'. Caddy's suffering increases with her marriage. Her husband, apparently deciding that the baby she bears is not his,

---

* Modern Library and Vintage Editions.

forces her to leave his house. Caddy's love for her baby, a dramatic contrast to her mother's inability to love, places her at the mercy of her brother Jason. She sacrifices herself to support the child, sending two hundred dollars every month for fifteen years and extra money whenever she can in the desperate and futile hope that she can buy her daughter a semblance of the family life that she herself is unable to provide.

Caddy is by no means a paragon of virtue, but whatever her weaknesses and her sins, she achieves stature because she opens her heart to those around her. In a dying family she is the only one who is alive, who is not afraid to live and to love. Ironically, it is this very quality that creates such disastrous effects for Benjy and Quentin.

» » Section I

In his first three sections, Faulkner presents three different images of modern man—a sterile idiot, a virgin suicide, a deliberately childless and cruel egoist. (The images are not three representations of an identical mood: in order of presentation they create an intensification of the nihilistic mood.) The three sections also create a thematic progression by presenting the human being in a different stage of his development: Benjy's is a child mind, Quentin's an adolescent mind, Jason's the mind of an adult.[3] This progression, ironically, represents a deterioration, which is, essentially, a loss of emotional response. Benjy is all feeling and no power of reason; Jason is rationalism triumphant over feeling.

Benjy's thought-flow evokes the feeling of a child's world—its security, order, and love—and, at the same time, the feelings accompanying the loss of that world. The majority of Benjy's recollections record the existence and then the loss of some important element of his childhood. Every change, destroying his sense of security and order, evokes a howl of protest.

What comprises Benjy's world before it is destroyed? It has love —Caddy is devoted to her baby brother. It has innocence—Caddy smelled like trees. It has fixed routines symbolized by his activities with Caddy and by the smooth bright shapes Benjy sees in the fire and when he closes his eyes to sleep. Each member of the family and household—his grandmother, mother, father, brothers, sister, and the Negroes who care for them—has a place in this ordered world in which Benjy grows up. Then gradually, incidents occur that shatter the patterns of his limited world. Death makes its first impression upon him when the mare, Nancy, breaks its leg falling into the ditch and must be shot by Roskus. Then Damuddy dies. Though Benjy's memory focuses upon Caddy rather than upon the death of the grandmother, the incident has made its impression upon him, as do each of the four deaths that take place. The change of his name from Maury to Benjamin remains in his memory primarily because Caddy becomes increasingly protective. The entire name-change scene, which takes place, for the most part, in the library, evokes a feeling of warmth and security. Benjy sits before the mirror, watching a reflection of the ordered world that he knows: Caddy fighting with Jason because Jason has cut up Benjy's paper dolls; Mr. Compson settling the quarrel and meting out justice; Caddy protecting Benjy from her mother's stupidity. In these two earliest scenes are portrayed the pattern of Benjy's child world. At the same time, both scenes record a loss. From this point on, each remembered scene, in its chronological order, depicts either a loss or an alteration that will lead to a loss. Most of these scenes are related to the central loss of Benjy's existence: the loss of his sister Caddy.

The routine of delivering messages to Mr. Patterson ceases suddenly the day Mr. Patterson intercepts the note and then blackens Uncle Maury's eye. At the age of fourteen, Caddy begins to use perfume. Benjy howls. The clean, innocent smell he associates with her is smothered. As long as Caddy is sexually innocent, she remains with Benjy; as soon as she loses her innocence, she goes out of his child world. Benjy seems to sense the threat, and he howls at each sign of her maturation. Caddy finally understands that Benjy objects to the perfume and she washes it off. When she once again smells like trees, Benjy's order and security are restored.

Benjy's own sexual development, which makes no discernible impression on his memory, produces an important alteration in his routine: he no longer can sleep in Caddy's bed. Sex, throughout the novel, is a threat to security and peace. When Caddy is fifteen, she becomes interested in boys and sits with Charlie in the swing. Benjy, sensing the threat, searches for Caddy, and when he finds her in the cedar grove, he howls. Again Caddy restores order for Benjy by washing her mouth. These incidents are preludes to the annihilation of Benjy's world. Each time, water restores innocence; but when Caddy loses her virginity, washing does no good. Caddy can never again smell like trees. Caddy's marriage completes the process that her affair with Dalton Ames started. Benjy's world no longer has a center.

All the other losses the idiot suffers are related to or are directly caused by his loss of Caddy. To pay for the wedding and for Quentin's year at Harvard, Mr. Compson sells the pasture that Benjy loves. After Caddy's wedding, Benjy continues his routine of waiting for his sister at the gate. He does not know precisely what he waits for, but he knows that something is missing. His sexual impulses get mixed up in this sense of loss; and after he chases the school girls, he loses his sexuality: he is castrated. Two months after Caddy's wedding, Benjy howls: his brother Quentin is dead. The deaths of his father and then of Roskus further alter his existence.

At thirty-three, Benjy's life consists of routines that reveal the way he has adapted to his losses. Everything that is meaningful to him in the present, in some way, is related to the past and the things he has lost. The Compson pasture has become a golf course. Benjy enjoys watching the players on the green putting and then driving. He follows along the fence, watching the golf balls and listening for the players' shout—"Caddie." In this routine, the dual losses of his sister and his own sexuality are merged. Benjy is also fond of playing with what Dilsey calls his graveyard—a bottle in which he sticks two stalks of jimson weed. This game unites symbols of all his losses. The mound is the cemetery with its adornment of flowers. Jimson weed, a weed with a nasty smell commonly known as stink weed, is an ironic symbol of the loss of Caddy who smelled like trees. The weed was used by Southern Negroes as a contraceptive medicine, and among hill people it was considered a symbol of the male sex organ. The two weeds in the bottle become a memorial to Benjy's sexuality. The fire continues to provide him with the bright smooth shapes of his lost world and ho oito bcforc it quictly. Holding the white satin slipper (probably one of Caddy's wedding slippers), provides him comfort. And the weekly trips to the cemetery also become a part of his adult routine.

In 1928, Benjy has been following these patterns for fifteen years. He does not comprehend what he has lost; he merely senses that something is gone. Because his routines express his feeling of loss, they are very important to him. Any deviation from the patterns he has established provokes a reaction. For instance, when Luster—whose search for the lost quarter dominates the action in the present and gives the clue to the theme of this section and of the whole novel—tampers with the jimson weed graveyard, Benjy howls. The smooth shapes of the fire and the smooth shapes Benjy sees when he goes to sleep become, for him, the same as the smooth shapes the trees and bushes and houses form as the carriage travels along the road to the cemetery. In Section IV, Luster breaks the flowing pattern by turning left at the statue, and Benjy's anguished outburst ceases only when the carriage moves again and the smooth shapes begin to flow in their accustomed pattern.

What Benjy really loses in his loss of Caddy is love. As the rest of the novel reveals, loss of love is the central cause of decay in modern society. All the other aspects of deterioration, social and moral, apparent in the juxtaposition of Benjy's childhood world and his adult life, are symptomatic. Around the turn of the century, the Compson house is still a mansion, surrounded by many acres of land, with its Negro quarters, its barn for cows and horses, its pigpen; the Compsons still retain the appurtenances of a plantation society family, with a whole family of Negroes to care for its needs. In 1928, the holdings have almost vanished. The pasture is gone, the barn, with a jagged hole in its roof, contains one old horse and a dilapidated carriage; the house is unpainted. Only Dilsey and Luster are left to work for the Compsons.

But even in 1900, the deterioration of the household and the

family is fairly advanced. In Benjy's earliest memories, Uncle
Maury is a wastrel and an adulterer who lives off his brother-in-law.
Mr. Compson is drinking heavily; Mrs. Compson is a hypochon-
driac. The adults of the family are lost souls, weak, ineffectual rel-
ics of a vanished society. In these early scenes, however, there is
still a residue of the traditional social and moral values. And most
important, there is love. Mr. Compson seems to provide his children with tender understanding; he has passed on to them the traditions which he himself lacked the strength to uphold. Caddy is
there to offer love to Benjy and Quentin. Nevertheless, the disintegration of the adults has already made considerable progress, and
the forces that will destroy the children are already in motion. At
the end of Section II, Quentin recalls a picture from a child's book
in which two faces are lifted out of shadows by a weak ray of light.
The picture has been torn out, and Quentin is glad: "I'd have to
turn back to it until the dungeon was Mother herself she and Father upward into weak light holding hands and us lost somewhere
below even them without even a ray of light." (191)

In Section I, the past that reveals the sterility of the present is
the immediate past of childhood. The Compson family is deteriorating socially and morally, but these aspects of decay have little
significance for Benjy. He suffers from the loss of Caddy, the emotional center of his childhood world. Essentially, Benjy's loss and
Quentin's are the same.

» » Section II

Quentin's is an adolescent mind in stasis. The normal adolescent
adjusts to the discoveries his increased awareness and his experiences force upon him, gradually bringing his idealized childhood
vision into adjustment with reality. Quentin, however, is emotionally unstable, and attempts to keep intact his youthful world, to
stave off the intrusion of reality.[4] He tries to isolate himself from
the "loud, harsh world," is unable to do so, and destroys himself.

Quentin's notion of the way life should be is not presented directly in the novel. It is possible to piece together his vision, however, by considering his reactions to the incidents he recalls and to the incidents that occur on the final day of his life.*

Mr. Compson undoubtedly contributes much to Quentin's youthful vision. Quentin sees himself as the inheritor of a tradition of nobility, in which gentility, chivalry, courage, honesty, and integrity are accepted and practiced virtues—the tradition of plantation aristocracy, refined and romanticized. One of the final acts of Quentin's life is to leave a complete outfit of clothing to Deacon, the Negro factotum of Southern students at Harvard. Quentin searches for Deacon before he goes to Boston for breakfast and then returns to the campus to continue his search. When he does find Deacon, he gives him a note with instructions to turn it over to Shreve the following day. In the note, Quentin has told his roommate to give Deacon the clothing he left. The meaning of this act, which seems so inconsequential for one about to commit suicide, becomes apparent when it is related to the thoughts about Negroes that absorb Quentin's attention. On the trolley, returning from Boston, he sits beside a Negro. Quentin ponders the relationship of white man and Negro, recalling his uneasiness when he first came to the North. He resolved the problem for himself by deciding that "a nigger is not a person so much as a form of behaviour; a sort of obverse reflection of the white people he lives among." (105) His thoughts shift to his trip home at Christmas time. His train is stopped at a crossing. Looking out the window, he sees an old Negro waiting patiently for the train to clear the crossing. Quentin throws him a quarter, after calling out "Christmas gift," a traditional Southern game. The old Negro responds, "Thanky, young marster. Thanky." (106) The familiar relationship between the races makes Quentin feel at home. By giving Deacon clothing, Quentin assumes the role of white patron, a role difficult to play with Deacon, a clever opportunist who makes profitable use of the Southern students' desire for the white-Negro relationship to which they are accustomed. Dressed in an Uncle

---

* See the Appendix, pp. 365-377, for detailed descriptions of the action in the present and of each remembered scene, and for a paginated guide to the identification of scene shifts in Section II.

Tom's Cabin outfit, Deacon meets the trains bringing Southerners to the campus. He makes himself useful, remaining for a time "ubiquitous and garrulous," but "his manner gradually moved northward as his raiment improved." (116)

Quentin is aware of Deacon's shrewdness, of his difference from the Negroes in the South, but for a moment when he tells Deacon that he is making him a present, Quentin has the satisfaction of seeing the Negro as he wants to see him: "I saw Roskus watching me from behind all his whitefolks' claptrap of uniforms and politics and Harvard manner, diffident, secret, inarticulate and sad." (118) Quentin desires the familiar relationship, but he also has a warm feeling for the Negro which he retains from his childhood, a secret admiration for their "timeless patience . . . static serenity," (106) for the way they "come into white people's lives . . . in sudden sharp black trickles that isolate white facts for an instant in unarguable truth like under a microscope." (189) It is Uncle Lou, the possum hunter, and Dilsey who provide Quentin on the final day of his life the only recollections of security and stability that he has. They remain part of that secure childhood world that he cannot relinquish.

Another aspect of Quentin's plantation-society ideal is revealed through the characters of Mrs. Bland and her son Gerald, Southerners from Kentucky. They come out of Quentin's tradition, but they are not of it. They are like the *nouveaux riches*, aping unfamiliar manners and customs. The Blands' ideal is English nobility. Mrs. Bland talks too much about her son's noble ancestry, his plantation, his Negro servants, and resents Spoade's lineal descent from a noble English family. Gerald rows on the river because Oxford students in England row on the river. Under his mother's tutelage, Gerald does everything a true gentleman should do. Mrs. Bland's concept of a gentleman demands birth below the Mason-Dixon line. Poor Shreve, unlucky enough to be a Canadian, is no fit companion for a Southerner, and Mrs. Bland tries to get Quentin a new roommate. The Blands are an absurd and amusing pair. Gerald can sit among his contemporaries and listen without embarrassment as his mother brags about his looks, his wealth, his abilities, and his amorous conquests.

To Quentin, the Blands represent a deterioration of Southern society, but despite his contempt for them, Quentin is drawn into their company, because they represent, however burlesqued, the traditional world he considers his heritage. When he thinks of Gerald and Mrs. Bland, Quentin frequently draws upon images of royalty. The images are tinged with irony, but the real irony in the presence of the Blands in the novel is that they are probably a closer representation of plantation aristocracy than Quentin's ideal ized vision of it. Gerald is crude, egotistical, arrogant, and immoral; and his mother is silly, superficial, and bigoted. Their life and values probably depict the reality of the dead society to which Quentin attributes the great and noble virtues. Quentin also equates the other Southerner, Spoade, with a decline in values. He associates Spoade with sexual immorality because Spoade has joked about Quentin's chivalric attitude toward women. In the scene of Quentin's arrest, Spoade acts intelligently and realistically. Of all the Southerners with Quentin at Harvard, Spoade is the only one who seems mature. Spoade's pronouncement about Quentin after the battle with Gerald is a true appraisal: " 'Oh . . . the champion of dames. Bud, you excite not only admiration, but horror.' " (185)

These idealized social and moral values are part of the vision that Quentin struggles to keep intact. He is not, however, simply an idealist who finds the real world too crude to be bearable. His ideals are allied to the emotional ties of his early years and it is emotional security he seeks. His emotional difficulties drive him to defy time and his own physical and intellectual development by remaining a child. He makes much, for instance, of sexual innocence, of Compson honor; but it is not merely sexual innocence that he wants. He finds comfort only in the thought of childhood sexlessness. The image of self-castration provides no release: "But that's not it. It's not not having them. It's never to have had them then I could say O That That's Chinese I don't know Chinese." (135) If adult sex were totally and completely alien to him, as it is in childhood, then it could not disturb him.

Quentin's struggle with reality reaches its climax when Caddy loses her virginity. In the traditional social code and in the religious code, which is also a significant element in Quentin's background, female purity is an important concept. But the intensity of Quentin's reaction to his sister's loss of virginity is by no means explicable by his adherence to such codes; a reaction that leads to suicide has its roots in deep emotional problems. Quentin's pitiful lament, *"If I'd just had a mother so I could say Mother Mother,"* (190) and the predominant role given to Mrs. Compson throughout the novel require consideration of the relationship between Mrs. Compson and her children.

Caroline Bascomb Compson is obviously neurotic. She has four children, but she can be a mother to only one of them—Jason. Dilsey has assumed the burden of caring for the children; Mrs. Compson retreats to her bedroom with psychosomatic headaches. She is completely self-absorbed, and she responds to all situations with self-pity. She is so cut off from her children that she can say to Caddy, " 'Are you going to take that baby out without his overshoes . . . Do you want to make him sick, with the house full of company.' " (28) She describes the suicide of her son as inconsiderate. It is suggested that her sense of social inferiority helps to make her what she is. Benjy's idiocy is her "punishment for putting aside my pride and marrying a man who held himself above me." (122) Quentin, who heard that remark, later asks his father about it: "do you think so because one of our forefathers was a governor and three were generals and Mother's weren't." (120-1)

Mrs. Compson splits the family into Bascombs and Compsons, with herself, her brother Maury and her son Jason aligned against Mr. Compson and the other children. She alienates herself from Quentin and Caddy because they are more Compson than Bascomb, and her division of the family is apparent in Quentin's thoughts. He invariably associates his mother, Uncle Maury, and Jason with anti-Compson characteristics. Whatever the source of her neuroticism, Mrs. Compson is in constant retreat from reality, retaining a vision of herself as a refined, naïve, fragile Southern lady. For a long time she refuses to accept the idea that she produced an idiot child. When she can no longer escape from the fact, she insists, over the opposition of her husband, upon changing the child's name from Maury to Benjamin as if she were freeing herself of responsibility by eliminating any relationship of Benjy to the

Bascombs.* She insists, also, after the failure of Caddy's marriage, that Caddy's name never be mentioned, as if she could efface her knowledge about her daughter by never hearing her name, though she has Caddy's bastard child in the house with her. By 1920, her conversation with Jason reveals that Mrs. Compson has been able to erase from her consciousness the knowledge that Caddy was two months pregnant when she married Herbert.

The traditional moral and social values that Mr. Compson inculcates in his son are not the values of Mrs. Compson. Like her son Jason, she is more concerned with appearances than with moral integrity. Her husband explains to Quentin: "you are confusing sin and morality . . . your Mother is thinking of morality whether it be sin or not has not occurred to her." (121) To Mrs. Compson, Caddy's transgression can be remedied by finding her a husband. The kind of woman Mrs. Compson is and the values she accepts are best revealed in the kind of man Jason becomes. Throughout her life, Mrs. Compson takes comfort in Jason: he is the only child who turns out as she wanted.

Quentin, Caddy, and Benjy do not grow up associating love with their mother. Caddy supplies the love that Mrs. Compson denies Quentin and Benjy. She provides her idiot brother with tender protection and comfort, and she becomes for the sensitive Quentin the object of all the affection he would have devoted to his mother. Quentin's childhood feeling for his sister is therefore stronger and more complicated than the normal emotional tie between brother and sister. There can be no question that Quentin's emotional instability is related to the failure of Mrs. Compson to provide her children with the love they required. Unquestionably, too, Quentin's disgust with his own initial sexual impulses is related to the emotional deprivation of his early years.

In the scene with Natalie, Quentin responds sexually to the adolescent girl. Caddy enters the barn and observes them. When Natalie leaves, Quentin throws himself into the pig trough, an ex-

---

* The use of the name "Benjamin" is ironic. In Hebrew it means "child of [my] right hand," a favorite son. Faulkner, however, chose the name for its association with the idea of being "sold into Egypt." The allusion is confusing. In the Bible, Joseph is sold into Egypt.

pression of revulsion against his sexual feelings. This reaction may be due, in part, to his moralistic and religious training, but, as his other responses to sex indicate, it has its source more in his fear that the sexual feeling threatens his relationship with his sister. In this scene, Caddy seems offended by Quentin's hugging the girl with whom she has just quarreled. Quentin tries to re-establish intimacy with his sister by taunting her to admit that she was offended. When she says she does not care what he does, he smears the mud from his own body on her. In this incident, his own sexuality—not Caddy's—becomes for Quentin a threat to the status quo of his child world.

He reacts in the same way to each manifestation of his sister's sexual maturity, each time trying to restore their previous intimacy. At fifteen, Caddy kisses a boy. Quentin slaps her and then, resorting to a child's game of "give up," he scours her head in the grass, insisting that she say "calf rope." (152) If Caddy had married Dalton Ames instead of having an affair with him, Quentin's reactions would probably have been equally violent. Right after her affair in the summer of 1909, he talks to his father about suicide; but he is still alive eight months later to attend Caddy's wedding. The wedding announcement, which he leaves unopened for three days and visualizes as a bier with its two candles and flower, is his death warrant. On the eve of the wedding he desperately begs Caddy not to marry Herbert but to run away with him and Benjy instead. He is concerned in that scene with losing her irrevocably, not with her honor. It is the loss of Caddy herself, far more than her loss of honor, that really disturbs Quentin. It is only when Caddy forces her brother, by her marriage, to recognize that their relationship can never again be what it was that Quentin must commit suicide.

Quentin's emotional dependence on his sister is so great that he centers all his idealism upon her. Religious and moral values are equated with her sexual innocence, and with her conduct. Thus only in his childhood relationship with Caddy can Quentin keep his world intact. As with Benjy, therefore, reality intrudes upon Quentin's dream when Caddy loses her virginity. Both brothers react initially with overt protest. Quentin, however, attempts to deal with the intrusion. His desperate proposals to Caddy on the day that the family discovers she has given herself to a man constitute a mad attempt to efface an ineffaceable reality.

The symbol of honeysuckle is introduced in the scene immediately following Quentin's discovery of Caddy's loss of innocence. Honeysuckle is not simply a symbol of Quentin's incestuous desire; it is a symbol of sex, of his and Caddy's sexual maturity. It is a pervasive odor from which Quentin cannot escape, just as he cannot escape the loss of his childhood relationship with Caddy. Sex threatens the world that Quentin must preserve. A close analysis of the scene at the creek shows that Quentin's sole desire is to keep his insulated world intact by denying the reality of Caddy's act. His suggestion that they have committed incest is only one of several insane proposals. He first insists that she admit that Dalton forced her and that she does not love the man. Then he suggests that she gave herself to him, not to Dalton. Finally, he proposes a suicide pact.

In the beginning of this creek scene, Caddy comes down to the kitchen where Benjy is eating. As soon as the idiot sees his sister, he renews his howling. With her brother's scream ringing in her ears, Caddy runs to the creek to sit in the water, a gesture of remorse, it later becomes clear, for having hurt her brothers. Her statements to Quentin and her actions reveal no sense of real guilt for having given herself to Dalton. Quentin follows his sister to the creek. In the conversation between them he shows no concern with Compson honor or with the morality of Caddy's act. He asks her if she loves Dalton. Her response is to place his hand on her chest to feel the thumping of her heart. Caddy, sensitive to her brother's anguish, says, "yes I hate him" and then without a pause, in the same breath, "I would die for him I've already died for him I die for him over and over." (170) She tells Quentin that he cannot understand what she feels because he has no sexual experience; he wildly insists that he has had experience and hysterically declares that they have committed incest and that he will tell their father what they have done. By saying it to their father it will become fact and then the two of them will be isolated from the world by their sin and the clean flames of their punishment.

The futility of his attempt to deny reality is clear to Quentin and he breaks down and cries. He recalls the day Damuddy died, when Caddy muddied her drawers in the creek and defied him by taking off her dress. Death, Caddy's independence, and the water merge together for Quentin. (It may be that in this fusion is explained his choice of death by water.) He takes out his knife and points it at Caddy's throat, proposing a union in death, a final blotting out of reality. Quentin does not have the strength or the will to kill his sister and himself. Death has not yet become his only possible means of obliterating reality. Caddy gets up to keep an appointment with Dalton. Quentin walks with her, leading her toward the ditch where the mare was shot by Roskus. He tries to re-establish their childhood intimacy by getting in front of her and holding her. "Im stronger than you," the eighteen-year-old Quentin says. But Caddy can no longer play games. Her childhood has ended. "I wont fight stop youd better stop," she tells him. (172)

While Caddy is with Dalton, Quentin walks around aimlessly, then returns to the branch. The smell of honeysuckle envelops him; he cannot escape from the fact of Caddy's sexual maturity. When his sister returns and offers to commit incest, he violently rejects the suggestion, shaking her hard and telling her to shut up. Incest, too, is reality; it would alter his relationship with Caddy. Quentin wants only to *say* that he committed incest. His sole desire is to isolate himself and Caddy somehow from the rest of the world as they were isolated during their childhood.

Quentin's meeting with Dalton is a disaster. His conception of himself in the traditional role of protector of women collapses, not only because he fails to accomplish his purpose but because he is forced to recognize his own weakness. Dalton is actually a reflection of Quentin's vision of himself: calm, courageous, strong, kind. The real Quentin does not measure up to the ideal Quentin, just as reality does not measure up to Quentin's romantic vision of what life should be.

Quentin's instability is due not only to emotional insecurity; there is also a character weakness, a lack of vitality and inner strength. Generation by generation the character of the Compson men has been attenuated. Mr. Compson and his son are not men of action as were their ancestors. Their withdrawal from life is a manifestation of their weakness. Quentin's attempt to stave off the intrusion of real life is not unlike his father's. Mr. Compson has passed on to his son a belief in an aristocratic code of conduct, and he must, therefore, at one time have believed sufficiently in these concepts to consider them worthy of inculcating in his children. His extreme cynicism and his alcoholism are obvious results of his own total disenchantment with life, with himself, and with the society he lives in. His cynicism is that of a disillusioned idealist. Though he seems to love his children and to offer them understanding and guidance, he is too weak a personality to provide them the security and strength they require. Since he passed on his nihilistic views to his adolescent son, it is no wonder that Quentin struggles so desperately to remain within his childhood world. The alternative is the nothingness of his father's views. In the discussions between father and son following the Ames episode, Mr. Compson tells Quentin that it is useless to try, as he is doing, to impose moral convictions upon life, not only because reality cannot measure up to such values, but because the values themselves are meaningless. Virginity is meaningless, and what is true about virginity is true about all human values. They are all created by man; they are not absolutes. Nothing in life has stability; everything is subject to the destructive force of time. Everything—men, their dreams, their ideals—is worn away by the clicking of tiny clock wheels. Mr. Compson tells his son not to fight time because "no battle is ever won . . . They are not even fought. The field only reveals to man his own folly and despair, and victory is an illusion of philosophers and fools." A watch recording the passage of time is "the mausoleum of all hope and desire." (95) Each tick brings man closer to death—the *reductio ad absurdum* of all human aspirations and experience. Time even annihilates suffering, and it will only be a matter of time before the anguish Quentin now knows will subside.

Quentin's enforced collision with fact through his sister's loss of virginity shakes the foundation of his beliefs. Recalling the odor of honeysuckle at night—the symbol of sex, of the force that destroyed his secure child world—Quentin thinks: "I seemed to be lying neither asleep nor awake looking down a long corridor of grey halflight where all stable things had become shadowy paradoxical all I had done shadows all I had felt suffered taking visible form antic and perverse mocking without relevance inherent themselves with the denial of the significance they should have affirmed." (188) Mr. Compson has told him that a man kills himself "only when he has realised that even the despair or remorse or bereavement is not particularly important to the dark diceman . . . it is hard believing to think that a love or a sorrow is a bond purchased without design and which matures willynilly and is recalled without warning to be replaced by whatever issue the gods happen to be floating at the time no you will not do that until you come to believe that even she was not quite worth despair." (196) Mr. Compson concludes the discussion with the observation that "was" is the saddest "word of all there is nothing else in the world its not despair until time its not even time until it was." (197)

There is a quality of defiance in Quentin's suicide.[5] He has not reached the stage of believing that Caddy is not quite worth despair, but he is not at all convinced that he will not reach that stage as time passes. Quentin, in effect, kills himself to stop time because time is the ultimate reality. Time has measured his own and Caddy's development into maturity. Their reaching maturity, symbolized by sex, has destroyed their childhood intimacy and undermined the stability of Quentin's existence. Quentin always thinks of death in images of stasis. One of these images with its childhood simile is particularly interesting: gulls motionless in air "like toys on invisible wires." (109)

Quentin equates time with reality, and that is why on the final day of his life he devotes so much effort to escape from the symbols of time. His own shadow is a reflection of passing time and he tries to avoid seeing it. He breaks his watch, symbolically stopping time. But as long as he remains alive he cannot escape from time. The position of his shadow, the sound of the bells, of the factory whistles, even the gnawing hunger pangs in his stomach remind him of time and reality. Only a sleep from which he will never awaken will stop the destructive effect of time, which wears away all values and beliefs and even deadens suffering.

Death by water, which Quentin thinks of in womb images—grottoes and caves of the sea—will offer the peace and stability he seeks. Water is Quentin's logical refuge. In his early years, it was the restorative whenever reality threatened. Caddy washed off her perfume; Quentin and Caddy washed off the mud from the pig trough after the Natalie incident; Caddy sat in the creek when her family discovered her affair with Dalton. For Quentin water does not absolve nor regenerate; it restores by effacing reality. It stops time.

The events of Quentin's final day dramatize the futility of his attempt to escape time. He is trying to suspend consciousness, to hold time in abeyance. He has to get through a number of hours before he can be at peace. He has been defeated; he has been forced to acknowledge that his world, with Caddy at its center, is irrevocably lost. He wants to avoid, during his final hours, anything that will remind him of his loss. But Quentin cannot isolate himself from life even during his few remaining hours. Everything that happens to him on June 2, 1910 stimulates his consciousness, and he relives the entire episode of his loss.

Shreve, for instance, asks him if he has dressed in his best clothes to attend a wedding or a funeral. Quentin, of course, is concerned with both: his sister's wedding causes his own funeral. Mrs. Bland invited him to a picnic. He associates the Blands with the memories he wants to keep suppressed. He does not open Mrs. Bland's invitation, but chance brings him into their party later in the day. On the bridge, which he has chosen for his suicide, he stares into the water. He sees a big trout that has defied the local fishermen. The trout becomes a symbol of stability in water, and he associates its shape with the clean flames that would isolate him and Caddy from the world.

The two central incidents of his afternoon activities lead him inexorably back to the childhood world he has lost. He becomes involved with the three young boys and then with the little girl. In the talk of the boys, dream and reality merge. They argue about the award for catching the trout as if it were already in their possession, an ironical reflection of Quentin's own predilection for living in a dream world. The boys exist in that untroubled state that Quentin has lost, but reality and pain intrude when they quarrel and the boy who cannot go swimming goes off by himself to sit

In the crook of a tree. The entire episode has to do with water. The boys fish; they argue about swimming, and finally two of them go off to swim. Their boyhood world and Quentin's merge through water.

There are several dimensions of irony in Quentin's involvement with the child whom he calls little sister. The episode becomes an inverted image of the experiences he is trying to keep below the level of consciousness. He has struggled to keep his own sister; now he cannot get rid of "sister." He has envisioned himself as the protector of women; now he is accused of assaulting a child. Sex has destroyed his own child world, and Julio's accusation justifiably makes Quentin laugh hysterically. The corrupt marshal and the justice of the peace reveal the gap between Quentin's ideals and reality. The series of events culminating in his meeting with the Bland party serve to force into his consciousness the memories he has been trying to keep submerged. Present reality and past reality come together. Quentin's attempt to isolate himself from the real world on this final day of his life is as futile as was his attempt to keep his child world intact.

As he becomes more involved with actual events, Quentin's absorption with the passing of time diminishes. In the morning he is conscious of every quarter-hour, of the sound of his watch ticking in his pocket, of the chimes and the whistles. When he is successfully suppressing his memories, his thoughts are concentrated on the symbol of reality, time. When his memories are irrepressible, he is involved with reality, and not its symbol.

The importance to Quentin of the order that he has lost is apparent in the way that he follows through the ritual—as best he can—of his suicide plans. Though he is in the vicinity of the spot he has chosen to kill himself, he takes the trouble to return to Cambridge solely to change his bloodied shirt and tie and to clean his vest. This ritual, like Benjy's rituals, reflects his lost world.[6] He must go into the water dressed as a gentleman. On the interurban trolley back to town, he remains socially aware and is shy about the black eye Gerald gave him. He avoids the stares of the other passengers by sitting on the left side of the car.

In the morning, Quentin's thought association is rapid. Brief al-

lusions to episodes flash across his consciousness, and as the day
progresses, he recalls entire scenes. In the evening, as his death
hour approaches, the tempo of his thought association becomes
very rapid. Water and death images are frequent. Many of the allusions that dominated his thoughts in the morning recur. Jesus
walking down the long and lonely light rays, an image of values
lost through time, is related to the memory of the story-book picture with the two faces in the single ray of light and below them
darkness. Jesus, religion, and the Negroes are momentarily fused.
Quentin's ironic vision of himself as an upholder of lost values is
reflected in his identification with Jesus. Thinking of the bloodied
tie he would be leaving for Deacon, the "tie was spoiled too, but
then niggers. Maybe a pattern of blood he could call that the one
Christ was wearing." (190) His final concentrated recollection before he leaves the dormitory room is the conversation with his father about suicide: "you are not thinking of finitude you are contemplating an apotheosis in which a temporary state of mind will
become symmetrical above the flesh and aware both of itself and
of the flesh it will not quite discard you will not even be dead."
(195-6)

Quentin's response is an incredulous "temporary," signifying
his refusal to accept Mr. Compson's view that his pain is only temporary, that it too will be effaced by time. He insists that he will
never come to believe that Caddy was not quite worth despair:
"nobody knows what I know." (196) Mr. Compson articulates
the mood of despair that predominates in Section II. However,
Quentin's suicide cannot be interpreted in metaphysical terms:
he does not kill himself because he agrees with his father that life
is meaningless or because he wants to shut off consciousness before
he comes to the point when he no longer suffers from the loss of
Caddy. His problem is emotional, involving his deepest psychic
bond—to his sister, whom he has lost.

Despite his weakness and self-involvement, Quentin is a sympathetic character. Section II is a heartfelt cry of despair, one of the
most moving expressions of disillusionment and suffering in literature. It dramatizes that state of mind and soul that existential-
ists have described and that Sartre has termed *l'angoise*, when man

knows absolute despair and either commits suicide or develops a vision that gives meaning to existence.

» » Section III

The third section of *The Sound and the Fury* is venomous and bitter. The theme of loss and disintegration reaches its dramatic climax and its general significance becomes clear. Jason Compson is a repulsive and cruel man; he is the reality that Quentin could not accept. And the life of the angry Jason, filled with sound and fury, is empty and utterly meaningless.

Jason is the only one of the Compson brothers who achieves functioning adulthood. He is, Faulkner informs us in the Appendix to the novel, sane, but this statement is ironic. Jason is not disoriented; he thinks in a logical manner; if these are the criteria for sanity, then he is sane. Jason's thinking, however, is a continuing process of rationalization, a logical justification of illogical desires and acts. Jason can live within society only because the values of modern society mirror his own. Indeed, this Compson is very sick. His alienation from the members of his family and from the people he works with, his excessive cruelty, his irrational acts give the lie to his facade of rationality. Jason's thinking also is divorced from reality. An action that is obviously cruel, that is motivated by an emotional need beyond Jason's control, becomes, in his thoughts, a necessary act justified by logic. Jason's pride in his practicality and rationality is, in itself, a manifestation of his illness.

One of the most despicable characters Faulkner ever created, Jason may very well rank with the most hateful villains in literature. He is man depicted at his lowest possible state. He values nothing, and cares only for surface appearances. He is not concerned with the morality of his niece's actions: his only objection is that the townspeople will talk and that her promiscuity will reflect upon him. The only value important to him other than social acceptability is money. At his own father's funeral, he looks at the flowers heaped on the grave and estimates that they must be worth fifty dollars. Conscience is meaningless to him: "I'm glad I haven't got the sort of conscience I've got to nurse like a sick puppy all the

time." (246) God does not exist; human relationships and feelings
have no signficance unless they are translated into monetary terms.
The one person with whom he is apparently at ease is Lorraine, a
whore. Even revenge is measured by money—the amount he extorts
from Caddy.

Jason can survive as an adult while his brothers cannot because
the vision of life that he brings out of his childhood approximates
the reality of the world. With his complete lack of human feeling,
Jason fits readily into modern society. But like his brothers, he, too,
is dominated by a sense of loss related to Caddy; however, whereas
Benjy loses love and security, Quentin his emotional anchorage
and his ideals, Jason loses nothing but a job in a bank. Herbert, the
man Caddy married, promised Mrs. Compson to give Jason a
position in a bank. When Caddy's marriage fails, Jason loses this
financial opportunity. As did his brothers, Jason howls in protest at
his loss. His protest takes the form of revenge. In 1928, it is eighteen years since he was promised the job. Jason's sense of loss has
not diminished. He continually measures his present condition
against what he might have been if his sister's marriage had not
collapsed, and if his father had given him the education Quentin
wasted.

Bitterness and hate dominate Jason's personality. Despite his
belief that his bitterness has its source in Caddy's failure, it becomes apparent that Jason is actually keeping alive his bitterness to
justify his own failure. It is obviously not the lack of education or
of job opportunity that keeps Jason a clerk in Earl's store as much
as his own lack of drive and practical shrewdness. Between the
facts of Jason's career and his own image of himself there is a great
discrepancy.

For fifteen years he has been taking two hundred dollars a
month from Caddy, for a total of thirty-six thousand dollars. What
has he done with all this money? The Compson house is run
down; a spot on the wall of the library marks the place where a
mirror hung in 1900; the carriage needs repair; the barn is empty
and dilapidated. None of the money he has received from Caddy
has gone into the upkeep of the house. The living standard of the
Compsons is hardly high, though Jason continually complains
about expenses. Jason, himself, does not live extravagantly. He

considers the forty dollars he gave to Lorraine a very generous gift. If he had been living on a scale higher than the one hundred and sixty dollars a month he earns at the store justifies, Earl and the entire small town would have been aware of it. Jason's reputation is hardly that of playboy.

At the end of fifteen years, all that Jason has saved from the money he gets from Caddy is, according to Faulkner's Appendix, approximately four thousand dollars. The other three thousand dollars that his niece Quentin takes from Jason are his own savings. Jasons thinks of himself as smarter than anyone else who speculates in cotton. On April 6, however, he loses two hundred dollars; and if it is into the cotton market that he has been pouring his stolen money, then this loss is hardly unusual. Jason's concept of himself as a practical businessman is also contradicted by his act of withdrawing a thousand dollars from Earl's business to buy a car. By doing so, he reduces his position from partner to clerk and buys a machine that causes him intense physical agony.

His purchase of the car, and use of it, despite the severe headaches the smell of gasoline causes him, are as irrational as most of his other actions. No man as practical as Jason considers himself would deliberately antagonize his associates and acquaintances, would go out of his way to be wantonly cruel. In practical terms, he has far more to gain by keeping his niece happy and satisfied than he does by antagonizing her. His gratuitous taunting of Earl serves no practical purpose at all.

Jason is driven by an intense inner fury that is completely uncontrollable.[7] Chasing his niece Quentin and the pitchman around the countryside is, typically, an irrational act. The pair has seen him; they know that he is following them. Under the circumstances, he has little chance of catching them in the love act, which seems to be his aim. Not one of the thoughts he records during the chase—though they all seem rational—provides an explanation of his action. When he sees his niece with the showman, he flies into a rage. The market is fluctuating wildly and he should be following it closely, but he dashes off on a senseless, futile chase.

When we have peeled away Jason's rationalizations, we see a man scurrying frantically around town all day long, searching for a blank check, rushing to the telegraph office, hurrying home to get his mother's signature on Caddy's check, rushing back to town to deposit the money, then dashing back home to get cash from his strong box to put into the market, and getting sidetracked into chasing his niece around the countryside. The grand finale of all this furious activity is that Jason loses money on the market and the next day loses not only his savings but also the source of his long standing illicit income when Quentin runs away.

Jason is sure that everything he does is purposeful, but his activity is utterly meaningless: he fails to make money and he fails to keep the townspeople from talking. The response of the sheriff to his demand for assistance in capturing Quentin, in Section IV, indicates Jason's status in the town.

One of the causes for the complete lack of meaning in Jason's life is his alienation from the past. He is like the representatives of modern society in Eliot's "The Waste Land," for whom the past holds no significance. Jason is the end-product of a society that has abandoned traditional humanistic values. Only such values can give meaning to life, and by cutting himself off from them, modern man becomes a Jason voyaging furiously for nothing.

Another reason for the lack of meaning in Jason's life is to be discovered in the distortion of his emotions. Jason's isolation from his fellow-man drives him, in his hatred and fury, to act irrationally. Self-love, achieving its *reductio ad absurdum*, becomes self-destructive. The normal emotional impulses that would have provided Jason with sufficient stability to make his life meaningful are distorted during his childhood, as they are for his brothers, by Mrs. Compson's inadequacy as a mother.

Mrs. Compson seizes upon Jason as the tangible evidence of her own separation from her husband and the Compsons. She makes Jason her ally against the enemy, and spoils him, setting him apart from his father and brothers and sister. Out of her own sense of inferiority, her own psychological limitation, she molds Jason to become the exact opposite of everything that the Compsons represent to her. She makes it impossible for Jason to establish an affectionate relationship with the other children, and the love that he might have given them is turned inward. Jason's extreme selfishness as an adult is a direct result of Mrs. Compson's tutelage. Everyone becomes an enemy to hate. Jason grows up to champion everything that his father and brother denounced, and to scoff at all they believed in. To them family tradition was important; Jason jeers at his ancestry. The chivalric code of the past is transformed by Jason into "Once a bitch always a bitch." (198) In Jason's feelings toward the Compsons there is bitterness about being excluded from the circle, which also contributes to his hatred.

When he no longer has any Compsons to hate Jason hates everyone: "all the rest of the town," Faulkner writes in the Appendix, "and the world and the human race too except himself were Compsons, inexplicable yet quite predictable in that they were in no sense whatever to be trusted." Jason becomes an exaggerated reflection of his mother, carrying to extremes her self-absorption, her superficial social and moral values, her alienation from people. Although the recollections of Benjy and Quentin reveal Mrs. Compson as devoid of maternal feelings, in comparison to Jason, she appears almost warm in her concern for her granddaughter and Benjy.

Jason's relationship with his mother also contradicts his conception of himself as a practical, logical man. His attachment to her is deep, and though he is frequently rude and unkind, he consistently defers to her wishes. He refrains from applying the strap to his niece when she appears, and he does not send Benjy to the asylum in Jackson for her sake. He also permits her to keep up the pretense of being the Southern lady. Jason, of course, is using his mother for his own purposes, keeping alive her feeling about Caddy so he can pocket the monthly checks that Mrs. Compson thinks she burns. But the depth of Jason's attachment to her is obvious in his fury at Earl's threat to tell her that the thousand dollars she invested in the business has been withdrawn.

The absurdity of Jason's and society's faith in reason is shown by the wide chasm between Jason's thoughts and his actions. Faulkner makes it clear that the forces governing human acts and human relations are emotional. When emotions are distorted, as they are in Jason, the result is a sterile existence.

In Section III Faulkner dramatizes the self-interest, the failure of love and compassion characteristic of modern man. At one end of the spectrum is Jesus, who preached love and died for his fellowman; at the other is his modern counterpart Jason, who hates his fellowman. Section III is a bitter invective against modern society, its commercialism, its inhumanity, its superficial social and moral codes, its devotion to mechanical contrivances. The section represents modern man, living a life of sound and fury signifying nothing. Though Mr. Compson and Quentin are weak and ineffectual, their disillusionment and despair are almost justified in Faulkner's evocation of the world in which Jason Compson functions.

» » Section IV

In the final section of *The Sound and the Fury*, the nihilistic tone of the preceding sections is not appreciably muted. Dilsey occupies a central position, but she is surrounded by Compsons. She is a humble servant; they are representative of modern society. Dilsey is one of those "who pardon one another for his love's sake, and who endure weakness and tribulation" and "who peaceably shall endure," but she is only one. The Compsons are many.

The climax of the action in this final section, which takes place on Easter day, is the Easter sermon. All the characteristics that Dilsey displayed in earlier scenes in the book are reinforced by her activities and attitudes on Easter morning. She reveals a solidity of character that defies the destructive force of time. Dilsey has served the Compsons through several generations. She has witnessed their fall from a position of importance, but she has continued to serve them loyally. During all those years she has remained the fixed center of the household, taking over the maternal responsibilities abdicated by Mrs. Compson, caring for the physical and spiritual needs of the entire family. She has served as a buffer between Benjy and his family, between Mrs. Compson and the facts of life, between Jason and Caddy's daughter Quentin. She is a servant, but she works with such devotion and responsibility that she has far more dignity than those she serves.

The source of Dilsey's strength is her humanity. She is incapable of thinking in abstractions, in terms of servant or employer, Negro or white; hers is a genuine response to individuals and to life. Aside from Caddy, she is the only person who insists upon Benjy's humanity, treating and respecting him as a child. On his thirty-third birthday, she makes him a cake, using her own funds for the ingredients, to forestall Jason's objections. Mrs. Compson seems unaware that it is her son's birthday. When Benjy burns his hand, his mother's reaction is to complain that his crying annoys her. To Jason, Benjy is a social nuisance and an unnecessary expense. To his niece Quentin, he is a repulsive annoyance. Dilsey's morality is her heart, her compassionate response to human beings.

Simple and uneducated, she presents a startling contrast to the sterile and doomed philosophizing of Mr. Compson and Quentin, and to the meaningless logic of Jason. In the heart, not the mind, is the salvation of mankind. The exuberant and vital response to being alive that characterizes the other Negroes in the novel—T.P. laughing wildly as he drinks champagne, Luster making music on the saw—is epitomized in Dilsey's mature acceptance of the pleasures and the pains of existence. She is the only person in the novel who seems capable of dealing with life.

The full significance of Dilsey's role is revealed by the Easter service. Benjy is the only Compson to attend services. Jason is chasing after his money; Mrs. Compson lies in bed with an unread open Bible beside her. At the beginning of the sermon, the preacher speaks in measured white-man tones. The congregation is attentive but unmoved. Gradually, however, as the tone shifts into Negro dialect and the sermon becomes a repetitive chant, the people begin to respond with intensity. The preacher utters no dogmas or intellectual concepts. His chant becomes a primitive expression of faith beyond intellect or rationality, and the response of Dilsey and the other Negroes is emotional and mystical. For the Compsons, father and son, the moral light rays emanating from Jesus have dimmed through time. But for Dilsey the rays burn brightly. The past and the present are united for her; the human values symbolized by Jesus are alive in Dilsey.

The only Compson who is at the service sits quietly. Benjy cannot respond, but on his own primitive level he feels, unknowingly, the love that Dilsey embodies. The Easter sermon, as a simple declaration of faith, is not unlike St. Francis's "Canticle of the Sun," with its expression of belief in salvation through unquestioning faith, humility, and love. Dilsey leaves the church, tears streaming along the furrows of her face, having understood and felt the tragedy of the Compsons. When she pronounces the demise of the Compson family, her words, resonant with Biblical overtones, seem to suggest the demise of modern man: " 'I've seed de first en de last . . . I seed de beginnin, en now I sees de endin.' " (313) It is with deep compassion that Dilsey makes her pronouncement. In contrast to her humility and faith are the pride and self-interest of the Compsons. Their love is directed inwards, isolating each of them from his fellowmen. It is a cancerous selfishness that eats away at their humanity, their strength, and their integrity. In the sterile waste land of the modern world, Dilsey is the symbol of resurrection and life.

Dilsey is the first of the primitives through whom Faulkner dramatizes the positive aspects of his views about life. But the central role given to Dilsey in the finale does not appreciably lighten the oppressive mood of despair in this masterpiece. There is a wide unbridgeable distance between the primitive Dilsey and social man. And though Dilsey stands as a symbol of hope, she is isolated from the complexities of the society that produces the Compsons and Sartorises, the Sutpens and McCaslins.

As I Lay Dying

As I Lay Dying (1930) is the story of a family on a six-day funeral journey through heat, flood, and fire.* Written shortly after the somber *The Sound and the Fury*, this short novel presents human existence as an absurd joke. At the end of the journey, Cash, thinking of his brother Darl's commitment to an insane asylum, muses:

* See the Appendix, pp. 377-382, for a chronology of events during the ten days of the story.

But I ain't so sho that ere a man has the right to say what is crazy and what ain't. It's like there was a fellow in every man that's done a-past the sanity or the insanity, that watches the sane and the insane doings of that man with the same horror and the same astonishment. (515) *

If there is any single clue to what Faulkner was about in this simultaneously horrifying and amusing, tragic and comic story, it is in the above statement. The nihilistic mood expressed in Shakespeare's lines—life "is a tale/Told by an idiot, full of sound and fury,/Signifying nothing"—that shapes *The Sound and the Fury* is also the mood of this novel, but here the meaninglessness of existence is viewed as a macabre joke. In an absurd world, who is to say what is sane and what insane? Surely, no reader of *As I Lay Dying* can unequivocally declare the Bundrens either heroic or idiotic, their funeral journey an epic or a burlesque.[1]

The subject of the novel is death; its central image the human corpse, generating furious passions and furious activity. At the center of motion is stasis. From this central paradox, a series of paradoxes proliferate, and before the novel ends, the distinctions between tragedy and comedy, being and non-being, reality and illusion, sanity and insanity have almost vanished.

Faulkner's remarkable success in this novel is achieved by an accumulation of incongruities. But these incongruities are apparent only to a detached observer. The reader remains detached because the fifty-nine short interior monologues that are used to tell the story permit him to identify with no single character; he is forced to view the individual characters in broad perspective.

Reader detachment is also created by Faulkner's choice and handling of rural characters. The doings of the Bundren family are of a piece with the avaricious enterprises of Flem and his relatives in the Snopes stories and novels. Many of their activities violate the generally accepted mores, but here their perpetrators are so blithely unconcerned with the proprieties that moral indignation is wasted upon them. If a member of an elite family were to perpetrate a fraud, we would be aroused to moral condemnation, but when a rural character does it, Faulkner has us rub our eyes incredulously and sit back to laugh at the human capacity for the outrageous. In

* Modern Library Edition.

The Sound and the Fury, Caddy's pregnancy before marriage is thoroughly serious, but in *As I Lay Dying,* Dewey Dell's predicament is comic to everyone but herself. It is a wonderful joke to Skeet MacGowan, the drug clerk. Dewey's bovine submission to his duplicity is the kind of incident that will swell the town's store of hilarious anecdotes about the bizarre doings of the rural folk. The funeral journey of the Bundrens, too, is an exquisite subject for local yarn-spinners—once the horrifying smell of the decaying corpse has become only a memory. The journey is so incredible that it provokes stunned amusement. Reading about the Bundrens is somewhat like watching monkeys; we identify with the lower primates in the zoo enough to make us simultaneously amused and uncomfortable. This comparison does not detract from Faulkner's very skillful and sympathetic rendering of the Bundrens as human beings, but shows how he achieves the detachment necessary to make the reader aware of incongruities.

Because the Bundren journey is a solemn, universal ritual of interment which reflects man's sense of his own dignity and his belief in a favored place in the hierarchy of creation, the absurd journey symbolizes the absurdity of human aspirations. In *As I Lay Dying,* death, as Mr. Compson observed in *The Sound and the Fury,* is the *reductio ad absurdum* of all human endeavor. Death, the stasis at the center of motion, makes life a gigantic joke. The joke is dramatically rendered by making the reader conscious of the incongruities, both particular and universal, of existence.

By its very nature, the internal monologue provides limited perspective, and as we move from mind to mind we realize the disparity between reality and the individual's perception of it. In these brilliant short monologues, Faulkner permits his speakers to characterize themselves. Each thought is shaped by the background and personality of the speaker. Darl's keen observation of detail and his intelligence unmistakably identify each of his monologues. Three levels of diction are used in the monologues. A realistic dialect records actual speech; a more formal diction records conscious thought, and a poetic imagistic language indicates uncontrolled thought. Except for the poetic sections, each of the characters speaks and thinks in his own language.

There is no author's voice in the novel. No single character can

be designated as a spokesman for the author, and no single character can be considered an objective recorder of events. Because each
character is so individualized, his monologues reveal only his personal view of an event. Anse's meditation on himself as an unfortunate man, for example, is clearly substantiated by the view we are
given of him in the thoughts of Vernon Tull and Darl. But there is
more to Anse than they have observed. He may say when his wife
dies, "'God's will be done . . . Now I can get them teeth,'"
(375) and reveal himself a self-centered, callous person, but we
have no reason to doubt the sincerity of his feeling as he tenderly
touches the face of his dead wife and clumsily attempts to smooth
the quilt covering her body. We know that he depends upon his
neighbors for help, but we also see him refusing the loan of a
wagon and mules to bring Addie's body to the graveyard in Jefferson as he promised her he would. Throughout the journey, he
displays an independence and fortitude that surprise his neighbors.

There are no villains and heroes in *As I Lay Dying*. The complexities and the contradictions of the human personality are
exposed and explored, and the ultimate result is the reader's awareness of the amusing and tragic incongruities between the individual's vision of himslf and his neighbors' views of him.

Cora Tull, for instance, who is a neighbor of Addie Bundren,
solicitously sits by the bedside of the dying woman. Though she is
acting the role of sympathetic friend, Cora has no thoughts but
for her own petty problem. She has used eggs to make cakes that
she could not sell, and she is disturbed by the possibility that her
husband will point up her failure. The self-righteous Cora is not
amenable to any view of herself as less than perfect and her failure
with the cakes has made her vulnerable. No sympathy for Addie is
registered in Cora's monologues; she is certain that the "eternal
and the everlasting salvation and grace is not upon her," because
Addie has not lived according to Cora's own moral code. (342)
In her three monologues, Cora's pietism makes the reader doubt
very much her chances of the salvation she is so certain she has
within her grasp. But Cora is a good neighbor to the Bundrens,
and though she is obviously wrong in many of her observations
about Addie, she is at times correct.

The important point is that Cora's certainties about herself and about life seem to the reader rather hollow manifestations of her ego, and we are amused by the difference between her view of herself and our own view of her. Vernon's meditation on his wife also provides an example of this type of humor:

I reckon if there's ere a man or woman anywhere that He could turn it all over to and go away with His mind at rest, it would be Ours. And I reckon she would make a few changes, no matter how He was running it. And I reckon they would be for man's good. Leastways, we would have to like them. Leastways, we might as well go on and make like we did. (391)

Most of the comic incongruities of the novel can only be described as grotesque. The entire journey is grotesquely humorous, but even before it starts, the corpse is mutilated by auger holes when the child Vardaman tries to provide air for the body that has been enclosed in the coffin. In Vardaman's monologues, we learn only how deeply the child is troubled by the death of his mother. It is Vernon Tull who discloses the atrocity the boy has perpetrated on the corpse in his attempt to provide air for his dead mother.

Of the fifty-nine monologues, sixteen are by neighbors or strangers, spaced throughout the novel to provide a different perspective on the activities being recorded in the thoughts of the Bundrens. To Jewel, the body in the coffin is his mother and therefore worth all the risk and sacrifice and effort. To the strangers, even to the sympathetic Samson and Armstid, the putrescent corpse is an outrage. To the reader, the devotion of so much anguish and physical effort to keeping above ground a mass of decaying matter for the purpose of fulfilling a meaningless promise to a dead woman becomes painfully absurd. The journey burlesques the burial ritual which, with solemn prayers consigning the soul to its maker, man uses to mask the reality of physical death. In the very process of honoring the dead, the Bundren's funeral journey, with its entourage of buzzards, is a grotesque proof of how dead the dead really are.

The journey is rich in irony. The neighbors never question the sincerity of Anse's desire to keep his promise to Addie, but Anse also wants to get to Jefferson to purchase teeth; Dewey Dell, who might have been able to persuade her father to bury the corpse at New Hope, supports the absurd journey only because she wants to get to a drug store in town. The ending of the story provides the most shocking incongruity of all. As soon as Addie is in the ground none of the family—except the insane Darl—devotes a single thought to her. After the expenditure of so much effort and passion, Jewel sits placidly on the wagon. There is no indication that either he or any of the other children have any objections to the new Mrs. Bundren. Vardaman, who has probably suffered more psychological disturbance than anyone but Darl, seems in his final monologue to have forgotten everything that occurred. In less than twenty-four hours after the burial, Anse has wooed and won a new wife. All the fury of their effort leaves nothing in its wake.

Among the many devices that Faulkner uses to make the funeral journey mirror the absurdity of human existence, the most important and effective is Addie's monologue. The burial journey is in its second day, and Jewel has just rescued the coffin from the swollen river; the mules have been drowned and Cash has a broken leg. The family has gone through the most hazardous day of the journey; the activity generated by the corpse is at its most furious, the suffering produced by Anse's promise to Addie at its most intense. It is at this point that Faulkner has Addie reveal the fact that the promise she exacts from Anse is meaningless to her. Her motive is revenge. She believes that Anse is incapable of responding to her real being, her reality, during her life, and she vindictively forces him to cope with the reality of her dead body.

Addie's monologue is so complex and rich that it requires careful analysis. Perhaps because so much is concentrated into so few words, the monologue is frequently ambiguous.

Her thoughts develop a number of variations on the central image of incongruity in the novel: stasis at the center of motion. Sex and death, which Faulkner describes in *Soldiers' Pay* as "the front door and the back door of the world" are the subjects upon which Addie's thoughts are concentrated. In the same way that Addie's death produces so much motion, during her own life, death generates all her activity. Her father's statement, "the reason for living was to get ready to stay dead a long time" serves as the touchstone of her existence. (461) Opposed to death is Addie's intense sex drive, the symbol not only of human continuity through the bearing of children, but of total absorption in life itself. Only through sex does Addie achieve the fulfillment and the feeling of being vitally alive that she craves. As a young school teacher, she feels life slipping by her. Her sexual frustration manifests itself as a need to achieve a sense of identity, feel the reality of being alive, by a total immersion of her identity in the identity of another person. She feels the separation between herself and the children whom she teaches, and she welcomes the opportunity to whip them. "Now you are aware of me! Now I am something in your secret and selfish life, who have marked your blood with my own for ever and ever." (462) Because her frustration is sexual, she suffers most in the springtime, and she is soothed only by going down the hill and lying on the ground by the spring where she can be quiet "with the water bubbling up and away and the sun slanting quiet in the trees and the quiet smelling of damp and rotting leaves and new earth. . . ." (461)

When Addie twice declares, "So I took Anse," that is precisely what she means. She does not wait to fall in love with him. He is an available male who she discovers is interested in her. She accosts him without subtlety. By inquiring around the village, she learns that he has a good house and farm, and as Anse stands awkwardly before her twisting his hat in his hand, she says, " 'A new house . . . Are you going to get married?' " (463) Anse takes the lure, and Addie gets a man. Anse, apparently, provides some sort of immediate relief, but when Addie becomes pregnant with Cash, she realizes that sex—with Anse at least—is not what it should have been: it has not violated her aloneness and therefore has failed to make her feel her own identity.

One of the major themes in the novel explores the meaning of being, the individual's awareness of his own identity. The theme, simply stated, presents the mystery of "I Am" against the unfathomable state of "I Am Not," "I Was." Contemplation of death, non-being, provokes meditation upon the reality of being: who am I? what am I? Right after the death of Addie, for example, Vardaman runs into the barn and goes into the stall which holds Jewel's horse. The child puts his hands on the horse to feel the "life in him." (376) Later, after he has beaten Dr. Peabody's team, he returns to the dark barn, and the effect of his mother's death upon his sense of himself is expressed in the following passage, as he responds to the presence of the live horse:

It is as though the dark were resolving him out of his integrity, into an unrelated scattering of components—snuffings and stampings; smells of cooling flesh and ammoniac hair; an illusion of a coordinated whole of splotched hide and strong bones within which, detached and secret and familiar, an *is* different from my *is*. I see him dissolve—legs, a rolling eye, a gaudy splotching like cold flames—and float upon the dark in fading solution; all one yet neither; all either yet none. (379)

In the barn, too, Dewey Dell undergoes a similar experience that is tempered for her by her pregnancy:

The dead air shapes the dead earth in the dead darkness, further away than seeing shapes the dead earth. It lies dead and warm upon me, touching me naked through my clothes. I said You don't know what worry is. I don't know what it is. I don't know whether I am worrying or not. Whether I can or not. I don't know whether I can cry or not. I don't know whether I have tried to or not. I feel like a wet seed wild in the hot blind earth. (384)

Darl's meditations on being and non-being are less imagistic because he is intelligent and he is capable of identifying the problem:

In a strange room you must empty yourself for sleep. And before you are emptied for sleep, what are you. And when you are emptied for sleep, you are not. And when you are filled with sleep, you never were. I don't know what I am. I don't know if I am or not. Jewel knows he is, because he does not know that he does not know whether he is or not. He cannot empty himself for sleep because he is not what he is and he is what he is not. (396)

The dependence upon emotional attachments and upon the identity of others for our own sense of identity is stressed in Darl's references to Jewel. Darl knows that Addie is dead, but Jewel does not; therefore Jewel, Darl muses, is what he is not. The identity that Jewel knows in his relationship with his mother no longer exists, though he does not yet know it. But Darl, knowing that Addie is dead, knows that Jewel "is what he is not." Lying in bed in the strange room, Darl attempts to moor himself to reality by identifying with the sound of the rain on the wagon "that is ours" outside. The load of wood on the wagon, however, has no identity because it belongs to no one. No longer does it belong to the people who cut it, nor to the people who bought it, nor to him and Jewel who are only carting it. But it does, in one sense, belong to them, because he and Jewel can hear the wind and rain shaping the wood to their ears when they are awake. Once they are asleep, though, it is not, "since sleep is is-not and rain and wind are *was*, it is not." Darl concludes that the wagon *is* because when he is asleep and the wagon is *was* then his mother will not be. "And Jewel *is*, so Addie Bundren must be. And then I must be, or I could not empty myself for sleep in a strange room. And so if I am not emptied yet, I am *is*." (396)

The dependence of self-identity with something outside of self is also illustrated by Vardaman's identification of his dead mother with a dead fish. The child is accustomed to the death of fish and animals, and it is his only means of dealing with the reality of his mother as *was*. Addie's death has so affected Vardaman's sense of being that he must continually identify with those around him: "Jewel is my brother . . . Darl is my brother . . . I am. Darl is my brother." (409).

Addie achieves a full sense of her own being by a complete identification with her child, Cash. When she bears him, she realizes, suddenly, that life was terrible before because she did not know and might never have known what being alive really meant. She also realizes the gap between words and the actuality the words attempt to express. When Cash is born she understands that "motherhood was invented by someone who had to have a word for it because the ones that had the children didn't care whether there was a word for it or not. I knew that fear was invented by someone that had never had the fear; pride, who never had the pride." (463)

Between the nothingness that is death and the reality that is life as she knows it with her child, there is for Addie a region that is neither one. This region of words and those who exist in it, Addie identifies with the air; her own region of reality, with the earth. And "the two lines are too far apart for the same person to straddle from one to the other." (465)

Anse belongs to this limbo of words, and when Addie realizes that he can never exist on her level, she knows only contempt for him; he is, for her, dead. Her second pregnancy produces a violent reaction in Addie, apparently making her aware once again of death, the negation of her reality. Her monologue is vague at this point. At first she wants to kill Anse because he tricked her, she says, by hiding behind a word. That word, which is probably "love," betrays her, because to a man like Anse it can only be a word. Then she realizes that what really tricked her were words older than "Anse" or "love," and that the same word that tricked her also tricked Anse. What that word is, Addie does not say; but it is likely that the word that she is thinking of, which tricks both her and Anse, is "death." The words that are "older than Anse and love" are perhaps those with which man deals with death. (464) At this point in her monologue, she seems to interpret her father's statement nihilistically.

One of the problems raised by Addie's monologue is the difficulty of determining if Addie's view of her father's statement alters as she grows older. My impression is that she does not believe in an after life. When Cora talks to her about the salvation of her soul, she says Jewel " 'is my cross and he will be my salvation. He will save me from the water and from the fire. Even though I have laid down my life, he will save me.' " (460) Addie identifies herself and her sense of being with the earth. The return of her body to the earth symbolizes the finality of death: Jewel can save only her corpse.

Addie's love affair with Whitfield reinforces her view of the gap between words and deeds. She decides that the reason for living is "the duty to the alive, to the terrible blood, the red bitter flood boiling through the land." (466) With Whitfield she knows the violation of her aloneness through sex that Anse failed to provide. Her experience achieves the intensity it does because Whitfield is a minister of God who talks about God's love and God's sin. Though this passage, too, is ambiguous, it seems to me that Addie is not discovering the reality of sin by committing adultery so much as she is discovering the emptiness of the word "sin." She describes the word as similar to the garments she wears to cover her nakedness. When she and her lover are together, they shed the garment and the word "sin" is dead. "I would think of the sin as garments which we would remove in order to shape and coerce the terrible blood to the forlorn echo of the dead word high in the air." (466) It is in Addie's response not to the codes or words that govern man but to the instinctual forces within her that gives her a vital sense of being alive. It is her nature as a woman that is fulfilled, which explains her emphasis on her children and the earth. "My children were of me alone, of the wild blood boiling along the earth, of me and of all that lived; of none and of all." (467)

Even Addie's final interpretation of her father's statement does not include preparation for an afterlife. After Jewel, her third child, is born, and the sexual forces weaken—"the wild blood boiled away and the sound of it ceased"—she cleans house. She does not prepare her soul; her duty remains to the alive. She now replaces for Anse the children she deprived him of during her affair with Whitfield: "I gave Anse Dewey Dell to negative Jewel. Then I gave him Vardaman to replace the child I had robbed him of." (467) Addie is a realistic, earthy woman who exists, unlike Cora, in the here and now.

In her monologue are concentrated all the paradoxes that flow from the central image of stasis at the center of motion: death and sex, non-being and being, illusion and reality. The irony of death creating life ("the reason for living was to get ready to stay dead"), the corpse generating motion, is the symbol of life's absurd paradox. The exploration of the meaning of being alive in Addie's monologue is counterpointed by an exploration of the meaning of death in the rest of the novel. Dr. Peabody declares at the beginning of the novel that he once thought death a phenomenon of the body but now he realizes that it is a function of the mind "and that of the minds of the ones who suffer the bereavement." (368) Dr. Peabody's statement points up the negative state that is death, and the reactions of the Bundren family to Addie's death are attempts to deal with the unfathomable, incomprehensible reality of non-being.

Anse, as Addie reveals, mouths words, and is satisfied. The responses of the children are shaped, as Olga Vickery points out, by their emotional relationship with their mother.[2] Cash and Jewel, whom Addie loved most, have the strongest grip upon reality. Absorbed in concrete details, Cash seems to think of death only in terms of the coffin he is building. Jewel, who has only one monologue, is presented mainly through the eyes of Darl. And what Darl perceives is that Jewel, secure in his love for his mother and her love for him, has created a relationship with his horse that duplicates his relationship with Addie. She whipped and petted Jewel more than any of the other children; and to Darl, Jewel's beating and caressing the horse mirrors that relationship. Because Darl is obsessed by Jewel as the living symbol of Addie's rejection of himself, it is difficult to ascertain what does go on in Jewel's mind. He seems to suffer from his loss, and his love is sufficient to sustain him through all the dangers and hardships of getting her corpse to Jefferson. Jewel does bring Addie through flood and fire, and it is through his efforts that Anse's promise is kept.

It is difficult to say, with any degree of certainty, whether Vardaman's violent reaction to his mother's death is due to an unconscious sense of his mother's lack of affection for him, or simply to the trauma of losing her. His monologues mainly emphasize his attempt to deal with the phenomenon of death. Dewey Dell, as she herself declares, is too absorbed by the problem of her pregnancy to be deeply affected. Darl's reactions are intense. His continual description of Jewel as "wooden" seems to reflect his knowledge of Addie's rejection of himself, and his concentration upon Jewel and the horse certainly demonstrates his obsession with Addie's failure to give him her love. Like Quentin Compson, in *The Sound and the Fury*, Darl has reason to cry, "If I only had a mother." If death is merely, as Dr. Peabody suggests, a function of the mind of the bereaved, and the response of each mind is different, then nothing real is left but the corpse. The importance of this theme of being and non-being, life and death, is indicated in the monologues of Darl and Vardaman, whose nineteen and ten sections, respectively, constitute about half of *As I Lay Dying*.

Through the monologues of Darl, our perspective is sufficiently broadened to make of the funeral journey a symbol of all human activity. Darl encompasses both the immediate and universal. Because his perception of realistic detail is so extraordinary, and because he is able to penetrate the secret thoughts of those around him, we tend to accept Darl's observations about life as valid. He incurs the hatred of Dewey and Jewel because he can communicate with them without words. He silently taunts Dewey by revealing to her that he knows about her pregnancy, and he forces Jewel to acknowledge the death of Addie while Jewel is trying to hide from the thought. In the same way, Darl impresses us with his power to see beyond the immediate and surface aspects of existence. He records scenes at which he is not physically present with sharp and convincing detail. Away on the wood-hauling trip when Addie dies, he describes her death. Thus Darl's mind functions, in a sense, free of the limitations imposed by his body. He is beyond time.

In Darl's monologues, Faulkner develops the image of stasis at the center of motion, giving it general significance. As in Addie's monologue, death and sex, non-being and being dominate Darl's thoughts. Darl sees Dewey Dell's leg as she climbs into the wagon, for example, as "that lever which moves the world; one of that caliper which measures the length and breadth of life." (410-1) And, later, the girl's wet dress shapes "those mammalian ludicrosities which are the horizons and the valleys of the earth." (458)

Darl's constant reference to Addie's extra-marital sexual escapade emphasizes sex as the source of life and motion, the antithesis of the nothingness of death. Only Darl registers a thought about Addie once she is in her grave, and that thought refers to her adultery: he recalls a French spy-glass in which was a picture of "a woman and a pig with two backs and no face." (527)

Time, in Darl's monologues, is the inexorable force leveling everything into insignificance. He envisions the funeral wagon moving not across space but through time, and he thinks of the movement of the wagon as "uninferant of progress . . . with an outward semblance of form and purpose, but with no inference of motion, progress or retrograde." (413, 504) All the fury and passion of their activities become meaningless, a mere repetition of the activities of human beings throughout history which lead nowhere and add up to nothing but motion:

How do our lives ravel out into the no-wind, no-sound, the weary gestures wearily recapitulant: echoes of old compulsions with no-hand on
no-strings: in sunset we fall into furious attitudes, dead gestures of
dolls. (491)

Darl, who ends up in an insane asylum, is, ironically, the most
practical member of the family. It is he who restrains Jewel from
attacking the man with the knife, who insists that Cash's leg be attended to immediately, and who cannot stand the intolerable in-
dignity of his mother's unburied corpse. As Cash observes, there is
much sanity in Darl's setting fire to the barn. "Insanity" for Darl is
inevitable: he sees too much. He cannot become blindly absorbed
in the immediate, minor problems and pleasures and routines
which fill the consciousness of most people, because he always sees
their meaninglessness and futility. Vernon Tull notes wisely that
when catastrophes occur, a man is forced to think about life, but
fortunately the mind need indulge in such thinking only infrequently:

Which is a good thing. For the Lord aimed for him to do and not to
spend too much time thinking, because his brain it's like a piece of
machinery: it won't stand a whole lot of racking. It's best when it all
runs along the same, doing the day's work and not no one part used
no more than needful. I have said and I say again, that's ever living
thing the matter with Darl: he just thinks by himself too much. (389)

And that is precisely Darl's predicament. He sees too much; he
perceives the ultimate absurdity of existence, the incredible incongruities that make up life. Like Captain Ahab, another solitary
thinker, Darl goes mad. In Cash's words, "This world is not his
world; this life his life." (532) Only when he is mad, Darl can say
"yes yes yes yes yes" to life.

In an absurd world, who is to say what is sane or insane? When
the distinctions between illusion and reality, between being and
nonbeing are so dependent upon the individual mind and that
mind itself has difficulty in making the distinctions, the line between sanity and insanity vanishes. Darl expresses the paradoxes of
life which have driven him mad in his image of the two-faced coin

with "a woman on one side and a buffalo on the other; two faces and no back." (527) Mad, Darl can finally laugh at the macabre joke that is life, and at the greatest joke of all: man's capacity to bear anything. As Darl thinks of his family sitting placidly in the wagon waiting for Anse and the new Mrs. Bundren, the "normal" part of him asks, " 'Is that why you are laughing, Darl?' " And foaming, he can say, " 'Yes yes yes yes yes yes.' " (527)

As I Lay Dying is one of Faulkner's easiest books to read, but it is also one of his most profound. It is highly poetic and probes deeply into the meaning of human existence in a ludicrous world.

Sanctuary

Though preceded by the two great works, *The Sound and the Fury* and *As I Lay Dying*, Faulkner's sixth novel, *Sanctuary* (1931), was the first work to attract a wide audience. Reader reaction to the lurid violence of the story made it a best seller and produced reverberations in Hollywood. Faulkner was invited to adapt his novel for the screen, and *Sanctuary* became *The Story of Temple Drake*, starring Marion Davies.

The aura of popular success has clung to the book and only recently have Faulkner critics begun to treat it as an important and significant novel.[1] Perhaps the author's own statement, in the introduction to the 1932 Modern Library edition, about setting out to write a potboiler has helped to obscure the book's merit. That entire introduction, which contains statements more fictional than factual, is characterized by a strange tone that combines bitterness, triumph, and contempt.* In effect, what Faulkner seems to

---

* The introduction has to be read with caution. If, for example, the galleys in the University of Virginia collection are indeed the galleys of the original version which Faulkner describes as "so terrible" that he "tore the galleys down and rewrote the book," then that statement is a gross exaggeration. The altera-

be saying is that *Sanctuary* is a sensational novel, but it is also no less a serious work than *The Sound and the Fury* or *As I Lay Dying*. Faulkner's estimate is accurate. *Sanctuary* is filled with sensationalism, and it is seriously marred by occasional stock characterizations, unevenness of tone, lack of structural and thematic unity, lapses into florid writing. But, despite these weaknesses, the novel is a brilliant and powerful expression of disillusionment and despair and deserves to be ranked just behind Faulkner's greatest works.

Thematically, *Sanctuary* is related to the Quentin Compson section of *The Sound and the Fury*. Its central character, Horace Benbow, is twenty years older than Quentin, but his despair has its genesis, too, in an adolescent reaction to the discovery that evil resides in the sanctuary, the temple, the dwelling place of purity and innocence—woman.[2] After forty-three years of life and ten years of marriage to the former wife of another man, Horace still has not shed his adolescent illusions. He has remained the dreamer and idealist who, in *Sartoris*, returned from World War I with glass-blowing equipment, hoping to capture strands of beauty through delicate creations. Quentin Compson struggles against the intrusion of reality, and Horace's antagonist is also reality.[*]

His journey into despair begins when his illusions about woman are exposed. He recoils from the sight of evil in this sanctuary, but his eyes are now opened and he discovers evil roosting in every other sanctuary that man, the dreamer, has created. Horace describes this process of recognition when he says, " 'there's a corruption about even looking upon evil, even by accident; you cannot haggle, traffic, with putrefaction.' " (152) † The corruption for Horace, personally, is not moral; it is spiritual. Once he accepts the pervasive reality of evil, he is forced inexorably to acknowledge that there is a "logical pattern to evil." (266) The idealistic Horace,

---

tions constitute, at most, a revision. The only truly important and major change is an addition, the final chapter, devoted to Popeye. That chapter, as I show in the analysis, is important because it broadens the significance of the story. Also, Faulkner's declaration in the introduction that he did not know and had not lived with people who wrote stories and novels ignores his friendship with Sherwood Anderson and his whole sojourn in New Orleans.

* See the Appendix, pp. 383-387, for a chronology of events.
† Modern Library Edition.

like so many of Faulkner's characters, is an absolutist. He vaults from one extreme to another. The snake cannot exist in the garden. If the snake is real, Eden is obliterated.

Those critics who have interpreted *Sanctuary* simply as an indictment of modern society tend to miss the moral significance of the novel. Unquestionably, Faulkner depicts the corruption produced by urban society. Popeye, the symbol of evil in the book, is described as having "the vicious depthless quality of stamped tin," of looking like a modernistic lamp. (2) He is so alien to nature that he is frightened by bird whistles. And Temple Drake seems to have many of the qualities that writers have associated with the "flappers" of the 1920's era. In contrast, Horace, the twentieth-century Don Quixote, is incapable of driving a car, of handling tools. The imprint of his and his sister's naked feet in the cement sidewalk represents the encroachment of modernity upon the simple innocence of childhood. But despite these references to modern society, the evil in the novel is not produced by the effects of modernity upon the human being. The sexual corruption, bigotry, social injustice, hypocrisy, cruelty, self-righteousness that Horace discovers, are evils that transcend time and place. Horace has existed in a state of childish innocence. It is life itself that he is out of touch with, not just the times in which he lives.

At the opening of the novel, Horace is in flight. His illusions have been menaced. His great romance with Belle Mitchell has deteriorated into a stale marital routine, symbolized for him by his weekly trips to the railroad station for shrimp. He reveals his spiritual crisis as he tries to explain to the uninterested group at the Old Frenchman place why he left his home in Kinston. He tells them about his wife and his stepdaughter, Little Belle. Horace, we discover, has been straddling two worlds—the world of his illusions and the world of his actual existence. Without his wife's knowledge, he used his own funds to maintain the Jefferson house in which he spent his boyhood; the house he lives in with Belle he bought with borrowed money. Disappointed in his wife, Horace has transferred his illusions to his stepdaughter, investing her with his ideals of female purity and spiritual beauty. But Little Belle is real and she is a woman. Horace tells about the day, the preceding week, he reproached her for bringing home a boy she met on the train. He recalls the moment when she flings herself into his arms to beg for giveness. Through a set of opposed mirrors in the room, he sees reflected on her face the insincerity of her act. This incident is only one of a series in which Little Belle betrays Horace's naïveté. Horace cannot escape the facts, but he flees from the truth. He is reluctant to acknowledge what he knows about Little Belle because if he does, the whole flimsy fabric of his idealism will collapse. His defense of Goodwin becomes a Quixotic defense of all his ideals. If he can prove that justice exists, then his belief in goodness and truth and beauty has validity.

Benbow's relationship with his stepdaughter has drawn the attention of critics. A number have argued that Horace's attachment to the girl is rooted in sexual desire. It is not. Structurally, *Sanctuary* has two central characters and two stories. Thematically, Temple Drake's story is subordinate to that of Horace, but the novel is almost equally divided between them. Faulkner joins the two stories with a number of links, some of which are too obviously contrived. Young Gowan Stevens, for instance, as the suitor of Narcissa, who is at least fifteen years his senior and the mother of a ten-year-old boy, is an awkward joint. The entire episode of young Snopes and his friend living at Miss Reba's without knowing it is a house of prostitution has little thematic or tonal relationship to the rest of the novel.* It serves the main narrative only by bringing the boy's uncle, Clarence Snopes, to Miss Reba's, where he discovers Temple, an unconvincing contrivance. The description of Clarence peeping through the keyhole into Temple's room does not explain how he learned that she was locked in the room. And Popeye's reaction to finding Clarence peeping—he sears his neck with a match—is much too mild a reaction for a killer.

There are many other such awkward connecting points between the stories, but the major thematic one is Horace's concern for his

---

* Even the novel's chronology is confused by this interpolated story. On the day Horace returns from Oxford and meets Clarence Snopes on the train, the two boys are leaving for Memphis. According to the story, the boys are at Miss Reba's at least two weeks before Clarence finds them, and according to Miss Reba, Clarence first came to the house two weeks before he disclosed to Horace that Temple was there. The lapse of a month between Horace's visit to Oxford and his visit to Temple in Memphis is not possible in the chronology of the novel.

stepdaughter. About the same age as the eighteen-year-old Temple, Belle is a carbon copy of Temple Drake. Each time that Horace discovers something about Temple, he thinks of his stepdaughter. When he first learns from Ruby, for example, that Temple and Gowan were at the Old Frenchman place when Tommy was shot, he goes to his sister's house and talks to Aunt Jenny. He makes no mention of Little Belle, but the perceptive Aunt Jenny says suddenly, " 'I'll declare, a male parent is a funny thing, but just let a man have a hand in the affairs of a female that's no kin to him. . . .' " To which, Horace responds, " 'Yes . . . and thank God she isn't my flesh and blood.' " (198-9) Returning to his house in Jefferson that evening, Horace looks long at a photograph of his stepdaughter, remembering her in the grape arbor with a boy, "the murmur of voices darkening into silence as he approached. . . ." He looked at the "familiar image with a kind of quiet horror and despair, at a face suddenly older in sin than he would ever be, a face more blurred than sweet, at eyes more secret than soft." (200)

Temple's adventure dramatizes the reality about women that Horace has avoided for forty-three years. Temple does not deteriorate morally; she responds to the evil of her nature—the evil that always existed beneath the deceptive trappings of convention and social status. The daughter of a judge, the sister of four brothers ready to defend her honor, Temple is, to the naïve male, the image of pure Southern womanhood. But what is she, actually? Her horrible corn-cob rape by Popeye does not initiate her moral collapse; it merely releases her from the restrictive conventions which society has imposed upon her. Before the rape, the evil in her asserts itself. She is callously indifferent to the effects her playing at sex has upon the town boys. But more important, as soon as she enters the lawless world of the Old Frenchman place, she knows that the conventions that have protected (or restricted) her do not exist. The knowledge terrifies her, but it also fascinates her. As great and real as is her terror, her continual, obsessive absorption with the possibility of rape indicates her desire for violation. Her wild, senseless running, as Ruby makes clear, incites the passions of the men. Like dogs, they react to a bitch in heat. She is, of course, an object of desire to men of this class because she is a college girl from an exclusive social strata. But Temple is provocative. That same qual-

Ity In her which produces the reactions in the town boys who cannot attend the college dance inflames these outlaws. Without that quality, Temple could have left the farmhouse safely. Popeye, sexually impotent, has managed to avoid the many whores who have sought his attention; Tommy is feeble-minded and apparently without sexual experience, with Ruby present, Goodwin is no real threat; and Van, perhaps the rampant male, is under the control of Goodwin. Ruby has lived among these men without provoking trouble, but within a few hours, Temple has them all intent upon raping her.

Naked carnal passion, a proclivity to evil, determine Temple's actions and reactions. To trace her desire to be violated to the undeveloped story she tells Ruby about her father killing her suitor, Frank, is to take over the role of novelist.[3] Faulkner offers no connection between this incident and Temple's character; if he originally intended that there be one, he seems to have abandoned the idea as Temple developed into a symbol of universal moral chaos.

This symbolic character of Temple's role first becomes apparent when the young girl is alone in her room at Miss Reba's. Faulkner shifts from the simple, almost Hemingwayesque style of the early chapters to one more typically imagistic. On the mantlepiece is a clock with its hands set perpetually at ten-thirty. Temple "watched the final light condense into the clock face, and the dial change from a round orifice in the darkness to a disc suspended in nothingness, the original chaos." (180-1)

The time it takes Temple to adjust to her violation is also indicative of her symbolic role. She is raped by Popeye on a Sunday morning. By ten-thirty that evening when "time had overtaken the dead gesture behind the clock crystal," she has already begun her recovery. (189) She eats, and she drinks the first of many future glasses of gin. She is not yet quite ready to accept Popeye, and her terror when he enters the room is genuine. The scene with Popeye drooling and moaning over her and the girl writhing in anguish on the bed evokes a feeling of sympathy for Temple and of overwhelming disgust and horror with Popeye. It is therefore a violent shock when we discover, in the next scene in which Temple appears, that she has completely adjusted to corruption. Only a few weeks have elapsed. Temple has not even, as yet, met Red and known a real sexual relationship; but she tells Horace what took place at the Old Frenchman place "in one of those bright, chatty monologues which women can carry on when they realise that they have the center of the stage; suddenly Horace realised that she was recounting the experience with actual pride, a sort of naive and impersonal vanity. . . ." (258-9)

Horace's interview with Temple produces for him the climax of his encounter with the reality he has tried to evade. "Better for her," he muses as he returns to his home in Jefferson, "if she were dead tonight . . . And I too; thinking how that were the only solution. Removed, cauterised out of the old and tragic flank of the world . . . Perhaps it is upon the instant that we realise, admit, that there is a logical pattern to evil, that we die, he thought, thinking of the expression he had once seen in the eyes of a dead child, and of other dead: the cooling indignation, the shocked despair fading, leaving two empty globes in which the motionless world lurked profoundly in miniature." (265-6)

Though Horace continues his fight for justice, he now knows that his old ideals are illusions. He has looked into the sanctuary and seen that goodness and truth do not dwell there; the only reality is evil. Horace's despair is cosmic. He once again stares at the picture of Little Belle, the symbol of his illusions, and he vomits.

In the final scene in which Temple figures prominently, there are interesting parallels with the scene at the Old Frenchman place. Approximately one month has passed. She has been with Red only four times. Her seething animal-like pursuit of him, despite her knowledge that she is endangering his life, her unabashed insistence upon sexual relief is not unlike the scene at Goodwin's hideout; this time, however, Temple is free of the conventions and the taboos; she can be openly the bitch in heat. The entire episode in the roadhouse, despite its lurid sensationalism, is brilliantly written, forcing the reader to feel disgust with female lust and human corruption.

The significance of the female as the sanctuary of male idealism and, therefore, as the source of disillusionment is reinforced by the actions and histories of the other women in the novel. Not only is Horace's stepdaughter a potential Temple Drake, but his sistor, too, plays a role that is a variation on the Temple theme. The righteous Narcissa, habitually dressed in white, some years previously receives (in *Sartoris*) anonymous love letters. Her reaction to these letters is not unlike Temple's to the possibility of rape. Disgusted by the thought that some unknown man thinks of her in that way, Narcissa is, at the same time, fascinated, and she preserves the letters. Eventually, they are stolen. The affair is concluded in the short story, "There Was a Queen," when Narcissa gives herself sexually to get the letters back, fulfilling the desire that originally prevented her from destroying them. The contribution of Narcissa to the destruction of Horace's idealism is almost as great as Temple's. She is moral righteousness incarnate, and believing that Horace is having sexual relations with Ruby, will not tolerate Ruby's presence in her family home in Jefferson. Ironically, far more corrupt than Ruby, the other righteous women of Jefferson hound Ruby—in the name of God and social morality—out of town and into the shack of an old crone, too demented to care who stays with her. By informing the District Attorney of Clarence Snopes's phone call to her brother, Narcissa helps to light the fire that destroys Goodwin. Narcissa differs from Temple only in degree.

The foil of these white women of good family, whom idealists like Horace envision as sanctuaries of innocence and purity, is Ruby—the one-time whore. Ruby does not escape the taint of sexual corruption that characterizes all the women—except Aunt Jenny—in the novel, but her history is one of self-sacrifice, and her prostitution is redeemed by her fidelity and love. Ruby is a realistic observer of life, and her opinions constitute a valid commentary on morality. Her statements to Temple about the morality of "good" women are validated by the actions of the "good" women in the novel. Her cynical acceptance of evil and corruption as the ineradicable condition of existence is the truth about life that Horace eventually must recognize. With her sickly baby in her arms, Ruby is the madonna. The whore as madonna is an appropriate symbol of a world in which all values are distorted.

Though Miss Reba is the stereotyped warm-hearted madam, her loyalty to her dead husband, her asthma, her dogs give her an unforgettable individuality. Her role in this novel of horror, violence, and corruption contributes to the evocation of despair. The episodes in which she appears do not provide comic relief so much as a moral commentary. In a world of moral chaos, prostitution is a source of humor, the whore house madam a warm, lovable person. Temple Drake shocks even Miss Reba. Because Miss Reba is so recognizably human and so sympathetic a character, her blasé acceptance of amorality as the norm of existence emphasizes evil as the predominating force in human affairs.

Female sexuality is not the only manifestation of evil in *Sanctuary* that contributes to the destruction of Horace's illusions. Gowan Stevens represents the corruption of a social class whose moral code is nothing more than an empty concept of the gentleman. As a character, Gowan is too simply drawn, but he is sufficient to dramatize the replacement of a vital moral code by a meaningless social code. Gowan's sole guide to conduct is that a gentleman educated at Virginia should know how to hold his drink. After his two-day drunk, he is so ashamed to have been seen drunk by Temple that he abandons her to the gangsters and runs away from the Old Frenchman place. His conscience responds only to his failure to live up to the code of the Virginia gentleman.

Goodwin, whom Benbow undertakes to defend in the name of justice, is a murderer and an ex-convict. His whole life is a mockery of Horace's ideals, but the chief irony is that he was just as intent upon raping Temple as were the other men, and would have, had not Popeye got to her first. Ruby left the house with her child when Goodwin refused to leave Temple alone. In the prison, the bootlegger's terror of Popeye is not consistent with the character revealed by his history and by his actions at the hideout. Nothing in Goodwin's past indicates that he is a coward, but his cowering attitude, when he is in the custody of the law, mocks the very thing Horace is fighting for—legal justice. Goodwin has no confidence in the power of law and order. The jungle law of the criminal world rules, and he has far more respect for that law than for Horace's concepts.

Eustace Graham, Horace's legal opponent in the trial and the duly elected defender of justice, also reveals the gap between reality and Horace's ideals. Fired by political ambition, Graham wants not only a conviction but a lynching, which he achieves. Another elected official, Clarence Snopes, member of the state legislature, is corrupt and vulgar. He occupies a shadowy zone between legal respectability and the criminal world of Popeye. He has no moral standards, but he is too petty in mind and character to be a thoroughgoing criminal. Though Clarence knows, for instance, that Horace has gone to Miss Reba's to talk to Temple, he is alert to the possibility of blackmail and pretends that Horace is going to make use of the house by advising him to try a cheaper place. Snopes is one of the best realized characters in the novel: everything about him, from his stained panama to his speech, is distasteful. His presence does much to help the reader share Horace's disgust with his fellow man.

Goodwin, Graham, and Snopes, in contrast to Popeye, are recognizable human beings. Popeye is outside the circle of the corrupt human fraternity, a link between human and cosmic evil. From the moment he is introduced, standing silently watching Benbow drinking at the pool, Popeye's peeping role is established. He is alien to the natural world and to the human species. Though a bootlegger, he cannot drink; though in constant association with whores, he is incapable of sexual relations. Of more importance, he does not experience human emotions. As a killer, he is not ruthless, but simply kills people who threaten him in the same passionless way he shoots Tommy's dog. Popeye cannot be described as immoral or even amoral. Throughout most of the novel, he horrifies us; but the final chapter, which Faulkner added when he revised the original version, considerably alters our feelings about him.

This final chapter seems, at first, an addenda: structurally, it is certainly awkward. The two major stories, of Temple and Horace, are finished. Horace loses his illusions; his despair is complete. He has even given up the idea of divorcing Belle. It would be a useless gesture in a world without meaning or hope. What, then, is served by our sudden involvement in the details of Popeye's life and death? Why does Faulkner want to bring us close to this man, even make us feel a reluctant sympathy for a corn-cob rapist and a killer, who, born on Christmas day, awaits his death with such apparent heroic calm?

The overall effect of the chapter, it seems to me, is to establish a more certain connection between human and cosmic evil. Popeye himself is a victim of blind cruel fate. The ultimate responsibility for the evil he perpetrates goes beyond him, beyond his syphilitic father and his demented grandmother. Popeye's sterility is more than sexual. He is also intellectually and emotionally sterile. We wonder what is going on in his mind as he sits in the jail, and we seek clues: is Popeye reacting to his failure as a man? is he, in some way, seeking punishment for his crimes? do his final words to the hangman, " 'Fix my hair, Jack,' " indicate courage? (378) What we finally realize, with a shudder, is that nothing at all is going on inside Popeye's mind and heart. He is not even indifferent, because indifference implies conscious recognition of alternatives. There is no motive, nor purpose, nor meaning to be discovered in his attitude.

The thematic relationship between this chapter and Horace's defeat then becomes clear. Just as we try to understand Popeye in terms of our own humanity, so we try to understand the ultimate forces at work in the universe. We try to find a meaning and a purpose in life, seek cause and effect relationships, search for a pattern of reward and punishment; but as with Popeye, there is no motive nor purpose nor meaning. If we find meaning, we have created it out of our need. This is the discovery that Horace makes when his idealism is shattered and he realizes that the ultimate sanctuary of man's hopes and dreams is a void. The ideals he believed in were human fabrications, created out of man's need for meaning, rather than reflections, as he thought, of an ultimate meaning in the universe.

Like the two novels that precede it, *Sanctuary* is a cry of despair. The grim image of life that it presents is unrelieved, unlike *The Sound and the Fury*, which has a contrapuntal theme to lighten the despair. Faulkner eventually acknowledged the imbalance of *Sanctuary* by writing a sequel, *Requiem for a Nun*.*

* Though *Requiem for a Nun* is both a narrative and thematic sequel to *Sanctuary*, I have chosen to discuss the novels separately because the ideas and their technique of presentation in *Requiem* belong to a later period. A discussion of the sequel at this point would confuse the presentation of the progressive development of Faulkner's ideas and the shifts in his moods that the chronological ordering of these analyses is intended to reveal.

» »

The common objections of many readers that the novel is filled
with sensationalism and violence, that it is disgusting and lurid
must be dismissed because it is precisely through violence and
lurid sensationalism that the necessary atmosphere for the feeling
of despair is created. A minor background figure, such as the blind
and deaf man at the Old Frenchman place, may seem to be a
stock Gothic-story prop, but in the context of the novel he becomes a symbol of death in life. Incidents such as Temple's encounter with the rat in the barn create the feeling of abject terror
that opens the soul to despair. Faulkner uses a variety of techniques, including humor, to achieve his effects. The humor is macabre because the laughter springs from a deep well of bitterness:
everything that man holds sacred becomes—since life is the way it
is—a fit subject for comedy. Even death is a macabre joke as the
corpse tumbles sedately out of its coffin and the wax plug in its
forehead is dislodged. Through such humor, our illusions of human dignity and human values are undermined. There are many
flaws in this novel, but they do not appreciably detract from Faulkner's achievement: to read *Sanctuary* is to experience despair at a
pitch of intensity rarely achieved in modern fiction.

Light in August

Thematically, *Light in August* (1932) is closely related to *The
Sound and the Fury* and *Sanctuary*. In this later novel, Faulkner
examines the absolutism that plunges Quentin Compson and Horace Benbow into despair; and he dramatizes it as a rigid, life-denying force that makes its victims seek death as a longed-for boon.

In structure, *Light in August* is very complicated, containing several distinct stories whose thematic relationship is not immediately apparent; but stylistically, it is relatively easy reading. The sentence structure is generally free of the spastic, breathless quality of the sentences to be found in *Absalom, Absalom!*, and the shifts from the present to the past pose little difficulty. The simplicity of the narrative technique, however, is deceptive, as the contradictory nature of the many intelligent and perceptive critical studies of the novel indicates.[1] The combination of stark realism with symbolic narration, the creation of highly complex characters, the resonance of the images and symbols, allusions and Biblical parallels—all tend to obscure the thematic unity of the stories of Lena Grove, Byron Bunch, Joe Christmas, Joanna Burden, and Gail Hightower.

Except for the final chapter, the action described in the present tense extends from a Friday in August through a Monday, eleven days later. Lena Grove, nine months pregnant by Lucas Burch, has hitch-hiked from Alabama to Jefferson, Mississippi. A simple soul with a simple faith, Lena is certain that she will find Lucas and that he will provide for her and her child. Her assurance stems not from a knowledge of Lucas's character or his whereabouts but from an unquestioning belief that the Lord will care for her. With her "inwardlighted quality of tranquil and calm unreason," her swollen belly and faded blue dress, she is a composite image of a pagan fertility goddess and a Christian madonna. (16) * Lena is all heart and body—simplicity and trust. She is troubled neither by logic nor worry about the future, abstract ideas nor traditions. And her "calm unreason" is her power and her protection. She comes directly to the town to which Lucas has fled. All the people whom she meets on the road are kind to her. Even a Martha Armstid, who would usually be vigorous in her denunciation of an unwed mother, treats her with kindness and generosity. The earth goddess is attuned to "the very immutable laws which earth must obey." (295) As Gail Hightower observes, she is of the "*good stock peopling in tranquil obedience to it the good earth.*" (356) In responding to her, Byron Bunch leaves the social world governed by taboos and traditions and enters the natural world she inhabits.

* Modern Library Edition.

When we last see Byron, he has quit his job and is on the road with Lena.

There is much humor in the Lena Grove-Byron Bunch romance, a humor derived from the effervescent life-force these country lovers represent. Before Lena's arrival at the mill on the fatal Saturday in August, Byron is a man who lives by the philosophy that idle hands sinners make. He keeps himself occupied by working overtime on Saturdays until he has just enough time to return to his boarding house, eat, bathe, dress, and ride on his mule thirty miles into the country to give religious instruction. By the time he returns to Jefferson, the mill is available once again to keep him busy. In a harmless fashion, Byron escapes from life. But he avoids the fate of his contemporaries in Jefferson and the South, as Faulkner here depicts them, by responding to the affirmative life-force of Lena so completely that he is freed from his preconceptions: he can ignore her pregnancy, her unvirgin state, and fall in love with her.

As Lena arrives at the mill, on the horizon rises the yellow smoke from Joanna Burden's intended funeral pyre. A week later, in a cabin close to the burned ruins of the Burden house, Lena gives birth to her child. Byron Bunch, friend of Gail Hightower and in love with Lena, is the link between the natural, bright, mindless, life-oriented natural world of Lena Grove and the taboo-ridden, dark, violent, death-oriented social world of Hightower, Joe Christmas, and Joanna Burden. Byron is everyman, potentially capable of existing in either world, free, though inexplicably, from a psychologically binding past. Byron can choose. He can follow Hightower's advice and turn away from Lena because she is an unmarried mother, or he can, as he does, respond to his feelings and follow her.

In terms of space, the Lena-Byron idyll is a minor story, but thematically it is of major importance because it illumines by contrast the significance of the Hightower, Christmas, and Burden stories. The key contrast is in the differing responses to life. Lena accepts life; the others resist it. Their personalities are twisted by childhood scars, by enforced submission to concepts and beliefs; they seek death, not life.

The supreme example of the life-negating force of mental abstractions, taboos, and conventions in the novel is racial prejudice. (*Light in August*, Faulkner's seventh novel, is the first in which he deals directly with the racial problem). By it, individuals are transformed into a robot-like lynch mob. As soon as the emotional switch—in the form of such words as "nigger and white woman" is thrown, individuals become automatons executing a precise and predetermined ritual. Even Gavin Stevens, with his Heidelberg Ph. D., accepts without question that the man who has lived in the town three years as a white man is a Negro, and he explains to the visiting stranger the flight of Christmas to Hightower's home in terms of Joe's mixed white and black blood. The murder of Joanna Burden produces, of course, a reaction of horrified fascination among the townspeople. But it is not until the shibboleth is uttered, until the generally recognized ne'er-do-well Brown says, " 'Accuse the white man and let the nigger go free,' " that the curtain on the lynch drama is raised. (85) At once, all the individuals become actors, their thoughts, statements, actions identical with the thoughts, statements, actions of those who played the roles before them. Like the Christian Passion Play, every statement and action in the lynch drama is familiar and inevitable. The individuals who, at the moment, happen to be playing the roles of crucified or crucifiers are unimportant; the drama itself remains the same. Faulkner's rendering of abstract idea transformed into a palpable force greater than any individual is a superb achievement. In his descriptions of the lynching, the familiar square and jail and stores of the town take on the unreal quality of a stage setting. The townspeople move as if in a trance, their speech stereotyped.

The most horrifying aspect of this drama is that its re-enactment strengthens and transmits the taboo that generated it. Each lynching reinforces the concept of white supremacy and intensifies the fear and guilt which mob violence expresses. The people whose participation in the drama is volitionless have been conditioned by their predecessors and their past, and their participation conditions their descendants.

The social tragedy of the lynch drama is a magnified version of the individual tragedies that are recorded in *Light in August*. The lynching serves as a thematic and structural framework for the histories of Hightower, Christmas, and Joanna Burden. Like the members of the mob, each of these characters is both victim of inherited taboos and abstract concepts, and crucifier. The lynching and the histories of each character illustrate the theme which Hightower articulates as he meditates upon the sonorous quality of Protestant music, which seems to him to be:

> . . . the apotheosis of his own history, his own land, his own environed blood: that people from which he sprang and among whom he lives . . . Pleasure, ecstasy, they cannot seem to bear: their escape from it is in violence, in drinking and fighting and praying; catastrophe too, the violence identical and apparently inescapable. *And so why should not their religion drive them to crucifixion of themselves and one another?* (322)

This passage is a succinct statement of the novel's theme: the destructive consequences of resistance to life, the inability to accept the pleasure and the pain that is the sum of human life. Resistance is a denial of life, hence a quest for death. The complex interaction of forces in the human personality is expressed in the final italicized sentence of the quoted passage. The refusal to accept life by the people Hightower describes makes a religion preaching this attitude attractive. By embracing such a religion they give their point of view supernatural sanction. In imposing their religion upon their children, they pass on their own attitude of denial.

As C. Hugh Holman has noted, Faulkner changes the normally Baptist-Methodist Yoknapatawpha County into a stronghold of Presbyterianism in this novel.[2] The shift to a Calvinistic religion is apparently intended to dramatize the residual effects of puritanical rigidity. In Faulkner's view, a child subjected to this religion is taught from birth to resist life, before he is able to respond naturally to experience. In the same way that racial concepts create victims who unwittingly crucify, religious concepts produce victims who crucify themselves and others. Except for Lena and Byron, the major characters in *Light in August* resist life's experiences; all, in varying ways, are self-destructive.

» » Gail Hightower

Gail Hightower, more obviously than the others, is an evader of life. He becomes a minister, gets appointed to Jefferson, and encourages his ostracism from the community so that he can relive each day in that moment between light and dark his grandfather's Civil War death charge on a chicken coop. Hightower's entire career is devoted to immuring himself safely away from the terrors of the "loud harsh world." But to escape the terrors, he must also deny himself the world's pleasures, and he is, in effect, removed from existence.

His birth to an aging couple helps to seal his doom. His father is past fifty when Gail is born, and there is no communication between father and son. His mother spends his formative years in her bed, dying. To the child, his parents are phantoms whom he can not, dare not approach. A third phantom of his childhood is the old Negro woman who, many years before, served his grandfather. She is a storyteller, and she embroiders into a legend the adventure of Gail's ancestor whose boyish exploit cost him his life.* Gail is a sickly, sensitive, and very imaginative boy. The childhood terrors from which he suffers become focused upon the black coat his preacher-father wore during the Civil War. When, at eight, he discovers the coat in an attic trunk, he is "almost overpowered by the evocation of his dead mother's hands which lingered among the folds." (410) One patch on the cloak is from a Yankee uniform. The boy stares at it with horror. That night he is physically ill, but afterwards he returns to the attic almost compulsively to stare at the blue patch. The solitary child, alone with his terrors, finds a refuge in the story of his grandfather's foolish, gallant chicken house raid. "He found no terror in the knowledge that his grandfather . . . had killed men 'by the hundreds' as he was told and believed . . . No horror here because they were just ghosts, never seen in the flesh, heroic, simple, warm; while the father which he knew and feared was a phantom which would never die." (418) He associates his father with the real world; the story of his grandfather releases him from the terrors of reality.

* This chicken coop raid is a revised version, apparently, of the anchovy raid of Bayard I in *Sartoris*.

"I tell you, they were not men after spoils and glory; they were boys riding the sheer tremendous tidal wave of desperate living. Boys. Because this. This is beautiful. Listen. Try to see it. Here is that fine shape of eternal youth and virginal desire which makes heroes. That makes the doings of heroes border so close upon the unbelievable that it is no wonder that their doings must emerge now and then like gun-flashes in the smoke, and that their very physical passing becomes rumor with a thousand faces before breath is out of them, lest paradoxical truth outrage itself." (423)

Like so many of Faulkner's young men, Gail Hightower develops into an abstracted idealist, and he identifies his idealism with the story of his grandfather's heroism. Entering manhood, he decides that "if ever there was shelter, it would be the Church; that if ever truth could walk naked and without shame or fear, it would be in the seminary." (419) His life as a minister in the church he visualizes in the image of Keats's Grecian urn, "intact and on all sides complete and inviolable, like a classic and serene vase, where the spirit could be born anew sheltered from the harsh gale of living and die so, peacefully . . . with scarce even a handful of rotting dust to be disposed of. That was what the word seminary meant: quiet and safe walls within which the hampered and garmentworried spirit could learn anew serenity to contemplate without horror or alarm its own nakedness." (419)

At the seminary each brush with the real world drives Hightower deeper into fantasy: " 'So this is love. I see. I was wrong about it too . . . Perhaps they were right in putting love into books . . . Perhaps it could not live anywhere else.' " The politics of the seminary and then his marriage intensify his need to escape: "*I see. That's the way it is . . . Yes. I see now.*" (421-2) By the time he arrives in Jefferson, his retreat from reality is nearly complete. All he requires is the physical isolation to match that of his spirit. Only after the death of Christmas does Hightower face the truth about his life and acknowledge that he betrayed his ministry and his wife because he would not establish contact with his parishioners and his wife on a human, personal level: he " 'did not see them.' " When he revealed to his wife not only the depth of his " 'hunger but the fact that . . . never would she have any part in the assuaging of it,' " he drove her to seek promiscuous relation-

ships and suicide. (427) She and his parishioners were his sole con-
tacts with the world, and so long as he remained exposed through
them, he was vulnerable. After his wife's death, he invited and welcomed the persecution that would seal him into a death-in-life. He
refused to give up his church and forced his parishioners to boycott
his wild, mad sermons. On his final Sunday as a minister, he left
the church with his face covered by a book. One photographer,
however, caught the mad expression of satanic glee that Hightower thought was hidden from view. He welcomed, too, the accusations and the beating that completed his immurement within
his psychic tower, high above the real terrors of ordinary existence.

When Hightower is drawn back into the world by Byron and
within a few days experiences the extremes of joy and pain that
living can provide—the joy of presiding over the birth of Lena's
child and the horror of witnessing the death of Joe Christmas—
he acknowledges human responsibility, in part at least, for the catastrophes which afflict man. He thinks that " 'there must be some
things for which God cannot be accused by man and held responsible.' " (427) He admits that in his own attempt to escape from
his fears, he created for others much pain and terror. The wheel
image, which Faulkner uses in this presentation of Hightower's
thought-flow, not only serves to capture the minister's reluctant
acceptance of truth (as the wheel of thought grinds through
sand), but also the cyclical pattern of victim becoming crucifier
which the novel dramatizes and which is exemplified in Hightower's life. The minister is not responsible for the conditions which
make him afraid of life. He is a victim of the character and the circumstances of his parents. He is their unwitting creation, the victim. But in his turn he becomes crucifier, driving his wife to her
death.

Hightower's climactic confrontation of truth is forced upon him
by his precipitate experience of extremes, those extremes which
he and "that people from which he sprang and among whom he
lives" cannot "seem to bear." He is torn from his refuge by Byron,
whose life bridges commitment and escape. On the day that Lena
arrives in Jefferson, Hightower senses that Byron, who has broken
his weekend routine to visit him, threatens his isolation. He perceives quickly that Byron is already in love with Lena, and he is

terrified for Byron and for himself. He sweats profusely as his visitor tells him of Lena's plight and of the events surrounding the death of Joanna Burden. The minister's relationship to Byron, perhaps the only human relationship he has ever experienced, makes him vulnerable. And he resists. At first, he listens to these stories of joy and horror, pregnancy and murder, "as though he were listening to the doings of people of a different race" (70); then, as he realizes Byron's involvement, his face registers an "expression of shrinking and denial." (73)

Hightower struggles to protect himself and his friend by trying to persuade Byron to run away, free himself from the girl and the commitment to life she represents. Hightower's anguish is that he welcomes as much as he fears the violation of his isolation. Byron, apparently, senses this ambivalence and confidently brings the grandparents of Joe Christmas to the minister to ask him not only to save their grandson from the lynch mob but to present himself to society as a homosexual by swearing that Christmas was with him on the night of the murder. When he delivers Lena's baby, Hightower is exhilarated. He even contemplates the future in the thought that the grateful mother might name her child after him. When he rises to prevent the execution of the man who sought refuge in his house, he experiences fully the terrors from which he has spent his life fleeing. And because, for the first time, he has known the full range—from ecstasy to catastrophe—of the human experience, he can understand his own death wish and that of his people. He recognizes the inexorable interlacing of past present and future; he realizes that, in a sense, he is the living personification of the past, and, as such, is " 'the debaucher and murderer of my grandson's wife.' " (430) No matter how the individual attempts to escape into isolation, the life of each individual is interlaced with the lives of others. In Hightower's vision "composite of all the faces which he has ever seen," his own among them, there is a composite face of victim and executioner, Joe Christmas and Percy Grimm. (430)

The human being perpetrates evil, creating anguish and suffering for others, but, he is also the victim. Hightower refuses to ignore cosmic responsibility for this moral paradox. He thinks, " 'I am dying . . . I should pray. I should try to pray.' " But Hightower does not try to pray, " 'With all air, all heaven, filled with the lost and unheeded crying of all the living who ever lived, wailing still like lost children among the cold and terrible stars. . . . I wanted so little. I asked so little.' " (431) Confrontation of truth does not, cannot, bring Hightower peace, because the peace which comes of accepting life as it is, with all its vicissitudes, cannot be achieved through thought. Through such an intellectual confrontation as Hightower experiences, the mind always moves to insoluble ultimates. The peace that passeth understanding is for the unthinking Lena Grove, and not for such as Hightower. He acknowledges man's responsibility for the human condition, but he also recognizes forces beyond man's control which must also be held accountable. Since the human mind cannot understand these forces, Hightower continues to resist life. His thoughts removed beyond the human sphere, he escapes once again into his dream: "It is as though they had merely waited until he could find something to pant with," to reaffirm, in resistance, his need of the phantom horsemen. (431)

Hightower does not die nor does he achieve salvation, as a number of commentators have argued.* Recognizing that Hightower escapes into his dream is essential to an understanding of the novel. Had Hightower achieved salvation and peace, it would have been through intellect, a possibility, as novel after novel shows, foreign to Faulkner's vision. Intellect in Faulkner's world prevents acceptance; it seeks answers to the unanswerable. Lena Grove and the other characters in Faulkner's novels who represent affirmation are essentially mindless, an almost alien breed from the typically sensitive, intellectual, and idealistic protagonist. The unbridgeable gap between the affirmative non-thinkers and the negative thinkers is dramatically apparent in the metamorphosis Byron Bunch undergoes. The Byron of the final chapter bears little resemblance to the sensitive, intelligent companion of High-

---

* In a session at the University of Virginia, Faulkner was asked specifically if Hightower dies. He replied: "He didn't die. He had wrecked his life. He had failed his wife. He had failed himself, but there was one thing that he still had —which was the brave grandfather . . . Everything else was gone . . . but he still couldn't take his own life. He had to endure, to live, but that was one thing that was pure and fine that he had—was the memory of his grandfather, who had been brave." *Faulkner in the University*, p. 75.

towor. Boforo ho can bocomo a fit lovor for tho oarth goddooo, ho must be transformed into a fool. The violence done to Byron's character in this final chapter is palliated, to some extent, by the technique of introducing a narrator whose view of Byron is presumably his own. Significantly, however, throughout the novel, Byron is kept at a distance. We are told nothing of his past, of the forces that have formed his character. To have done so would have been to make Byron the central figure in the book because he would have portrayed the road from negation to affirmation, a journey Faulkner did not, probably could not, describe. *Light in August* deals with extremes—resistance and acceptance; it does not bridge the two.

» » Joe Christmas

Like Hightower, Joe Christmas and Joanna Burden are victims of their childhood. Two absolutist concepts mold and destroy both Joanna and Joe: in the case of the former, a Calvinistic division of men into the damned and the elect; in Joe's case, a racial division of men into black and white.

Joe Christmas's life-long anguish is that he must but cannot identify himself as Negro or white. He cannot accept race as incidental to his individuality, to his humanity. He must know what he can never know, and his life is a process of self-crucifixion. Joe thinks as he does because of the absolutism of his grandfather and his foster-father.

His grandfather, Joe Hines, is perhaps the most obvious example in the novel of the escapee Hightower describes. Before his daughter's escapade with the circus man, Hines's tensions are expressed through violence. As Mrs. Hines tells Hightower, " 'Even before we were married, he was always fighting.' " (326) On the night his daughter Milly is born, he is in jail for brawling. His daughter's sexual adventure provides a focus for his tensions, and his violence is transformed into a blend of religious and racial fanaticism. Milly's seducer must be a Negro, Hines decides, and her outraged father must become the avenger of the Lord and of the white race. During Milly's pregnancy, Hines interrupts services in a Negro church to preach white supremacy. When she gives birth, he sees himself as the instrument of God's wrath. Sex and evil are, of course, equated for him; and he, in effect, kills his own daughter, the symbol of "bitchery and abomination." Her child, whom he considers Negro, he spares as proof of God's abomination of "lechery."

In his newly acquired mission, the once violent Hines can now sit quietly in the orphanage for five years to watch his grandson. Formerly a competent and capable workman, a foreman, he destroys his effectiveness and usefulness and embraces a life of poverty and degradation. Obsessed, he becomes the pursuer of his grandson, Joe Christmas. Like all the pursuers in the novel, he is, in reality, the pursued. Hines's fanaticism serves him as the vision of galloping horses serves Hightower: it makes him a ghost.

McEachern, Joe Christmas's foster-father, is the victim of a religious concept that equates life's pleasures with evil. According to the Calvinistic belief, man is predestined as one of the elect or the damned, and his proof of election is abstention from sin. The greatest temptation is, of course, sex; therefore lechery is the greatest sin. The good life is a form of self-flagellation, of rigid discipline, hard work, unceasing prayer. Life itself is a stage one must get through—an unfortunate but necessary prelude to death and union with God. Life becomes, in effect, an extended self-crucifixion for those who interpret the dogma in this way. A victim of this life-denying concept, McEachern, in his turn, creates victims.

These two extremists leave their ineradicable mark upon Joe Christmas. Though Faulkner provides only a summary of the formative influences upon Gail Hightower and Joanna Burden, he reveals in dramatic detail the process of forming an escapee from life by depicting the crucial traumas of Joe's early years.

Two soul-searing incidents occur at the orphanage in which Hines places his grandson on Christmas Eve. Over the years, by watching him constantly, Hines makes the child feel isolated from the other children:

"Because he didn't play with the other children no more now. He stayed by himself . . . and old Doc Hines said to him, 'Why dont you play with them other children like you used to?' and he didn't say nothing and old Doc Hines said, 'Is it because they call you nigger?' and he didn't say nothing and old Doc Hines said, 'Do you think you are a nigger because God has marked your face?' and he said, 'Is God a nigger too?' and old Doc Hines said, 'He is the Lord God of wrathful hosts, His will be done.' " (335-6)

The troubled child studies the Negro gardener and when the Negro reacts to his scrutiny, the boy asks, " 'How come you are a nigger?' " Angrily, the Negro says, " 'Who told you I am a nigger, you little white trash bastard . . . You dont know what you are. And more than that, you wont never know. You'll live and you'll die and you wont never know.' " (336) Thus is raised for Joe the central question of his life. Though Faulkner does not emphasize the fact, Joe is being raised in the South as a white Southerner. He is therefore inheritor of the concept of racial division and of white supremacy. In the Southern world, as Faulkner shows again and again, actual relationships between Negro and white transcend racial barriers. But the concept exists apart from the reality of human relationships. And as soon as the issue is raised or challenged, the concept automatically takes precedence. This absolutist concept is part of Joe's inheritance.

When the boy is five the incident that ends his stay at the orphanage occurs. In this incident, sex and Joe's racial origin are fused and seared into the child's memory. Joe has somehow discovered that the toothpaste in the dietician's room is sweet and pleasant-tasting. Trapped by the entrance of the dietician and her lover, the child hides behind the washstand curtain. He is terrified and compulsively eats toothpaste as he hears without comprehension the sounds of love-making. The toothpaste sickens him and he vomits. The woman, horrified at the thought of public exposure, is furious. Seeking the vilest possible epithet to express her rage, she calls the cowering, terrified child a "nigger bastard." Like the Jeffersonians who, thirty years later, automatically accept Brown's statement that Christmas is a Negro, the dietician accepts her wild designation as fact. The shibboleth simplifies by categorizing. It curtains guilt: the anger that should be directed inward finds a convenient external object. The dietician seeks out the janitor whom she has noticed, without consciously registering the fact, watching the boy.

Hines, made almost clairvoyant by his own obsessions, knows she is guilty of lechery. He is convinced that the child—to him the living symbol of God's abomination of lechery—is an instrument to expose the woman's sin.

The five-year-old Joe, already adapted to the discipline of the institution, anxiously awaits the release of being punished for wrongdoing. But the dietician, imputing to the child an adult awareness, is certain he delays exposing her sin to extend her torture. Finally, she approaches him. Gratified that the punishment he awaits is to be administered. Joe is shocked and confused by her offer of money. It denies him the security of the sin-and-punishment ritual which absolves and releases him from guilt. The insecurity and confusion he knows as the furious woman curses him will be connected for the rest of his life with woman. He comes to prefer the certainty of McEachern's whippings to the faltering kindness of his foster-mother. His violent disposal of the food offered him by Mrs. McEachern and later Joanna Burden are probably related to this original fusion of sickening toothpaste, woman, and anxiety. After his day-long resistance to McEachern, he takes the tray of food his foster-mother brings him and throws it into the corner. Twenty-five years later, after his first night with Joanna, he angrily ponders the ambivalence of Joanna's sexual submission and throws the dishes of food she has prepared for him against the wall.

In adulthood, Joe will not understand why he acts as he does because "Memory believes before knowing remembers." (104) Nevertheless, the source of his future anguish, his self-crucifixion and his public execution, lies in these two incidents and several others that occur during his years with McEachern. Already at five, Joe can be described as a "shadow," the image Faulkner uses repeatedly for those people who are phantoms, shadows of their past.

Joe's life-long struggle to establish his identity begins on the day he leaves the orphanage with McEachern. He decides that he will keep his own name, but his attempt to define for himself the "I-Am" of his individuality is doomed to failure not only because he is an orphan, but because the fanatics who mold him make him an absolutist, and he must therefore fit himself into a category to establish his identity.[3] In contrast to Lena Grove, who is attuned to the natural, Joe is alienated from nature. Though brought up in the country, he can look up at "the stars of which he had been aware for thirty years and not one of which had any name to him or meant anything at all by shape or brightness or position." (92) In the description of Joe's final hours of freedom, Faulkner emphasizes this alienation: "For a week now he has lurked and crept among its secret places, yet he remained a foreigner to the very immutable laws which earth must obey." (295) Lena's response to life is natural, Joe's unnatural. Lena accepts; Joe resists. Joe can respond to experience only in terms of the abstractions imposed upon him. Molded by a fanatical victim of a religious concept, McEachern, Joe Christmas learns to oppose his foster-father's fanaticism with an equal fanaticism.

At eight, he asserts his individuality by refusing to learn the catechism. The boy is described, in this episode, as a monk submitting to the flagellation of his flesh, almost with exaltation. At the end of the day-long ordeal, he kneels at McEachern's command, but he does not pray. He listens to the man "requesting that Almighty be as magnanimous as himself, and by and through and because of conscious grace." (133) Joe hates his foster-father, but the cold, almost impersonal rigidity of the invariable routine of punishment for wrongdoing appeals to him more than the tendered sympathy of his foster-mother. In resisting McEachern, Joe becomes as extreme and rigid as the man he hates. When he is beaten his "body might have been wood or stone; a post or a tower upon which the sentient part of him mused like a hermit, contemplative and remote with ecstasy and selfcrucifixion." (139-40)

The religious fervor of McEachern, and Joe's resistance to it dramatize that quality Hightower hears in Protestant music: "deliberate and without passion so much as immolation, pleading, asking, for not love, not life, forbidding it to others, demanding in sonorous tones death as though death were the boon." (321-2) Under McEachern's tutelage, Joe has little chance of learning to respond to life naturally, of accepting life as he finds it. When he strikes down McEachern in the dance hall, for instance, he rides off on the horse exultant; like Faust, he has sold his soul to the devil, which means to Joe that now he is unequivocally among the damned. He has been trained, in other words, to think in terms of absolutes, mutually exclusive categories—the damned and the elect, black and white—into which he must but can never place himself.

Another aspect of his absolutism is revealed in his initial encounter with sex. Though it is very difficult to reconcile the adult Joe Christmas with the young boy portrayed in these scenes, the adolescent Christmas is, apparently, a sensitive idealist, very similar to Quentin Compson and Horace Benbow, who envision woman as inviolable perfection and beauty. Joe's reaction to hearing about the menses is so violent that he is impelled to kill an animal and dip his hands into the blood. Years later, the first time he is alone with Bobbie Allen, the waitress, she tells him that she is sick. She has to explain to her naïve and innocent companion what she means. When Joe finally understands, he runs from her and seeks refuge in the dark woods. Again using the Keatsian urn image, Faulkner describes the boy's revulsion:

In the notseeing and the hardknowing as though in a cave he seemed to see a diminishing row of suavely shaped urns in moonlight, blanched. And not one was perfect. Each one was cracked and from each crack there issued something liquid, deathcolored, and foul. He touched a tree, leaning his propped arms against it, seeing the ranked and moonlit urns. He vomited. (165)

This episode reveals clearly, it seems to me, the relationship between *The Sound and the Fury* and *Light in August*. Both novels have their genesis in the extreme reaction of the adolescent idealist to reality. But the later novel is a dramatized argument against the rigidity of such idealism and its resultant disillusionment. The idealist vaults from one absolute to another. He resists the impurity, the evil, the terrors and pain that are all part of human life. His resistance to the reality he discovers constitutes a denial of life. Death becomes a longed-for boon. Like all the major characters, except Lena and Byron, in *Light in August*, Joe Christmas becomes a self-crucifier and a crucifier of others. Interestingly enough, the Keatsian urn image is also applied to Lena Grove. In the opening scene, her journey is "a long monotonous succession of peaceful and undeviating changes from day to dark and dark to day again . . . like something moving forever and without progress across an urn." (6) As the character who accepts life, who is responsive to the earth, Lena symbolizes the timelessness evoked by Keats's ode.[4]

Joe's reactions are always violent and extreme. At fourteen, he is already a victim of his past. When he enters the shed in which the Negro girl awaits, his sexual desire is associated with a need to vomit. "There was something in him trying to get out, like when he had used to think of toothpaste." (137) His reaction to sex and to the Negro girl are somehow related to his traumatic experience at five. His swings from one extreme to another are apparent in the different stages of his affair with the unattractive prostitute who doubles as waitress in the backstreet restaurant. Completely innocent and inexperienced, he falls deeply in love with Bobbie. For the first and last time in his life he knows love, and he is able to communicate with another human being. He even reveals to her his doubts about his racial heritage. His discovery that Bobbie is a prostitute transforms him from naïve rube to companion and imitator of the underworld pimps she serves.

Bobbie's violent rejection of Joe for exposing her to McEachern's denunciation of her as a harlot results in her taking refuge, like the dietician, behind the shibboleth and denouncing Joe to her companions as a Negro. The episode provides a violent finale to Joe's education and his youth. Though he strikes down McEachern, he can never be free from the fanatical absolutism that he hated. His refuge is motion. He enters a road that extends for fifteen years, a road of self-flagellation and of flight from himself. He torments himself, for instance, by living with a black-skinned woman:

At night he would lie in bed beside her, sleepless, beginning to breathe deep and hard. He would do it deliberately . . . trying to breathe into himself the dark odor, the dark and inscrutable thinking and being of Negroes . . . And all the while his nostrils at the odor which he was trying to make his own would whiten and tauten, his whole being writhe and strain with physical outrage and spiritual denial.

He thought that it was loneliness which he was trying to escape and not himself. But the street ran on . . . he might have seen himself as in numberless avatars, in silence, doomed with motion, driven by the courage of flagged and spurred despair; by the despair of courage whose opportunities had to be flagged and spurred. He was thirtythree years old. (197)

A racial extremist, Joe nearly kills a white prostitute who offers herself to Negroes as well as whites. The knowledge that a white woman would give herself sexually to a Negro shocks and revolts him so much that he does not recover from the experience for two years. During his years on the road, Joe combines lechery and confession that he is Negro as if he were trying to achieve the security of being both damned and inferior. The two dreaded categories are fused in his mind. On the evening preceding his murder of Joanna, he walks through the Negro quarters of Jefferson and, panting, feels as though he "had been returned to the lightless hot wet primogenitive Female." He runs wildly up the hill into the "cold hard air of white people," and stares down at the unlighted Negro quarters. "It might have been the original quarry, abyss itself." (100-1) Joe can escape neither the fanatical racism of his heritage (embodied in his grandfather, Hines) nor the fanatical religiousness of his foster-father. Female (the symbol of man's fall from grace), and Negro are linked, for him, with damnation.

Joe remains at the Burden place, just outside of Jefferson, for three years before he is almost literally crucified.* Tempted frequently during that period to re-enter the street of flight and motion, Joe cannot leave. Just as he can never escape from himself, he cannot leave Joanna, who mirrors the polarities between which he is stretched.

» » Joanna Burden

For Joanna, too, race and religion are inextricably linked. Like Hightower and Christmas, she is a victim of her predecessors. At twelve, her grandfather, Calvin Burden, ran away from the New

---

* Though most interpreters of *Light in August* have assumed that Joe is thirty-three when he is executed, the evidence is not clear-cut in the novel. Faulkner concludes his brief description of Joe's experiences "on the road" with the statement: "He was thirtythree years old." (197) He then describes his entrance into Jefferson. The crux of the ambiguity is whether the three years in Jefferson are to be considered as part of those years in which "the street ran on" or apart from them. Joe's continual reference to the road as a refuge from his relationship with Joanna would seem to me to indicate that the two are separated, and that therefore Joe is thirty-three when he arrives in Jefferson and thirty-six, three years older than Jesus Christ, when he is executed.

England of his minister-father. But he fled too late. Already he was stamped by the absolutism of his father's religion, which Faulkner describes as Unitarianism but which seems closer to the rigidity of Calvinism. In the manner of the rebellious absolutist, Calvin moves from one extreme to another. He becomes a Catholic and spends a year in a monastery. Ten years later, at his wedding to a Huguenot girl, he denounces Catholicism and slavery in the same saloon speech. He reverts to the religion of his father and teaches his son "the bleak and bloodless logic" he learned as a child. A violent man, Calvin kills an opponent in an argument over slavery. To his three children he declares: " 'I'll learn you to hate two things . . . hell and slaveholders.' " (212)

This violence and extremism Calvin passes on to his son Nathaniel, who, in his turn, runs away from home. Nathaniel returns sixteen years later with a Mexican woman and a son. He has not married the mother of his child because he would not be married outside the religion of his father. This Mexican woman, whom Nathaniel chooses to live with, is described as a replica of his mother. Reunited with his father, he joins in the struggle against slavery. After the Civil War, father and son get a commission from Washington to help freed Negroes in Mississippi. Calvin Burden and Nathaniel's son are killed by Colonel Sartoris over a question of Negro voting. Nathaniel buries them in unmarked graves to avoid possible desecration and mutilation of the bodies by the enraged white supremacists of Jefferson. When he is fifty years old, Nathaniel sends to New Hampshire for a woman to replace his dead wife. The woman dispatched to him by relatives becomes the mother of Joanna.

In later life, Joanna cannot remember her father very clearly. He is, like Hightower's father, a phantom to the child. What has seared Joanna's memory is a visit, when she is four, with her father to the grove of cedars where her grandfather and half-brother are buried. The fear that grips her is not caused by the grove itself but by something in her father. Nathaniel enjoins his child to remember that the dead were murdered " 'not by one white man but by the curse which God put on a whole race . . . A race doomed and cursed to be forever and ever a part of the white race's doom and curse for its sins . . . None can escape it.' " (221)

Joanna tells Christmas that after that day Negroes became for her " 'a shadow in which I lived, we lived, all white people . . . the black shadow in the shape of a cross.' " (221) When she tried to inform her father of her obsessive need to escape from the shadow, he replied that there is no escape: " 'You must struggle, rise. But in order to rise, you must raise the shadow with you.' " (222) Thus God's curse and the Negro is unsealed for Joanna by her fear: the white man is cursed and his salvation can only be achieved by helping to raise the Negro. Of utmost significance to Joanna's thinking and feeling later in life is her father's belief that the Negro is inferior to the white. In order to rise, he tells her " 'you must raise the shadow with you. But you can never lift it to your level.' " (222)

Joanna assumes the burden imposed upon her, but since that day in the grove, she cannot see the Negroes " 'as people, but as a thing, a shadow.' " (221) They are the cross she must carry. She works with Negroes for their benefit, but she cannot associate with them on a human level. Because she assists Negroes, she is isolated from the white people of the community. Joanna lives a self-immolating existence, symbolized by the submergence of her femininity. Her stern devotion to her crusade makes her man-like. Over forty when Christmas enters her house, Joanna struggles with her sexual desire. She does not surrender to Joe so much as to the long-suppressed need that rages within her. As does she, Joe identifies her desire to submit with her femininity, her moral resistance with her masculinity. Her fierce sexual struggle reflects the polarities of her character. Her duality, which mirrors his own character, enrages Joe, and the night following his first encounter with her, he rapes her. His attack ends their sexual relationship for six months. Joe does not re-enter the road; instead he works at the planing mill and sleeps in a cabin on Joanna's land. Though he thinks of leaving, Joe cannot, apparently because he recognizes in Joanna a spiritual counterpart, a being like himself spreadeagled between extremes. Certainly, Christmas is not the kind of man to wait six months simply to renew a sexual relationship.

When her own six-month battle has ended, Joanna plunges herself into sex—evil and damnation—with a need as intense as that which drove Joe to live with an ebony-skinned woman. For neither one is there a middle ground. Joe must be black or white, Joanna evil or good, one of the damned or one of the elect. Joanna's nymphomania is a reaction to her years of denial and devotion, but it is so extreme that it is masochistic. Her daily existence reflects the mutually exclusive absolutes between which she is divided. In the light of day, she sits at her desk, man-like in her dress, steadfast in her devotion to the cause of raising the Negro and saving her own soul. In the darkness of the night, she wallows in the throes of insatiable sexual desire and of sin. She whispers "Negro" into the ears of her lover, plunging herself into damnation with the very symbol of her salvation.

At first it shocked him: the abject fury of the New England glacier exposed suddenly to the fire of the New England biblical hell. Perhaps he was aware of the abnegation in it: the imperious and fierce urgency that concealed an actual despair at frustrate and irrevocable years, which she appeared to attempt to compensate each night as if she believed that it would be the last night on earth by damning herself forever to the hell of her forefathers, by living not alone in sin but in filth. (225-6)

The hypnotic fascination that Joanna holds for Joe is probably her ability to plunge herself into the extremes from which he must eternally withdraw but toward which his absolutist personality yearns. When Joanna enters the third stage of their relationship, she swings from one polarity to another. Obsessively, she prays for forgiveness, seeking salvation. She must have the man with whom she has sinned achieve salvation with her by assuming the identity of a Negro and share her work to raise the black race. She asks him to do what he tried but could not do: identify himself once and for all as a Negro. For Joe, Negro and damnation are identical; for Joanna, Negro and salvation are fused.

Both are volitionless victims of their absolutism, and violence is inevitable. Joe is repelled by Joanna's praying, which reminds him of McEachern's. He is also repelled by her continued insistence that he declare himself a Negro, as well as by her loss of sexuality. Again he thinks of the road as a welcome release, but he cannot leave. Joanna embodies all the furies that have driven Joe throughout his life. He will not kneel and pray, but he cannot leave the room; he must stand and watch her. He cannot become Negro as she demands, but he cannot declare her mad and leave. His tension increases, and the need to strike out at the embodiment of all the forces that have tortured him becomes obsessive. The impulse to destroy, however, is actually self-destructive, because Joanna merely embodies what he can never escape. Joe and Joanna become for each other alter-egos. Joanna prepares two bullets. The self-crucifixion which has been their lives thus reaches its climax: death is the physical and ultimate expression of the self-immolation of their existence. The denial of life which Hightower hears in the Protestant music and which their lives dramatize reaches its symbolic conclusion in their violent ends.

» » Conclusion

Joe's actions after he slashes Joanna's throat are not those of a man trying to escape. He invites chase and capture by appearing in the Negro church, where he utters his final violent repudiation of the concepts—religion and race—that molded and destroyed him. Joe's body retains its hold upon life longer than his spirit, but he finally goes passively to the boon he sought so long.

In Faulkner's description of Joe's final days, the parallels between the story of Joe Christmas and the New Testament story are too obvious to ignore.[5] Throughout the novel, many details evoke the story of Jesus. The day, for example, on which Hines brings Joe to the orphanage is Christmas eve, and his initials are those of Jesus Christ. The circumstances of Joe's birth and some incidents from his early years are recounted, but the years of early manhood are obscure. As in the Christ story, the final three years and the crucifixion are fully presented. Lucas Burch, who is identified as Joe's disciple, betrays his master. Wandering around after the murder, Christmas must suddenly know the day of the week, and when he discovers it is Friday, he goes directly to Mottstown to be captured.

Some interpreters of *Light in August* have seen in Joe a Christ figure; others, who rightly find it difficult to identify the character of Joe with that of Jesus, have denied the parallels or ignored them. The pertinence of the Christ analogies is clear, however, when one recognizes that Faulkner divorces crucifixion from salvation. The parallels in the novel with the New Testament emphasize the self-immolation of Jesus and his crucifixion by the people. Faulkner's story dramatizes the excessive emphasis in the Southern brand of Protestantism upon suffering and death as the road to salvation. The effect of viewing life as a process of self-crucifixion, and death as the gateway to eternal joy, is to turn the eyes of these dogma-ridden people away from life. This view tortures them because it denies the value of being alive, a value their very instincts affirm. Instead of trying to live fully, instead of enjoying their short span of consciousness, they look toward death as the longed-for boon.

The parallels with the New Testament are ironic. Not salvation, but a continuation and strengthening of the fanaticism that produced it, result from the execution of Christmas. Death brings Joe the personal release he sought, but it in no way suggests the salvation inherent in the Christian crucifixion. Guilt sears the death of Christmas into the memories of his executioners. Percy Grimm, the crucifier, is a volitionless victim of a racist concept. The fear and guilt of his society, which initially produced the concept, are reinforced by his act, and the concept will be imposed, during childhood, upon the heirs of the executioners and make these victims, in their turn, executioners.

Light in August is not a realistic study of Protestantism and racism; its subject is the crippling clutch of abstract concepts upon the mind and soul of the human being. These concepts, imposed in childhood, enshroud the individual's attitude toward life, making him incapable of responding naturally to the full scope of human experience. The concept of racial superiority, with its attendant fear and guilt, molds and controls the individual, just as the Calvinistic-rooted religion, with its emphasis upon sin and punishment, death and damnation, steers him away from life by directing his gaze toward death. Though the novel deals with the particular forces at work in the South and upon the Southerner, it is fundamentally a study of the effect of any absolutist view that makes the human being its servant and victim.

Light in August encompasses extremes. It is like an altar triptych with a large central canvas of the crucifixion, dark, somber, and violent. The small sidepieces, hinged to the major canvas, are bright, joyous, placid scenes of the mother and child and of the holy family. One of the remarkable achievements of the novel is the consistency with which Faulkner creates these opposing canvases. The stories of Hightower, and Joe Christmas, and Joanna Burden are narrated with images of darkness, pain, crucifixion, and death. The Lena Grove story is bathed in warm sunlight and filled with images of timelessness and affirmation. The title, which is resonant with meaning, seems most appropriately associated with the warm life-glow that haloes Lena.

With its brilliant portraits of a variety of grotesques, victims of their past and their society who in their turn create victims, *Light in August* is unquestionably one of Faulkner's greatest novels. A fascinating story, masterfully told, of the South and Southerners, it transcends the specific to reveal the human being as his own executioner and victim.

Pylon

In writing *Pylon* (1935), Faulkner turned his attention from the particular problems of Yoknapatawpha County to the general problem of life in the age of the machine.* Ostensibly a story about flying and fliers, the novel is a scathing indictment of twentieth-century American society. Written in a rich and brilliantly allusive

---

* Faulkner's interest in flying is reflected in his earliest piece of published fiction, "Landing in Luck" (See *Early Prose and Poetry*, Carvel Collins, ed.), and is apparent in the number of war stories about pilots that he wrote. After the success of *Sanctuary*, he bought an airplane, but he gave up flying when his brother Dean was killed in a plane crash. Two early stories, "Honor" (1930), and "Death-Drag" (1932), contain the germs of the situation and characters developed in *Pylon*.

style, *Pylon* is exciting and evocative, but it provides an unsatisfying, almost irritating, reading experience. Faulkner seems unable to decide whether the group of airmen upon whom he centers his story are "spiritual and moral waifs," or prototypes of new humanists in the age of the machine. As a result, reader sympathy is unfocused. Also, the imposition of the techniques of modern poetry upon the narrative form frequently produces confusion and obscurity. Description of character, for example, is sometimes rendered in bizarre juxtaposition of images. Hagood, the newspaper editor, visualizes the Reporter's mother as a train engine preserved as a museum piece; then, immediately following this image, her "fine big bosom" is described as similar to "one of the walled impervious towns of the Middle Ages whose origin antedates writing, which have been taken and retaken in uncountable fierce assaults"; her teeth are like "those of a horse"; and, finally, Hagood sees her as "a canvas out of the vernal equinox of pigment . . . a canvas conceived in and executed out of that fine innocence of sleep and open bowels capable of crowning the rich foul unchaste earth with rosy cloud where lurk and sport oblivious and incongruous cherubim." (57) *

Such a profusion of images creates a stippled impression that obscures rather than creates character. Extensive use of imagery, symbolism, allusions, and Joycean wordmergers expand the boundaries of narration into the domain of poetry. The effects are very often excellent, but *Pylon* is primarily a novel, and the storyteller is subverted by the poet. Hagood seems to be some kind of father figure, but why he feels impelled to underwrite the Reporter and what relation his paternal attitude bears to the action of the novel, it is impossible to determine. Neither as character nor symbol is he comprehensible. In fact, of all the characters, only one, Jiggs, seems a real person. The Reporter, through whose consciousness much of the narrative is presented, never emerges from poetic shadows; and the airmen, Schumann, Laverne, and Holmes, though they at least have names, are kept at such a distance that we cannot know and understand enough about them to think of them as real people.

* Signet Edition.

Like *As I Lay Dying*, this novel too is a poem in narrative form. It expresses a vision of the modern world similar to that of T. S. Eliot's in "The Waste Land." [1] Faulkner's own description of the novel in a seminar discussion at the University of Virginia probably provides a clue to his initial intention. In response to the question, "Mr. Faulkner, do you regard *Pylon* as a serious novel, and what were you driving at in that novel?" he said,

To me they were a fantastic and bizarre phenomenon on the face of a contemporary scene, of our culture at a particular time . . . They were ephemera and phenomena on the face of a contemporary scene. That is, there was really no place for them in the culture, in the economy, yet they were there, at that time, and everyone knew that they wouldn't last very long, which they didn't. That time of those frantic little aeroplanes which dashed around the country and people wanted just enough money to live, to get to the next place to race again. *Something frenetic and in a way almost immoral about it. That they were outside the range of God, not only of respectability, of love, but of God too. That they had escaped the compulsion of accepting a past and a future, that they were—they had no past.* They were as ephemeral as the butterfly that's born this morning with no stomach and will be gone tomorrow.[2]

I have italicized several lines in this statement because they sum up succinctly a major theme of *Pylon*. The entire statement also reveals the ambivalent attitude toward the fliers that mars the novel. Sympathy for them in their isolation from society merges with antipathy for them as rootless beings beyond the range of God and love.

The central symbol of the novel is the pylon—a symbol of speed and of sex, the equivalents of God and love in the waste land of the mechanical age. The major characters, both the airmen and the citizens of New Valois, are "moral and spiritual waif[s]" driven by spiritual needs that they do not understand and that, in a society cut off from the past, cannot be fulfilled. (73) The ephemeral sensations the waste land dwellers seek in speed and sex manifest their spiritual aridity. The speed their dials register increases "steadily toward some yet unrevealed crescendo of ultimate triumph whose only witnesses were waifs." (54) They live in and for tho momont; thoy laok a oonoo of human continuity; they are without religion, without moral and social traditions.

The airmen, Roger, Laverne, Jack, their child Jack, and the mechanic Jiggs, have no place they think of as home. Constantly on the move, traveling across the country from one air meet to another, they are a self-contained group with no binding ties to the past, to society, to any other human being. Their entire existence— their location at a particular moment, their subsistence, their routine, their moral and spiritual values—is determined by the machines they serve. They are monstrous products of a mechanized age, and their submerged humanity is in "gargantuan irrelation" to the "vicious" machines they fly. (7) Schumann, the leader of the group probably because he is the one who actually flies the machine, is described as "single-purposed, fatally and grimly without any trace of introversion or any ability to objectify or ratiocinate, as though like the engine, the machine for which he apparently existed he functioned, moved, only in the vapor of gasoline and the filmstick of oil." (103-4)

Dedication to the machine creates and unites the group. Human relationships are subservient to relationships created by the necessity of servicing the machine. The son that Laverne, Jack, and Roger share is no focal point of unity. The marriage of Roger and Laverne was a concession to a custom that means nothing to them. Laverne does not know whether Roger or Jack fathered her child. To provide the boy a last name, the two men tossed dice. The "ménage à trois" is not disturbed by the civil ceremony which couples Roger and Laverne as man and wife. There is little indication that love has any role in their lives. Even Jack's antagonism to the Reporter appears motivated not by jealousy but by anger at the thought that Laverne might give herself to him to repay his favors to the group. These people do experience feelings that are recognizable: occasionally, Laverne expresses a desire for stability and continuity; at times, Jack seems to resent Roger's primacy as Laverne's legal husband, but these eruptions are minor and do not interfere with the functioning of the team. If Laverne knows maternal love, it is not strong enough to foster any alteration in the nomadic life of the group. It is she who initiates the game of goading the child to strike out wildly at the taunt, "Who's your old man?" The human and familial ties of these people, in short, are incidental to their unity as a machine-servicing team. And when they lose their machine and its flier, the group disintegratoo.

The airmen feel isolated from society, but, in reality, they carry to an extreme but logical conclusion the tendencies prevalent in a mechanized world. Their isolation is a question of degree not quality. The Reporter, who in many ways represents the waste land society, shares many of the airmen's characteristics. He, too, is a waif, (he even becomes "the patron . . . saint of all waifs"— 110) "a creature who apparently never had any parents either and . . . who apparently sprang fullgrown and irrevocably mature out of some violent and instantaneous transition like the stories of dead steamboatmen and mules." (27) The Reporter's mother, who looks like a retired Madam, has changed her last name frequently, and there is little indication that she provided her son with a home or even indentifiable paternity.

The Reporter's macabre physique evokes the image of a dead society. He is a breathing skeleton, a refugee from a doctor's cupboard dressed in garments snatched from "an etherised patient in a charity ward." (15) Jiggs, who is prompted to humorous gibes by the cadaverous appearance of the Reporter, calls him Lazarus, an appropriate identification of the man who seeks to raise himself from the grave of spiritual death.

The Reporter serves to reveal the similarity between the world of the airmen and the waste land society. Through the consciousness of this character, Faulkner describes that society (with a rich array of images, symbols, and allusions) as being equally rootless and traditionless, as substituting ephemeral excitation for God and sex for love, and as existing for and in the moment. To list and identify all the symbols and allusions is unnecessary. A few will illustrate the general meaning of most of them. One that recurs frequently is the stack of newspapers, with a watch resting face down upon the headlines, in the coffin-like elevator of the newspaper building. The newspaper headlines are a "crosssection out of time-space," (47) the "dead instant's fruit of forty tons of machinery and an entire nation's antic delusion." They feed the "eye, the organ without thought, speculation, or amaze. . . ." (68) The newspaper headlines record the present, severing human events from the past and the future, ignoring, as do the compulsive newspaper readers, the continuity of time and of human history. The headlines provide a "cryptic staccato crossection of an instant crystallised and now dead two hours, though only the moment, the instant: the substance itself not only not dead, not complete, but in its very insoluble enigma of human folly and blundering possessing a futile and tragic immortality." (53)

The newspaper symbolizes the society's emphasis upon the ephemeral and its denial of continuity through time. In the same way, the Mardi Gras, which serves as background for the events in the novel, reveals another aspect of this severance from the past. The celebration, which initiates the Lenten season, has been stripped of its religious significance and merely provides, like the air show, meaningless excitation. The "cryptic shieldcaught (i n r i) loops of bunting" all over the city recall the scroll on the cross of the crucified Jesus, but in the traditionless modern world, the purple and gold bunting, the confetti and serpentine are the "tinseldung of the stars." (38) The medieval world, which Faulkner frequently evokes in oblique references, produced the great Gothic cathedrals dedicated to God. The great structure of the Godless machine age, the airport, "Raised Up and Created out of the Waste Land," is dedicated to the Chairman of the Sewage Board, H. I. Feinman. (11) Instead of religious symbols, the modern structure is decorated with Feinman's initial. On the base of the four sides of the airport lampposts are *F*'s, and the runways form a gigantic *F*.

Godless and traditionless, the waste land is also loveless. Vulgar sex characterizes modern life. Throughout the novel images of death and love are merged: "Momus' Nilebarge clatterfalque." (48) Telephone booths are " 'ranked coffincubicles of dead tail.' " (41) Hotels are the homes of traveling salesmen: "legion homeless and symbolic: the immemorial flying buttresses of ten million American Saturday nights, with shrewd heads filled with tomorrow's cosmic alterations in the form of pricelists and the telephone numbers of discontented wives and highschool girls." (38) (This description with its allusion to the flying buttresses of Gothic cathedrals and probably to Eliot's "The Hollow Men" in the "shrewd head" phrase is typical of the poetically allusive style in the novel.) These and many more images in *Pylon* create the vision of a society which Eliot called the Waste Land and which Faulkner, utilizing many of Eliot's symbols and images, describes in a similar tone of disillusionment.

Like the unnamed protagonist of Eliot's poem, the anonymous Reporter in Pylon seeks salvation. Though he does not know the source of his malaise nor even that he is a seeker, the Reporter is in quest of escape. Apparently a frustrated writer, he sought, when he first arrived in New Valois, quarters in the bohemian section of the city, the Vieux Carré. He scours antique and junk shops with "the eager and deluded absorption of a child hunting colored easter eggs" to furnish the bohemian apartment he rents in a street called "*The Drowned.*" (56) When he encounters the airmen, he clings to them like a drowning man to a life buoy. Shocked by their unconventional existence and at the same time irresistibly fascinated, he formulates, out of his own desperation, an image of them that has little basis in reality. Somehow, he comes to envision them as his salvation. He fantasies becoming a member of their group and escaping from the "day after tomorrow and the day after that and after that and me smelling the same burnt coffee and dead shrimp and oysters and waiting for the same light to change." (106) Returning to the airport to watch the wreath being dropped over Roger Schumann's lake-grave, the Reporter realizes that there is to be no escape. From the moving taxi, he could:

. . . still see the city, the glare of it, no further away; if he were moving, regardless at what terrific speed and in what loneliness, so was it, parallelling him. He was not escaping it; symbolic and encompassing, it outlay all gasolinespanned distances and all clock-or sun-stipulated destinations. It would be there—the eternal smell of the coffee the sugar the hemp sweating slow iron plates above the forked deliberate brown water and lost lost lost all ultimate blue of latitude and horizon . . . tomorrow and tomorrow and tomorrow; not only not to hope, not even to wait: just to endure. (170-1)

Like Schumann, who drops out of the sky and sinks in the water, the Reporter loses all "ultimate blue of latitude and horizon."

His dream of escaping from meaninglessness evaporates and he must endure in the world of the submerged dead.[3]

The dreadful irony of the Reporter's dream of the airmen as salvation is that he so little understands his own spiritual needs and his quest that he can discover hope in an existence that actually mirrors his own dead world. Like the airmen, the Reporter responds to the ephemeral sensations of speed and sex. He is not in love with Laverne; he thinks of her always as a sexual object. He is fascinated by the thought that this Lady of Situations shares the bed of two men. Like an adolescent with an obscene picture, he dwells upon the thought of her bizarre sex life. The significance of the Reporter's obsession with sex is revealed by its similarity to the incident that occurs when Laverne makes her first parachute jump with Schumann piloting the plane. Out on the wing, preparing to jump, she suddenly undergoes some kind of terrifying spiritual experience, which seems to be an overwhelming sense of aloneness, of desperate isolation. On her face, Schumann sees an expression that is not fear of death but a "wild and . . . mindless repudiation of bereavement." Her response to this soulshaking experience is sexual: she climbs back into the cockpit and straddles Schumann with a "blind and completely irrational expression of protest and wild denial on her face." (117) A short while later, Laverne herself becomes the object of the same kind of violent sexuality. In the face of the law officer who sees in the descending half-naked female, the "ultimate shape of his jaded desires fall upon him out of the sky," (118) it is not lust that Schumann perceives but the "counterpart of that terror and wild protest against bereavement and division which he had seen in Laverne's face. . . ." (120-1)

In the waste land world, the spiritual loneliness and despair of people for whom love does not exist and who are isolated from one another and from God is expressed by sex. The Reporter's sexual obsession with a woman totally indifferent to him is another manifestation of the buried and thwarted needs that produce the compulsive behavior of these lost souls. Jiggs's buying boots he has not tried on and that he cannot afford, and Jiggs and the Reporter beyond physical and moral control in indecent and disgusting states of drunkenness are symbols of lost and driven souls. Rootless and traditionless, without moral values and without a sense of human dignity and continuity, modern man, like Jiggs, struggling futilely against his need to drink, is "a moral and spiritual waif shrieking his feeble I-am-I into the desert of chance and disaster." (73)

The airmen are as compulsion-ridden and as lost as the other inhabitants of the modern world, and the Reporter's quest for salvation through them, therefore, must end in failure: the sound and the fury of the airmen's lives signifies nothing. Faulkner's continual reference to the nihilistic passage from Shakespeare beginning "Tomorrow and tomorrow and tomorrow" and his continual allusions to Eliot's waste land and Prufrock poems, plus his use of so many of Eliot's symbols and images indicate clearly the thematic direction of *Pylon*.*

But Faulkner does not keep his novel on course. His vision of the airmen as living a frenetic life that puts them beyond the range of respectability, love, and God is considerably blurred by his sympathy for their dedication to something beyond self. He seems to lose sight, temporarily, of the fact that movement for the sake of movement is meaningless. He veers off course when he begins to contrast the dedication of the airmen to the selfishness of society. The money-grubbers and the self-seekers like H. I. Feinman make the airmen seem like humanists whose sense of loyalty to one another and whose lack of interest in both money and personal glory make them victims of a rapacious society.

Trying to reconcile our sympathy with them as victims and our antipathy for them as monstrous exemplars of a traditionless and Godless society is impossible. Reader ambivalence toward the fliers is rooted in the ambivalence of the novel. Several critics have made the attempt to discover in *Pylon* a fundamental unity of vision.[4] In doing so, they have been forced into the untenable position of presenting the airmen as victims of society and as symbols of regeneration for the world of the waste land. The temptation to seek and find thematic unity in a Faulkner novel is almost irresistible, but in *Pylon*, the quest is not rewarding.

To illustrate one of the enigmas that Faulkner's ambivalence

* This Shakespearean passage, Keats's "Ode on a Grecian Urn," and Eliot's "The Waste Land" are drawn upon continually in the earlier novels.

creates, we can consider briefly the inferences that can be drawn
from the circumstances of Schumann's death. The Reporter initiates the chain of events that ends in the crash and Schumann's
death by drowning. Had the Reporter left the group alone, Jiggs
would not have begun to drink and might have finished the work
on the valves before the Friday race. And it is the Reporter's ef
forts that secure Schumann his death plane. Now, if the Reporter
can be seen as a representative of society, then certainly the airmen are victims of that society. But the fact is that the Reporter is,
in part, motivated to help the airmen because he is angered by the
callousness of society.

When his plane begins to disintegrate in mid-air, Schumann
chooses to avoid the spectator-filled field and uses his last measure of control to head toward the lake. We do not know if he
would have escaped death had he crashed on the ground, but his
choice does imply heroism and perhaps the sacrifice of his life. Does
his choice of death by water, a symbol of regeneration in "The
Waste Land," symbolize sacrifice and hence hope for mankind? In
the scenes following the crash, water is not given any regenerative
significance, and when we consider the effects on those for whom
Schumann presumably sacrifices his life, we are forced to view his
death as meaningless. His flying team disintegrates. Jiggs generously gives up his boots to offer something to Laverne, but Jiggs
does not go back to his wife and two children, whom he has
abandoned. Laverne and Jack callously, and with inhuman coldness, leave the boy Jack with Roger's father, who wants proof that
the boy is his son's. One of the reporters in the chapter entitled
"The Scavengers" suggests that Laverne and Jack must get rid of
the child because he will be a constant reminder to them of Roger.
Why they should want to eliminate a reminder of Roger is not at
all clear. The incontrovertible fact is that they give up the child so
they can go on living the irresponsible nomadic existence of circus
airmen. And the Reporter has surely gained nothing from Roger's
death. In the final scene, when he attempts to find meaning in the
death and to express it, he tears up his copy, writes a bitter account
of the wreath-dropping ceremony, and goes off to get drunk in the
red-light district.

There are a number of other images, incidents, and statements in the novel that also seem latent with symbolic meaning, but they too lead to thematic confusion rather than unity. Any full appraisal of *Pylon* must recognize the ambiguities fostered by Faulkner's ambivalence, and by his failure to create characters who emerge as individuals. My impression is that Faulkner was probably fascinated by the type of airmen he described in this novel but that he really did not know them as people, and when he needed, as he himself indicated, a respite from the real people he was creating in *Absalom, Absalom!*, he turned to these airmen. Marred as it is by ambiguity, lack of thematic unity, and weak characterizations, *Pylon* must be listed as a failure; nevertheless it is a frequently brilliant and always stimulating (if occasionally irritating) experiment in poetic narration.

Absalom, Absalom!

Absalom, Absalom! (1936) examines the malaise that afflicts twentieth-century Southerners and the origin of that malaise in the crime of slavery. In the character and history of Thomas Sutpen, Faulkner penetrates to the truth behind the Southern legend to assess the moral responsibility of the pioneer who created a replica in Missisippi of the ante-bellum Southern society and helped provoke the destruction of that society. The descendants of this pioneer, generation after generation, re-enact their father's crime, and, plagued by guilt, they are shadows of the past, incapable of coping with the reality of the present. The novel, spanning four generations, is an incisive history of the South; it is also a perceptive study of American individualism, and the need of each living being to be recognized as an individual. Because it encompasses so much, mainly through masterful but unconventional nar-

SUTPEN GENEALOGY

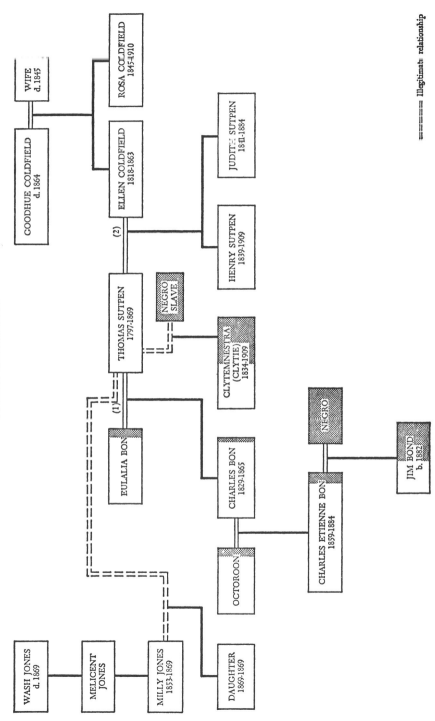

==== Illegitimate relationship

ration, the novel is difficult, and it might be well to begin this analysis by discussing the narrative structure and techniques.

» » Narrative Structure

The tragic story of Thomas Sutpen and his children is told by four narrators—Rosa Coldfield, Mr. Compson, Quentin Compson, and Shreve McCannon, Quentin's Canadian roommate at Harvard. The hero of their story died in 1869, forty years before the day in September of 1909 that Rosa Coldfield calls Quentin Compson to her house to tell him her version of the Sutpen tragedy. Rosa is the only one of the narrators who was an actual participant in the drama, and even her role was a limited and minor one which ended forty-three years earlier with her sudden departure from Sutpen's house. The storytellers are dealing with people long dead and with events about which they have little first-hand information.

There are certain facts that are generally known by the people of Jefferson. Twelve miles outside the town is a decayed mansion built in 1835 by Thomas Sutpen. In this remnant of plantation grandeur live a ninety-year-old mulatto named Clytie and a twenty-six-year-old Negro idiot. In Jefferson proper lives Rosa Coldfield, the sister-in-law of Thomas Sutpen. Many years before, she was engaged to her widowed brother-in-law, but she broke the engagement and has lived ever since, alone and in poverty, in the house she inherited from her father. She is known to the townspeople as Miss Rosa. One detail about the Sutpen family has become a part of local legend: that at the gates of the Sutpen mansion, at the close of the Civil War, Charles Bon, a New Orleans man, was killed by Henry, the son of Thomas Sutpen.

During the three hours of the September afternoon which he spends with Miss Rosa, Quentin discovers some of the facts about this legend and the people involved in it. On the evening of the same day, his father gives him more details and presents his version of the story. When he goes to Harvard, Quentin tells Shreve about Sutpen; and on the day that Quentin learns of Miss Rosa's death, both boys work out their own version of the tragedy, filling in gaps in the narrative, discarding conclusions of the other narrators that do not fit the facts or that the boys do not consider valid. These four people, in other words, are not merely telling a story; they are trying to reconstruct the past, seeking to understand not only the sequence of events and the human motivations that culminated in the tragedy, but also the meaning of Thomas Sutpen's rise and fall. Much of their narrative is therefore speculation, influenced greatly by their own interests and personalities, and by the degree of their emotional involvement in the drama. Quentin, who does most of the listening, knows many details of the story. The narrators, aware of his knowledge, refer to incidents not previously mentioned and jump from event to event without regard for chronology. Within the first few pages of the novel, for instance, reference is made to "the son who widowed the daughter who had not yet been a bride," a reference which Quentin understands but which mystifies the reader. (11) * Faulkner himself recognized the difficulty of his novel and in the Modern Library edition provided a brief chronology of events.†

Not only are the facts of Sutpen's history presented without regard for chronology, but the versions of the narrators also are not presented in integrated units. Rosa's narration opens the novel, but it is not completed until Chapter V when Quentin recalls her account of the period following the murder of Charles Bon. Quentin's contributions are interspersed throughout the other narrations, usually in the form of interior monologues. (Italics are used to distinguish thought from speech throughout the novel). The versions of the four narrators are presented in nine chapters in the following sequence:

CHAPTER I The scene is Miss Rosa's house in Jefferson on a September afternoon in 1909. She and Quentin are in the musty room called the office. Rosa tells Quentin about Sutpen's early days in Jefferson, his marriage to Ellen, his fighting matches with his Negro slaves.

---

* Modern Library Edition.
† See the Appendix, pp. 387-392, for a detailed chronology of the history of Thomas Sutpen and his family.

CHAPTER II It is evening of the same day. Quentin, waiting until it is time to pick up Miss Rosa and go out to the Sutpen house, listens to his father's account of Sutpen's early days in the town and of his marriage to Ellen Coldfield.

CHAPTER III The scene is continued. Sitting on the porch of the Compson house, Quentin listens to his father, who gives his version of the relationship between Rosa Coldfield, Thomas Sutpen, and the Sutpen family.

CHAPTER IV The scene is continued. Mr. Compson brings out the letter that Judith Sutpen received from Charles Bon, and he speculates about the relationship of Charles, Judith, and Henry. His narration ends with his account of the scene in which Judith brings General Compson's wife the letter. Quentin reads the letter and imagines the scene in which Bon was murdered.

CHAPTER V Quentin is still on the Compson porch. The imagined scene of the murder evokes the memory of Miss Rosa's account of the events that took place after Bon's death. Quentin recalls Miss Rosa telling of Sutpen's return from the Civil War, his proposal of marriage to Rosa and then his suggestion that she prove herself capable, before marriage, of bearing him a male heir.

CHAPTERS VI-IX The scene is the room which Quentin shares with Shreve at Harvard. It is the evening of the day that Quentin receives a letter from his father, dated January 10, 1910, announcing the death and burial of Rosa Coldfield. Quentin sits with the letter before him, recalling the September evening when he listened to his father and then went out to the Sutpen place. He reads part of his father's letter. Shreve begins his account of the story. Quentin does not finish reading the letter for several hours (about 174 pages). The evening wears on; the heat is turned off, and finally the roommates get into their beds. In the darkness, Shreve asks Quentin, " 'Why do you hate the South?' " Quentin, "panting in the cold air, the iron New England dark," replies, " *'I dont. I dont! I dont hate it! I dont hate it!'* " (378)

Though the structure of *Absalom, Absalom!* and the narrative techniques are complicated, they are not, as some readers and

critics have declared, supererogatory, or the fanciful experimenta-
tions of a virtuoso.[1] Faulkner's structure and techniques are organic
—essential to the development and meaning of his novel, as significant to the story as the details of Sutpen's childhood. Revealing
the relationship between structure and meaning is no simple task,
but by examining the narrative techniques and then analyzing
the meaning of the novel, the organic nature of that relationship
can be established.

» » Narrative techniques

Thomas Sutpen is the hero of the novel. It is his story that the
narrators are telling, but in their differing versions, they are also
telling another story—their own. By using multiple narrators,
Faulkner is able to incorporate two stories: Sutpen's life, and the
effects of his life on the narrators. (The design of the central story
follows, as we shall see, the pattern of Greek drama). Aside
from the device of multiple narration, Faulkner uses several other
significant techniques. All of the storytellers, despite differences
in background and character, employ an identical rhetorical, impressionistic language. Also, the narrative is developed without
chronology; there is frequent repetition, and crucial data is consistently withheld.

The author reserves for himself a minor role. Only one scene
in the story of Sutpen—the details of the hero's arrival in Jefferson
in Chapter II—is presented by the author. He sets the scenes
for each chapter—at Miss Rosa's or on the porch of the Compson
house or in the Harvard dormitory room—but the rest of the
novel is, for the most part, a continual flow of talk. About ninety
percent of the narrative is, in fact, set off by quotation marks.
And in all that talk it is difficult to distinguish the individual
voices of the narrators. When Quentin and Shreve speak to each
other, they use colloquial speech, but as soon as they resume the
narration, they sound like Miss Rosa and Mr. Compson. As
Quentin musingly listens to his roommate, he observes that
Shreve sounds just like his father, and when Quentin is narrating,
Shreve interrupts to make the same observation.

Only in imagery and in tone are the narrations colored by the personalities of the speakers. Miss Rosa draws steadily upon hell and its diabolic inhabitants for her images. Mr. Compson's knowledge of the classics and particularly Greek drama provides him with many allusions. And Shreve's version, to a great extent, reflects his reading and his romantic imagination. In tone, Miss Rosa's narration has a breathless, outraged, emotional quality so overwhelming that it dominates the reader's imagination throughout the entire novel, despite the fact that her version occupies only two of the nine chapters. Mr. Compson's account is generally ironic in tone, but his detachment is not sustained. When he creates the scene of Charles and Henry in New Orleans, he becomes imaginatively involved in his creation.

Such differences in the language and tone of the narrators does not appreciably detract from the singular sound pattern of the novel, which is created by loose, long sentences, with qualifying phrases added to qualifying phrases, clauses attached to clauses. This kind of cumulative sentence structure creates the effect of thought-flow, the mind ranging free, working over a fact, speculating about it, rejecting one possibility, considering another, rushing ahead more quickly than words can be uttered. It is the technique of the interior monologue or stream of consciousness, vocalized. The replacement of verbs by verbals—"sitting there, telling it, remembering," rather than "he sat there and told it and remembered," produces a sense of immediacy and continuity as the narrators mull over events of the past.

The narrators' diction is poetic and erudite beyond the educational and intellectual level of any of them except, perhaps, Mr. Compson. Like Quentin, who does so much of the listening, the reader feels himself caught up in a flow of language with a current so strong that he cannot keep himself above the surface. He is pulled inexorably to a level below conscious thought, where chronological time is not important and word sounds convey feelings beyond rational expression. It is precisely by means of the powerful current created by the flood of words that the reader is involved with Sutpen's story and its general significance. After being subjected to these rhythms for several chapters, the reader's own thoughts begin to form in similar patterns.

The lack of chronology in the development of the story also serves to draw the reader into the world the narrators create by forcing him to participate in their search for meaning. The storytellers are not so much interested in learning what happened as understanding why it happened. Though they know facts that the reader does not know, they do not have all the necessary details, and they are trying to establish connections, to discover motivations, to find meaning. Provided with scraps of information, the reader is drawn into the investigation. He actually becomes a fifth investigator, experiencing sudden illuminations with the discovery of new facts, formulating theories and then discarding them. Involved in this way, he participates in the narrators' search for meaning in Sutpen's story.

Sutpen's history, in itself, is not Faulkner's primary concern. He is dramatizing the meaning of that history, and that is why present time in the novel is 1909, forty years after the death of the major character. It is also one of the reasons for employing multiple narration. The four speakers, separated in varying degrees by time and by immediate involvement from Sutpen's story, are in one way or another victims of his history, and in their various versions of Sutpen's life, they reveal the meaning to them of his tragedy.

Of all the narrators, Miss Rosa is the one most closely connected with Sutpen's story, and by first examining the significance to her of his story, we shall begin to see how structure in the novel conveys meaning and how meaning determines structure.

» » Rosa Coldfield

In 1866, Thomas Sutpen, nearly sixty, returns from the Civil War. His son, Henry, has murdered a man and disappeared. His plantation is in ruins. Three months after his return he proposes marriage to his twenty-one-year-old sister-in-law. Two months later he makes a suggestion that so horrifies her, so outrages her that for the next forty-three years she dresses in black and lives apart from the world. In effect, Rosa Coldfield dies at the moment that she grasps the significance of Sutpen's suggestion. When she tells her story to Quentin, in 1909, she is still outraged, still befuddled by the event. She has lived with it, and time has done nothing to abate her fury and assuage her hurt. She can think of Sutpen only in terms of a demon—a demon rising straight out of the pit of hell, producing devil's progeny, bringing the tortures of the damned to everyone who moves into his orbit of evil.

Sutpen's suggestion that Rosa prove herself capable of bearing him a male child before they marry is immoral and outrageous, certainly shocking enough to jolt a twenty-one-year-old girl brought up in the nineteenth-century Southern tradition. And yet, despite Rosa's puritanical upbringing in a household dominated by a man who weighed everything and everyone in a moral balance, it is not the sexual immorality of Sutpen's suggestion that produces in her so violent a reaction. When she describes Sutpen's formal proposal of marriage in the presence of Clytie and Judith, Rosa admits to Quentin that if Sutpen had taken her that night she would not have resisted. With her sister Ellen's ring on her finger, she sat there and listened to him and told herself, " '*Why, he is mad. He will decree this marriage for tonight and perform his own ceremony, himself both groom and minister; pronounce his own wild benediction on it with the very bedward candle in his hand: and I mad too, for I will acquiesce, succumb; abet him and plunge down . . . If I was saved that night . . . it was no fault, no doing of my own. . . .*' " (165) Rosa's is therefore not simply the voice of outraged puritanical morality; her wound is more profound.

Her description of her childhood as "*that warped and spartan solitude . . . which . . . taught me (and little else) to listen before I could comprehend . . .*" (140) provides the clue to her violent reaction and to the central theme of the novel. She is born when her sister Ellen is already seven years married. Her middle-aged mother dies at her birth, and Rosa grows up hating her father for this loss. Goodhue Coldfield is a cold, rational man who judges human beings in terms of an abstract moral code. He lives in a tightly enclosed, drab moral counting-house, tabulating his spiritual balance against the day when he will present his sight-drafts on self-denial and fortitude. In nailing himself into his attic at the beginning of the Civil War, he merely follows the pattern of withdrawal from life that has characterized his whole existence. His self-incarceration is a gesture of moral protest which is commensurate with the immorality of war against the Union. Coldfield's sister, who helps him to care for Rosa, is a bitter, vindictive woman who hates Thomas Sutpen and hates the people of Jefferson for not having attended Ellen's wedding.

In this mausoleum adult world, Rosa grows up, catching occasional glimpses of her sister and her older niece and nephew, hearing snatches of conversation she does not understand, listening at doors. She is too young to be a part of the only world that is open to her; and the parental love that would have created a world for her does not exist. Even when her aunt runs off with a horse-trader, Rosa's role as mistress of the house gives her little feeling of importance. Her eager desire to become involved with others leads her to make her naïve offer to sew Judith's wedding dress. Her proferring is met with laughter from her sister. Her separation from immediate experience and her need for emotional involvement are most clearly and pathetically demonstrated in the way she responds to the love of Charles Bon and Judith. "*I who had learned nothing of love, not even parents' love—that fond dear constant violation of privacy, that stultification of the burgeoning and incorrigible I which is the meed and due of all mammalian meat, became not mistress, not beloved, but more than even love; I became all polymath love's androgynous advocate.*" (146). She falls in love with love, in love with Charles whom she has never seen. Informed of his death, she rushes out to Sutpen's Hundred to keep her promise to her dead sister that she will protect Judith. But her niece is dry-eyed, completely self-sufficient. Rosa has not seen her nephew, Henry, for four years; she does not see him after the murder; she is not even allowed to look at the dead face of Charles whom she enveloped with fanciful amorousness. She is kept on the periphery of this violent drama, though she wants desperately to be a participant.

After the burial of Charles, Rosa stays with Judith and Clytie at the plantation, waiting, with them, for the return of Sutpen. The great moment of her life occurs three months after his return. She is hoeing in the garden. "*I looked up and saw him looking at me. He had seen me for twenty years, but now he was*

looking at me; he stood there in the path looking at me. . . ."
(162) For the first time in her life, Rosa feels wanted, feels as if
one of the people in that adult world from which she was excluded
is recognizing her as a person. In another context, she declares, in a
statement that can provide us terms to discuss the significance of
this experience to her:

*Because there is something in the touch of flesh with flesh which abro-
gates, cuts sharp and straight across the devious intricate channels of
decorous ordering, which enemies as well as lovers know because it
makes them both—touch and touch of that which is the citadel of
the central I-Am's private own: not spirit, soul; the liquorish and ungirdled mind is anyone's to take in any darkened hallway of this earthly
tenement. But let flesh touch with flesh, and watch the fall of all the
eggshell shibboleth of caste and color too.* (139)

Rosa speaks here of her struggle with Clytie when she is prevented from rushing up the stairs to Judith after the murder of
Charles Bon. She describes her recognition of Clytie as a fellow
human being, as an individual entity, a recognition of a Negro's
individuality by a white that is usually prevented by the shibboleth of color. The shibboleth exists in the "liquorish and ungirdled
mind." Clytie's "central I-Am" is her individuality, her unique consciousness of self. In the garden, when Sutpen looks at her,
Rosa feels, for the first time, that someone is recognizing her individuality, her "central I-Am." She knows it is not love that Sutpen feels for her, but she is satisfied. Two months later, Sutpen's
suggestion, uttered as if he *"were consulting with Jones or with
some other man about a bitch dog or a cow or mare"* reveals that
she does not exist as an individual for him. (168) It is not the self
of Rosa Coldfield, the human being who is only incidentally
capable of bearing children, that Sutpen addresses. Her power to
bear children is her total significance to him. In effect, he denies her humanity, her integrity as an individual. It is this denial
that constitutes the immorality of his proposal and that wounds
Rosa so deeply. Sutpen's death three years later cannot assuage her
feelings; in fact, *"that's what she cant forgive him for: not for the
insult, not even for having jilted him: but for being dead."* (170)

Nothing but some kind of act, some kind of revenge that would be an assertion of the individuality he denied her could soothe her wound. With Sutpen dead, the balm can never be applied.

What Rosa does not know is that she has been only one of many victims of the same crime. In her forty-three years of asking and listening to that "Why and Why and Why?" she has only her own relations with Sutpen to work with; she knows nothing about Sutpen's design and about the others whom he has treated in the same way. Rosa's vision is limited; her image of him as a demon is a distortion of the truth, but there is truth in it because she has been a victim of that moral flaw in Sutpen that causes his tragedy. In that "notlanguage" that flows from her, she speaks for all those who suffered as she did. Sutpen died, but the effects of his immorality remain. In the portraits of Sutpen drawn by the other narrators, as different aspects of his character and his career become visible, Rosa's distortions are mitigated, but the core of truth in her portrait is in all of them.

» » Thomas Sutpen

Mr. Compson's narration clears the air of the hell-fire smoke. The towering figure of Sutpen as demon becomes the towering figure of Sutpen as tragic hero. The design of classic tragedy is clearly discernible in the narration of Mr. Compson. Sutpen is one of the powerful of the earth—courageous, strong, independent—who strides to success without faltering. Like the Greek heroes, Sutpen embodies the characteristics of his time and his nation. He is the rugged individualist of nineteenth-century America. He possesses those qualities associated with the development of the nation—the fierce ambition, the self-assurance, the iron will, the individualism, the ability and willingness to endure hardship and hard work. In an American setting, Sutpen is the closest possible approximation to the kind of character essential to classical drama. His tragedy, played out against a historical backdrop, is caused by a fatal flaw in his character, a human flaw that gives universal significance to his downfall.

Mr. Compson's narration serves also to equate Sutpen's rise and fall with the development of the South and its destruction in the holocaust of the Civil War:

Because the time now approached (it was 1860 . . .) when the destiny of Sutpen's family which for twenty years now had been like a lake welling from quiet springs into a quiet valley and spreading, rising almost imperceptibly and in which the four members of it floated in sunny suspension, felt the first subterranean movement toward the outlet, the gorge which would be the land's catastrophe too. . . . (73-4)

As a victim, by heritage, of the Civil War, Mr. Compson, in seeking the Why of the Sutpen tragedy, is seeking the Why of his own. His image of Sutpen as a Greek hero defying man and gods betrays his own involvement in the legend of the South's grandeur. His inability to discern the full significance of Sutpen's flaw is a result of his confusion about the past and its effects upon the present in which he exists. Mr. Compson's detachment and irony are a defensive facade, but they serve him, and in some measure, save him, from the fate of his son Quentin, who several months after the closing scene of this novel commits suicide.*

Quentin's personality affects his narration.

[Quentin's] very body was an empty hall echoing with sonorous defeated names; he was not a being, an entity, he was a commonwealth. He was a barracks filled with stubborn back-looking ghosts still recovering, even forty-three years afterward, from the fever which had cured the disease, waking from the fever without even knowing that it had been the fever itself which they had fought against and not the sickness, looking with stubborn recalcitrance backward beyond the fever and into the disease with actual regret, weak from the fever yet free of the disease and not even aware that the freedom was that of impotence. (12)

Quentin's psychological state forces him to focus his attention with morbid consistency upon the image of Henry's killing Charles to protect the honor of his sister, Judith, and thereby upholding the

---

* In *The Sound and the Fury.*

traditional code of the Old South. Most of his contributions to
the narrative reveal his hopeless struggle to free himself from the
past. Of the four narrators, only Shreve is sufficiently removed
from the immediate effects of Sutpen's tragedy to understand its
general significance. What becomes clear in the Canadian boy's
version is that Sutpen's tragic flaw is that quality in him which
could annihilate Rosa, making her a ghost, and in broader perspective, as a representative sectional flaw, annihilate the South.

According to General Compson, "Sutpen's trouble was innocence." (220) The meaning of that word "innocence" applied
to Sutpen is difficult to grasp without understanding fully the
significance to Faulkner of individuality.[2] Judith's single long
speech in the novel sounds the important theme of individuality. She has brought Bon's letter to Mrs. Compson and tells her
either to keep it or throw it away as she likes.

"Because you make so little impression, you see. You get born and you
try this and you dont know why only you keep on trying it and you are
born at the same time with a lot of other people, all mixed up with
them, like trying to, having to, move your arms and legs with strings
only the same strings are hitched to all the other arms and legs and the
others all trying and they dont know why either except that the strings
are all in one another's way like five or six people all trying to make a
rug on the same loom only each one wants to weave his own pattern
into the rug; and it cant matter, you know that, or the Ones that set up
the loom would have arranged things a little better, and yet it must
matter because you keep on trying or having to keep on trying and then
all of a sudden it's all over and all you have left is a block of stone with
scratches on it. . . ." (127)

Judith Sutpen here expresses a view, common in Faulkner's
novels, of man's insignificance in time and the universe and of
his desperate need to fight against that condition by asserting his
own importance, by achieving some kind of expression of his
individuality and of his very existence. Man knows that his struggle is futile, and born out of that knowledge is his furious need
to "make that scratch, that undying mark on the blank face of
the oblivion to which we are all doomed." (129)

By applying this statement about the human condition to

Sutpen's story, we can understand the psychological impulse of his design, the precise character of that design, and the source of his fatal flaw: his inability to recognize, as Judith does, that each man seeks to weave his own pattern on life's loom, and that the strings that one man uses are hitched to the arms and legs of others who are also seeking to weave their individual pattern.

Thomas Sutpen is born in the mountains of the area later to become West Virginia. In the primitive mountain community, distinctions between men are established on the basis of what a man is, not on the basis of possessions. During the slow journey of the Sutpen family down the mountain, Thomas loses track of time. The trip becomes a symbolic journey from a primitive to a civilized world. The closer the family comes to civilization, the more aware the boy becomes of social castes. He encounters for the first time a Negro slave; he senses tensions between the poor whites and the Negroes, but in his innocence, these sensations do not penetrate his consciousness. With the family settled in a shack on the Virginia plantation, Thomas spends much of his time furtively watching the rich man lying in the swing, constantly attended by Negro slaves. He does not envy the man. He brings from the mountains a belief that it is a matter of luck that one man possesses things that other men do not. He "could not have conceived of the owner taking such crass advantage of the luck which gave the rifle to him rather than to another as to say to other men: *Because I own this rifle, my arms and legs and blood and bones are superior to yours. . . .*" (228 9) Sent by his father with a message for the owner, he approaches the front door of the plantation house. His hair is unkempt, his clothes are dirty and ragged, but he has no doubt that the owner will be happy to show him the rest of his possessions. Being told by the Negro servant to go around to the back door is an annihilating experience because it denies his individuality. The Negro is not telling the boy Thomas Sutpen to go around to the back door; he is addressing a ragged nonentity, an unkempt emanation of a landless class. Standing there in shock, the boy sees himself through the eyes of the laughing Negro and the plantation owner. He sees not the person whom he is aware of as an individual—Thomas Sutpen—but one of a herd of "cattle, creatures heavy and without grace, brutely evacuated into a world without hope or purpose for them, who would in turn spawn with brutish and vicious prolixity, populate, double treble and compound, fill space and earth with a race whose future would be a succession of cut-down and patched and made-over garments bought on exorbitant credit . . . with for sole heritage that expression on a balloon face bursting with laughter which had looked out at some unremembered and nameless progenitor who had knocked at a door. . . ." (235) Where he expected immediate human contact, the boy is greeted by words that declare him nonexistent, by eyes that see not him, but a ragged member of a shiftless, worthless group.

The parallel between Sutpen's experience at fifteen and Rosa Coldfield's at twenty is striking. Their immediate reactions are identical. They both retreat physically, Rosa to her house in Jefferson, Sutpen to a cave in the woods. Both are shocked and outraged by this refusal of another human being to acknowledge in them the "I-Am," the central citadel of their individuality. Psychologically, both never leave their retreats. Rosa spends the next forty-three years of her existence cut off from life. Sutpen's ability to respond emotionally is amputated. As he sits in his cave, he listens to two inner voices debate. One wants to kill; the other counsels against it because killing would serve no purpose. The debate between the emotional and the rational goes on until the boy receives a second shock, a still further revelation of his own insignificance. Neither his father nor the plantation owner cares that he has not delivered the message. His realization of their indifference seals the tomb on his emotional responses; the purely rational part of Sutpen wins the debate and formulates the design.

In his childhood innocence, Sutpen had never judged as either good or bad his idea that possessions have nothing to do with a man's worth. When he undergoes his crucial experience, he makes no moral judgment: he does not decide that his view was good, the one that could cause him such pain, bad. He does not think in moral terms. He simply discards his childhood view as incorrect. Life is not the way he thought it was. He was guilty of an error and he corrects it. Mere existence does not guarantee a man recognition by his fellow man, as he thought. Each man has to fight for recognition. The boy's experience reveals to him a world in which there are laughing balloons—Negroes; cattle—poor whites; and lords of the earth—plantation owners.

Sutpen's experience not only illuminates for him the reality of the social structure, but also reveals the insignificant role of the individual in the overall pattern of existence. In the quoted passage, in which Sutpen sees himself as a nameless progenitor who knocked at a door, is embedded an important Faulknerian concept of time and humanity. Faulkner conceives of time as indivisible, a continuum. A particle of time comes into momentary identity as, say, the third hour of the sixteenth day of the eleventh month of the one-thousand-nine-hundred-and-twenty-secondth year A.D. At the end of its existence as a separate hour, it recedes into the continuum of time. The human being, like an hour of time, is born into individual identity. He is merely a particle in the continual flow of humanity. He dies, but the race continues. What individual man does, during his hour, becomes a part of history. The individual ceases to exist, but history does not; history is the manifestation of human continuity. It is the continuum out of which the individual person emerges, the way the hour emerges out of the continuum of time. History, the actions of those who came before, is the heritage of each single identity. What Sutpen does, as we shall later see, becomes part of the common heritage of all who follow him.

Sutpen's vision of his own transience outrages him as much as his recognition of his insignificance in the social structure. His design, therefore, is a defiance of the scheme of things. He will assert his individuality among men by becoming a king, and make his mark upon the blank face of oblivion by producing a dynasty.* If he, Thomas Sutpen, must die, his identity will not; it will flow in the veins of future generations of Sutpens.

To Sutpen, wealth and respectability are tools toward this end. His goal is the assertion of his individuality in a society based upon ownership of property. And his desire for an heir is a defiance of

---

* Replying to a seminar question at the University of Virginia concerning the goal of a writer, Faulkner used terms reminiscent of those he used in Judith's speech. A writer, he said, "knows he has a short span of life, that the day will come when he must pass through the wall of oblivion, and he wants to leave a scratch on that wall—Kilroy was here—that somebody a hundred, a thousand years later will see." *Faulkner in the University*, p. 61.

the gods (the Greeks called it *hubris*). In a lecture, Faulkner described Sutpen as wanting to become a king among men.[3] The description explains Sutpen's repudiation of Eulalia Bon and the infant Charles when he discovers that they have Negro blood. In the
world of the South—the only one he knows—marrying a woman
with Negro blood would be even worse than the marriage of a king
to a commoner in a monarchical society.

Before he is turned away from the plantation door, Sutpen's
ideas about human existence are based chiefly upon feelings. Afterward, they are based upon "reason." His feelings betray him, lead
him to a disastrous collision with reality. He becomes an opportu-
nistic rationalist, formulating a design in accord with the social
reality he discovers. Actually, the design is a defense, guarantee-
ing that he will never again be subjected to so devastating an emotional experience. With a social blueprint to follow, logic is his
guide. Any such abstract code, whether like Sutpen's or Goodhue
Coldfield's (a well-chosen name) moralistic one, is the product of
mind. The heart is incapable of creating or adhering to an abstract
design. Before his crucial experience, Sutpen could respond with an
open heart to life. At fifteen, he shifts to a rational approach to
life. And in the shift he dooms himself. Ultimately, Sutpen's tragedy is caused by a lack of feeling, a failure to recognize the feelings
of others.

He is so intent upon asserting his own individuality that he is
unaware of the identical need for recognition in each of his fellow
men—white or black. In Haiti, that island halfway between civilization and "the dark inscrutable continent from which the black
blood, the black bones and flesh and thinking and remembering
and hopes and desires, was ravished," which might have "been
created and set aside by Heaven itself . . . as a theater for violence and injustice and bloodshed," Sutpen works and lives for
several years. (250) He is completely impervious to the human
tragedy of men denied their humanity because of their color.
Lacking compassion, Sutpen's only morality is the cold logic of
theoretical justice. He can put aside his wife and child with an
easy conscience because he provides them with a just compensation
—all the property he received from Eulalia's father and everything
else he earned since his arrival. Marriage is equivalent to a busi-

ness transaction. Eulalia's father withheld a vital fact, and the contract is therefore null and void. Under such circumstances, Sutpen considers himself magnanimous in giving up everything he earned in Haiti and placing himself in the position of having to start all over again. Thirty years later, when his world is toppling around him and he seeks the cause of his failure, he can pass over this incident without realizing its significance. By repudiating Eulalia, he denied her humanity, just as years later his suggestion to Rosa denies her existence as an equal human being with feelings and desires and a need for acceptance. As Rosa is to do, and as Sutpen himself has already done, Eulalia will react with fury. In Shreve's reconstruction of her role in Sutpen's history, she uses her son, Charles Bon, to gain her revenge. Sutpen cheats Rosa of whatever satisfaction her fury requires by getting himself killed, but Eulalia Bon enjoys vengeance.

Rejection, such as each of these undergoes, is so devastating an experience that its effects never diminish. It makes its victims almost inhuman, almost monomaniacs who must dedicate themselves to affirming the individuality that was denied them. Sutpen, however, has no particular person on whom he can vent his rage. The Negro and the plantation owner are merely representatives of a system; therefore he must show "them"—society, men, the gods— "more than all the human puny mortals under the sun that might lie in hammocks all afternoon with their shoes off. . . ." (238)

For each of these victims, the reaction to rejection is identical and the effects upon them are the same. To understand this reaction to rejection is to understand the theme of *Absalom, Absalom!* and also the significance of much of Faulkner's Christian symbolism. Sutpen is a victim of a crime that goes back through history —the denial of equal human status to men of different color, or religion, or social and economic rank, or nationality, or tribe, or family. When Jesus preached compassion, love of one's fellowman, he preached mutual recognition of a common humanity. In this novel, as in many of Faulkner's works, crucial scenes are, ironically, enacted on those days that are dedicated by men to the memory of Christ and his doctrines. On Christmas eve, Sutpen forbids the marriage of Judith and Bon. During the Christmas season, Rosa Coldfield finally decides, after three months, to bring the sheriff out to the Sutpen place to arrest Henry. Charles Bon, Charles the Good, is thirty-three when he is murdered. Charles seeks only recognition of his common humanity. The murder of Charles, like the murder of Joe Christmas in *Light in August,* is a re-enactment of the crucifixion of Christ, who is the symbol of love and suffering among men. The universal tragedy of rejection is that its effects extend through time. The violated becomes the violator, the crucified the crucifier. The boy Sutpen, expecting immediate acceptance at the door, is rejected and becomes the man Sutpen, blind to every other human being, compounding in his own acts the wrong from which he suffered.

Throughout his life, Sutpen is detached from those around him, incapable of recognizing a shared humanity. He holds his architect captive until his mansion is completed. When the Frenchman tries to escape, Sutpen hunts him down as if he were an animal. As soon as the mansion is furnished and he is ready to take the next step to fulfill his plans, he chooses a wife, marrying Ellen Coldfield because she can provide him the respectability that he requires. The townspeople of Jefferson react to his blanket rejection of them and accuse him of getting his furniture illegally, a crime which he did not commit. In all his years in the County, he possesses a confidant, General Compson, but no friend.

Independent, shrewd, iron-willed, and powerful, Sutpen towers above his fellow men, but he is doomed. His lack of compassion destroys his design and provokes Wash Jones into killing him. When Charles Bon arrives at Sutpen's Hundred, the retributive wave that Sutpen set into motion nearly thirty years earlier is about to engulf him. His refusal to recognize his son is an ironical re-enactment of the whole tragic episode of rejection at the plantation owner's door. Actually, the rejection of Charles is anticlimactic. Nothing that Sutpen could do, could now stem the forces of retribution. This is apparent if we consider how easily Sutpen might have eliminated Charles as a threat to his design. Henry and Judith had lived their entire lives with Clytie. Their half-sister, she holds a subservient position in the household because she is a Negro. If Sutpen had simply told his children that Bon was Negro, they would hardly have accepted him as suitor and friend. Sutpen's failure to use this strategy is significant. Though he will never recognize the fact, he is no longer in control of his destiny. From the moment that Charles appears, he has lost control; forces stronger than he have him in their grip. He detonates the explosion that destroys his design when he tells Henry at the end of the War that Charles is Negro, but his act merely confirms the inevitable. His dream was doomed at the moment he repudiated Eulalia Bon, just as the catastrophe of the Civil War was initiated by secession but had its beginnings on the day the first slave was landed on American shores. When he returns from the War, Sutpen still believes that courage, shrewdness, and will are all that he needs to begin a third time. He never loses his conviction because, like the Southerners he represents, he cannot understand that his downfall is caused by the violation of a design for human existence far more basic than the design of plantation aristocracy.

Five months after his return, Sutpen admits that he can save only one mile of his land. On that same day he suggests that Rosa prove herself capable of bearing him a male heir. His suggestion indicates that he recognizes only one force working against him—time, his advancing age. In his blindness, Sutpen is more fortunate than his heirs will be. He suffers because he failed. They will suffer not only failure but the oppressive burden of guilt. In the final years of his life, Sutpen is a pitiable old man. He opens a crossroads store and spends his time haggling over nickels and dimes and deriving nourishment for his ego in the companionship of the man who, at one time, was not allowed inside his mansion. His one last desperate attempt to make his mark on the face of oblivion by seducing Wash Jones's adolescent granddaughter with scraps of bright ribbon is a final revelation of his continued detachment from his fellow man. The child and all the other people with whom he has dealt are nothing more than instruments, to be preserved, like Ellen, if they serve their purpose, discarded, like Eulalia, if they fail.

The final act of Sutpen's life is an act of rejection, identical with the act that set the whole tragedy into motion. By telling Milly Jones that if she were a mare he could give her a stall, he negates her humanity and, at the same time, the humanity of her grandfather. The shiftless Wash Jones, who has considered Sutpen one of the greats of the earth, reacts in the inevitable pattern of the violated. After he kills Sutpen and awaits the sheriff, Wash, according to Mr. Compson, begins to understand how the South, led by such great men as Sutpen, could have been defeated, how it had been possible "for Yankees or any other army to have whipped them—the gallant, the proud, the brave." (290) Wash grasps the significance of Sutpen's and the South's tragedy. The lack of compassion in Sutpen mirrors the lack of compassion in the South. It brings Sutpen to a violent end as it brought the Old South to a violent end. Wash's insight gives him stature and dignity. He refuses to run away. He cuts the throats of Milly and her child, sets fire to the cabin, and, scythe in hand, charges the loaded rifles of Major DeSpain's posse.

Like King David in the Biblical story from which Faulkner derived the title of his novel, Thomas Sutpen rises through his own power to high station among men, breaks the moral law and brings suffering upon his children. In both the house of David and the house of Sutpen, retribution takes the form of violent crimes by the children—revolt, incest, fratricide. The parallels in the stories are not extensive, but sufficient to indicate a continuity in the human condition through centuries of time. The crimes of David and Sutpen give birth to the crimes of their children; the effects of their sins extend into future generations.

» » Sutpen's children

It is this extension through time of the effects of Sutpen's wrong that Faulkner is dramatizing with his technique of the multiple narrators. What happens to Sutpen's children reflects the fate of the post-War Southerner. Sutpen's story has the aura of legend, but Sutpen himself is a fully delineated character. The forces that drive him are analyzed in detail, and he stands out as a living human being. His children, however, are not so clearly presented; they and their drama cannot be extricated from the historical drama of the South. *Absalom, Absalom!* is not a realistic novel. The characters, particularly the children of Sutpen, are stylized. If they come into sharp focus for a moment, they quickly recede into the panorama of history.

Only a few facts about Henry and Charles are available to the narrators. Henry murdered Bon at the gates of the plantation after five years of close friendship. The two attended law school together, visited Henry's home three times, then went off to New Orleans. They joined the same company at the beginning of the Civil War and fought together for four years. Right after the murder, Henry disappeared. One other fragment is at the narrators' disposal: the letter Charles wrote to Judith to tell her they have waited long enough to marry. All the narrators except Rosa focus their attention upon the murder. Their investigations begin and end with it. The murder is actually the dramatic center of the novel. All the details uncovered about Sutpen and his children lead toward the solution of the mystery: why Henry killed Bon. Not until the final pages does Faulkner reveal the vital fact that Bon has Negro blood. It is the one fact needed to clarify the mystery of the murder and the significance of Sutpen's history to the narrators. The meaning they have sought in his tragedy exists in this fact, because it relates the past to the present, the tragedy of Sutpen to the tragedy of the South.

The speculations of Mr. Compson and Shreve concerning the relations of Charles and Henry serve to intensify the dramatic impact of the final revelation. Their two versions produce a crescendo effect. In the first version, Mr. Compson pictures Henry as a country bumpkin, completely fascinated by the suave, worldly man he meets at the law school. His attachment to Bon is so strong that he repudiates his father and his birthright when Sutpen forbids the marriage of Charles and Judith. Mr. Compson decides that when, in New Orleans, Henry discovers that Bon is married to an octoroon, he is revolted at the thought of his sister being married to a man who has as a common-law wife a woman with Negro blood. Having a mistress is one thing, but a morganatic marriage to such a tainted woman shocks Henry. During the war, he struggles to accept this situation and finally does, as Charles's letter indicates. Mr. Compson realizes, however, that this speculation is hardly sufficient to explain the murder.

In the next version, Henry's problem is intensified. He knows that Charles is his father's son. What he must accept if he sanctions the marriage is incest. For four years, while he fights the bat-

tle of the South, he struggles with his conscience. His love for Bon
finally overcomes his moral scruples and the letter to Judith is
written with his blessing. When the final clue is revealed, we realize that Henry could sanction an incestuous marriage but not a
miscegenetic one. Henry loved and admired Bon. He repudiated
his birthright and his conscience for him, risked his life in battle
for him, but all his love could not withstand the ultimate taboo.

The chronology of events in the personal drama of Charles and
Henry is identical with the chronology of the War. They meet in
1859, fight the Yankees together for four years, and when the South
is defeated and the war to end slavery is done, Henry discovers
that Bon has Negro blood and he kills him. The murder takes
place less than a month after Lee surrendered at Appomatox. The
moral crime which initially brought on the war is thus repeated.
Henry's crime is basically the same as Sutpen's, but Henry is not
blindly innocent; he is involved with Charles as a human being.
He cannot ignore the moral responsibility of his act. In Faulkner's
version of the Greek *Oresteia*, Henry is pursued by the furies for
forty years. No one knows what Henry does during the years of his
exile from Jefferson. It is appropriate that those years remain a
blank. Like so many of the Southerners who people Yoknapatawpha County, Henry ceases to exist in the present. He becomes a
ghost, absorbed by the tragedy of the past, confused and burdened
by an omnipresent heritage of guilt. He finally returns to the house
of his father and the scene of his crime, sick and wasted, to allow
his body to join the spirit that died forty years earlier.

Judith comes into sharper focus than Henry, but she, too, cannot escape the legend into individuality as Sutpen does. We get no
closer to her than Rosa can when she rushes out to Sutpen's
Hundred and is met by a dry-eyed, cold-faced woman at the top of
the stairs. The sustained image of Judith is the image of woman
suffering. Her individuality exists in the characteristics she inherits
from her father—strength, courage, independence. Only intimations
concerning the motives for her actions are provided, however. The
effect is that she looms larger than life. She is Electra, a figure in a
legend whose acts illuminate the legend rather than her own individuality.

Is it love that motivates her to bury Charles in the Sutpen burial

plot? She has seen Charles only a very few times—a total of a little over two weeks in five years, and not once from the moment
he leaves with Henry on Christmas Eve, 1860, until he lies dead
on her bed in 1865. If we can accept love as the motivation for
burying Charles in Sutpen's place beside the grave of Ellen, can we
also accept it as sufficient to explain her rushing to General Compson with the money for a gravestone for Charles's son, even before
the son, Charles Etienne, arrives from New Orleans, and Judith has
a chance to grow fond of him? The impression Judith gives is of a
woman atoning for a crime; and yet we never know if Henry told
her why he killed Bon, or if she ever realizes that Bon was her father's son. Whatever the motives, the results of Judith's actions are
a series of ironies that add dramatically to the central theme of
rejection. Beside the grave of Ellen she buries Charles, the son
whom Sutpen refused to recognize. When her father is killed,
she buries him beside Charles and uses the money from the sale of
his store to assure Charles's son a gravestone. Charles Etienne is
buried on the other side of Sutpen. By chance, Judith's own grave
is set apart from the others; and in death, Sutpen is surrounded by
the descendants of the woman he repudiated because she had Negro blood. When Clytie sets fire to the remnants of his mansion,
destroying herself and Henry, only the Negro idiot, Jim Bond (formerly Bon) remains to mark Sutpen's dream of a dynasty.

The greatest irony, perhaps, is that the man Judith loves has
Negro blood, and though she devotes and sacrifices her life to his
son, she is at the same time capable of denying Charles Etienne's
equality because he is a Negro. Judith's suffering, her loss of
Charles and of her brother at the same moment, stems directly
from her father's crime. She, too, stops living in the present. All her
acts during the twenty years left of her life derive from that event
in 1865. Love and guilt are inextricably blended and deprive her of
the freedom to live in the present. In the complicated mixture of
feelings that characterizes her relations with Charles Etienne, she
represents the post-War South. She brings the twelve-year-old boy
from New Orleans and lets him sleep on a trundle bed between
her, the white woman on the bed, and Clytie, the mulatto on the
floor. In contrast to Henry, who, like so many of Faulkner's male
characters, does not inherit the strength of his pioneering father,

Judith shares some of the heroic proportions of Sutpen. She cannot, however, escape her heritage of racial prejudice, and by her attitude dooms Charles Etienne as surely as if she rejected him outright.

Charles Bon's role in the legend reveals the extremity of racial prejudice. Not only is he, to all appearances, a white man; he is also the first-born son of Thomas Sutpen. It is the abstract idea of Negro that rules Sutpen and his son, Henry. Charles seeks nothing more than a sign of recognition from his father. He may be the agent of his mother's vengeance, but he himself is not, at first, vindictive. It is clear that he would disappear from the world of the Sutpen family if he could get some indication that his father acknowledges him. He asks for very little, but he is Negro and he can therefore get nothing. Charles waits patiently for four years. And it is only when he is certain that his desire is hopeless that he acts. From that moment on, he follows the pattern of the rejected, determined to assert his individuality by an act of vengeance.

Knowing what he does about his relationship to Judith and Henry, Charles commits a ruthless act when he writes his letter proposing marriage. It is an act calculated to bring upon his father the greatest possible suffering. If Bon, as Shreve and Quentin decide, does love Judith, he would, it is obvious, have sacrificed that love if his father had acknowledged him. And also, if he does love her, it is a strange love that would bring him to marry his own sister without telling her that she will be committing incest. To avoid the unpleasant truth about Charles, Shreve and Quentin weave a romance of love and heroism; but Charles has been rejected, and his actions are an expression of an overpowering need for revenge. After five years of close friendship with Henry, he knows the depth of Henry's feeling for him. He is merciless, however, when Henry returns from the visit to his father's tent. He hands Henry his pistol, fully aware of the anguish he is causing his brother. And it is not difficult to imagine the terrible struggle that Henry goes through on that ride to Sutpen's Hundred, delaying until the final possible moment committing the act that will destroy both him and his brother. Charles actually gives Henry no alternative. All his acts are those of a man determined to bring pain and anguish, at no matter what cost, upon the Sutpen family. Carrying the picture of his octoroon wife and child is a defiant declaration of his identity rather than an attempt, as Shreve romantically conjectures, to spare Judith the pain of mourning him. Charles acts out of the fury that grips all victims of rejection.

His son, Charles Etienne, represents a refinement of the reaction-to-rejection pattern. In a society that denies human equality to the Negro, that makes race rather than a common humanity the basis of recognition, Charles Etienne is both Negro and white —and, at the same time, neither Negro nor white. He is cut off from the only two available social groups and is thereby isolated from everyone. He is a man without fellow men. Nothing visible sets him apart from the white community. An abstraction, intangible but real, threatens his identity as a white person. We never know whether it was Clytie or Judith who tells him he has Negro blood. (One of them had to. Ultimately, it is Judith's responsibility. If she had accepted him, Clytie would not have been free to tell him.) That indefiniteness is symbolic of his whole life. He does not suffer a definite rejection. He alone knows what he is; however, he has no target but himself. By associating with Negroes, by marrying the most Negroid woman he can find, he seeks to make concrete the abstraction that tortures him. For a Charles Etienne, there is no release from suffering. His anguish, too much for human flesh to bear, is not transmitted: his idiot child is impervious to the pain human beings inflict upon one another.

Of no little significance is the blood relationship of all these characters. Sutpen fathers the white children who reject their blood relations and who suffer the moral consequences of this act; he also fathers the Negro children who are rejected. The familial tragedy of Sutpen becomes the tragedy of the human family. Henry and Judith are only the initial victims of their father's crime, which reflects the crime of the South. The moral consequences of a crime extending through time become a part of the heritage of the human race. Though intelligent and sensitive, Mr. Compson and Quentin are oppressed by the past, by a sense of guilt that they do not fully understand or that they refuse to face. In Sutpen's story they seek the source of their own problems. In one of the interpolative thoughts in which Quentin observes how much Shreve sounds like Mr. Compson, an image is developed that shows the relation between the past and the present. The same image can serve as a final revelation of the integration of theme and structure in the novel.

Maybe nothing ever happens once and is finished. Maybe happen is never once but like ripples maybe on water after the pebble sinks, the ripples moving on, spreading, the pool attached by a narrow umbilical water-cord to the next pool which the first pool feeds, has fed, did feed, let this second pool contain a different temperature of water, a different molecularity of having seen, felt, remembered, reflect in a different tone the infinite unchanging sky, it doesn't matter: that pebble's watery echo whose fall it did not even see moves across its surface too at the original ripple-space, to the old ineradicable rhythm thinking Yes, we are both Father. Or maybe Father and I are both Shreve, maybe it took Father and me both to make Shreve or Shreve and me both to make Father or maybe Thomas Sutpen to make all of us. (261-2)

The theme of *Absalom, Absalom!* is rejection and its moral consequences. These consequences, like the ripples in Quentin's image, extend in ever-widening circles through time, to become part of the common heritage of man. Beyond the accidents of time and place, men are united by a common humanity and heritage. In the single language-flow of the narrators, Faulkner unifies the consciousnesses of these individual people, because Sutpen's history is their common heritage.

The concept of time that shaped Sutpen's thinking is also inherent in Quentin's image. Fragmented time, measured in years and days and minutes, is a surface illusion. Quentin is separated by many years of chronological time from Thomas Sutpen, but when he thinks about Sutpen's life, or about Henry Sutpen, the past and the present merge. Physically, the human being exists in fragmented time, but when he thinks, he is in the realm of indivisible time. Rosa, for instance, can link in one thought events separated by forty years; in her mind these events exist in a continuum. The lack of chronology in the narrations and in the novel as a whole mirrors this characteristic of human thought.

Absalom, Absalom! is a novel of man thinking, not man doing. The characteristics of human thought determine its form. The narrators are seeking meaning. Thomas Sutpen's crime, again using Quentin's image, is the pebble thrown into the water that sets up the current of ever-widening ripples. Each of the narrations represents one of those circles—of a different molecularity and tone. Each is fed by the circles closer to the initial force. The actual narrative movement of the novel, however, is centrifugal, rather than centripetal as the image would indicate. We move ever closer to the center until we finally understand what Sutpen did. His crime, any crime, is the pebble thrown into the stream of human life, and the inexorable moral consequences of the crime form the umbilical between the ever-widening circles. Forced to participate in the process of piecing together the evidence and, at the same time, assimilating the effects of the crime, the reader, as fifth investigator, actually represents another concentric circle—of a different molecularity and temperature certainly—but involved, at least as much as the Canadian Shreve, in the meaning of Sutpen's life.

Absalom, Absalom! is Faulkner's analysis of the effects of slavery on the conscience and consciousness of the South, but through his structure and narrative techniques, his theme of rejection takes on universal significance. The profundity of that theme and the superb craftsmanship with which it is handled make this work Faulkner's greatest novel and surely one of the masterpieces of contemporary literature.

The Wild Palms

Though *The Wild Palms* (1939) does not concern Yoknapatawpha County and its inhabitants, it does continue to develop the themes of the preceding books, and it does reveal the development of Faulkner's ideas by its elevation, for the first time, of a primitive character to the role of protagonist. The concept of the "natural man," dramatized in Dilsey and Lena Grove, is worked out more fully in "Old Man," one of the two stories in the novel. By juxtaposing a tale of man in nature with one of man in society, Faulkner sets into relief those characteristics of the modern world that make society unnatural and that alienate modern man from his own nature and from the natural conditions of existence.

"Wild Palms" and "Old Man," probably known to most readers as separate stories, were originally published as one book, entitled *The Wild Palms*. Each story is divided into five sections, which in the original book Faulkner alternated, beginning with the first chapter of "Wild Palms." The book was recognized as an experiment in literary counterpoint, and with that concession to Faulkner's intentions, the stories were subsequently reprinted separately. The separation, which the author apparently accepted with his usual indifference to the treatment of his works, destroys a novel of remarkable depth and startling ingenuity.

In actuality, the book is a bold innovation in the technique of the novel, a variation and extension of the multiple-point-of-view technique by which the novelist tells his story through the consciousness of several characters without obvious authorial interference. In previous books, the technique was effectively employed. *Absalom, Absalom!*, as we saw, has four narrators who tell the same story from differing viewpoints. The reader, who must sift each version to discover the truth, becomes another investigator, another consciousness. *The Wild Palms* pushes the technique of reader participation one step further. The main story, a tragic love story, is told entirely from the point of view of one of the lovers. In alternate chapters, a completely different, though related and, in a sense, parallel, story is interjected. The reader is forced, by this technique, to become an active participant in the process of literary creation. He must establish the thematic relationship of the stories, recognize the parallels and discover the truth. Whether the burden that Faulkner places upon his reader is excessive is a matter for debate. For the moment, it is sufficient to suggest that Faulkner may have added another dimension to the modern novel by permitting his reader to indict himself for sympathizing with the kind of romantic love the author is satirizing.[1]

Few readers of the story "Wild Palms" can escape a deep sense of sympathy for Harry and Charlotte; and yet one cannot feel for them as one does for other tragic lovers in literature, like Romeo and Juliet, or Catherine and Frederick in A *Farewell to Arms*. The reason is that, despite our almost instinctive sympathy for love and lovers, our literary conditioning to stories of ideal love in good or cheap literature, and our empathy with the lovers of "Wild Palms," we are unable to ignore the unnatural and sordid elements in the love of Henry and Charlotte. Our awareness of these elements does not destroy our sympathy, but it does temper it. As a result, we finish the story with a feeling of confusion and dissatisfaction. When the story is read in conjunction with "Old Man," however, much of this confusion is dispelled. The sane, realistic attitude of the protagonist of "Old Man," the convict, and the humor with which his story is told, permit us to withdraw, at least temporarily, from the plight of the lovers. Our perspective broadened, we become aware not only of their extravagances, but of the excesses that our own sympathies have led us into.

There are many indications in both stories that the genesis of *The Wild Palms* may have been an annoyed reaction to the tendency in literature to romanticize love excessively. There is even much evidence that Faulkner may have had his contemporary, Ernest Hemingway, in mind. There are a number of interesting parallels between Charlotte and Harry's love affair in "Wild Palms," and Catherine and Henry's in A *Farewell to Arms*.[2] A number of the settings that Faulkner chooses—the lake and the isolated mining camp, for example—seem arbitrary until they are compared with Hemingway's settings. The cryptic reference to Hemingway by the newspaper reporter McCord in his strange and irrelevant response to Charlotte's strange and irrelevant toast may be a clue to the inspiration of *The Wild Palms*:

"Drink up, ye armourous sons. Keep up with the dog."
"Yah," McCord said. "Set, ye armourous sons, in a sea of heming-waves." (52)*

* Despite my objection to the separation of the stories in the Signet Edition, I have quoted from it because it is the only readily available edition of the novel.

There are several incidents and statements in other scenes in which McCord appears that seem to have no discernible connection with the development of the love story. Charlotte's search for an iron dog, for instance, seems comprehensible to the newspaper reporter, but Harry is as mystified by the whole ritual as is the reader. While it is impossible to determine the precise relevance of such incidents and references, it appears that Faulkner is not only condemning a general tendency in our society to take romantic literature as literal truth, but that he is also quarreling with Hemingway's concept of the nature of reality. In *A Farewell to Arms,* the hero escapes the firing squad by jumping into the Po River. When he emerges he is cleansed of his romantic notions about war and about life, but not, obviously, of his romantic notions about love. Though this may seem far-fetched, I would suggest that Faulkner's double story can be viewed as an extension of this crucial moment in *A Farewell to Arms.* The hero of "Old Man" remains in the river and discovers reality; the hero of "Wild Palms" pursues romantic love to its ultimate tragic conclusion.

The protagonist of "Old Man" is a victim of literary romanticism. The escapade that makes him a convict is inspired by pulp-fiction. The simple hill man accepts as truth every detail of these stories, and he is so outraged by the ignorance and gullibility of the pulp-story writers when his train robbery fails that he dreams of suing them for using the mails to defraud. The protagonist of "Wild Palms," listening to the cry of a loon, muses "how man alone of all creatures deliberately atrophies his natural senses and that only at the expense of others; how the four-legged animal gains all its information through smelling and seeing and hearing and distrusts all else while the two-legged one believes only what it reads." (58)

But we need not depend upon allusions to literature in the novel to recognize that the love Charlotte and Henry seek is romantic love carried to excess. The real evidence is in the story itself. Harry Wilbourne, the man who gives up everything for love, is probably the most incompetent, silly, and unmanly lover in all literature. As McCord points out, Harry lacks the courage of his fornications. At twenty-seven, and four months away from being a full-fledged doctor of medicine, he is in a retarded state of adolescence. His ideas about the nature of the female are, to be kind, immature. He is stickily romantic—truly, a "ninth-rate Teasdale," as McCord observes. (56) As a lover, Wilbourne is an insult to the entire male sex.

The sexual relationship he establishes with Charlotte is so unmasculine that it borders on sheer comedy. He is continually being attacked by his virile partner. Charlotte is usually stripped before Harry even realizes that he is being set upon. She holds him close to her "hard body"; she helps him out of his clothes. And in bed, Harry is constantly suffering, without remonstrance, from Charlotte's hard elbow in his chest and from being shaken by the hair as he gets a vigorous lecture on love. Charlotte so continually makes love to Harry, and Harry so continually submits to her attacks with his breathless "Yes, Yes, Yes," that it is not without shock that we discover it is Charlotte who becomes pregnant.

Charlotte, too, as heroine of a tragic love story lacks romantic appeal. It is perhaps possible to accept her aggressive sexuality as an unconventional and honest response to her desires, but one need not be anchored in bourgeois morality to be disturbed by her neat intellectual somersault when she justifies abandoning her two children. She has discovered, she declares, that something she read in books is true: " 'that love and suffering are the same thing and that the value of love is the sum of what you have to pay for it and any time you get it cheap you have cheated yourself. So I dont need to think about the children.' " (32)

Viewed objectively, the love Charlotte and Harry seek is the romantic love, idealized to the point of absurdity, of pulp-fiction. More significantly, their idea of love—or at least Charlotte's—is a creation of the human imagination, a by-product of the very civilization that the lovers consider their enemy, rather than an ideal which the civilization has cheapened. The combined stories in the novel constitute a satire on romantic love, but they are also much more: they dramatize a view of reality and human existence; they indict our culture for substituting symbol for reality; and they study, in something like mythological terms, the mysterious relationship of the male and the female.

As in all his best works, Faulkner's vision encompasses man in time and simultaneously man outside of time: the individual and the type, the specific and the universal. In 1927, the convict in

"Old Man" is twenty-five years old. He is a tall man with blue eyes. But he is also Adam, Everyman, man in any age trapped in an alien universe that he cannot understand but must exist in. Faulkner broadens the novel's scope of vision by combining the realistic story of Charlotte and Harry, two sophisticated modern people living within the confines of a world created by civilized man, with a fable that begins, "Once there were. . . ." The fable is about simple, inarticulate people in an environment that seems to evoke that of Genesis. Below the surface details of the story are elemental patterns and types. These serve, as did the ancient mythological stories about gods and goddesses, to explain the unknown forces within man and the unknown forces in his universe. Historical events in each story anchor the narratives in time—the Mississippi flood of 1927, and the economic depression in the United States during the 1930's. But the convict is also out of historical time. In his battle against the flood, he is elemental man struggling to provide safety, food, and shelter for the child-bearer, the earth-mother. And Harry Wilbourne is elemental man bewitched by the demon goddess Lilith.

The central characters in each story are a man and a woman who are two aspects of the essential male and the female. The pregnant woman in "Old Man" is Eve the mother. Charlotte in "Wild Palms" is Eve the temptress. And Harry and the convict are Adam, on the one hand, tempted by Eve, and on the other hand, Adam trapped into caring for Eve the mother. As in most mythological stories, the viewpoint is masculine. The two women seem to embody the extremes of "the female principle": the mother and the Lilith.* Between these alien forces—oppressive responsibility that he does not want, and bewitching seduction that destroys him—the male seems to be trapped. Like Adam, both of Faulkner's heroes are dragged from the serene security of Eden to face the outrages of a fearful and violent existence. The world beyond Eden is a veritable no-man's land in which the male is whirled about so violently that he is numbed into a state of shocked

---

* Lilith is a favorite allusion of Faulkner's. In Talmudic tradition, Lilith is identified as Adam's wife; in other mythologies, she is a demon of the night, the mother of the empusae who, in the form of bewitching maidens, suck the vital juices of men until they die.

lethargy. It is a world without peace, where the male is doomed and damned.

In both stories, the principal male characters are continually described as being in a state of amazement or incredulity or outrage; and both are somehow a victim of the mysterious female principle that seems to represent uncontrollable forces. Rittenmeyer, Charlotte's husband, and Wilbourne are Charlotte's victims. The fat convict of "Old Man" prefers one hundred and ninety-nine years of prison to facing the female whom he transported across a state line. The sole desire of the tall convict is to get rid of the pregnant woman and to "turn his back on her forever, on all pregnant and female life forever and return to that monastic existence of shotguns and shackles, where he would be secure from it." (178)

In the alien world into which he is dragged by the female, the male's sole source of power is his maleness, his instinctive moral integrity. If he asserts his maleness, he can, as the tall convict does, know a limited fulfillment, a limited success. If he does not, he is, like Harry, doomed. Relevant to this emphasis on femaleness and maleness are the joking references in each story to the union of the male and female in one organism—hermaphroditism. In "Wild Palms," when Charlotte and Harry leave their Chicago apartment to go to Utah, the manager of the house shakes hands with both of them and then with McCord. Wilbourne, who never before or after in the story even smiles, let alone makes jokes, says to the manager: "'Just two of us . . . None of us are androgynous [hermaphroditic].'" (74) And in "Old Man," the convicts who listen to their cell mate's adventures on the river define the term the doctor on the riverboat used to describe the convict's nosebleeds: "hemophilic." One of the convicts suggests that it is "'a calf that's a bull and a cow at the same time.'" The plump convict responds, "'Hell fire . . . He's got to be one or the other to keep from drounding.'" (204) When it is isolated from the whole novel, the convict's statement about drowning if "it" is not either male or female is incomprehensible. In terms of the conjoined narratives, however, it sums up succinctly the difference between the tall convict's and Harry's responses to their separate but similar encounters with an overwhelming force—the roaring flood waters

and the raging passion of love. Both men begin and end their ad
ventures in a monastic world; both are unusually naïve about
women; both are uprooted, by chance, from a secure, routine
existence; and both, in the end, choose the all-male world of prison.
Together, they have spanned the extremes of the female principle,
from mother Eve to Lilith Eve. The convict asserts his maleness
and retains his integrity; the romantic lover sacrifices his integrity
and, figuratively speaking, drowns.

Considered separately, the two stories in *The Wild Palms* have a
number of loose ends. The emphasis upon the convict's attitude
toward women in "Old Man," for instance, is hardly substantiated
by the narrative. Even if a woman did contribute to his getting
into prison, his experience with the female sex is so limited that
his vehemence is unwarranted. The emphasis in the story is on his
heroic struggle against the forces of nature, and the line with
which the tale concludes " 'Women——!' the tall convict said,"
seems irrelevant. (239) As the final line of the combined stories,
however, it is meaningful. Read separately, "Wild Palms" is confusing. Without the balance provided by the subsidiary story, for
example, we may easily fail to recognize that Harry is the filter-
ing consciousness rather than the spokesman of the author. His
thoughts are entirely his own, ruminations, for the most part, of a
confused and harassed man who cannot quite keep up to the
woman he loves. For one thing, he is male, and for another, he is
so confused by passion that his thoughts are illogical, his observations frequently contrary to the obvious facts, and his perceptions
often imperceptive. If Harry's thoughts are accepted as Faulkner's,
as many readers and critics tend to do, the obvious parallels
with "Old Man" must be ignored, and "Wild Palms" becomes a
silly paean to sterile love.

A full appreciation of Faulkner's book depends upon the recognition that Harry's thoughts must be approached warily. Two days
after they arrive in Chicago, for instance, Harry awakens to discover that Charlotte is not beside him. At once, he begins to muse
about the nature of woman:

*It's not the romance of illicit love which draws them, not the passion-
ate idea of two damned and doomed and isolated forever against the*

world and God and the irrevocable which draws men; it's because the
idea of illicit love is a challenge to them, because they have an irresisti-
ble desire to . . . take the illicit love and make it respectable. . . .
(41-2)

Harry's thinking sums up perfectly his own romanticism, but his generalization about women hardly applies to Charlotte. When she returns she informs him that she has found an apartment for them, and shaking "his head again with that savage obliviousness," she gives him another lecture on love. (42) Seeing the apartment, Harry discovers that it was not chosen to make their love respectable since *"It's only incidental that there is a place to sleep and cook food. She chose a place not to hold us but to hold love. . . ."* (43) Charlotte has neither the inclination nor the desire to mask their illicit relationship. It is Harry, himself, who seeks respectability, who has to keep fighting against his desire to be a husband.

Of a piece with this type of obtuse observation is Harry's: *"I dont believe in sin. It's getting out of timing. You are born sub-merged in anonymous lockstep with the teeming anonymous myriads of your time and generation; you get out of step once, falter once, and you are trampled to death."* (36) This state-ment has so romantic an appeal that our impulse is to accept it as true. It has often been cited as evidence that Faulkner's theme in "Wild Palms" is that society has no place in it for love. The truth is that Charlotte and Harry are not harassed by society be-cause they are living in sin. On the contrary, almost everyone, in-cluding Charlotte's forsaken husband, goes out of his way to abet them.

The only external force that poses a real threat to their love is poverty. The lovers are victims, as were most Americans living in or out of sin during the 1930's, of a collapse in the national econ-omy. Except for one brief period, the lack of money haunts them throughout their year together. But poverty is far less a threat to them than their slavish romanticism. Even ignoring the historical fact that by 1938 the economy was beginning to recover, their decision to leave Chicago and go to the lake and love until star-vation overtakes them or McCord finds one of them a job is a species of sentimental bravado that borders on the stupid. It *is* "ninth rate Teasdale," a sentimental absorption in self-pity. Why, one must ask, did they not do anything—sweep streets, work for WPA, go on relief, if necessary, since all they wanted in life was enough to be together to love. Hunger, Charlotte preaches to Harry with several painful pokes in his stomach, is not in the stomach, it is in the heart. Poverty, in point of fact, is not their nemesis. After their idyll at the lake, Harry is able to "beat poverty": he puts Charlotte to work dressing store windows, and he sits home writing stories for confession magazines.

When society fails to ostracize them morally and socially, and poverty no longer can bolster Harry's romantic image of "two damned and doomed and isolated forever against the world and God," he resorts to respectability. What is this "respectability" that threatens their love so much that it can be preserved only in the forty-below-zero cold of a Utah mining camp, where deservedly, one almost feels, they get no chance to make love for six weeks? Harry's image of "respectability" is children. As he explains it to McCord: " 'I would be waked in the mornings by the noise of children passing in the street; by the time spring came and the windows would have to stay open I would have been hearing the fretful cries of Swede nursemaids from the park all day long and, when the wind was right, smell the smell of infant urine and animal crackers.' " (77)

It is not society, but Harry's own bourgeois instincts that pose this absurd threat to their love. He sums it all up when he says, " 'I had turned into a husband.' " (75) But why, one must ask, go all the way out to a mine in Utah to escape respectability? Why not just move out of the comfortable bourgeois apartment and into a bohemian apartment in a bohemian section of the city, where it might even be cheap enough so that Charlotte can stay home with Harry while he writes his pulp-magazine stories to provide for their simple wants?

Responding to McCord's cynical questions, Harry declares that there is no place for love " 'in the world today.' " (78) The statement is romantic self-pity that the facts contradict. Harry and Charlotte are not out of step with their generation and time. They are so much in lockstep with it that they are out of step with life itself. They are personifications of their society, carrying to an extreme one of the symbols that their culture has substituted for reality. Most aspects of human society are rooted in fundamental human needs. Working, for example, provides essential subsistence, and, as the convict of "Old Man" learns, working for money can even provide a sense of accomplishment and fulfillment. But in our society, the making of money has become an end in itself. We do not work for the symbol of subsistence, but the symbol of status and power. The same thing is true of security, morality, respectability, and love which have been abstracted from function.

Love, for instance, as Charlotte conceives it, is an ideal separated from its roots in the natural sexual function of the human being. It becomes an end in itself, expressed through sexual contact but isolated from the natural purpose of sex. Love, for Charlotte, is a god that must be served by nothing less than immolation. Such love, as the tragedy of Harry and Charlotte proves, can only end disastrously not because it violates society but because it violates life, nature. It can only exist under unnatural conditions, and anything that anchors it to normality threatens it.

Charlotte is the fanatical high priestess of this religion, and Harry is her acolyte. For eight of the twelve months of their union, Harry works hard to overcome his natural reluctance and to become a worthy fanatic. A naïve neophyte, he is swept up by Charlotte's passion. And, as he declares, he clings to her until he has himself learned how to swim. Harry's first eight months of love are, in many ways, parallel to the convict's initial experiences on the flooded river.

Like Harry, who is helpless under the piercing yellow of Charlotte's eyes, the convict is helpless against the raging yellow waters of the flood. Though he struggles to steer and to control the skiff, he is powerless against the force of the abnormal upstream current. His sense of outrage at the terrifying power that whirls him about like a moth in a tornado is augmented by the bitter irony that makes him—a reader of pulp romances—protector of a woman in the final stage of pregnancy. Among all the females in the world with whom he might have been isolated after seven years in prison, it has to be a woman whose swelling body mocks his dreams and forces upon him a responsibility he fears and does not want. He has to keep fighting down the thought that he could easily free himself from the oppressive burden by putting the woman back into a tree or even arranging for her to fall overboard. After a while, the convict, because of his determination to fulfill the mission with which he was entrusted, begins to take control, and he eventually fulfills his responsibilities. Harry, too, learns how to swim, but his adventure ends tragically. The paradox of these companion tales is that the fable deals with reality and the realistic story deals with the fabulous. "Old Man" presents the human tragedy comically; "Wild Palms," the human comedy tragically.

The humor in "Old Man" is not unlike that in a slapstick movie in which the comedian is knocked about so continually, is battered so excessively that his predicament becomes comical. Each time the convict is certain that he has faced the most incredible outrage possible, another comes along even more outrageous. As Faulkner describes him, at one point, he feels like the man who is narrowly missed by a falling safe only to be struck by a paper weight. The humor in the story, to be sure, is not the overflow of a gay and joyful spirit; it is the grim humor of a lacerated and outraged sensibility. From the vantage point of his belief in man's endurance, Faulkner can describe, with amused incredulity, puny man's encounter with the terrifying conditions of existence.

"Old Man" is essentially a parable. The forces in nature that control the conditions of human existence are embodied in the majestic Mississippi river, the Old Man. The colloquial term for father applied to the father of waters carries with it the suggestion of deity, God the Father. The convict, who is deliberately unnamed, is Man, and his unnamed companion is Woman. Though the convict has lived within a short distance of the river all his life and has spent the last seven years working close to it, he has never seen it. Faulkner uses a series of insect images to convey the convict's impression of the river's magnitude and power, and of man's fragility in the presence of such force. For instance, when the convict realizes that what he is hearing is the rushing water, he is described as suddenly becoming aware "that he had been hearing it all the time, a sound so much beyond all his experience and his powers of assimilation that up to this point he had been as oblivious of it as an ant or a flea might be of the sound of the avalanche on which it rides. . . ." (164) The convict is uprooted from his peaceful, secure routine, as any man might be by a chance occurrence, and thrust alone upon the raging waters, where he encounters facsimiles of those terrible and unaccountable disasters that men can and do undergo. He has so little control that the only decision that he can deliberately make is to keep struggling against the overwhelming forces, or quit and be submerged by them. The convict's head is literally bloodied and bowed. He is awed by the incredible force and power he faces and by the recognition of his own weakness. His situation is, in effect, the classic existential moment when a human being is pulled out of the protective sheath of routine life and discovers for himself the tragedy of the human condition. Significantly, no prayer for mercy ever flashes across the convict's consciousness. His sole source of strength is his desire to endure and his determination to fulfill his mission. It is his moral strength that guarantees his survival.

This confrontation of the human being with the naked powers of nature or the universe severs him from all contact with society. Like Job and every other man throughout time who has faced a spiritual crisis, the convict is alone in his hour of trial. Twice, before the woman's child is born, he seeks help from society, but twice he is rejected. Faulkner's style in this section of the story serves to convey more than the convict's situation; it conveys the sense of Man's naked confrontation of the forces of the universe. The very texture of the swelling sentences in the descriptions of the cresting flood evokes the terrible power of the Old Testament God and sweeps us, with the Man and Woman in the skiff, beyond time and temporal civilization.

The Indian mound on which the convict finally lands is the earth in the reptilian age, emerging from the waters. Here, in this prehistoric world where the snake predominates, the human female fulfills her childbearing function, and the male assumes the responsibility of caring for mother and infant. As the earliest men must have done, the convict fashions a paddle by burning a tree to size and by shaping the wood with fire. And later in the bayous, protected only by a loin cloth and armed with a mace and knife, he grapples with that vestige of prehistoric time, the alligator, to provide for his charges. In short, the convict is primitive man—

man stripped of the accumulated layers of civilization, to expose man's fundamental relationship to the natural world. Like a surgeon, Faulkner has cut through the layers of accumulated fat and exposed the heart of human existence. His story presents a basic reality of human life: the struggle for existence, and man's power to endure by means of his innate qualities of fortitude and integrity. And in this natural situation, the roles of the male and female are unmistakable. Each fulfills the task which he is by nature equipped to fulfill. The male provides subsistence, the female bears and cares for the child and keeps house. She is passive, the male is active; she accepts his decisions and his leadership.

In contrast to the natural response of this simple man and simple woman to the elemental conditions that are—no matter how disguised by civilization—the conditions of human life, Charlotte and Harry dedicate themselves to an ideal, a mere abstraction. For eight months, Harry resists because he cannot obliterate his maleness. Charlotte is in orbit, but Harry is still earth-bound by his desire to provide for his mate, to be a husband. Even when he does surrender to Charlotte's ideal of romantic love, he is motivated by an impulse different from Charlotte's—fear. As he puts it to McCord, " 'I found out one day that I was afraid.' " (78) Harry is afraid that he is too normal to love as Charlotte does, so he has to escape from an environment that induces him to think "My wife must have the best." According to Harry, however, the gods cannot tolerate love. By deciding to go to the mining camp in Utah, he escapes the danger of money and respectability, but the gods have other weapons: " 'So I am vulnerable in neither money nor respectability now and so They will have to find something else to force us to conform to the pattern of human life which has now evolved to do without love—to conform, or die.' " (81)

Harry's gods of conformity of course find their destructive weapon in Harry himself. He is the one who trembles at the idea of abortion and whose hand therefore performs faultily. Abortion is the logical finale of this love that is, from the outset, so abnormal that the natural male-female roles are psychically reversed. Its abnormality is apparent, too, in the personal relationship of the lovers, who actually have nothing in common but their romantic enslavement to the idea of love and its manifestation in sex. Their conversation is limited to the subject of love; when they are not talking about love or making love, they move on parallel but separate tracks. In Chicago, for example, Harry is unaware for some time what Charlotte intends doing with the plaster of paris and glue she sets on her work table. And she does not know for many days that he has lost his job at the clinic. Charlotte gathers around her a circle of friends who spend their evenings in the love-nest. Harry frequently observes, with no show of regret or frustration, that there is a part of Charlotte that remains isolated, that he cannot approach. At the lake, when they are completely alone, they seem to have less in common than ever. Charlotte goes for a swim every day while the weather permits, but Harry remains in bed. Afterwards, she goes off by herself to draw and paint, and Harry stays behind in the cabin with nothing to do but worry about their dwindling food supply. Finally, he admits "quietly to himself, *I am bored. I am bored to extinction. There is nothing here that I am needed for. Not even by her. I have already cut enough wood to last until Christmas and there is nothing else for me to do.*" (62) What a sad thought for a man who has given up all for love! And the country, as well as the city, fails to provide a haven for the lovers. Harry comes to think of nature as a whore seducing him into a lethargy that nearly destroys them. It never occurs to him that he could replenish their larder, keep them alive to love, by fishing or even hunting. When he really gets desperate, he rushes off to the village to see if McCord has found them a job. Always the melodramatic romantic, on his return, Harry informs Charlotte that she must return to the city alone; he will stay at the lake and starve to death. This statement earns him another good shaking and a lecture. In their respectable apartment in Chicago, their lives seldom cross: "he was awake mostly while she slept, and vice versa." (69) Their second foray into the world of nature ruins them. They are kept apart by the forty-degree-below-zero cold. Too fastidious to make love with the Buckners present, they must abstain for six weeks. The very first time that they are alone, the cold bursts Charlotte's douche bag, the perfect symbol of nonfunctional love, and Charlotte becomes pregnant. She does not tell her doctor-lover that they have no contraceptive,

and he never even notices. Their tragic finale begins with her
pregnancy, the natural consequence of male-female love, and ends
by a failure of abortion, an attempt to destroy life.

When Harry decides to leave Chicago for Utah, he has capitulated completely to Charlotte's concept of love. His capitulation
gives him, for a time, an unusual strength. He becomes decisive,
active, even aggressive. But by submitting to Charlotte's idea of
love, he denies his maleness by fighting against his nature, his
irrepressible desire to serve as husband, protector, and provider.
In his impassioned justification of love to McCord at the railroad
station, Harry has to admit that Charlotte feels no threat to their
love in the city; he alone is afraid. There are times in this vale-
diction to civilized life when Harry sounds like a refugee from a
Hemingway novel: " 'the wisdom to concentrate on fleshly pleasures—eating and evacuating and fornication and sitting in the
sun—than which there is nothing better, nothing to match, nothing else in all this world but to live for the short time you are loaned
breath, to be alive and know it—oh, yes, she taught me
that. . . .' " (76) Harry's obsession with the romantic idea of
doomed love is set into perspective by McCord's realistic reactions:
" 'There's the damned horse. . . . After ten minutes we sound
like *Bit and Spur*. We don't talk, we moralise at each other like
two circuit-riding parsons. . . .' " (79) His response to Harry's
description of his eight-month resistance to Charlotte's idea of love
as a prolongation of the orgasmic climax effectively undermines
Harry's verbal orgy: " 'Sweet Jesus,' McCord said. 'Holy choriated
cherubim. If I am ever unlucky enough to have a son, I'm going
to take him to a nice clean whore-house myself on his tenth birthday.' " (80)

Although they represent a *reductio ad absurdum* of the romantic
fallacy, Charlotte and Harry are not alien to their culture; they are
its epitome. Theirs is the tragedy of a culture that has lost sight of
its relationship to nature, that has falsified values by abstracting
them from function. The woman and the convict in "Old Man"
also struggle for survival, but they are not led astray and confused
by any shibboleth of society. They follow their natural impulses
and respond to the needs of their beings. In contrast, Harry violates his instinctive moral sense. So strong is his revulsion to abor-

tion when he vainly resists Charlotte's pleas that he thinks, "*I have thrown away lots, but apparently not this. Honesty about money, security, degree,* and then for a terrible moment he thought, *Maybe I would have thrown away love first too* but he stopped this in time. . . ."(93)

Harry's moral integrity is put to the ultimate test by Charlotte's insistence that he perform an abortion. Tragedy befalls them because he does not resist her pleas. Harry's failure at abortion is clearly a failure to give himself to love as completely as does Charlotte. He bungles the operation because he cannot make his moral instinct subservient to her ideal. Had Charlotte been put to a similar test, she would doubtless never have faltered. But the difference in their ability to become absorbed in love is not so much traceable to a difference in their characters or personalities or past experiences as it is to their difference in sex. The middle-aged doctor, who studies Charlotte sitting outside the cottage that he has rented to the lovers, discerns in her eyes a "profound and illimitable hatred," that he decides is directed "at the race of man, the masculine." (12) He feels the same hatred directed at him as is directed at Harry. It is the masculine in Harry that ultimately destroys Charlotte and her perverse ideal of love. She remains, until she slips into unconsciousness, constant to her ideal, more devoted to love, certainly, than to her lover. She begs her husband not to prosecute Harry if anything should happen to her, not for her lover's sake nor for her own, but for " '*the sake of all the men and women who ever lived and blundered but meant the best and all that ever will live and blunder but mean the best.'* " (114)

Though the lovers have been selfish, silly, and blundering, their suffering gives them some stature, and the final chapter contains some of the finest writing in this story. Harry's anguish throbs in the lines. Death becomes palpable, choking off breath. The palm outside the jail, suddenly shaking though there is no wind, becomes a symbol of the wild, short love Harry shared with Charlotte, and the black wind that blows in from the sea is the death of their romantic idyll. If the love that this couple tried to achieve is unnatural, anguish is not; and Faulkner, for the first time in the story, communicates intensity and conviction.

The lyrical power of the final chapter, however, should not obliterate for the reader the meaning of Harry's final choice of prison over death. As the bereaved lover sinks deeper and deeper into suffering, his individual identity begins to fade (the deputy addresses him continually by a different name), and he becomes Man Suffering. The new convict first chooses not to jump bail and then rejects suicide, both opportunities offered him by Charlotte's husband. Harry chooses to keep memory alive. The choice is not, as it at first seems, an absolute triumph for love. In the prison awaiting trial, Harry spends much of his time looking out of his cell window. One day, he notices the concrete hulk of a ship and identifies it as an emergency ship begun in 1918 and then abandoned. A man and woman have made the hulk their home, and Harry's thoughts focus on the ship as a place that he and Charlotte might have spent their final four days and saved ten dollars. On the day that he is able to think of Charlotte as dead and buried beneath the earth, he muses:

Only that cant be all of it, he thought. *It cant be. The waste. Not of meat, there is always plenty of meat. They found that out twenty years ago preserving nations and justifying mottoes—granted the nations the meat preserved are worth the preserving with the meat it took gone.* (142)

This strange and startling reference to the war to end all wars, to the war that revealed to a generation the hollowness of its ideals, places Charlotte's death on a par with the death of those who died in vain. Harry protests the waste, and he grasps desperately at the thought that memory remains beyond death: "*Surely memory exists independent of the flesh,*" but immediately he recognizes that it is not true. "*Because it wouldn't know it was memory,* he thought. *It wouldn't know what it was it remembered. So there's got to be the old meat, the old frail ineradicable meat for memory to titillate.*" (142) Harry's insight is, in effect, a refutation of Charlotte's concept of love as an absolute that does not die but leaves you if you are not worthy of it. Neither the love nor the mere reflection of it in memory exists without the living human flesh that created it. Harry's decision to remain alive—so contrary to the lover's traditional desire to join his loved one in death—is an expression of despair, a recognition that as soon as both he and Charlotte are not, nothing remains.

With this evocation of World War I and of a disillusioned generation—a generation which fought desperately for certain romantic ultimates—one is almost tempted to rename "Wild Palms" and call it "A Farewell to Love." Faulkner's story carries Hemingway's *A Farewell to Arms* one step further and sets the love of Catherine Barkley and Frederick Henry into the same category as those other ideals that Frederick Henry emerged from the Po River cleansed of forever. This double-storied book clearly dramatizes the fundamental disagreement of Faulkner and Hemingway on the nature of reality. Hemingway seeks reality in the integrity of feeling; Faulkner seeks it primarily in the immutable conditions of human existence, in man's functional relationship to nature and his fellows.

Because of the outcome of "Old Man" and "Wild Palms," Faulkner's vision remains, in this book, essentially tragic. Yet, despite the dominance of the tragic view, *The Wild Palms* is a kind of turning point in Faulkner's career. The affirmation embodied in the concept of the convict as primitive man, which had been present but muted in the previous novels, is developed into a major motif and will continue to be developed in future works. And the skillful use of the techniques of myth in "Old Man" becomes an increasingly important aspect of the future work.

Go Down, Moses

Faulkner's subject in *Go Down, Moses* (1942) is once again the Southern racial problem. *Absalom, Absalom!* deals with the crime of the white's rejection of the Negro as an equal human being and its punishment. *Go Down, Moses* traces the history of race rela-

McCASLIN GENEALOGY

===== Illegitimate relationship
( ) approximated date

tions and the impact of that history upon the life of the novel's protagonist, Isaac McCaslin. Only three of the seven stories in the book represent Faulkner at his best, but all seven are cemented together by theme into a remarkably unified novel.[1]

As usual in Faulkner's work, the specific problem is made to reflect a general problem. The "curse of his fathers" which descends upon Ike McCaslin's cousin, Roth Edmonds, in "The Fire and the Hearth" is not only the white Southerner's inherited racial bias but the white race's heritage of accumulated moral guilt. Roth is the great-great-great-grandson of the pioneer, Lucius Quintus Carothers McCaslin, Until he is seven, Roth plays, eats, and sleeps with his friend and relative, the Negro Henry Beauchamp. "Then one day the old curse of his fathers, the old haughty ancestral pride based not on any value but on an accident of geography, stemmed not from courage and honor but from wrong and shame, descended to him." (111)* No incident occurs that precipitates the seven-year-old's sudden decision not to allow Henry to sleep in the same bed, as was their custom. He does not understand why he insists that the Negro boy remain on the pallet beside the big bed, but Roth must lie alone "in a rigid fury of the grief he could not explain, the shame he would not admit." (112)

What Roth does, in effect, is to re-enact his ancestor's initial repudiation of the Negro as an equal human being. The act is symbolic of the extension from one generation to another in the South of the separation between the races, each generation re-establishing the old pattern. "Then one day he knew it was grief and was ready to admit it was shame also, wanted to admit it only it was too late then, forever and forever too late." (112) It is too late because Henry has reacted, withdrawn from the role of friend into the role of Sambo—his protection against the humiliation imposed upon him—and the pattern of the traditional Negro-white relationship is newly established.

The incident is more than an explanation of the continuity from one generation to another of the racial barrier. By the time a child reaches the age of seven, he might very well have been

* The Modern Library Edition.
  See the Appendix, pp. 393-396, for a chronology of significant events.

indoctrinated and hence act as Roth does, but Roth's action is described as being impelled by forces below the level of consciousness: "the old curse . . . descended. . . . So he entered his heritage. He ate its bitter fruit." (111, 4) Roth's act is similar to the first cough of a child in a tubercular-ridden family. He does the coughing, but his proclivity to the disease is transmitted to him by his parents. In the same way, the white Southerner is born into a heritage of guilt, and in the same way, the whole human race is born into a heritage of accumulated guilt since the first man and woman sinned.

Faulkner traces, in the first three stories of the novel, the increasing complexity of racial relations in Southern society. "Was," the initial story, describes in the manner of a legend the codified relations of the races in the ante-bellum society. As is usual in Faulkner's ante-bellum stories, the mood of "Was" is nostalgic. The characters are handled with compassion and humor: essentially, however, the story is horrifying. A Negro boy, the half-brother of his white masters, is in love with a slave girl from a distant plantation. Whenever he can, the love-sick boy runs off to be with the girl, whom he cannot marry because the plantation owners cannot decide who will buy which slave for what price to bring the couple together. Each time the slave runs off, one of his two white masters hunts him down as if he were an animal. Such a summary does not serve to convey the spirit of the story Faulkner actually tells. The catalyst that transforms a horror story into a humorous warm, nostalgic tale of the Old South is a feeling of security rooted in the formalized and accepted pattern of Negro-white relations. On the McCaslin plantation, the Negroes live in the plantation house that Lucius Quintus Carothers McCaslin built. Buck and Buddy, his twin sons and heirs, move out of the plantation house after the death of their father. They live in a cabin, while the Negro slaves occupy the big house. The twins, we discover later in the novel, are enlightened men who see the wrong in slavery and who are expiating their father's crime. In this story, however, no motive is given for the twin's choice of residence. In a legend, motive is not important. All that is important is the ritual that the brothers go through each evening of latching the front door of the big house into which all the Negroes have been ushered. The back door is open and the Negroes are free to do as they please, but the daily ritual, symbolizing a formal and hence simplified relationship between white and Negro, is religiously followed. Hunting down the love sick Tomey's Turl is also a ritual. As soon as the twins discover that the boy has run off, Buck puts on his tie and the hunt begins. There is no malice in the pursuit. The brothers expect that periodically Tomey's Turl will run off and that Buck will give chase. To Turl it is a game with formal rules, and to Buck it is a dangerous nuisance because it brings him into the lair of Sophonsiba Beauchamp, who wants a husband. The chase after the Negro, the formal sparring between Buck and Hubert Beauchamp to get Buck to marry Sophonsiba, are as much a part of the codified life as the toddy before the afternoon dinner and the nap afterwards. Buck is almost trapped by the formal social code when he stumbles unwittingly into Sophonsiba's bed. The gentlemanly settlement of a situation involving human beings by a game of poker is fascinating in its simplicity. Emotional and moral questions are subservient to the code.

In contrast to this ritualistic, legendary tale is the third story in the volume, a realistic, beautifully written, deeply moving story of inconsolable grief. With its setting about 1940, the story shatters the image of the Negro that the white Southerner has created to prevent his prejudice from foundering on his sensibilities. The sheriff has witnessed the Negro's display of humanity. Made uncomfortable by what he has seen, he is impelled to describe the incident to his wife and, in the process, recreate the protective image that he needs. He prefaces his story by saying:

"Them damn niggers . . . I swear to godfrey, it's a wonder we have as little trouble with them as we do. Because why? Because they aint human. They look like a man and they walk on their hind legs like a man, and they can talk and you can understand them and you think they are understanding you, at least now and then. But when it comes to the normal human feelings and sentiments of human beings, they might just as well be a damn herd of wild buffaloes." (154)

If the sheriff recognizes the Negro as a fellow human being, he creates for himself an intolerable situation. His segregationist attitude can be maintained only if he insists upon the fundamental difference between the quality of the Negro's humanity and his own. The sheriff is a "little hysterical" as he recalls the Negro, Rider, ripping up the iron cot in the jail and tearing the steel bars out of the wall, resorting to violence to escape thinking of his dead wife. (154) The sheriff obviously recognizes the inconsolable grief of the Negro. He must, therefore, restore the protective image of the Negro as not quite human by recasting each display of anguish he has witnessed or heard about as proof of the Negro's lack of humanity.

"His wife dies on him. All right. But does he grieve? He's the biggest and busiest man at the funeral. Grabs a shovel before they even got the box into the grave they tell me, and starts throwing dirt onto her faster than a slip scraper could have done it." (155)

With its ironic title, "Pantaloon in Black"* is a dramatic and moving portrayal of the Negro. If *Go Down, Moses*, with its related but independent stories, may be said to have a climax, this story serves the climactic function. The preceding stories are preludes to it; the four stories that follow are thematically derived from the basic recognition of the equal humanity of the Negro.

In the second story, "The Fire and the Hearth," the process which dissolves the formal and simple code governing the relations of the races is traced. The formal pattern of the ante-bellum society was based upon the mutual acceptance by the two races of the Negro's inferiority. The solidity of the racial code in this society is perhaps best revealed by the indifference of Negro and white to the blood relationship of Tomey's Turl and the McCaslin twins. They are all sons of the same man, and despite the enlightened and sympathetic attitude of Buck and Buddy, they treat Tomey's Turl not as a brother but as a Negro.

Many decades pass between the events of "Was" and those in "The Fire and the Hearth." The racial pattern is no longer capable of withstanding the strain placed upon it by the complicated interrelationships of Negro and white. Lucas Beauchamp, son of Tomey's Turl, and hence grandson of Lucius Quintus Carothers McCaslin asserts his integrity and individuality by acting as a man

---

* *Pantaloon* is a *buffoon*.

rather than a Negro. The Edmondses are descended from McCaslin's daughter. Lucas is a direct descendant of the patriarch, but because he has Negro blood, he must live and act as a Negro. Just as his son Henry is to grow up with Roth Edmonds, Lucas grows up with Zack, his cousin. When Zack's wife dies in childbirth, Zack takes Lucas's wife, Molly, into his house to care for the baby. For six months, because he is a Negro, Lucas accepts this violation of his home. Then he goes to Zack and demands the return of his wife. Molly does come back to her own house, but now Lucas can never know if Zack has exercised his seigniorial rights and used Molly sexually. Lucas decides that he must kill Zack and accept the consequences of his action. In asserting himself against the white man, Lucas is violating the pattern of the society. In the encounter, Zack treats Lucas as an equal and therefore he, too, breaks through the racial barriers. Zack's son, Roth, is nursed and raised by Molly and, as he grows older, his emotional involvement with the only mother he ever knew makes compliance with the traditional racial pattern difficult.

Despite its rather silly and makeshift plot, the story does effectively reveal that the racial code in the modern South lacks the firm foundation of the code in the ante-bellum society. Because the white man is so frequently forced to recognize that the code lacks justification, he insists upon it with hysterical blatancy. The Negro continues to accept the role assigned to him, but not with the unquestioning resignation of Tomey's Turl, who not only refuses the legacy left him by his father, but refuses the opportunity for freedom that his brothers, Buck and Buddy, offer him.

Living under such social patterns results in a fracturing of personality. A man like Roth Edmonds accepts the code as his heritage: he is white first and human being afterward, rather than a human being who happens to have white skin. But the Negro perhaps even more than the white man suffers internally. He has had to bury his real self beneath the assumed mask of Sambo. Unlike the white, however, he is closer to his primitive sources in nature. He works the land and he lives by the sweat of his body. Lucas gambles nothing except his own sweat for his subsistence. In contrast, the product of Roth's labor is an abstraction—money. He does not pit himself against the land, but expends his energy work-

Ing with figures in ledgers and with bank statements. The white man, individually and collectively, is cut off from the land. He has been for so many generations, even centuries, that the way he thinks and acts is alien to the basic pattern of existence. The Negro consciousness, only a few generations removed from the forests of Africa, is not buried under so many layers of civilization. In his primitive religious rituals, for example, he comes closer to a God whose living presence he can feel than does the white man, whose God is an abstraction approached rationally. Furthermore, the Negro has not yet camouflaged the reality of the life-death pattern through the use of soothing concepts that tend to distort the truth. He is therefore attuned to the vicissitudes and uncertainties of existence and accepts what the white man vainly fights. He can endure. Because he is more primitive, the Negro is more responsive to the deep wellsprings of his emotional being. The passion that grips Rider in "Pantaloon in Black" terrifies the white sheriff not only because he must recognize the humanity of the Negro but also because he must face what his white tradition has taught him to deny: the boiling cauldron of primitive responses deep within his own being. These responses are so deeply buried in the white consciousness that they can be exhumed only through disciplined ritual such as Ike submits to in "The Old People." Being closer to his primitive association with the world of nature, the Negro follows a pattern of life that is not at variance with the pattern of existence in nature.

In "The Fire and the Hearth" (the title combines an elemental force of nature with the symbol of elemental human relationship, the family), the solidity of Lucas's relationship with Molly is threatened when he violates the land. Lucas digs into the Indian mound to hide his still. The overhang sloughs, and as he leaps back from the falling dirt, Lucas is struck "a final blow squarely in the face with something larger than a clod—a blow not vicious so much as merely heavy-handed, a sort of final admonitory pat from the spirit of darkness and solitude, the old earth, perhaps the old ancestors themselves." (38)

Obsessed by the dream of finding buried gold, Lucas sacrifices his work on the land, and only when his wife nearly kills herself carrying away his divining machine does he come to his senses.

Molly refuses—after so many years of marriage—to live with him until he gives up his search for the gold. In explaining to Roth why she must have a divorce, she declares "'Because God say, "What's rendered to My earth, it belong to Me unto I resurrect it. And let him or her touch it, and beware." And I'm afraid. I got to go. I got to be free of him.'" (102) Lucas's temporary aberration, his separation from the pattern of existence imposed by working and living close to the land, nearly destroys his marriage, puts out the fire that has burned in the hearth of his home since the day he married Molly. His wife's uncompromising belief in the inviolability of the land saves him and their marriage.

Roth argues with Lucas, threatens him, and finally arranges for the divorce Molly wants. Roth's attachment to Molly, his realization that something occurred between his own father and Lucas over a woman, involve him so deeply in the lives of the Negroes that the formal barrier between white and black is continually threatened. Despite the penetration of the pattern, Roth treats the Negroes as children. And his allegiance to the racial code remains strong enough for him to be amazed at "the old man who had emerged out of the tragic complexity of his motherless childhood as the husband of the woman who had been the only mother he ever knew, who had never once said 'sir' to his white skin and whom he knew even called him Roth behind his back, let alone to his face." (130-1)

This conflict between an inherited racial code and the actuality of human relations is symbolic of the complexities and tensions that tear modern man apart. It is this pattern of tension and guilt that is Isaac McCaslin's heritage. In the two hunting stories that follow in the volume, the demarcation between the woods and civilization is sharp. In Ike's puberty ritual, Faulkner dramatizes an antidote to the terrible effect of modern society upon the soul of man. The alienation of social man from the land in his pursuit of money and the social values it buys impels the search for wholeness and peace recorded in these two stories. That search for the real human being buried beneath the social man is also brought on by the destructive fragmentation of personality such as that produced by the relationship of Roth and Lucas, and by the unresolvable conflicts and tensions of ambivalent feelings—the Negro as "nigger," the Negro as fellow human being.

The hunt itself is a condition of natural existence: the strong feeding upon the weak, the weak utilizing innate resources of coloration or cunning, agility or intelligence for self-preservation. In such elemental conditions, the human animal, too, must develop and utilize innate resources. In the woods, man, within the pattern of natural existence, strips away the layers of artificiality imposed upon him by society and bares the vital forces of his inner being. By confronting his essential self, he acknowledges his relation to the world of nature, its cyclical pattern of death and regeneration, and hence his own role in that pattern.

This moment of confrontation constitutes a profound religious experience, a transcendence of time and place, a union with God. It is this experience that leaves young Isaac trembling at the end of "The Old People." Faulkner dramatizes the moment of confrontation by structuring his story upon a puberty ritual, the full meaning of which he expounds through a central symbol—blood. The story is developed around two major scenes. The first is a tableau, set in the forest. Rain is falling; the woods are somber and gray. Lying on the earth is a dead deer, the blood from its slashed jugular flowing into the earth. On the face of the initiate, Ike, the blood of the slain deer has been daubed by the hand of his sponsor, Sam Fathers. Blood unites the initiate, the sponsor, the dead deer, and the earth. This union in blood makes meaningful the final rite of the initiation. In this second major scene, Sam Fathers raises his arm and greets a buck: " 'Oleh, Chief . . . Grandfather.' " (184) As he utters his greeting, Fathers, who has stood behind the initiate, steps to Ike's side, signifying that the boy has become a man, has understood and accepted the code of his sponsor.

The meaning of what has taken place is clarified by a comment that Ike's cousin, Cass Edmonds, makes to Ike about Sam Fathers. " 'When he was born, all his blood on both sides, except the little white part, knew things that had been tamed out of our blood so long ago that we have not only forgotten them, we have to live together in herds to protect ourselves from our own sources.' " (167)

The bloods of three races flow in Sam's veins. His father was a Chickasaw Indian chief, his mother a quadroon. Because of his mixed heritage, Fathers reflects the confusion of the South. He is not " 'betrayed by the black blood and not wilfully betrayed by his mother, but betrayed by her all the same, who had bequeathed him not only the blood of slaves but even a little of the very blood which had enslaved it; himself his own battleground, the scene of his own vanquishment and the mausoleum of his defeat.' " (168)

Sam is only one-eighth Negro, but that drop of Negro blood compels him to live as a Negro in the former slave quarters on the Edmonds plantation. He thinks of himself as a Chickasaw Indian, but so long as he remains within the white social structure, he must assume the status of an inferior. Fathers, like most people living in the South, is super-sensitive on the subject of his blood heritage. Though he lives with the Negroes, he keeps apart from people both white and black, befriending only the young Ike and the full-blooded Chickasaw, Jobaker, who comes in from the woods for a monthly visit to Sam. Fathers, says Cass Edmonds, is like

". . . an old lion or a bear in a cage . . . He was born in the cage and has been in it all his life; he knows nothing else. Then he smells something. It might be anything, any breeze blowing past anything and then into his nostrils. But there for a second was the hot sand or the cane-brake that he never even saw himself, might not even know if he did see it and probably does know he couldn't hold his own with it if he got back to it. But that's not what he smells then. It was the cage he smelled. He hadn't smelled the cage until that minute. Then the hot sand or the brake blew into his nostrils and blew away, and all he could smell was the cage." (167)

Sam's battle with his mixed blood lasts until Jobaker dies. Then, as the last living Chickasaw in the area, though his blood is tainted, Sam Fathers claims his heritage. Taking nothing with him, even refusing transportation, he breaks out of the cage in which he was born and goes to live in the woods. Sam Fathers returns to his sources.

For Sam, the return is easier than for the white boy Isaac. Sam is only a few decades removed from the jungle of his African ancestors and the forest of his Indian progenitors. Ike McCaslin's is an ancient, civilized heritage, and therefore what is close to the surface in Sam Fathers is buried deep within Ike. The indoctrination process preceding the puberty ritual must strip away the accumulated layers of inherited artificiality and reveal to him the forces in his unconscious, "the things that have been tamed out" of his blood.

From his first brief sojourn in the woods when he is ten, Ike brings back "an unforgettable sense of the big woods—not a quality dangerous or particularly inimical, but profound, sentient, gigantic and brooding, amid which he had been permitted to go to and fro at will, unscathed, why he knew not, but dwarfed and, until he had drawn honorably blood worthy of being drawn, alien." (175-6) Ike's uninitiated state is not the only thing that makes the boy an alien in the woods. Like Sam Fathers, whose allegiances are revealed in a trinity of blood lines, Isaac's are revealed in a trinity of fathers. His own father, Uncle Buck, nearly seventy when Ike was born, binds him to the past, to the heritage of guilt that his race incurred by enslaving a people. His cousin, Cass Edmonds, sixteen years his senior and more father than cousin, trains him to assume the responsibility of the plantation and to accept his place in the white society. Sam Fathers (whose name is meaningful) teaches him the code of the natural world and leads him back to his sources in nature.

Ike eventually tries to choose the pattern of existence that Sam Fathers offers rather than the social pattern that is Cass's and his own heritage. Sam indoctrinates the boy by telling him stories "about the old days and the People whom he [Sam] had not had time ever to know and so could not remember." (171) Sam talks about what he himself has never consciously experienced. The knowledge he offers the boy is the knowledge of his blood. Blood connects the past and the present and the future, destroying chronological time.

. . . to the boy those old times would cease to be old times and would become a part of the boy's present, not only as if they had happened yesterday but as if they were still happening, the men who walked through them actually walking in breath and air and casting an actual shadow on the earth they had not quitted. And more: as if some of them had not happened yet but would occur tomorrow, until at last it would seem to the boy that he himself had not come into existence yet, that none of his race nor the other subject race which his people had brought with them into the land had come here yet; that although it had been his grandfather's and then his father's and uncle's and was now his cousin's and someday would be his own land which he and Sam hunted over, their hold upon it actually was as trivial and without reality as the now faded and archaic script in the chancery book in Jefferson which allocated it to them and that it was he, the boy, who was the guest here and Sam Father's voice the mouthpiece of the host. (171)

Isaac's indoctrination leads him back through time, beyond the crimes of his immediate ancestors and beyond the crimes of his civilized heritage, back to his sources—the forest, the earth. The people in Sam's stories who cast "an actual shadow on the earth they had not quitted" are Chickasaw Indians, the Old People of the earth, pristine man, as the title of the story indicates.

When he shoots his first deer, drawing blood worthy of being drawn in an honorable manner, and his sponsor steps to his side, Ike enters his true heritage. The forest "tremendous, attentive, impartial and omniscient . . . the eye of the ancient immortal Umpire" becomes "less than inimical now and never to be inimical again since the buck still and forever leaped." (181, 178) At the same moment, Ike feels the existence and presence of God, experiencing a transcendence of time and place and of individual identity. His breathing stops. There "was only his heart, his blood, and in the following silence the wilderness ceased to breathe also, leaning, stooping overhead with its breath held, tremendous and impartial and waiting." (182) When Sam greets the buck, Ike "marked . . . forever one with the wilderness" by the blood on his face has experienced a oneness with all life through all time. (178) That night, his cousin, who was also initiated by Sam, puts into words the boy's spiritual experience. Time and death do not exist, Cass says. Out of his "instant of immortality, the buck sprang, forever immortal." All the blood, " 'hot and strong for living, pleasuring' " has soaked back into the earth, and the " 'earth dont want to just keep things, hoard them; it wants to use them again.' " (186)

Isaac has accepted death as part of life. With the blood of the buck that the boy has slain, Fathers "consecrated and absolved him from weakness and regret . . . not from love and pity for all which lived and ran and then ceased to live in a second in the very midst of splendor and speed, but from weakness and regret." (182) This code, evolved from a confrontation of the true pattern of existence in nature, is the code that Ike chooses.

"The Old People" is one of the most imaginative expressions in contemporary literature of the buried need in modern man for religious faith, and an understanding of it also clarifies the symbolism of "The Bear." As an introduction to the meaning of "The Bear," two aspects of "the Old People" require emphasis. The return of Sam and of Ike to their sources is clearly an attempt to plunge deep into the unconscious and face the essential human being and his relation to the essential pattern of nature. Ike retrieves what has been tamed out of his blood, and by doing so discovers a code to live by—acceptance of natural conditions with pity and love but without weakness and regret. This code is further elaborated in "The Bear." The virtues of the code are those which touch the heart: honor, pride, pity, justice, courage and love. These virtues of the heart are knowable only when the artificialities imposed by society are peeled away and the essential man is bared. What is particularly significant is that the process of getting down to essentials must be executed away from the civilized world. Society is the enemy; it warps man and it warps his life. In the world of nature, the pattern of existence is clear and simple, and man's relation to the pattern is obvious. In society, however, pattern is superimposed upon pattern until essentials are indistinguishable and almost unknowable. Social man's relations to these imposed patterns and to his fellow men are so complex, so mixed up with feelings and ideas, traditions and mores, that he is necessarily pulled in many opposing directions and whatever he does produces conflict and confusion.

Anyone who is born and brought up within society is necessarily divided. Deep within him is the natural man; superimposed is the social man. Between society and the woods, between social man and the buried natural man, there is an unbridgeable gap. Ike uncovers the natural man within him, but he is never able to fuse into one harmonious being the social and the natural aspects of his personality. In "The Bear" this gap is symbolized by Ike's failure not only to create a new world, a society cleansed of its guilty heritage, but also by his failure to have any effect at all on the society which he feels he has to repudiate. When Ike tries to live in society by the code he learns in the woods, his attempt founders on the very complexity it should have simplified.

"The Bear" is a difficult short novel because it is filled with symbolism and because the relationship of the long fourth section to the hunting story is not immediately apparent. However, keeping "The Old People" in mind, we can recognize that the hunting sections of "The Bear" depict a return to the essential in man and nature, a stripping away of the imposed social artificialities and a baring of the natural man.

The group in Major DeSpain's party are hunters because they respond to a primitive desire to confront the natural. On their semi-annual trips they cut themselves off from the civilized world, its attachments, routines, obligations, and codes. They take with them only enough food for the first few meals. After that they are dependent for food upon their skill as hunters. They join the other animals in the forest in the pursuit of subsistence, accepting the brutal pattern of nature and adopting codes of conduct and thought in accord with that pattern. Their pilgrimages are a ritualistic observance of primitive instincts so far below the level of social consciousness that color and blood, so important to their lives in society, are meaningless. Among the hunters, a class system exists, but men are not ranked according to birth or race, but according to the skill and courage displayed in the hunt. Ash, the Negro cook, is not at the bottom of the hierarchy because he is a Negro, but because he is not fit, as he proves when he goes out with Ike, to be a hunter. Boon, who has a trace of Chickasaw blood, is not automatically a woodsman and a hunter because he is part Indian. He is, in fact, fit only for the role of retainer because he is unskilled and incompetent. Sam Fathers, who in society must live in Negro quarters, is the chief of the hunters. He has the skills and virtues necessary for supremacy.

Away from the artificialities of social life, these men cannot ignore the rules imposed by nature. They are "ordered and compelled by and within the wilderness in the ancient and unremitting contest according to the ancient and immitigable rules which voided all regrets and brooked no quarter." (191-2) If the attenuated consciousness of civilized man turns away from the brutal facts of existence in nature—the struggle for survival and inevitable death—the facts are not altered. Social man is merely weakened by his attempt to gloss over the truth, or ignore it, or deny it. The truth is fearful and to accept it takes courage. Fear induces respect for the truth, and it initiates the process of developing the skills and virtues necessary for survival.

In the hunt, man returns to his sources. The ritual of indoctrination and initiation that Ike goes through in "The Old People" is repeated in "The Bear." Not until Ike has taken off his watch and discarded his compass is he worthy of seeing the bear "which ran in his knowledge before he ever saw it."

He had already relinquished, of his will, because of his need, in humility and peace and without regret, yet apparently that had not been enough, the leaving of the gun was not enough. He stood for a moment —a child, alien and lost in the green and soaring gloom of the markless wilderness. Then he relinquished completely to it. It was the watch and the compass. He was still tainted. (208)

In the critical scene in which the fyce attacks the bear, Ike learns the meaning of courage, but more significantly, when he comes so close to the old bear that he can see a tick on its leg, he undergoes a profound spiritual experience to which he and his cousin eventually attribute his repudiation of his inheritance. To put into words the meaning of that experience, Cass reads Keats's "Ode on a Grecian Urn," the poem which encloses in its lines the finite and the infinite, the transitory and the permanent. Ike's experience is religious, a repetition of the scene in "The Old People" in which the boy knew a oneness with nature, opened his soul to truth and understood that the dead "buck still and forever leaped."

This profound religious experience is dramatized in "The Bear" by the use of myth. The major participants in the story are rendered bigger than life. The old bear is the biggest, craftiest, strongest of all bears, and he is bigger, craftier, and stronger still in the imaginations of the men who pursue him. Lion is a savage, wild dog, more lion, more wolf, than dog. He is a "cold and almost impersonal malignance like some natural force." (218) Sam Fathers is "the chief, the prince." Ike, more at home in the woods than any of the older hunters because he has opened his soul to what they can only sense, is second only to Sam Fathers. The hunt for Old Ben and his death is a mythical rendition of the life-and-death pattern in nature. Ike develops a reverence for the old bear, one of the mighty in nature, and though he "should have hated and feared Lion," he cannot, because the pattern of nature is unalterable; and Ike is learning to accept it with pity and love for the slain but without weakness and regret. (209)

The experience of essence is confined to Ike and Sam. The other hunters remain tainted, fettered by their ties to the other world. The participation of the clumsy Boon in the killing of Old Ben, the death of the bear, and the collapse of Sam Fathers at the moment the bear dies (all of which takes place in an isolated area) symbolize the isolation of Ike's spiritual experience. It cannot be transferred to the realm of social consciousness. Sam Fathers prepares for his own death by training Lion, and Ike surmises that the Indian is ready to die. Sam Fathers, who has led Ike back to his sources to confront what was tamed out of his blood, who in effect embodies Ike's knowledge and skill, is solitary and childless. Why Sam must die is revealed in the passage in which Ike ponders Sam's willingness to die. "*He was old. He had no children, no people, none of his blood anywhere above earth that he would ever meet again. And even if he were to, he could not have touched it, spoken to it, because for seventy years now he had had to be a negro. It was almost over now and he was glad.*" (215)

Sam Fathers is isolated by his Negro blood. And it is precisely Ike's inability to apply the code he learned in the forest to the racial situation in society that isolates the spiritual experience that Sam represents. Both Old Ben and Sam die in seclusion. Old Ben crosses a river before he is bayed. Present at the kill are Lion and the dogs, and Sam, Ike, and Boon, "the plebeian," the shiftless retainer, one of the insignificant in the natural hierarchy of the primitive world. (222) Boon is the one who drives the knife into the old bear's heart, not out of courage but out of fidelity to the brute an-

inial the bear has in its clutches. Boon, an image of weak and frail
humanity, helps to bring to a close the experience represented
by the hunt. It is also indicated that he serves Sam Fathers as he
had the bear.

Throughout the story, society is a threat to the woods. It "claws"
at the natural world, gradually encroaching upon it. At the same
time, throughout the story, nature is referred to continually as a
constant, as immemorial and eternal. It is not the woods themselves, nor the natural world, therefore, that is overrun by society,
but the spiritual experience Ike undergoes in the "tremendous, attentive, impartial, and omniscient" deep woods. (181) The sale of
the hunting camp right after the death of Old Ben to the logging
company, except for the small area containing the graves of Sam
and Lion and the bear's paw, symbolizes the encroachment of social
commitment. When in the final section of the story, Ike, still in
his teens, returns once more to the woods, the logging train which
has always been there, which long before should have symbolized
the eventual destruction of the woods, but which seemed to Ike a
toy, now becomes a destructive symbol. The impressionistic style
of the description indicates the loss, not specifically of the woods
but of an experience that has left its mark but cannot be sustained.

It had been harmless then . . . They would hear it going out, loaded,
not quite so fast now yet giving its frantic and toylike illusion of crawling speed, not whistling now to conserve steam, flinging its bitten la-
boring miniature puffing into the immemorial woodsface with frantic
and bootless vainglory, empty and noisy and puerile, carrying to no des-
tination or purpose sticks which left nowhere any scar or stump as the
child's toy loads and transports and unloads its dead sand and rushes
back for more, tireless and unceasing and rapid yet never quite so fast
as the Hand which plays with it moves the toy burden back to load the
toy again. But it was different now. It was the same train . . . yet this
time it was as though the train (and not only the train but himself, not
only his vision which had seen it and his memory which remembered it
but his clothes too . . . had brought with it into the doomed wilderness even before the actual axe the shadow and portent of the new mill
. . . and he knew now . . . that after this time he . . . would return
no more. (320-1)

On this final visit to the woods, Ike visits the grave of Sam and places tobacco and candy in a tin box for the spirit of the Indian. On his way to find Boon, he salutes an old snake (whose fangs he escapes) as " 'Chief . . . Grandfather.' " (330) And in the final scene, Boon, forever incompetent, comprehending nothing of the experience in which he has participated, is surrounded by squirrels that he is hunting while he hammers wildly and hopelessly at his dismantled and useless rifle. In a hoarse, strangled voice, he warns Ike off: " 'Get out of here! Dont touch them! Dont touch a one of them! They're mine!' " (331) Boon's illusion of possession is the illusion of mankind.

It is an illusion because neither Boon nor any other man can possess anything in nature. The link between Ike's experience in the woods and his experience in the world of society is the land. The pattern of existence which he has understood and accepted in the woods, and the virtues he has developed in accord with his acceptance, are not the pattern and virtues extant in society. Social man's initial error is to think that he can own the land. That error alienates him from truth and from himself. Only by recognizing his own role in nature can he live truly. His illusion that he can possess things culminates in his attempt to possess other human beings. The falseness in the social pattern, mirrored in the relations of Negro and white, is clear to Ike after he has experienced truth. Between the day at twelve that he kills his first deer, and the day at twenty-one that he renounces his patrimony, Ike discovers the extent of guilt in his heritage. In the old ledgers kept by his father and uncle he learns that his grandfather fathered a child by Tomasina, his own illegitimate half-breed daughter. Lucius Quintus Carothers McCaslin was so impervious to the humanity of the Negro that he could treat his own daughter, because she had Negro blood, as if she were a possession to be used and discarded. Tomasina's mother, Eunice, drowns herself on Christmas day, apparently when she learns that Tomasina is pregnant by her own father. The incredulous entry in the ledger by Uncle Buddy questioning his brother's notation about Eunice's death, "*Who in hell ever heard of a niger drownding him self*," reveals the attitude toward the Negro's humanity of even these enlightened men who freed their slaves before the Civil War was fought. (267)

In the woods, Ike learned the oneness ot all nature, and he learned that blood does not matter, that Sam Fathers, Negro, white, and Indian, is Sam Fathers, a man. He also learned love and pity for all that lived. In repudiating the crime of his grandfather and therefore the crime of his society, Ike is sincerely trying to live by the code of nature. But during the discussion on that October evening in the commissary of the plantation, Cass Edmonds suggests that Ike is not facing his responsibilities, that he is escaping them. In a significant exchange, Ike maintains, " 'I am free.' " Cass, however, declares, " 'No, not now nor ever, we from them nor they from us.' " (299) Cass speaks the truth; though Ike sacrifices everything, including his marriage, to expiate the violation of the land and of man, he is not free of the curse of his heritage. At the very moment that he acknowledges that the Negro is better than the white because he is not oppressed by a heritage of moral guilt and because he is close to his sources in the earth, Ike's social conditioning is operating. He pauses almost imperceptibly before making his declaration that the Negro is better than the white: ". . . it was not a pause, barely a falter even, possibly appreciable only to himself, as if he couldn't speak even to McCaslin, even to explain his repudiation, that which to him too, even in the act of escaping (and maybe this was the reality and the truth of his need to escape) was heresy: so that even in escaping he was taking with him more of that evil and unregenerate old man who could summon, because she was his property, a human being because she was old enough and female, to his widower's house and get a child on her and then dismiss her because she was of an inferior race . . . than even he had feared." (294)

Ike does take with him too much of Old Carothers to fulfill the destiny that he declares God chose for him.[2] In his historical approach to his repudiation, Ike envisions God as reserving the new world on the American continent as a place where mankind can start all over again, free of his guilty heritage of rapine and enslavement, to create the kind of world he should have created from the beginning. But on the new continent, man again fails; he commits the same old sins. Cod, fortunately, is patient, and provides man another opportunity to start afresh—the Civil War, a baptism of blood to cleanse the old sins. Again man fails. This time it is not the Southerner who is primarily at fault. It is the carpetbagger, says Ike, who comes to the defeated region, creating a reign of terror, sowing the seeds of lasting bitterness, and bringing with him the worthless men who will become the Ku Klux Klanners. Ike's own father and uncle, with God's help, saw the light and made a move in the right direction by freeing their slaves. Now Ike sees himself as God ordained to start the new world. But Ike takes too much of Old Carothers with him to serve as Moses leading the Negroes out of bondage.

Ike is an old man in "Delta Autumn." He has lived within society for many years, each autumn going into the woods, which he must travel farther and farther each year to find. When he meets Roth's mistress and discovers that though she looks white she has a drop of Negro blood, Ike's reaction is almost instinctive. The social man, the product of his social conditioning, is stronger than the natural man, exposed and nurtured by Sam Fathers. Ike pleads with the girl to go to the North and marry someone of her own race. The girl's response, " 'Old man . . . have you lived so long and forgotten so much that you dont remember anything you ever knew or felt or even heard about love,' " effectively dramatizes the reason for Ike's failure. (363) He has not been able to eradicate his prejudice. And when the girl leaves, he lies shaking and cold. By repudiating his inheritance, he made an attempt at personal expiation, but he was not able to resolve the conflict of social man.

And the tragedy is that Ike is far more sensitive and far more advanced because he has come closer to the natural within himself than the other white men in the South. In the final and title story, "Go Down, Moses," Gavin Stevens, with his doctorate from Heidelberg, is continually surprised and continually exasperated by the Negroes, treating them as children, as inferiors. He is kind and gentle and generous, but he can feel no true rapport with them. He is too much the social man to understand a person like Molly, who, close to her primitive sources, can respond to the feelings of her blood. Before her grandson is executed, and though she has had no word from him or of him for a long time, Molly knows that he is dying or dead. She walks seventeen miles into Jefferson to seek help. Molly is reacting to promptings far below the level of consciousness. This blood response which is, for the most part, ig-

noted by the whites, is the Negro way of life. Ike describes this response in "The Bear," when he speaks of the Bible's direct appeal
to the heart. The simple Biblical tales express fundamental human
experiences that the mind may not be able to grasp, but which the
heart understands. The ritualistic chant of Molly and her companions for the dead is an ancient, primitive expression of grief. It is
not a prescribed ritual so much as a natural response to feeling, like
the unconscious wringing of hands in despair or the slow swaying
of the body in anguish. The lament, equating the death of the
boy with the enslavement of the race, articulates the racial grief of
a people torn from its natural habitat and brought into an alien
world. Roth Edmonds, on whose plantation Molly's grandson
was raised becomes, in the lament, the symbol of the white race
that sold the Negro into bondage. Had Ike not rejected his patrimony, he, rather than Roth, would have been the symbolic oppressor. Significantly, however, in the lament, the Negro still awaits
a Moses. Ike has failed in his God-ordained mission. Roth, as symbol of the oppressor, is particularly interesting because he typifies
the complexity of racial relations in the modern world. Ironically,
Molly, who condemns him, is the only mother Roth knew, and his
emotional attachment to the old Negro woman is very deep. Roth
also could love a girl with Negro blood, enough to go and live with
her, at least for a short time, while he tried to decide if he could
marry her. His allegiance to the traditional racial code is too strong,
and he cannot take that final step. By this woman, who is his own
distant relative, he has an illegitimate son. Basically, Roth's crime
is the same as his ancestor's. But Roth cannot blithely deny the humanity of the Negro as could Lucius Quintus Carothers McCaslin.
The complexity of the racial relations is dramatized also in the feeling of intrusion that Gavin experiences when he walks into the
room of the lamenters. Gavin knows that he does not belong there.
He is too much a product of social conditioning to enter suddenly
the emotional world of the Negro. The important distinction here
is that Gavin is an intruder not because he is white and Molly is
black. Miss Worsham comes from the same background that
Gavin does, but she has lived with Hamp and his wife. To her, the
Negroes are fellow human beings. When Gavin apologizes for in-
truding, Miss Worsham says: "It's all right . . . It's our grief."

(381) Miss Worsham is a minor character with a minor role in the novel, but she is a symbol of the Southerner who has thrown over the traditional code that separates the races.

Five stories in *Go Down, Moses* concern the relations of the races, and these enclose the two hunting stories. The very structure of the novel reflects the isolated experience that Ike undergoes in the woods: social man and natural man cannot merge. And they never really do in Faulkner's novels.

Go Down, Moses marks the end of Faulkner's great period of creativity. It deserves inclusion in that period mainly because it contains "The Bear," one of his greatest stories. Qualitatively and quantitatively, the work of the next twenty years does not compare with the artistic achievement of the short period between the publication in 1929 of *Sartoris* and the publication in 1940 of *The Hamlet*.* The technical reasons for the comparative failure of the later works I shall attempt to point out in the succeeding chapters. Why Faulkner reached his artistic peak relatively early in his career, however, must remain a matter of speculation, until we learn more than we now know about the writer's personal life. Possibly the reason is that once Faulkner worked his way out of the personal despair recorded in his early and greatest works, his novels tended to be inspired by idea more than feeling. Generally, as we shall see, the art of the later period fails to achieve the fusion of theme and story, idea and feeling that characterizes *The Sound and the Fury, Light in August,* and *Absalom, Absalom!*

* *The Hamlet* is discussed later as a volume of the Snopes trilogy.

Intruder in the Dust

Intruder in the Dust (1948) is Faulkner's most provincial novel.[1] It is, in fact, the only novel that he wrote which can be classified as a regional novel. In this book, his vision does not penetrate beyond the specific Southern problem. Faulkner here limits himself to an exploration of the soul-rending dilemma of the intelligent, sensitive white Southerner who recognizes the Negro as equal human being but who cannot free himself from the racial prejudice of his Southern heritage.

Faulkner's analysis of the Southern consciousness illuminates the complex psychological and social forces that make the intelligent white Southerner a unique phenomenon of the twentieth century. But because Faulkner treats his subject as a special regional problem—everyone not born a white Southerner is an Outlander—the significance and value of his book as art is minimal. Of even more importance, perhaps, in accounting for the failure of the novel as a work of art is Faulkner's assumption of the role of spokesman for the South. He sacrifices his art to social analysis and preaching. The result is a propaganda novel. The melodramatic plot in which two boys—a Negro and a white—and an old woman open a grave to prove that the Negro, Lucas Beauchamp, about to be lynched for the murder of a white man, is innocent, is too slight a story to sustain the weight of the rhetoric Faulkner heaps upon it. Aside from the sensitive and brilliant analysis of the young hero's racial consciousness, the only scenes which have artistic merit are those in which Faulkner creates the lynch atmosphere of the town. These scenes are superbly rendered.

Intruder in the Dust combines two types of stories, both Faulkner favorites—the murder mystery and the transition of a young

STEVENS GENEALOGY

boy to adulthood. The young protagonist's role in the mystery drama precipitates his maturation. At the end of the novel, Southern Boy has become Southern Man. This regional drama of social maturation has three stages. The first begins when the twelve-year-old Chick Mallison, indoctrinated since birth into the traditional code governing race relations, encounters Lucas Beauchamp. In the second stage, Chick saves Lucas from being lynched and rejects his society and its racial code. In the third stage, the young man is reconciled to his society and his heritage.

The central conflict is psychological rather than social. Chick is torn between the impulses of his heart and his allegiance to the racial code. The truth the heart reveals is the Negro as equal human being; the code proclaims the Negro inferior. The two are irreconcilable, for once the assurance of white superiority is shattered, the prescriptions of the code are illogical, immoral, and unjustifiable. The sensitive Southerner, like Chick, is therefore torn between an unshakable allegiance to a tradition, and a conviction that the tradition is unjustifiable.

Charles Mallison, Jr., who is identified by the narrator only once or twice throughout the novel, is Southern White Boy, brought up in a society in which the servility of the Negro is not merely a pattern of racial relationship but a doctrine. The childhood companion of Southern White Boy, in this and a number of other Faulkner novels, is a Negro boy. The white child adapts very early in life, therefore, to the dichotomy of Southern social existence. The child, incapable of logical distinctions, unquestioningly accepts these irreconcilables as the natural order of things. By the time he achieves maturity, he is impervious to logic. In *Go Down, Moses*, Faulkner describes that critical moment when Southern White Boy and his Negro friend realize that the code supersedes friendship. Inevitably for a boy like Chick Mallison the racial code is an invisible aspect of his personality. As Southern Boy, his character is naturally shaped by a sense of continuity with the past and a strong feeling of belonging to his community. He is nourished on stories of his ancestors' lives, their actions, attitudes, and beliefs. He is made aware of the family's role in the history and life of the community. For him, the community becomes an extension of his own family. Like a fly being inextricably woven into a spider's web,

Southern Boy is bound in a tight mesh of allegiances and loyalties. Every child, of course, is; but the web encasing the Southern child is tighter and more intricate. Its design is inspired by that sense of vanished glory which intensifies a need for communal and familial justification.

Unfortunately for Chick's peace of mind, he is impressionable, sensitive, and honest. Despite his social indoctrination, he cannot ignore the truth his heart perceives. He tries hard, but fails. His initial encounter with Lucas occurs when Chick is twelve. Hunting rabbits on the Edmonds plantation, he falls into a creek. The old mulatto, Lucas Beauchamp, a descendant of Lucius Quintus Carothers McCaslin, the founder of the plantation, witnesses Chick's dunking and brings the boy to his cabin.* Lucas is a strong, arrogant personality. He takes pride in his ancestry, and though in his conduct he observes the forms imposed by the racial code, his personality blazes through the Negro mask that he wears.

Something in the old Negro's attitude toward him reminds Chick of his own grandfather. Lucas treats the white boy as if they were of the same race, separated only by many years. In the absence of Edmonds, who invited Chick to hunt on the plantation, Lucas assumes the role of protector and host. Sitting before the fire in the cabin, Chick suffers a moral and psychological crisis. As a boy of good breeding, he respects and obeys his elders; as a shivering wet hunter, he responds to the brusque, kind hospitality of Lucas; as a hungry twelve-year-old, he submits when Lucas orders him to eat. At the same time, the Negro cabin, the "smell of Negro" permeating the comforter covering his naked body forcibly remind him that he is a white boy and that Lucas's attitude and manner violate the established pattern of racial relations. Instinctively, Chick responds to Lucas as he would to his own grandfather, but the code decrees that the Negro must be servile to the whites. Chick forces himself to establish the proper relationship between white and Negro by proferring money to pay Lucas for his hospitality. Lucas refuses to be Negro. He stares coldly at the boy. Chick throws the money on the floor. Immediately, he is ashamed and angry—ashamed because by offering money, he violated the dictate of his heart, and angry because as a white boy he was humiliated

* See the McCaslin Genealogy, p. 231.

by a Negro. Lucas orders Chick's Negro hunting companion to pick
up the coins and return them to Chick. He then sends the boy off
with the admonition, " 'Now go on and shoot your rabbit . . .
And stay out of that creek.' " (16)* Chick deliberately refrains
from shooting a rabbit, and he throws the coins into the creek.

For a long time afterwards, "writhing with impotent fury, he was
already thinking . . . as . . . every white man in that whole section of the country had been thinking . . . for years: *We got to
make him be a nigger first. He's got to admit he's a nigger. Then
maybe we will accept him as he seems to intend to be accepted.*"
(18) Chick's failure to uphold the racial code remains an open
wound. By failing to make Lucas act as a Negro, he "had debased
not merely his manhood but his whole race too." (21) For two and
a half years, the boy is tormented by the experience. He tries to
erase his shame by sending a gift to Lucas's wife as a substitute for
the coins Lucas refused to accept. But some time later, Lucas sends
Chick a jug of molasses. The jug is delivered by a white boy, and
Chick is right back where he started. Then, one day on the town
square, Chick sees Lucas. The Negro passes him without any sign
of recognition. Chick feels liberated until he learns that, at the
time, Lucas's wife had just died. Though he does not realize it, the
incident helps to loosen the shackles of the code by intensifying his
response to Lucas as a human being. He muses: *"She had just died
then. That was why he didn't see me. . . .* thinking with a kind of
amazement: *He was grieving. You dont have to not be a nigger in
order to grieve. . . ."* (25) Chick haunts the square when it is time
for Lucas's annual visit to town. Lucas passes him and looks him in
the eye without the least indication that he recognizes him. Finally,
Chick feels "free, the man who for three years had obsessed his
life waking and sleeping too had walked out of it." (26) Now,
Chick would be "carrying into manhood only the fading tagend of
that old once-frantic shame and anguish and need not for revenge,
vengeance but simply for reequalization, reaffirmation of his masculinity and his white blood." (26)

Actually, Chick is not to escape so easily. Lucas, the man, has
penetrated his consciousness. He is too much Lucas Beauchamp for
Chick ever to think of him as Sambo. The boy's awareness of the

* Random House, 1948.

man beneath the colored skin creates the crisis of the second stage
in his maturation. When Lucas is accused of murdering a white man
all the white people become automatons, mindless and volitionless agents of the code. The murder is not merely the grave crime
of one man depriving another man of life. A Negro has killed a
white: the prescribed ritual is lynching. When the old Negro is arrested, his name, his individuality, his personality no longer count.
He is not Lucas Beauchamp but "threatening Negro."

Chick's trouble is that the abstraction "Negro" does not obliterate his awareness of Lucas, the man. Chick is sixteen when Lucas is
taken into custody, and he thinks of jumping on Highboy, his
horse, to ride away from Jefferson and stay away until the Negro
has been lynched. Even this impulse to flee, to disassociate himself from the traditional lynch ritual, is a betrayal of his heritage.
The abstraction "Negro" should block out his awareness of the
man's individuality as it does for Mr. Lilley, the storekeeper who
serves and helps Negroes daily, but who, in this crisis, "has nothing
against what he calls niggers . . . All he requires is that they act
like niggers." (48) Chick's uncle, Gavin Stevens, more enlightened
than the Mr. Lilleys of the town, comes to the defense of Lucas,
not, however, because he is aware of the man. Gavin interposes
the abstraction of due process of law upon the abstraction Negro.
He opposes the traditional method but not the code. Gavin does
not doubt, even momentarily, that Lucas is guilty. He does not seek
justice, merely due process. Lucas understands Gavin's attitude, and
when the lawyer visits him in the jail and gives him a lecture instead of asking questions about the murder, Lucas is perfectly justified in telling Gavin that he would prefer to get some sleep.

Accompanying his uncle to the jail, Chick, at first, takes comfort
in the thought that Lucas is "*just a nigger after all.*" (58) Unlike
his uncle, however, the boy's heart remains open and he can respond to "the mute unhoping urgency of the eyes." (69) Though
the impulse to jump on his horse remains strong, he returns to the
jail, ostensibly to bring Lucas tobacco, but actually to get the message of the eyes translated into words.

Fortunately for Lucas, the boy has not yet become a slave to abstractions, concepts; he can still respond to truth. As the old Negro,
Ephraim, explained to Chick some years earlier when he offered

to find Mrs. Mallison's lost ring by consulting a fortune teller, " 'Young folks and womens, they aint cluttered. They can listen. But a middle-year man like your paw and your uncle, they cant listen. They aint got time. They're too busy with facks . . . If you ever needs to get anything done outside the common run, dont waste yo time on the menfolks; get the womens and children to working at it.' " (71-2)

And an old woman and two children do save Lucas from being lynched. Mrs. Habersham (Miss Worsham of *Go Down, Moses*) and Chick have known Lucas, as have all the townspeople, for years. These two are certain, as everyone else should be, that he is not a murderer. And they work together to unearth the evidence to save him. When they have presented the proof of his innocence that sends the lynch mob scurrying out of town, the second stage in Chick's maturation process reaches its climax.

The full impact of the horror he has averted shocks him into a violent rejection of his tradition and society. Because they cling "blindly to the vices of their ancestors," his fellow townsmen would have murdered an innocent man. Chick's reaction is triggered by the sight of the lynch mob dispersing. The identity of the murderer is now known. He is a white man. The lynchers have no further cause for action. The murder of white by white is not their affair. Their concern is not with justice, but with keeping the Negro servile.

In the third stage of his development, Chick becomes a man: he re-allies himself with his tradition and society. This third stage is presented by tracing the steps the renegade takes back into the fold. Chick's rehabilitation becomes, in effect, a defense of the separate but equal theory. The sixteen-year-old boy's rejection of his people makes him acutely aware of the land and the tradition he is repudiating. It "had bred his bones and those of his fathers for six generations and was still shaping him into not just a man but a specific man, not with just a man's passions and aspirations and beliefs but the specific passions and hopes and convictions and ways of thinking and acting of a specific kind and even race." (151) Beyond this land and culture is an alien world "not north but North, outland and circumscribing and not even a geographical place but an emotional idea, a condition of which he had fed from his mother's milk to be ever and constant on the alert not at all to fear and not actually anymore to hate but just—a little wearily sometimes and sometimes even with tongue in cheek—to defy." (152) Chick recalls a childhood image of a high wall enclosing the South. On the wall, looking down at him, were people with the same faces as his own and with similar names as those he knew, but between him and them "no longer any real kinship and soon there would not even be any contact since the very mutual words they used would no longer have the same significance. . . ." (152)

Though Chick is repudiating his people for the same reason that Northerners criticize them, he still thinks of the North as "outland." Gavin intensifies Chick's identity with the South by arguing that the South is unique and homogeneous and its homogeneity must be preserved:

"Only a few of us know that only from homogeneity comes anything of a people or for a people of durable and lasting value—the literature, the art, the science, that minimum of government and police which is the meaning of freedom and liberty, and perhaps most valuable of all national character worth anything in a crisis. . . ." (154)

In all the United States, only New England once had a homogeneous culture like that of the South, but when it absorbed the "coastal spew of Europe," its homogeneity was destroyed. (153) Within the South is a second homogeneous group, the Negro, whose homogeneity must also be preserved. The South, Gavin tells his nephew, is not defending its politics or its beliefs but its precious homogeneity. Despite its cultural isolation from the rest of the nation, the South remains an integral part of the United States; and the aim of the enlightened Southerner is to preserve the union of states. That union is to be preserved by fighting on two fronts: externally, by resisting the legislative interference of the North; internally, by fighting the unenlightened Southerners who would deny the Negro his legal, constitutional rights.

Chick's intensified awareness of his allegiance to the South does not efface the feeling of horror his fellow Southerners produced in him by their near murder of an innocent man simply because his skin was dark. But he recalls something his uncle said some years before: Time is a continuum: "yesterday today and tomorrow are Is: Indivisible: One." The past determines the present and the future. "Yesterday wont be over until tomorrow and tomorrow began ten thousand years ago." (194) What happened to the South a hundred years earlier, Chick therefore realizes, shaped the people and the attitudes that nearly cost Lucas his life; the past also shaped Chick to save Lucas's life. And what Chick has done now will help to determine what happens in the South tomorrow.

Gavin helps Chick take another step toward rehabiliation by explaining why the mob hurried away without even an apology to Lucas. Gavin declares that the county will be apologizing to Lucas for years. The lynchers did not run away to avoid apologizing to the Negro; they ran away to express their repudiation of Gowrie, a murderer who killed his own brother. Kin murdering kin is the worst of all possible crimes. If Gowrie sheds Gowrie blood, then there is no hope that mankind will ever reach a stage when *"Thou shalt not kill at all"* is an accepted and honored commandment. And only at that stage will Lucas Beauchamp's life " 'be secure not despite the fact that he is Lucas Beauchamp but because he is.' " (200-1) So horrible is the crime of fratricide, lynching the murderer would not be a sufficient expression of the people's revulsion. " 'If they had lynched him they would have taken only his life. What they really did was worse: they deprived him to the full extent of their capacity of his citizenship in man.' " (202)

Gavin also suggests that the people whom his nephew is condemning were not really going to lynch Lucas. They milled outside the jail, but they were merely waiting for the murdered man's relatives and friends from Beat Four to do the actual lynching. When these people appeared, they would have provided the catalyst necessary for a lynch mob; however, Lucas was still safe because with the arrival of the Beat Four group, there would have been too many people for a lynch mob. There is, explains Gavin,

"a simple numerical point at which a mob cancels and abolishes itself, maybe because it has finally got too big for darkness, the cave it was spawned in is no longer big enough to conceal it from light . . . Or maybe it's because man having passed into mob passes then into mass which abolishes mob by absorption, metabolism, then having got too large even for mass becomes man again conceptible of pity and justice and conscience even if only in the recollection of his long painful aspiration toward them, toward that something anyway of one serene universal light." (201)

Chick recognizes this statement as a declaration of faith in man. Gavin elaborates his view by indicating that he does not place his faith in individual man but in Man. Pity and justice and conscience are attributes of the human being; they are constants, like legs and arms. If they are smothered in individuals or in groups, they are smothered only temporarily because they cannot be extinguished. So long as man is left free, these innate attributes will lead him toward that "serene universal light." When Chick objects to his uncle's faith in Man by declaring ironically, " 'So man is always right,' " Gavin declares:

"No . . . He tries to be if they who use him for their own power and aggrandisement let him alone. Pity and justice and conscience too— that belief in more than the divinity of individual man (which we in America have debased into a national religion of the entrails in which man owes no duty to his soul because he has been absolved of soul to owe duty to and instead is static heir at birth to an inevictible quit-claim on a wife a car a radio and an old-age pension) but in the divinity of his continuity as Man. . . ." (202)

Two conflicting views of democracy are being described in the rather vague rhetoric of this statement. Debased democracy, that practiced in the United States, is concerned with man as a physical being, providing each man with a minimum economic security. This kind of democracy not only ignores man as a spiritual being but shows a lack of faith in man. True democracy takes for granted that the human being has the innate attributes, capability, and power to attain to that state which is the aim of democracy. Government exists only to guarantee the freedom in which man's inherent pity and justice and conscience can operate to move him along the road he has been traveling ever since he broke free from the tyranny of rulers and oppressive governments. If one believes

In the human being and recognizes that his history, despite all its setbacks, reveals a progression toward democracy, then it is possible to retain one's faith in democracy despite the temporary and immediate displays of cruelty and injustice of man to man. Left alone, the common man can and will achieve his democratic destiny: peace, tranquility, and justice for all.

Applied to the specific situation in the South, Gavin's theory sees the Southerners as victims of their history. Over the years since the Civil War, their innate pity, justice, and conscience have begun to operate, the proof of which is the presence and actions of people like Chick and Gavin and Mrs. Habersham. But the past cannot be effaced quickly and easily. Eventually, pity and justice will come to dominate as more and more Chicks and Gavins are born and bred, and the unjust treatment of the Negro will lessen and finally be eliminated. The important point, according to Gavin, is that only this inevitable, gradual emergence of conscience can eliminate injustice and cruelty. Legislation cannot. Legislation, in fact, will serve only to bury the awakening conscience of the South.

"I'm defending Lucas Beauchamp. I'm defending Sambo from the North and East and West—the outlanders who will fling him decades back not merely into injustice but into grief and agony and violence too by forcing on us laws based on the idea that man's injustice to man can be abolished overnight by police. Sambo will suffer it of course; there are not enough of him yet to do anything else. And he will endure it, absorb it and survive because he is Sambo and has the capacity. . . ." (203-4)

Gavin cautions his nephew against allowing demonstrations of man's inhumanity to man to blind him and destroy his faith in Man. To denounce his fellow-man as Chick is doing is to set himself above man, to ignore his own fallibility. Chick is a man. In him, therefore, is the same potential for inhumanity as in the lynchers. And in them is the same potential for right and justice that led Chick to save Lucas. The young man's disgust with his fellow-man is finally checked completely when his uncle tells him that he is being righteous. Chick's cheeks redden with shame. Later, the homely act of eating anneals "the proud vainglorious minuscule which he called his memory and his self and his I-Am into that vast teeming anonymous solidarity of the world. . . ." (207)

By the time he has finished eating, Chick has not only accepted his society once again, but has "expiated his aberration from it, become once more worthy to be received into it." (209) The intensity of his bitter denunciation of his fellow townsmen reflected, he realizes, his basic unity with them. They "were his and he was theirs," and so great is his pride in them that he could be furiously intolerant of "any one single jot or tittle less than absolute perfection." Because he is one of them, he can "excoriate them himself without mercy," but he will defend them "from anyone anywhere." (209) Thus Chick advances, in the banal phrasing of his uncle, from "Tenderfoot Dont Accept" to "Eagle Scout Dont Stop." This promotion signifies his acceptance of his heritage and his people, his faith in the fundamental pity and justice and conscience of the human being, and his determination to feed the small flame of pity and justice in the South until it is warm and bright enough to reach the outcast Negro.[2]

Intruder in the Dust is a propaganda novel. Judging from Faulkner's letters to newspapers and other public statements, the ideas that Gavin expounds are Faulkner's own. Because the story and the characters in the novel are subservient to the message, I have attempted in this analysis to set forth, with as much impartiality as possible, Faulkner's defense of the South. In a few years, most of the argument may have only an historical interest. One of the concepts, however, the one which Gavin describes as the divinity of the Continuity of Man, is important to an understanding of Faulkner's ideas. The doctrine, which is based upon a faith in innate attributes, follows logically from the concept of the natural man of the earlier works. Because of these inherent attributes, the human being can endure temporary afflictions such as political tyrannies, or temporary aberrations such as a mechanized, industrialized society, and he can endure the unchanging inimical conditions of existence itself. The individual dies, but his essence is transmitted, and therefore Faulkner can say "Man Endures." In his next two works, this aspect of the human spirit occupies him increasingly.

Requiem for a Nun

In 1951, twenty years after the publication of *Sanctuary*, Faulkner presented a thematic sequel to the story of Temple Drake and Horace Benbow. *Requiem for a Nun* focuses upon those moral and philosophical aspects of *Sanctuary* that are obscured, for many readers, by the sensationalism and the violence. The earlier novel depicts human evil as a manifestation of cosmic evil. The later book returns the responsibility for evil to man and places upon him the burden of his own salvation. *Sanctuary* contains no note of hope, but its sequel does. *Requiem for a Nun* is to *Sanctuary*, belatedly, what the Dilsey chapter is to *The Sound and the Fury*, and the Lena Grove story to *Light in August*. Actually, because during the intervening years Faulkner's ideas developed, it does more. In the early novels, primitive characters like Dilsey, who embody affirmation, are completely isolated from those products of social conditioning like Quentin Compson. But in *Go Down, Moses*, the natural man and social man are united in one character, Ike McCaslin, and presented as two antithetical aspects of the human personality. The battle between these antitheses is implied by Ike's failure, but it is not dramatized. *Requiem for a Nun* and *A Fable* dramatize the struggle. Temple's quest for peace sets intellect against spirit. Temple seeks within herself the peace that Nancy Mannigoe, one of Faulkner's primitives, has achieved.

Temple's quest is presented in terms of an ancient myth. In this re-examination of man's moral plight, Faulkner starts from the very beginning and retells the story of Genesis. Gowan and Temple are Adam and Eve after the fall, trying to understand what has happened to them and why. The same basic questions that are raised by the original story of man's fall from grace are raised in Faulkner's version. Why does man sin? Why does Eve take the apple; why did Temple jump off the train that day eight years ago? Nancy says about sinning. " 'You aint got to. You cant help it.' " (332)* Man, in other words, is free; he can choose not to sin, but evil is real and man is weak. Temple declares that you must not only " 'never even look on evil and corruption,' " you must be prepared long in advance against it. " 'You've got to be already prepared to resist it, say no to it, long before you see it; you must have already said no to it long before you even know what it is.' " (252-3)

But even if man is free not to sin, should he bear the responsibility for his sin? Why, after all, did God put Satan in the garden? And why did God create man so weak that he could not resist temptation, and then exile him for his sin to an existence of pain and anguish and death? *Requiem for a Nun* provides no answers to these questions about God. Such questions are intellectual problems, and man cannot rationally justify God's ways to man. During the eight years since she jumped off the train, Temple and Gowan have suffered the consequence of their "original" sin. In the course of the drama, Temple assumes the responsibility for her act and for its consequences. Significantly, each time she mentions God, Temple adds, " 'if there is a God.' " Whether God is ultimately responsible is not man's concern. It is a theoretical, unanswerable question. Man's concern is with the actuality of his existence. Like Adam each man is evicted from the Eden of childhood innocence. And each man like Adam must create for himself a modus vivendi to deal with reality in his fallen state. The suffering produced by sin is a reality. The consequences of sin (to repeat Quentin's image in *Absalom, Absalom!*) are like the ripples in a pond created by a falling stone; they spread in ever-widening circles. The sins of the father are visited upon the children. Human history proves this to be a fact. How then does man deal with this crucial problem of his moral existence? He recognizes that when he sins, he commits the action and that he is responsible for that sin and for its consequences. But what does he gain by accepting moral responsibility? Does his acceptance stop the ever-widening circles

---

* The Signet Edition: *Sanctuary with Requiem for a Nun.*

of suffering produced by his sin? It may, but there is no guarantee of it. The suffering goes on tomorrow and tomorrow and tomorrow. Why then should he accept responsibility? The answer is contained in a quotation from the New Testament: "Suffer little children to come unto Me." As Gavin interprets the quotation, it does not mean *permit* them to come unto Me, but *suffer* so that they will be guaranteed their few years in Eden, suffer so that " 'little children, as long as they are little children, shall be intact, unanguished, untorn, unterrified.' " (295) It is no wonder that Camus found *Requiem for a Nun* so appealing that he adapted and staged it. His own insistence upon cutting through all traditional concepts, asking the ultimate questions parallels Faulkner's in this book.

The preceding general summation does not touch upon many important aspects of Faulkner's thinking here. For these we must turn to the context of the story itself. Faulkner chose, perhaps because he was expounding ideas, to write this sequel to *Sanctuary* as a dialectic in the form of a three-act drama, with historical introductions for each act. The drama is not a congenial medium for Faulkner's style, and Temple's long Dostoyevskian confession lacks narrative tension. Most of the first act and part of the second hang upon the question: Will Temple face her guilt? The answer is inevitable, and though Temple's evasive tactics are thematically meaningful, they are dramatically repetitious. The second act moves too slowly dramatically and too fast intellectually. The complicated relationship between Temple and Gowan is merely summarized by Gavin; it is not dramatized. The relationship is difficult to grasp even in a careful reading, and so direct a summary of their complex feelings, as made by Gavin, provides a theater audience no opportunity to digest the significance of Temple's experiences, let alone participate in her suffering. The major weakness of *Requiem* is that the basic human forces that drive Temple are submerged beneath the dialectic. As readers or as theater audience, we are engaged intellectually, but seldom emotionally. One almost forgets, for instance, that Temple is the mother of an infant who has recently been murdered. Her feelings of guilt and her preoccupation with moral responsibility seem more dominant than the anguish of loss. There is a tragic story in the drama, but

Faulkner's interest is focused upon the philosophical rather than the emotional tragedy, and the appeal of *Requiem* is to the mind, not the feelings.

» » Act I

The historical sections preceding each act serve to set the scene, but their major task is to provide historical perspective, to place Temple's moral crisis against the background of man's moral history. In Act I, Temple must decide to face her guilt, accept moral responsibility. The historical introduction to the act presents the founders of Jefferson facing a similar problem. The history of Jefferson, as a town, begins on the day that a gang of bandits is captured and placed in the settlement's sole public building, the jail. This makeshift structure is generally used to house minor disturbers of the frontier peace. The one lock in the settlement, brought by Holston from Carolina, is usually used on the U. S. mail bag. It is requisitioned by the town fathers to secure the bandits in the jail. In the morning, not only are the bandits gone, but one whole side of the jail is missing. The door and the lock have disappeared. A minor crisis erupts; it turns out that Holston was not asked permission to use his lock on the jail door, and he wants it back. The leaders of the settlement hold a conference. They decide to pay Holston fifteen dollars and to charge the sum to the U. S. government by entering it on the Indian accounts. The federal mail rider, Thomas Jefferson Pettigrew, informs them that because they have been using the lock on the mail bag, the lock is the property of the U. S. government. If they charge the cost of the lock to the Indian Department, he tells them, they are charging one Department of the government for property belonging to another Department of the same government. Pettigrew's trouble, the conferees decide is that he is " 'a damned moralist.' " (192) They win over Pettigrew by naming the town after him. Their problem then is that they have no town. That very day they set to work building a courthouse, and when it is done, the frontier settlement has become the town of Jefferson.

They never do get around to charging the government the fif-

teen dollars that they had to give to Holston, though the possibility
of doing so remains an irritant for a long time. This history of Jefferson's origin, with its broad and exaggerated humor, has many
elements of the American frontier tall tale. It is also, however, a
kind of parable. These simple men, faced with a moral dilemma,
have the choice of absolving themselves of responsibility by placing the burden upon an unknown higher authority, or accepting
the responsibility and resolving the problem themselves. The product of their decision is the log courthouse, and eventually the big
courthouse, symbol of justice, "protector of the weak, judiciate and
curb of the passions and lusts, repository and guardian of the aspirations and the hopes." (200) It is also the symbol of men working and living together, creating through their labor something
"bigger than any because it was the sum of all and, being the sum
of all, it must raise all of their hopes and aspirations level with its
own aspirant and soaring cupola." (201) The settlers are satisfied
with their decision about the lock and with their accomplishment, but there remains a nagging uncertainty that they may
have committed a fatal and irremediable error by assuming the
responsibility. As Ratcliffe phrases it,

"It's like Old Moster and the rest of them up there that run the luck,
would look down at us and say, Well well, looks like them durn pecker-
woods down there dont want them fifteen dollars we was going to give
them free-gratis-for-nothing. So maybe they dont want nothing from
us. So maybe we better do like they seem to want, and let them sweat
and swivet and scrabble through the best they can by themselves."
(202)

The town develops, suffers the ravages of the Civil War, becomes modernized and neonized, but the courthouse remains the
"center, the focus, the hub," the symbol of man's never-changing
moral problems. (200) And each hour, as the clock in the courthouse tower strikes, the birds explode out of the belfry as though
"the hour, instead of merely adding one puny infinitesimal more
to the long weary increment since Genesis, had shattered the
virgin pristine air with the first loud dingdong of time and doom."
(204) There are few direct parallels between this history of Jefferson and the story of Temple Drake, but it does convey the idea

of continuity in the moral dilemma of man. For each generation and each individual, the pristine air is shattered, and each individual in each generation must face his dilemma and seek his salvation.

The curtain of the drama arises upon the Jefferson courtroom where Nancy Mannigoe, a Negro, is being sentenced to die. Her " 'Yes, Lord,' " in response to the death sentence indicates that the justice that has brought her salvation is not the justice administered by the court. What that justice is, we eventually learn through Temple's search for peace.

Temple Drake is a tortured being, engaged in a desperate moral battle. Her second child has been smothered in its crib; the murderer of her baby is to be hanged for the crime. Temple is not merely a bereaved mother, the victim of Nancy's crime: the death of her child and the impending death of Nancy are direct consequences of her past. She knows the guilt is hers, but she cannot face and accept the terrible responsibility of acknowledging her guilt. Her evasive maneuvers with Gavin objectify her inner struggle. Stevens is not, as some critics have asserted, Temple's antagonist, prodding her for the sake of justice. The lawyer's role shifts during the drama, but in these early scenes he is the embodiment of Temple's conscience, the force in her which is driving her to confession. Stevens's personality is underplayed in the first act. When Temple tells Gavin, for instance, that he can say goodbye in two words if he tries hard, the insult is meaningless to anyone who is not aware from other books that Stevens tends to be loquacious. Except when he analyzes Gowan's effect upon Temple during the second act, Gavin always speaks briefly and succinctly. In those scenes which lead Temple to the governor's office Stevens merely vocalizes Temple's conscience.

Her sense of guilt is so overpowering that her self-defenses are necessarily almost impenetrable. She first adopts the role of bereaved mother and insults Stevens because he served as attorney for the murderer. Stevens does not defend himself; there is no need, for Temple herself strips off the mask of victim. If she were not involved in Nancy's crime, she could easily think of Nancy as a whore, dope fiend, murderer. But the role of bereaved mother is too obviously false. Temple knows why Nancy killed the child, and she knows that the Negro is not "stinking." What Nancy forces Temple to acknowledge is that people can be both good and bad. Temple wants to believe that people are "rotten." If she could believe that, then she would have an excuse for being rotten herself. But it becomes clear that she is already trying to find a reason for facing her own guilt when she declares, "Maybe it wouldn't be so hard if I could just understand why they dont stink—what reason they would have for not stinking." (214)

Temple and Gowan first appear on stage as the innocent, bereaved victims of a Negro servant's inexplicable crime. By the time Temple leaves the stage in this act, we are aware that she is deeply involved in the crime. And we also know that Gowan has helped weave the web of guilt. Gowan is willing and psychologically able to connect the death of his child with his own past sins. His attitude, in contrast to Temple's, is an interesting revelation of the psychological effects of moral awareness. Temple is fully aware of the extent of her responsibility in the tragedy, and she has therefore created all kinds of defenses to protect herself from admitting her guilt. Gowan, however, is unaware of the full extent of his responsibility until he hears his wife's confession in the governor's office. He considers the death of his daughter a punishment for his sin eight years earlier when he ran off and left Temple at the Old Frenchman place. He has, he says bitterly, been given a bargain: he had two children and he only had to pay one as the price of immunity. Stevens, whose task is to make Gowan aware of his full responsibility, tells him there is no such thing as immunity. Sin and guilt can never be paid off, absolved, because there is no such thing as past. In human consciousness, the past and the present are indivisible. What a man has done in the past determines what he is in the present. There is neither escape nor immunity from the past. The marriage of Gowan and Temple illustrates perfectly Stevens's theory. Gowan married Temple to right a wrong. Their relationship as a married couple, which actually produces the death of their child, is determined by their original sin. Gowan, as he sees himself, magnanimously offered the redeeming security of marriage to a woman who had not only spent a month in a Memphis whorehouse, but who had loved being there. Gowan's attitude toward his wife, though he is not yet aware of it, contributes directly to the tragedy that befalls them. Neither Gowan nor any man can escape the past.

In the final scene of the first act, Temple continues her evasive tactics. She tries to explain her return from California, just before Nancy's execution, as the result of coincidence. She received a telegram from Stevens, she says, and her boy, Bucky, asked where they would go when Nancy was executed. But she knows and admits that such incidents were not really influential in bringing her back; it was her own conscience. Her insistence that she returns to save Nancy is another attempt at evasion. She is fully aware that Nancy cannot be saved from execution, that if Stevens could have saved her through legal maneuvers, he would already have done so. When, finally, Temple speaks of possible benefits from confession, she has not only accepted the inevitability of confession but has also recognized why she must face her guilt. Her confession before two strangers will not help Nancy; it will only help Temple Drake, it will be "for the good of my soul—if I have one." (228) Temple's skepticism about the existence of her soul and the existence of God throughout the drama is very important to an understanding of Faulkner's theme. If she believed she had a soul and if she believed in God, Temple would, through confession, be making peace with God. Her moral responsibility would then be to God. But by emphasizing her skepticism, as Faulkner does, the author makes clear that the human being must bear full moral responsibility for his acts simply because he alone is responsible for them and their consequences. Temple's decision to confess, therefore, is made with no illusions about possible benefits— either for herself or Nancy. She wants to save the Negro woman, she hopes to save her, but she does not confess to save Nancy because she knows that Nancy is doomed irrevocably to execution. The confession may ultimately save Temple herself, but its immediate end is justice—the assessment of moral responsibility.

» » Act II

The subject of the introduction preceding Act II, in which Temple confesses, is justice, symbolized by the courthouse in

Jefferson, in the introduction to Act I, and by the golden dome of the state's capitol in the introduction to Act II. Unlike the town of Jefferson, Jackson was not established by settlers. A commission of three was sent out to locate a site for the capital of Mississippi. The golden dome in Jackson, therefore, was not the product of community cooperation, it was predetermined, imposed as the highest authority in the state. This difference between the origin of justice in the town of Jefferson and the origin of justice in the state capital serves to juxtapose human with a higher justice. The symbolism is developed in the poetic passages describing the history of the universe with the "gilded pustule" already decreed in the beginning. Since creation, this "tiny gleam, this spark, this gilded crumb of man's eternal aspiration, this golden dome preordained and impregnable" (233) existed and survived through all the physical changes of the world, then through the conquest of the great land mass of the United States by the "tumultuous and eupeptic" frontiersmen, and its settlement by those who followed them. The three men commissioned to find a state capital brought in their canoe "not the meek and bloody cross of Christ and Saint Louis, but the scales the blindfold and the sword," establishing "in the wilderness a point for men to rally to in conscience and free will." (237, 236)

This introduction to Act II seems almost to establish justice as an absolute, existing beyond time and man. In the context of the drama, however, the symbol of man's eternal aspiration, "the golden dome preordained and impregnable," seems to be related to human salvation—salvation through justice—though not justice in the ordinary sense. When Temple enters the governor's office and sits before the symbolic throne and the symbolic figure ("no known person, neither old nor young; he might be someone's idea not of God but of Gabriel perhaps, the Gabriel not before the Crucifixion but after it"), she is confronting justice. (240) She faces not God, nor a judge, but herself—her conscience. Ultimate justice rests within each individual. The courthouse, with its golden dome, symbolizes man's collective conscience, but human courts and human law only superficially assess moral responsibility. Nancy and Temple are both beyond the dictates of the courts. Nancy has broken a law; therefore the court in Jefferson tries and sentences her. But long before she appears in court, Nancy confronts justice, assesses her responsibility, and accepts the consequences of her act. She appears before the same bar that Temple faces in the governor's office—her own conscience. That is the reason no one—not Temple, nor Stevens, nor the governor—can help Nancy; her sentence is irrevocable. In contrast, Temple has broken no law. As far as the law and the courts are concerned, she is guiltless. No one but Temple can assess Temple's guilt. She seeks, by facing her guilt, the peace Nancy has found.

In her confession, Temple insists that she alone is responsible for the acts eight years earlier that led to her present condition. She was free, she declares; she could have left Gowan at any time during their drunken ride, and she could have climbed down the drainpipe to escape from the room in which Popeye kept her. The bad in her "was already there waiting," she says, when Popeye brought Red to her and, "I fell what I called in love with him and what it was or what I called it doesn't matter either because all that matters is that I wrote the letters—" (262, 259)*

Gowan and Temple, like Adam and Eve after the fall, were brought together by a sense of mutual guilt. Temple is sincere in her desire to make her marriage work. All she wants is peace, and the "no shame" of love. She believes that she and Gowan have much to build a life upon—mutual forgiveness. But guilt corrodes. As Stevens explains, Gowan marries to right a wrong. Repentant and magnanimous, he forgives Temple for whatever in her past requires forgiveness. She is grateful for the forgiveness, and she is certain that she is strong enough to continue to give her husband the increasing amounts of gratitude he requires. For Gowan, however, says Stevens, "the forgiving wasn't enough . . . after about a year, his restiveness under the onus of accepting the gratitude began to take the form of doubting the paternity of their child." (264-5)

Pregnancy makes Temple's problem critical. Before she becomes pregnant, she can always leave Gowan if she feels she can no

---

* Faulkner probably introduces the idea of some kind of love here to mitigate the unbridled lust that Temple exhibits in *Sanctuary*. It is made clear, however, that sex, not love, was the basis of her relationship with Red. She says later, "I didn't even fall, I was already there: the bad, the lost. . . ." (260).

longer satisfy his growing appetite for gratitude. The child cuts off her escape. And then she finally learns that "everyone must, or anyway may have to, pay for your past; that past is something like a promissory note with a trick clause in it which, as long as nothing goes wrong, can be manumitted in an orderly manner, but which fate or luck or chance, can foreclose on you without warning." (268) She also learns that man can endure anything. In the years since her marriage she has discovered that she is capable of coping with her own suffering, but with a child coming, she is now terrified that the child too will have to suffer because she sinned. According to Stevens, who analyzes Temple's fears and thoughts during her pregnancy, she makes some sort of pact with fate or God, in which she promises that if her child is spared from suffering for its mother's past, she will have no other child who too might become a victim of her sins. She is willing to undergo any suffering that fate might inflict if she can, by doing so, protect her child. After the birth of Bucky, Temple struggles hard to keep her part of the bargain, employing "one hand to offer the atonement with and another to receive the forgiveness with and a third needed to offer the gratitude, and still a fourth hand more and more imperative as time passed to sprinkle in steadily and constantly increasing doses a little more and a little more of the sugar and seasoning on the gratitude to keep it palatable to its swallower. . . ." (270)

And she is so preoccupied with the atonement and the gratitude, according to Gavin, that she becomes pregnant again. Her pact has been broken; there will be another potential victim of her past. Temple knows then that she has lost her battle and that she is doomed. She knows it fifteen months before the blackmailer, Red's brother, appears with the letters. All she can do during those fifteen months is wait and wonder what form the doom will take. And when Pete finally appears with the letters, Temple experiences, says Stevens, a feeling of triumph. She waited all those months for inevitable destruction without once cringing. Then, however, she quits; collapses morally. She is even willing to sacrifice both her children by leaving Bucky with a father who questions the boy's paternity and by bringing her daughter to a man who might, at any moment, throw mother and child into the gutter. Stevens offers two possible reasons for Temple's abject capitulation. He suggests that not only did Pete resemble his brother Red, but that Red probably resembled Gowan. So the attraction, or whatever it was that Temple felt for Red, was re-awakened. The second suggestion is that Temple struggled so long and suffered so much to appease Gowan that she welcomed a "man . . . after six years of that sort of forgiving which debased not only the forgiven but the forgiven's gratitude . . . a man so single, so hard and ruthless, so impeccable in amorality, as to have a kind of integrity, purity, who would . . . never need nor intend to forgive anyone anything. . . ." (273)

In this tragic story of sin and punishment is recorded the moral history of mankind. There is nothing that man can do to alter the pattern that he himself has created. One generation does not merely suffer the consequences of the sins of the preceding generation; in each new generation, man, like Cain, sins and, in effect, re-enacts the original sin. Thus in each generation, man falls from grace and must face, as did the first man and woman, the consequences of his sin. He loses salvation, and he must find it again himself. The quest for salvation must begin within himself. He must accept the outcome of his acts because only by doing so can he offer his children those few years of unanguished childhood before they too fall from grace. In the very attempt to spare his children may lie some sort of salvation.

For Nancy Mannigoe, at least, the access to salvation comes through her compassion for Temple's child. She sacrifices her own life and the life of the infant to force Temple to accept her responsibility and to guarantee Bucky the unanguished years of his innocence. Nancy tries everything she can think of to prevent Temple from running off with Pete. When she finds the money and the jewels that Temple has prepared to take with her, she hides them. She reasons that Pete will get disgusted and leave without Temple or the money, or perhaps that the delay will give Temple time to come to her senses. Pete, however, is shrewder than Nancy imagines. The possession of Temple and her child will provide him a steady source of income, and he twice offers the letters to Temple, telling her she is free to destroy them. Twice Temple refuses the letters because, with the letters destroyed, she would again have to choose between fleeing and resuming the struggle of marriage to Gowan. When Nancy is certain that nothing reasonable will dissuade Temple from abandoning her child, she reverts to the only remaining means she can think of to force Temple to stay: she smothers the baby in its crib.

Nancy acts with full moral awareness; it is as if she arises out of the swift-flowing tide of life, and, individually, determines to dam up the irresponsible drift of those caught in the undertow of guilt. In the introduction to Act III, Faulkner is preoccupied with the theme of individuality being submerged in the fast and swiftly-moving course of modern life.

» » Act III

In a brilliantly-written recapitulation of the history of Yoknapatawpha County, Faulkner captures, in one continuous sentence, the rush of time and events: "Going fast now . . . That fast now . . . Moving faster and faster." In the rushing pace of modernity, individuality is submerged:

. . . one universe, one cosmos: contained in one America: one towering frantic edifice poised like a card-house over the abyss of the mortgaged generations; one boom, one peace: one swirling rocket-roar filling the glittering zenith as with golden feathers, until the vast hollow sphere of his air, the vast and terrible burden beneath which he tries to stand erect and lift his battered and indomitable head—the very substance in which he lives and, lacking which, he would vanish in a matter of seconds—is murmurous with his fears and terrors and disclaimers and repudiations and his aspirations and dreams and his baseless hopes. . . . (315-6)

And when a stranger, Faulkner writes, perhaps one from the North, tries to understand why a cousin or friend or acquaintance has elected to live "here—not specifically here, of course, not specifically Jefferson, but such as here, such as Jefferson," he cannot understand, until he finally feels, in the small town, the continuity of human life, "the vast weight of man's incredible and enduring *Was.*" (318,297) And perhaps if he has will enough, he may even see "the face itself three hundred years after it was dust—the eyes, two jellied tears filled with arrogance and pride and satiety and knowledge of anguish and foreknowledge of death, saying no to death across twelve generations, asking still the old same unanswerable question three centuries after that which reflected them had learned that the answer didn't matter, or—better still—had forgotten the asking of it. . . ." (297)

In an era and a land in which a man's survival no longer depends upon his ability to drive a straight furrow or to fell a tree, in which the government itself seems designed to help the citizen to a point where he may be in danger of losing his ability and independence, in which all communities are made one by the train and the plane, and all homes made one by the waves of sound, the sense of personal integrity and individuality is intensely threatened. But it is the individual human being who creates history, the individual human being who must stem the rushing flood of irresponsibility. It is this sense of the importance of the single individual that the small town provides, through contact with a time when identity was not destroyed by modernity. It is this sense of individuality that is evoked by the memento on the windowpane of the old jail—the name "Cecilia Farmer," and the date, "April 16th 1861," scratched with a diamond on the pane by the daughter of the jailkeeper as she stood at the window and watched the Civil War rage through the town. Her face drew a soldier back to Jefferson after the war to seek her as wife and bring her to his Alabama farm to be the mother of his sons. A stranger, perhaps from the North, looking at it, may come to understand and hear the "clear undistanced voice . . . from the long long time ago," saying " 'Listen, stranger; this was myself: this was I.' " (324)

The tragedy of twentieth-century American life is the loss of the individual's sense of identity and the concomitant loss of moral responsibility. In this book, and in his other novels, Faulkner recognizes that social and psychological forces coalesce to make man their victim. He does not, however, see individual man as simply a victim. The individual is an entity whose personal sense of identity depends upon his recognition of his freedom. Temple asserts that she was free to leave Gowan and Popeye; she did not, and hers is therefore the responsibility for the consequences of her actions. Does such acceptance by the individual of his freedom and moral responsibility lead to salvation? It does for Nancy, but it does not for Temple. *Requiem for a Nun* offers no simple, happy solution. Salvation, which seems to mean simply the peace that passeth understanding, is possible for some people; for others it is not. Temple accepts and confesses her guilt, but she does not achieve peace nor release from suffering. She discovers that peace is possible for the human being: Nancy is at peace. But Temple is not Nancy, and when she leaves the jail cell in the final scene, Temple is far from certain that she will ever be at peace. Temple is too intellectual and too complicated a person to achieve salvation as Nancy has achieved it.

In this contrast between the complex white and primitive black, in *Requiem*, as in the preceding books, intellect is viewed as inimical because it causes resistance to life rather than placid acceptance. Nevertheless, intellect is an inexpugnable part of man. What the final act seems to say is that the only way to peace is through unquestioning acceptance and total submission to faith, but for those who think, such submission is impossible. The intellect demands explanations, and it cannot accept a God whose ways cannot be justified. Temple wants desperately to believe as Nancy does, but she cannot. Her problem is pinpointed for us by her recollection of the Negro whose bride of two weeks died ("Pantaloon in Black"). The anguished man tried walking in the fields so he could sleep, then he tried drinking and fighting, and finally he cut a white man's throat. When he awoke in the jail, six men were needed to hold him down. Pinioned beneath them, he cried out, "'Look like I just cant quit thinking. Look like I just cant quit.'" (288) Like Temple, the Negro cannot submit to the anguish he must bear, and so long as he seeks to understand why his wife had to die, he can know no peace.

In the exchange between Temple and Nancy in the jail cell, Temple keeps asking questions that Nancy cannot answer. Temple's confession has brought her neither peace nor absolution; it was "just for me, just for the suffering and the paying." (330) Temple has decided that she will return to Gowan and make a home for Bucky, but the decision has not eased her suffering, and she knows that her suffering will go on and on. How, she asks

Nancy, is she to endure the suffering. "Trust in Him," Nancy replies. In the light of what He has done to people, Temple asks, why should she trust Him? Nancy has no answer: "But you got to trust Him. Maybe that's your pay for the suffering." Stevens interposes with, "Whose suffering, and whose pay? Just each one's for his own?" And Nancy replies, "Everybody's. All suffering. All poor sinning man's." Stevens, trying to understand what she means, suggests, "The salvation of the world is in man's suffering. Is that it?" Nancy replies, "Yes, sir." But when Stevens asks how salvation is in man's suffering, Nancy can only declare again, "I dont know." (331)

Temple, then, pursues the argument, asking why salvation must come out of suffering. If God, she says, is omnipotent, why did He have to make man suffer, and if suffering is necessary, why cannot each man, at least, suffer only for his own sins? Why must an innocent child "suffer just because I decided to go to a baseball game eight years ago?" And she continues, "Do you have to suffer everybody else's anguish just to believe in God? What kind of God is it that has to blackmail His customers with the whole world's grief and ruin?" (331) Nancy's reply, in the form of a parable, begs the question. God is like a man with too many mules, she says. The mules will work in harness but when they are let loose in the pasture, they are free and they will commit all kinds of mule sins. Man does the same thing; he does not have to sin, but he cannot help it. He can, however, suffer for his sins. God "gives you the best He can think of, that you are capable of doing. And He will save you." (332) Temple then tries to discover what being saved means to Nancy by asking her if there is a heaven. Again, Nancy replies, "I dont know. I believes." (334)

This exchange emphasizes the fact that Nancy does not know rationally what she believes in. She is not saved by an acceptance of the doctrines of Christianity. She does not know if she has an immortal soul or if there is a literal heaven. Her belief in Jesus is symbolic of the mystical submission of her spirit. Nancy has faith, but she cannot justify God's ways to man. In other words, there is no attempt in the drama to explain the questions that the intellect poses. The mind cannot be satisfied; but salvation can be achieved only when the intellect is subdued so completely by spirit that it no longer requires answers. For Temple this is impossible, and she sums up the human tragedy when she says "Even if there is one [a heaven] and somebody waiting in it to forgive me, there's still tomorrow and tomorrow. And suppose tomorrow and tomorrow, and then nobody there, nobody waiting to forgive me . . . Anyone to save it. [her soul] Anyone who wants it. If there is none, I'm sunk. We all are. Doomed. Damned." (335-6) And Stevens agrees that without the possibility of salvation after death, man is damned. "Of course we are. Hasn't He been telling us that for going on two thousand years?" (336)

In *Requiem for a Nun* Faulkner continues the exploration of his concept of man's duality, of what we termed earlier the conflict between social man and natural man. Natural man, here as in the preceding books, accepts the conditions of existence unquestioningly and knows peace. Social man resists and suffers. What is particularly significant in this book is that Faulkner has followed his concept through to its logical conclusions and indicated that his vision of natural man has only limited validity. Nancy, and the other primitive characters of the earlier novels, are symbols, incarnations of the spiritual potential in the human being. That potential Faulkner believes in, and it is the basis for his belief in man. The characters in whom he embodies this potential, however, are generally non-intellectual, and they are isolated from society and its complex problems. The representatives of the complex human beings in ordinary life are characters like Temple. She has within her the spiritual potential that Nancy symbolizes, but Temple cannot ignore her intellect. She cannot shut her eyes to death and to suffering and to all the afflictions of mankind. Through her, Faulkner seems to be saying that, though man possesses within his own being the possibility for salvation, the peace that passeth understanding is not really available to the complicated, intelligent person. This tragic dichotomy in the human being and the complexities and paradoxes it creates, Faulkner further explores in *A Fable*.

A Fable

A Fable (1954) is a philosophical book expressing in the form of a morality Faulkner's matured and comprehensive ideas about human character and human life. Essentially, Faulkner depicts a fundamental dualism in the nature of man which produces continuing conflict and tension. The generalissimo in the novel defines the dualism:

"we are two articulations . . . [of] two inimical conditions . . . I champion of this mundane earth . . . you champion of an esoteric realm of man's baseless hopes and his infinite capacity—no: passion— for unfact. . . ." (347-8) *

In his Nobel prize speech, which he delivered while at work on *A Fable*, the novelist urged young writers not to forget the "problems of the human heart in conflict with itself which alone can make good writing because only that is worth writing about. . . ." The human heart in conflict with itself defines precisely the subject of *A Fable*. The various characters and episodes present a composite image of man at war with himself. The supreme general and the corporal are of the same flesh and blood. This conflict between father and son symbolizes the eternal conflict between flesh and spirit, the practical and the ideal. This dualism in human nature is not in itself a complicated idea, but its effect upon the way men live and upon the values that they live by is very complicated. For one who recognizes this dualism, moral judgments are difficult because the distinctions between good and evil be-

* Random House, 1954.
  See the Appendix, pp. 396-401 for a detailed chronology of events.

come lazy. The corporal, for example, by choosing martyrdom causes the death of General Gragnon. And the supreme general can preserve his own power only by executing the corporal; but by making the corporal a martyr, he strengthens the inimical force the corporal epitomizes. Jesus, himself, did not convert the world: " 'it was pagan and bloody Rome which did it with IIis martyrdom.' " (363) Such paradoxes abound in the novel.

Because of his dual nature, man is his own enemy. The institutions that oppress and repress him are his creations, and they endure only because man himself endures. The military hierarchy, which in the novel represents all institutions that wield power over individual men, is the creation of man. The group commander, Bidet, tells General Gragnon: " 'It wasn't we who invented war. . . . It was war which created us. From the loins of man's furious ineradicable greed sprang the captains and the colonels to his necessity. We are his responsibility. . . .' " (54)

Man's greed and rapacity, his drive for self-aggrandizement, produce wars and the military. The self-interest of his personal life is reflected in his society. Egoism isolates the individual from his fellow-men and it isolates nation from nation. All that is necessary to obliterate the military, says the group commander, is the " 'simple effacement from man's memory of a single word . . . Fatherland.' " (54) The military hierarchy, throughout *A Fable*, is cited as the enemy of man, but even as a symbol of man's rapacity, the military reflects man's dual nature. Dedicated to self-preservation and the extension of its mundane power and glory, it also expresses the human capacity for sacrifice and honor and fidelity.

Faulkner's overall view of human existence is not optimistic. His basic view, as it is presented in this novel, is that the forces of self-interest have always dominated and will continue to dominate, but, at least, these forces will not rule supreme. These antitheses in the human being are ineffaceable, and the struggle will never cease. In the final scene of the novel, the corporal's disciple is horribly scarred and maimed, and he is beaten by the mob, but he cries out. " 'I'm not going to die. Never.' " (437)

The plot of *A Fable* develops from a sudden upsurge of the submerged humane spirit and the resulting struggle of the mundane to re-establish the status quo. Present action in the book extends over a period of one week during the spring of 1918. On Monday morning, a French regiment, inspired by a corporal and twelve disciples, refuses to respond to an order to attack. The supporting forces remain in the trenches, and the enemy does not initiate a counterattack. By noon, the entire French front is quiet, and by three in the afternoon, all firing has ceased on the Western front. The cessation of activity on both sides of no man's land is, in reality, by secret arrangement between the Allied commanders and the German military commanders. They have learned of the enlisted men's desire to lay down their arms, and they arrange a meeting to decide upon a plan to counter the rebellion among the men on both sides of the battle line.

General Gragnon, a French division commander, places the entire regiment of mutinying men under arrest, and he demands permission from his superiors to execute the three thousand men. On Wednesday morning the regiment, including the corporal and his twelve disciples, is brought to Paris and placed in a hastily-constructed compound.

An English message runner, a follower of the corporal, discovers that a convoy of trucks heading for the front lines carries dummy ammunition. He deduces that the military hierarchy is plotting to render ineffective the corporal's influence. He urges a sentry for whom the men in the English battalion have a strange allegiance to lead the unit into no man's land. The runner hopes to carry on what the corporal initiated and by an ineradicable demonstration of unity between the men on both sides of the battle line below the rank of sergeant to prevent the military from carrying out its plan. The sentry, however, is violently unreceptive, and he beats the runner unconscious. The runner regains his senses and witnesses the arrival of the German general over allied territory. He realizes that the blank ammunition fired at the plane is to prevent the soldiers from thinking that the German general has come to discuss the peace that the common soldier has temporarily achieved by asserting that he was tired of war and laying down his arms. The English runner rushes to Paris to appeal to an American Negro for help. The Reverend Sutterfield knew the English sentry for nearly three years in the United States. The Negro minister and the English runner return to the front lines.

Though the sentry remains uncooperative, he does go over the top
with the Negro and the runner. The battalion follows, and from
the German trenches, unarmed soldiers rush out to meet them.
But the two groups never meet. An artillery barrage from both
sides destroys them.

The barrage is ordered by the German and Allied commanders.
They have conferred and agreed to conceal the mutiny by treating
it as if it had never occurred. To achieve this aim, they need to
eliminate only two men: General Gragnon if he continues to demand that the regiment be executed for mutiny, and the corporal
if he refuses to cease his opposition to the military. General
Gragnon remains adamant, and he is executed. The supreme
general of the Allied armies attempts to bribe the corporal to betray the men who followed him. His attempt fails. On Friday, the
corporal is executed in the company of two other soldiers guilty of
robbery and murder. The General gives the corporal's two sisters
and his fiancée permission to bury the dead man. The sisters
bring the body to the family farm and bury it in a land bank
separating two farms. Before dawn the next morning, an artillery
barrage tears up the farm, and the body of the corporal disappears.
In the scene describing the mission of the special detachment to
pick up a body to be buried in the tomb of the unknown soldier, it
is strongly suggested that the corporal's body is the chosen one.

In the allegorical scheme of the novel, the common soldier, led
by the corporal, threatens the power of the military, led by the supreme general. The peace the men seek is specifically the end of
World War I, but, symbolically, it is the peace on earth, good will
toward men that Jesus preached—a union of man with man in a
universal brotherhood of the heart, which is to be achieved by a
dissolution of selfish interests on all levels, from the aggrandize-
ment of nations to the selfishness of individuals. The opponents,
represented by the corporal and the supreme general, are the antithetical forces that exist in every man. By means of a variety of
characters and a variety of incidents, Faulkner identifies the character and power of these inimical forces. With the corporal and
the common man, he associates the human "passion for unfact,"
ranging from the profane to the divine, man's capacity for belief,
hope, sacrifice, love, unselfishness—all the manifestations of what

Faulkner in his public speeches during the final years of his life seemed to refer to as "the human spirit." With the supreme general and the military hierarchy, he associates man's passion for worldly success and glory—power over others, wealth, rank—all the pursuits that nurture the ego and thereby separate man from man, nation from nation. Because the contending forces are encompassed in one organism, the human being, they are not mutually exclusive. Among the officers are believers like the quartermaster general, and among the common men is Polchek, the Judas of A Fable.

Before I attempt to show how the characters and events in the novel illuminate the dualism of human nature, it might be well to establish that Faulkner is not writing a religious allegory. A few critics have noted that though the life and death of the corporal are obviously intended to parallel the life and death of Jesus, the corporal's personality does not suggest the Biblical Jesus. As Hyatt Waggoner declares, "the supernatural is in effect, though probably not in intention, ruled out." [1] Despite the misleading crosses that adorn the 1954 edition, Faulkner utilizes the Christian story only as a myth. In A Fable, Jesus is not the son of God; he is the son of Man. What he preached and epitomized in his death is inherent in all men. Jesus is the pure incarnation of that part of human nature which is opposed to the rapacious. The myth of Jesus, like all myths, embodies in a personality certain universal qualities, and therefore the entire story of Jesus can be enacted over and over so long as human nature remains the same. The corporal works no miracles and makes no claims of divinity, but he achieves what Jesus achieved and expresses what Jesus expressed because he articulates, or at least personifies, the potential inherent in all men.[2] The corporal is an alien, and among his twelve disciples there are some who do not even speak French. The corporal does not, however, need to preach to the soldiers. His mere presence, even among the German soldiers, is sufficient to bring to the surface their common desire for peace and unity. Because the corporal personifies the repressed generosity and good will of the men, he can silently interrupt their gambling, take their money and give it to a young couple who must marry. The men adopt the couple and provide a wedding. There is nothing miraculous in this version of the Cana wedding; the corporal does not convert

the men; he simply translates potential into action by embodying
in a pure state the unselfishness and brotherliness that exist in all
men. Such universal Christ-qualities are generally repressed by the
dominant antithetical qualities of self-interest. The corporal's symbolic embodiment of one part of man's nature is emphasized in
the scene in which the officers of three nations identify him as
men whom they saw dead. The characteristics and capabilities that
he personifies transcend individual men; they are the immortal
heritage of mankind.

But the antitheses of these characteristics are also man's immortal heritage. The quartermaster general, who dreams of man's
salvation, bitterly reviews human history as proof of man's enduring rapacity:

"Rapacity does not fail, else man must deny he breathes. Not rapacity:
its whole vast glorious history repudiates that . . . Not just one family in one nation privileged to soar cometlike into splendid zenith
through and because of it, not just one nation among all the nations
. . . but all governments and nations which ever rose and endured
long enough to leave their mark as such, had sprung from it and in
and upon and by means of it became forever fixed in the amazement
of man's present and the glory of his past; civilization itself is its pass-
word and Christianity its masterpiece . . . rapacity . . . endures, not
even because it is rapacity but because man is man, enduring and immortal; enduring not because he is immortal but immortal because he
endures: and so with rapacity, which immortal man never fails, since it
is in and from rapacity that he gets, holds, his immortality. . . ."
(259-61)

Faulkner, dramatizing universal human characteristics, utilizes
ancient myths to reinforce those he is creating. His major characters are not, as most commentators have noted, breathing human beings. They are probably not intended to be. As mythical
characters, they are supreme expressions of particular aspects of
the human personality. Throughout his career, but to an increased
degree in his later work, Faulkner tended toward the creation of
myth. In the Snopes trilogy, as we shall see, Eula Varner Snopes
is an incarnation of sexuality. In her being, sexuality is elevated to
a state so pure that its incarnation expresses what in the normal

human being is necessarily tempered and alloyed. In many novels, Faulkner depicts the adulation which men offer to anyone who isolates a common attribute and perfects it. It is the adulation, the almost fanatical response engendered by a great singer who raises the human voice to a level of perfection and beauty, or by the great artist in any media, or by the runner or jumper breaking all records of previous human performance, or by the fearless hero. Such elevation of human potential is the source of legend and myth, and it is with legend and myth that Faulkner, in this novel, portrays human capabilities. By direct or implied allusions to Biblical, or mythical, or legendary figures, he elevates his characters into archetypes: the quartermaster general is Isaiah or Man Hoping; the supreme general is Man Conquering and Man Ruling, reincarnation of Alexander, or Caesar, or Napoleon; the English runner is Man Seeking Faith. And though he writes within the Western tradition, Faulkner equates all religious beliefs as expressions of hope. Like Nancy in *Requiem for a Nun* who simply believes, the English runner declares, " 'Maybe what I need is to have to meet somebody. To believe. Not in anything: just to believe.' " (203) In a speech to the youth of Japan, Faulkner made a similar statement: ". . . man himself will prevail over all his anguishes, provided he will make the effort to; make the effort to believe in man and in hope—to seek not for a mere crutch to lean on, but to stand erect on his own feet by believing in hope and in his own toughness and endurance." [3]

What Faulkner means by believing in hope is clarified in *A Fable*. So long as there is belief in the hope of salvation, the lamb in man contends with the wolf. The novel, in effect, argues that man holds his salvation within his own being, but it also shows why man has failed and continues to fail of its achievement: the wolf remains ascendant over the lamb, the mundane over the humane.

Faulkner's use of the New Testament story as a myth is most clearly established by the similarities between the horse-groom story and the story of the corporal. [4] Both reveal man's "passion for unfact," his response to a personification of his own potential for love and sacrifice. Just as the corporal, on one level, unites the soldiers in a brotherhood opposed to the military hierarchy, the horse and groom, on another level, produce a similar unity among the country people against the pursuing authorities.

The hero of this strange, symbolic legend is an English groom, a foul-mouthed, repulsive creature "to whom to grant the status of man was merely to accept Darkness' emissary in the stead of its actual prince and master." (158) But this lowest among men, without becoming outwardly any more acceptable or amiable, undergoes a spiritual transformation, which is symbolized by his baptism into the Baptist religion and his initiation into the secret order of Masons. Assigned to care for a fine race horse, the groom establishes a relationship with the horse "which was no mere rapport but an affinity, not from understanding to understanding but from heart to heart and glands to glands." (152) The rapport of man and horse is so complete that the horse will not even run "until—whatever the communication was: voice, touch, whatever —the man had set it free." (152) Purchased from its English owner by a wealthy Argentinian, then by an American, the horse and its groom are brought from England to South America and then to the United States via New Orleans. The American owner dispatches one of his own grooms, a Negro named Sutterfield, to bring the new acquisition to the racing farm. Accompanied by his young son, Sutterfield joins the horse's entourage. On the way from New Orleans, a trestle break plunges the railroad car into a swamp. The horse breaks a leg, and the three caretakers spirit the horse into hiding. The English groom, Harry, who has discovered that he possesses a gift with dice, gambles with the railroad crew to get food and whatever necessary to set and care for the horse's leg. Five separate organizations begin a two-and-a-half-year pursuit of the horse and its grooms. The Federal government, several state governments, the insurance company, the railroad, and the owner of the horse cooperate on the futile chase. When the horse is mobile, its three grooms leave the swamp and race the horse in small, isolated communities. Even on three legs, the horse responds to the groom and outdistances his competitors. The incredible performance of the animal, the strange and mysterious rapport between man and animal, and the sacrificial devotion of the three men to keep the horse from being returned to its owner and turned into a stud inspire the hundreds of strangers who see them to become their conspirators. The pursuers can get no information about the group. When they reach a town in which the horse has raced, all the inhabitants are dumb. Faulkner's own rhetoric is necessary to describe the nature of this inspirational group.

. . . the runner five years afterward was seeing what the Federal deputy marshal had five years ago while in the middle of it: not a theft, but a passion, an immolation, an apotheosis—no gang of opportunists fleeing with a crippled horse whose value, even whole, had ceased weeks back to equal the sum spent on its pursuit, but the immortal pageant-piece of the tender legend which was the crowning glory of man's own legend beginning when his first paired children lost well the world and from which paired prototypes they still challenged paradise, still paired and still immortal against the chronicle's grimed and bloodstained pages: Adam and Lilith and Paris and Helen and Pyramus and Thisbe and all the other recordless Romeos and their Juliets, the world's oldest and most shining tale limning in his brief turn the warp-legged foul-mouthed English horse-groom as ever Paris or Lochinvar or any else of earth's splendid rapers: the doomed glorious frenzy of a love-story, pursued not by an unclosed office file nor even the raging frustration of the millionaire owner, but by its own inherent doom, since, being immortal, the story, the legend, was not to be owned by any one of the pairs who added to its shining and tragic increment, but only to be used, passed through, by each in their doomed and homeless turn. (153-4)

It is, in short, immortal love, transcending the individuals who have experienced it because man's capacity to love—to be so inspired by a passion that career, wealth, throne, life itself are sacrificed to it—is, like rapacity, man's immortal heritage. In the legend, the pursuing authorities parallel the military of the main story, and the Federal deputy marshal plays a role identical with that of the English runner. The marshal, like the runner who was an architect student, is a mute poet. Troubled from the beginning in his role as pursuer, the marshal gives up the pursuit when he finally recognizes why it was that "a minister, a man of God, sworn and dedicated enemy of man's lusts and follies, yet . . . from that first moment had not only abetted theft and gambling, but had given to the same cause the tender virgin years of his own child as ever of old had Samuel's father or Abraham his Isaac." (159)

When the marshal resigns, the horse's owner offers a fantastic sum of money for the capture of the horse and the grooms. The reward disseminates "the poison faster than they advanced, faster even than the meteor-course of love and sacrifice." (161) The betrayal for silver is at hand. The marshal thinks of offering a higher sum to prevent the capture: "Mammon's David ringing for a moment anyway Mammon's Goliath's brazen invincible unregenerate skull." (162) And musing upon the power that money wields over men, the marshal thinks:

> . . . how it was no wonder that man had never been able to solve the problems of his span upon earth, since he has taken no steps whatever to educate himself, not in how to manage his lusts and follies; they harm him only in sporadic, almost individual instances; but in how to cope with his own blind mass and weight: seeing them—the man and the horse and the two Negroes whom they had snatched as it were willy nilly into that fierce and radiant orbit—doomed not at all because passion is ephemeral (which was why they had never found any better name for it, which was why Eve and the Snake and Mary and the Lamb and Ahab and the Whale and Androcles and Balzac's African deserter, and all the celestial zoology of horse and goat and swan and bull, were the firmament of man's history instead of the mere rubble of his past), nor even because the rape was theft and theft is wrong and wrong shall not prevail, but simply because, due to the sheer repetition of zeros behind a dollar mark on a printed placard, everyone . . . would be almost frantically attuned to the merest whisper regarding the horse's whereabouts. (161)

The reward produces its Polchek-Judas. The pursuers close in. At the final moment before capture, the English groom shoots the horse. The marshal hires a famous lawyer to defend the fugitives, but the lawyer is not necessary. The English groom disappears, and when the Negro and his son are taken into custody, the mob that has gathered at the jail and the courthouse releases them. The introduction of the lawyer provides Faulkner an opportunity to expatiate on another aspect of the human spirit that has been demonstrated in this unified response to the horse and groom against the force of authority. During the French Revolution, the common man responded to his own impulse to be free, and unifying into an active force, asserted himself against the status quo. The same spirit created and maintained the American nation. The lawyer, watching the people quietly freeing the prisoners, muses upon the power of the common man:

. . . neither in lust nor appetite nor greed lay wombed the potency of his threat, but in silence and meditation; his ability to move *en masse* at his own impulse . . . none knew this better than the lords proprietors of his massed breathing, the hero-giant precentors of his seething moil, who used his spendthrift potency in the very act of curbing and directing it, and ever had and ever would. . . . (187)

The English groom returns to the mountain community that made him a Mason, and he remains there until he hears of the war in Europe. When he leaves the United States, he severs himself completely from his past experience, reverting to the insolent, self-centered creature he was before his human potential for giving himself was activated by his love for the horse and then destroyed by the pursuing authorities. In the army, he establishes a business in which his fellow soldiers borrow a sum, let us say twenty dollars, on the condition that they repay it at a dollar a day for thirty days. The men do not object to the exorbitant interest because the sentry-groom is, in effect, gambling that they will be alive to repay the loan. Though Harry very cold-bloodedly is working on mathematical percentages, his loan to each man constitutes an act of faith in that individual's survival. The routine of lining up each day to repay Harry one-thirtieth of the loan becomes a religious ritual. The runner, at first shocked by the rate of interest, finally understands its spiritual worth, and he spends the money he borrows "with the single-mindedness of a Roman Catholic at his devotions or expiating a penance." (148)

When they are separated from the English groom by their arrest, Sutterfield and his son begin a search for him that lasts for several years, and that brings them from the South to New York and finally to Paris. Sutterfield, the Negro minister, functions as a central and multi-faceted symbol in *A Fable*. He serves as a link between the horse-groom story and the corporal's, but more significantly, he is Man Believing. In a colloquy with the American lawyer, the Negro responds to the lawyer's question, " 'Are you an ordained minister?' " with the statement:

"I dont know. I bears witness."
"To what? God?"
"To man. God dont need me. I bears witness to Him of course, but my main witness is to man."
"The most damning thing man could suffer would be a valid witness before God."
"You're wrong there," the Negro said. "Man is full of sin and nature, and all he does dont bear looking at, and a heap of what he says is a shame and a mawkery. But cant no witness hurt him. Some day something might beat him, but it wont be Satan." (180)

Most of the major characters in the novel offer their views of the human being, but only two characters, Sutterfield and the supreme general, recognize and accept man's dual nature. The supreme general chooses to champion the mundane; the Negro champions the spiritual. The English groom, called "Mistairy," embodies the extremes of sinfulness and spiritual exaltation; and the Negro's continuing faith in Harry symbolizes his faith in the spiritual potential of man despite his propensity to sin. The most significant demonstration of the Negro's faith in man is his acceptance of the repulsive and uncooperative groom as the symbol of the savior. Sutterfield is not an ordained minister; his doctrine is simply a belief in man, and his is a vital faith because it encompasses antitheses. He is willing to abet gambling and become a refugee from the law because in the sacrificial love of the groom for the horse he recognizes man's potential for salvation. Sutterfield's faith is simple and intense, and as he searches for Harry, he becomes the cynosure of all those who blindly hope. Backed by rich women whose sons are fighting, he becomes the head of an organization that does nothing except serve as an expression of hope. In France, Sutterfield becomes known as Tooleyman, a corruption of the final phrase of his organization's title: *Les Amis Myriades et Anonymes à la France de Tout le Monde*. His skin coloring is of no significance because he is Man Believing and Hoping. It is to this man that the runner, who is also a seeker, comes and rediscovers his faith in man.

This runner, an Englishman, having displayed courage and leadership in battle, was sent to officer's school. After five months as a lieutenant, he decides to return to the ranks. His motives are not clearly established, but it would appear that though years before, he lost his faith in man, he has still not lost his need for faith. He explains to his company commander that he cannot tolerate the knowledge that simply because he wears bars on his shoulder, he can " 'tell vast herds of man what to do' " with the " 'impunitive right to shoot him with my own hand when he doesn't do it.' " Such power makes him realize, he says, that man is worthy of " 'fear and abhorrence and hatred.' " (61-2) The very intensity of the runner's disillusionment reveals his need to believe in man, and his decision to resign is, in reality, a symbolic act placing him on the side of man and against the military hierarchy. By returning to the ranks, he asserts his opposition to the mundane power represented by the military. Once in the hierarchy of power, however, he is not permitted to resign. He has to stage a gross moral violation to regain membership in the ranks of the common man. The aura of his former status remains a barrier between him and the soldiers, and for some time he does not learn about the corporal. Finally, an old man who joined the army to search for his missing son tells him of the corporal's activities and the reaction of the soldiers below the rank of sergeant. The old man's search for his son symbolizes a search for faith in the Son of Man. When the corporal's regiment mutinies, the old man tells the runner that he knows that his own son is dead, and that the blank ammunition being brought up to the front is to welcome His Son.

Throughout the novel, the father-son theme reflects the contending forces in the nature of man. The son is equated with youth, freedom, hope, belief, and rebellion; the father, with disillusionment, loss of faith, acceptance of the status quo, and mundane power. Those who seek faith await the rebellion of the son, the assertion of that fresh, uncorrupted belief in man which is the privilege of youth. When the runner, for example, decides to go to Paris to find out more about the Negro minister and the mysterious Harry, his trip becomes a "pilgrimage back to when and where the lost free spirit of man once existed." In Paris, where he once studied architecture, "with the ghost of his lost youth dead fifteen years now, he retraced the perimeter of his dead life when he had not only hoped but believed." (148) And after he hears Sutterfield's story about the horse and the English groom, the runner discovers his need to believe, not in anything, but just to believe. The mutiny, which is led by the corporal, who is the son of the supreme general, becomes a rebellion of son against father, youth against age, hope and belief against cynicism. The runner defines the struggle between the authorities and the men as a struggle between belief and the hierarchy of established power: *"It's not that we didn't believe: it's that we couldn't, didn't know how any more. That's the most terrible thing they have done to us. That's the most terrible."* (73)

The runner finally becomes a believer, and with the help of Sutterfield, leads the sentry and the battalion into no man's land. The Negro, who for some time has been wearing a French corporal's uniform, symbol of the corporal's presence in Everyman, is killed in the artillery barrage that the military hierarchy orders. Harry dies too, but not before he sees the men coming behind him and joins in their cries of hope and exultation. At the same moment that he hears the artillery fire, he screams, " 'No . . . no! Not to us!' not even realizing that he had said 'we' and not 'I' for the first time in his life probably, certainly for the first time in four years. . . ." (321) The sentry finally feels the bond "between or from man to his brother man stronger than even the golden shackles which coopered precariously his ramshackle earth." (165) He dies with his eyes on the runner and his ears filled with the runner's cry " 'They cant kill us! They cant! Not dare not: they cant!' " (322) The runner is the only man who escapes with his life. His wounds make him an image of man's dual nature. Flame envelops half his body "neatly from heel through navel through chin." (322) On the scorched and seared side, his eye socket is empty, his mouth paralyzed, an arm and a leg are missing. The mundane power is triumphant; the spiritual has been scarred and maimed, but it is alive because it is immortal.

The antitheses of these common soldiers, these believers in man, are the military representatives. The first soldier introduced in the novel is an unnamed sergeant who is impatient at "the stupidly complicating ineptitude of civilians at all times," and who, surrounded by a crowd of people, suddenly recognizes that he is the alien, not they. (7) By "relinquishing volition and the fear of hunger and decision . . . he had sold his birthright in the race of man." (9-10) This same recognition is experienced by General Charles Gragnon when he arrives at Chaulnesmont to request the generalissimo's permission to execute the regiment. As he leaves his car, Gragnon, knowing that he and his career have been sacrificed by his superiors, stands for a moment looking at the crowd containing the families of the regiment. He is "solitary, kinless, alone, pariah and orphan both from them whose decree of orphanage he would carry out, and from them whom he would orphan; repudiated in advance by them from whom he had bought the high privilege of endurance and fidelity and abnegation with the forfeiture of his birthright in humanity, in compassion and pity and even in the right to die. . . ." (135-6)

This separation of the professional military leaders from the race of ordinary man clearly establishes Faulkner's design of depicting two inimical forces. On the side of man, as we have seen, are aligned belief and hope, the manifestations of man's spiritual potential. On the side of the military, as we shall see, are marshaled those qualities which prevent the human being from realizing his full spiritual potential. The servants of the organization created to serve man's rapacity sacrifice their humanity by offering themselves to an institution whose very existence requires that rapacity, selfishness, and greed create men's values. Despite the courage, abnegation and fidelity of which the soldier is capable, his allegiance to the military is governed by self-interest. The sergeant sells his birthright in the race of man for guaranteed lodgings and food, and freedom from decision and worry. Gragnon's sole interest is his personal advancement and all the power and privilege inherent in high rank. It is for the sake of his reputation that he demands that the entire regiment be executed. He views man as nothing but a fighting machine. The rebellion of his troops is a soul-shaking experience for Gragnon. When he returns from the headquarters of the group commander, technically under arrest, he is in a state of shock. Leaving his aide, he plunges into a thicket to listen for the sound of a cicada, a sound which, during his childhood, expressed his inconsolable desire for a mother.[5] The priest in the

Catholic orphanage insisted that the Blessed Mother was his mother too, but that was not enough for the child, "because he didn't want the mother of all nor the mother of Christ either: he wanted the mother of One." (42) During those early periods of grief, he would lie on the earth and whisper the word "mother," listening for the reply of the cicada. Forty years later, when he loses his security for a second time, he again whispers the word and hears the sound "such as he imagined might be made by the sleeping untoothed mouth itself around the sleeping nipple." (42-3)

Gragnon obviously found in the military life the ordered security he lacked in childhood, and at this crisis, he is so disturbed that he becomes aware that he is alienated from his fellow men. He recalls a book which one of his aides, now dead, read continually. The aide wanted to be a writer and told Gragnon that he would write when he learned enough about people. He wanted to learn, he said, about " 'honor and sacrifice, and the pity and compassion you have to have to be worthy of honor and sacrifice, and the courage it takes to pity, and the pride it takes to deserve the courage—' " Gragnon asked, " 'Courage to pity?' " And the aide replied, " 'Yes. Courage. When you stop to pity, the world runs over you. It takes pride to be that brave.' " (45)

To Gragnon, courage and sacrifice are simply attributes of a fighting machine. The idea that it takes courage to pity is incomprehensible to him. After his arrest, Gragnon remembers his aide (who was killed attempting to warn a civilian car out of a danger area), because his sense of security has been so shaken that he begins to wonder if there is not more to life and people than he realized. Returning to his own headquarters, he finds the dead aide's book, *Gil Blas*, and reads it through carefully and attentively. Gragnon, however, is too insulated, and the insights into human motive and character in the novel make little impression upon him. The characters are to him "inventions and naturally he didn't believe them—besides being in another country and long ago. . . ." (48)

This theme of another country, Faulkner uses to dramatize the denial of the human spiritual potential by those who have no faith in man. During that period, for instance, when the runner has no faith but wants desperately to believe, he recalls a verse he read while at Oxford. During a week of battle, the verse serves as a substitute for the harassing ordeal of thinking:

> lo, I have committed fornication.
> But that was in another country; and besides,
> the wench is dead (70)

The lines, from Marlowe's *The Jew of Malta*, Faulkner may have derived directly from Eliot's poem, "Portrait of a Lady," where they serve as an epigraph. The feeling they convey of a nagging sense of guilt and a desire to evade personal responsibility is utilized by Faulkner to show that the military hierarchy is actually destroying part of itself by destroying man's hope. When the runner discovers the blank ammunition, he keeps searching for a thought. The one that dominates because he would like to believe it is appropriate for the occasion is "*In Christ is death at end in Adam that began.*" This thought reflects the runner's hope that the mutiny of the corporal has achieved man's salvation. But then finally comes the thought that is appropriate, "the right one . . . smooth and intact and instantaneous, seeming to have been there for a whole minute while he was still fretting its loss:

> —but that was in another country;
> and besides, the wench is dead" (83)

It is this thought that sums up his knowledge of the military plan to efface the mutiny. Just as Gragnon shrugs off the truths in *Gil Blas* as of another country, the military hierarchy plans to obliterate the ineffaceable mutiny of the men. Gragnon's insistence that the regiment be executed is dictated by selfishness. The death of the three thousand men will serve as a personal exoneration of his reputation. Ironically, Gragnon's life is sacrificed by the higher echelons for the very same purpose. To preserve the military institution, the commanders decide to treat the mutiny as if it had not occurred. Gragnon's execution by the three American soldiers is one of the most vivid and gruesome scenes of the novel. Inflexible to the end, Gragnon insists that he be shot from the rear so that his body will record that his own men shot him, rather than obey his order to attack. The military hierarchy, however, must have Gragnon shot from the front, and his body must yield a German bullet. The cold, pitiless determination of the military institution to preserve itself even at the sacrifice of a devoted servant, and the ruthless inhumanity of man to man are painfully palpable in the execution scene. Gragnon succeeds in being killed from the rear, but his executioners prepare to plug the bullet hole behind his ear with wax and to shoot him as they have been ordered to do. Perhaps the most horrifying aspect of this scene is the tragic waste of human potential. Gragnon dies with dignity and courage for an ephemeral, meaningless cause—his personal reputation. The very qualities which heroically serve self-interest might have been harnessed to serve Man.

Gragnon's view of man is shared by his immediate superiors. The corps commander, Lallemont, has a greater respect for man's mass potential, but he considers this potential as actually inimical to the common man and to his military leaders. To him, man is a malleable mass capable of responding to the directions of a great military leader, but as soon as the reins are slackened, the purposeful mass dissolves "'faster and faster flowing and seeking back to its own base anonymity.'" Referring to the mutiny, Lallemont declares, "'. . . in one more little instant they might have changed the world's face. But they never do.'" (30)

Bidet, the group commander, earned his rank and name by a "cold, scathing, contemptuous preoccupation with body vents and orifices." In presenting the view of man held by this army commander, Faulkner also offers his own contrasting view. Bidet's preoccupation with man is "not as an imperial implement, least of all as that gallant and puny creature bearing undismayed on his frail bones and flesh the vast burden of his long inexplicable incomprehensible tradition and journey, not even in fact as a functioning animal but as a functioning machine in the same sense that the earthworm is. . . ." (51)

Each commander is fascistic, accepting implicitly the need of the people for a strong leader. Though Faulkner does not deal with civil authority, the political implications of his story are clear.

Strong governments, as he states explicitly in other books, abrogate the inherent rights and privileges of political man; and they deny his right and his ability to decide, *en masse*, his own destiny.[6]

Even the quartermaster general, who dreams of man's salvation, thinks in terms of a great leader to save mankind. What this general conceives of as salvation is not made clear, but like the Old Testament Isaiah, he awaits the coming of a savior. On his first meeting with the future supreme general at St. Cyr, he envisions him as the incarnation of his hope. After graduation, his belief is strengthened by the new lieutenant's refusal to use his family's powerful military connections for immediate advancement. To the surprise of everyone, the lieutenant requests an insignificant assignment to a remote African outpost. Later, the future quartermaster general, a Norman, voluntarily replaces his friend in the desert outpost. In his interview with the mysterious man who chose military anonymity rather than the high rank his family connections guaranteed him, the Norman confesses his dream that the lieutenant will save mankind. From the desert outpost, the lieutenant goes to the Middle East to enter a mountain monastery. The Norman accepts this action as proof that the lieutenant is preparing by prayer and contemplation for his great mission.

On his return to France, the Norman is confined to a hospital, where he is visited by an unnamed captain. They discuss the lieutenant's role in an affair that occurred in the remote desert station before the Norman replaced his friend. A native girl was assaulted and murdered. The local chieftain demanded that the officer in charge of the military post turn over the guilty man, warning that unless the request were honored, the tribe would destroy the entire post. The lieutenant knew the identity of the murderer, an international refugee who came to the remote outpost to escape prosecution for similar crimes. The lieutenant requested a volunteer to sneak away during the night to seek help. He knew the culprit would seize the chance to escape in the guise of hero. The lieutenant, apparently, informed the native chief that he was sending the guilty man to him. That night, the murderer was captured and tortured and his body returned in the morning. By sacrificing the guilty man, the lieutenant prevented a local war.

As he retells the story, the captain emphasizes that the lieutenant sacrificed a man's life. The Norman, obviously trying to keep intact his dream of the lieutenant as the savior of mankind, insists that the lieutenant sacrificed a murderer. When his visitor leaves, however, the Norman, in tears, admits, " 'Yes, he was a man.' " But he seeks to find excuses for the lieutenant's action: " '. . . he was young then, not much more than a child.' " To the hospital attendants, nevertheless, the Norman says, " 'These tears are not anguish: only grief.' " (271)

This episode at that desert outpost, described by the Norman as "not Golgotha of course but Gethsemane," is a version in miniature of the major incident in the book in which the corporal is sacrificed to preserve the military hierarchy. (258) The Norman, blinded by the imperious needs of his dream, continues to envision the future supreme general as the savior. When his friend is elevated to commander of the Allied armies, he accepts the appointment as quartermaster general. His dream is finally deflated when he realizes that the generalissimo intends to sacrifice the corporal. The quartermaster general, like the other idealists in the novel, puts his faith in a concept but not in man. He is ineffectual because he fails to recognize the complexity of the human being and the inevitable alloying that ideals must undergo when transformed into action. His conversation with the generalissimo after he discovers the intended purpose of the dummy ammunition reveals the weakness of the idealist, the dreamer.

He hands the generalissimo his resignation, declaring that his superior is afraid of man and has proved it by planning the elaborate hoax of camouflaging the arrival of the German general in order to save " 'our whole small repudiated and homeless species about the earth who not only no longer belong to man, but even to earth itself, since we have had to make this last base desperate cast in order to hold our last desperate and precarious place on it.' " (327) The generalissimo replies that he does not fear man. He respects him as " 'an articulated creature capable of locomotion and vulnerable to self-interest.' " (331) He responds to the quartermaster's argument that man would have saved himself had not the military interfered by informing him that one of the corporal's disciples, Polchek, had informed the authorities of the planned mutiny.

The quartermaster general, who has not accepted the dual nature of man, continues to repeat that the supreme general is afraid of the " 'simple unified hope and dream of simple man.' " (331) But finally, the supreme general reveals to his subordinate the paradoxes inherent in any real action, and the quartermaster general, shrinking from this truth, meekly leaves without resigning. In the colloquy that defeats the quartermaster general, the leader of the Allied forces points out to his friend that he has only come to him to resign his commission; he has not made a plea to spare the corporal's life.

"He wont accept that life!" the other cried. "If he does—" and stopped, amazed, aghast, foreknowing and despaired while the gentle voice went on:
"If he does, if he accepts his life, keeps his life, he will have abrogated his own gesture and martyrdom. If I gave him his life tonight, I myself could render null and void what you call the hope and the dream of his sacrifice. By destroying his life tomorrow morning, I will establish forever that he didn't even live in vain, let alone die so. Now tell me who's afraid?" (332)

The idealist is defeated by the antitheses which make up human existence. Like the quartermaster general, the young aviator Levine is destroyed by his uncompromising idealism. The sections describing the boy's dream of heroism are the least integrated episodes in the novel and they are much too long.* But the slow-burning Sidicott, set afire by the blank tracers, unquestionably represents the inevitable corruption of a tested dream. The mature Bridesman accepts the situation, but the immature Levine cannot, and finally kills himself.

In contrast to these idealists, the generalissimo accepts the double edge of reality. His vision of man and of life, like Sutterfield's, is comprehensive enough to encompass man's dualism. Sometime during his years in Africa and the Middle East, which served as his Gethsemane, the general made a choice. In the original Gethsem-

---

* The intense frustration of Levine is very much like that of Julian Lowe in Faulkner's first novel, *Soldiers' Pay*. Both characters, separated by so many years, seem to reflect Faulkner's own unquenchable sense of frustration at being cheated by the armistice in 1918 of a chance to fly in combat.

ane, Jesus suffered the anguish of decision and made his choice. The general makes an opposite choice. He recognizes and acknowledges the spiritual potential of man which the corporal epitomizes, but he also has gauged correctly the relative weakness of this potential in relation to self-interest. In the everlasting battle of the human heart with itself, the balance of power rests with self-interest, and the general has chosen to be on the side of the stronger. When he confronts the corporal and offers him the gifts of the mundane world—liberty, unlimited power, existence itself—he knows that the corporal will refuse, because the general realizes that the human "passion for unfact," which he calls man's deathless folly is, like rapacity, man's immortal heritage. And therefore he can say:

"I dont fear man. I do better: I respect and admire him. And pride: I am ten times prouder of that immortality which he does possess than ever he of that heavenly one of his delusion. Because man and his folly—"

"Will endure," the corporal said.

"They will do more," the old general said proudly. "They will prevail. . . ." (354)

More than any character in the novel, the general reveals the choice which every man must face. The quotation from Marlowe, with its theme of suppressed guilt, sums up the supreme general's career. In another country, he got a woman with child and deserted her. She died in childbirth, but it is the corporal whom the general fathered. His evasion of moral responsibility for the woman and child symbolizes his decision to pursue the glories of the world and repress his own moral and spiritual impulses. These, represented by the corporal, are inexpugnable.

Faulkner also depicts man's dual nature in the mob scenes, spaced throughout the novel to remind us that the individual characters are images of all men. The majority of these scenes, significantly, reveal man motivated by self-interest. In the opening scene of the novel, the terrified kin of the mutinous regiment heap vituperation upon the corporal who led their relatives into the abyss of death. In another scene, the sisters and the fiancée of the corporal (whose roles are almost entirely symbolic—to present the parallels with the Christ story and give essential background about the supreme general), are vilified by the mob because they are related to the corporal. The other side of man in the mass is presented in the scene in which the mob releases Sutterfield and his son.

Even Faulkner's shifts in style from abstract and symbolic narration to realistic detailed storytelling express the dualism of man. His version of the last supper, for instance, is startling in its realism. It is our first close-up view of the corporal and his twelve disciples. They have, before this, been presented through the minds of others and have generally been treated as a reincarnation of Christ and his disciples. Thus it is a shock to encounter these rough and crude men whose conversation is dominated by discussion of their pending execution. There is nothing otherworldly in this scene.

Faulkner's vision of man's dual nature and his mature recognition of the complexity of moral judgment are successfully transformed into art. If the book is approached as a morality rather than a novel, it provides a rich, provocative experience. Having said this, however, I hasten to add that Faulkner's penchant, during this stage of his career, for abstract statements about man and life produces, in *A Fable*, too many exasperatingly obtuse passages and too many dull abstract speeches that induce more irritation than thought.

The Snopes Trilogy

In 1957, at one of the University of Virginia sessions, Faulkner declared that a Snopes chronicle had occurred to him about thirty years earlier. He had thought of the "whole story at once like a bolt of lightning lights up a landscape." [1] Not until 1940 did the

SNOPES GENEALOGY

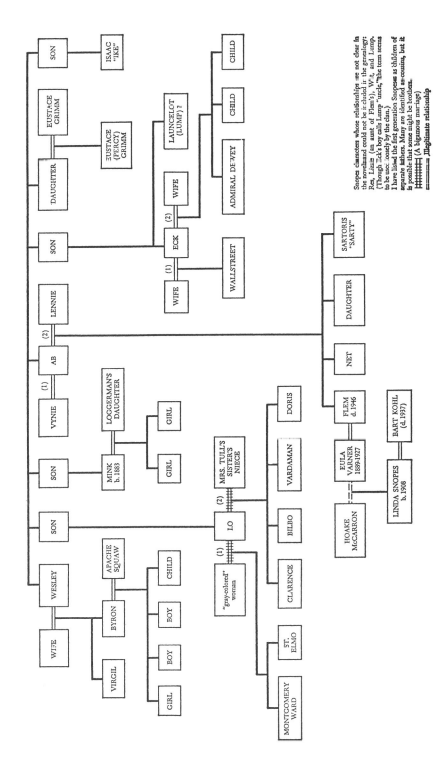

Snopes characters whose relationships are not clear in the novels could not be included in the genealogy: Res, Lizzie (an aunt of Flem's), Wat, and Lump. (Though Eck's boy calls Lump "uncle," the term seems to be used loosely by the clan.)

I have listed the first generation Snopeses as children of separate fathers. Many are identified as cousins, but it is possible that some might be brothers.

╫╫╫╫╫ (A bigamous marriage)

═════ Illegitimate relationship

first volume of the chronicle, *The Hamlet*, appear. Seventeen years elapsed before its sequel *The Town* saw print. The final volume, *The Mansion*, was published two years later in 1959.[2]

In many ways, the trilogy does support Faulkner's statement about its conception. Stories which he published in the early 1930's and probably wrote some years earlier appear, sometimes with few revisions, in the trilogy. The Flem Snopes of the 1932 story "Centaur in Brass" is the same character of the novels. The affair in that story between Flem's wife and the mayor of Jefferson is an integral part of *The Town*. Flem's rise from sharecropper's cabin to ante-bellum mansion is clearly part of Faulkner's original idea. During the many years separating the conception and its execution, however, Faulkner's moral vision changed. As a result, the trilogy has a basic story unity, but it lacks thematic unity.*

The Hamlet

Written during Faulkner's great period of creativity, *The Hamlet* is by far the best book in the trilogy and deserves a place beside *Sanctuary* just below Faulkner's greatest novels. The book throbs with passion and with life. Its stories range from the mock-heroic to the grotesque, encompass comedy and tragedy, and introduce some of Faulkner's most memorable characters. Structurally, the novel is centered upon Flem Snopes. At the beginning, he arrives in Frenchman's Bend; at the end he leaves, having wrested from the hamlet not only all the success that it can offer him but the tools he will need to become an important citizen of Jefferson: experience in usury that will lead him into banking, a beautiful wife whom he can barter for social position, and a half-interest in a restaurant that provides him access to the town. As central character, Flem obviously presented Faulkner with a technical prob-

---

* See the Appendix, pp. 401-403, for a chronology of significant dates in the Snopes trilogy.

lem: building a novel around a character who must himself be kept in the background. Flem seldom speaks; his financial operations are seldom dramatized. His step-by-step rise in the hamlet is, for the most part, recorded as accomplished fact. After an absence from the village, Ratliff discovers that Flem has moved to the village and rides Jody Varner's horse. After another absence, Ratliff returns to discover that Flem goes about with old Will Varner in his buggy and that he lives at Varner's house. In only a few scenes of the novel is Flem an active participant: his encounter with the Varners, when he blackmails Jody into making him his clerk and when he insists that Will pay for his chew; his temporary and minor defeat at the hands of Ratliff in the goat trade; the finale of the horse trade; and the scene of the buried treasure. Throughout the novel and the whole trilogy, Faulkner never provides a closeup view of Flem's mind, an analysis of the forces that drive him.

The technical problem posed by such a central character, Faulkner resolves by an ingenious and effective method of tonal and thematic contrasts. As a number of critics have recently shown, the early criticism of *The Hamlet* as merely a collection of short stories is without validity.[3] Episodic the novel certainly is, presenting as it does the stories of many characters, some of whom (like Labove and Houston) have no contact with Flem; but the book as a whole is unquestionably unified, each episode revealing directly or indirectly the character of the central figure.

Faulkner's reason for keeping Flem at a distance rests in the genesis of the whole concept of Snopesism in the writer's imagination. The Snopes tribe represents not so much specific and specialized Snopesian sins as a general social and moral pollution.[4] There are few sins which any Snopes commits in *The Hamlet* that Will Varner has not also committed. Even the Snopes reputation for breeding is undeserved by comparison with Varner's sixteen children. The Snopes proclivity for multiple bed-partners, in the case of I.O., at least, makes him a bigamist, but not a Varnerian seducer of mortgagees' wives. As soon as Faulkner approaches a Snopes closely and presents him individually, the individual becomes detached from the tribe. Eck, who is the first Snopes that Flem brings into the hamlet, is an affable, pleasant, and kind person. When Ratliff demands that Ike's relatives deal with the problem of sodomy, Eck gives twenty dollars for the cow and, moved by pity, buys a toy replica for the idiot to hold.[5] We learn later in the trilogy that Eck wears a brace around his neck. He incurred the crippling injury when he refused to let a log that he was holding slip and crush a Negro. This Snopes is so good that when Montgomery Ward Snopes thinks about him, in *The Mansion*, he decides that Eck must have been the product of some extra curricular night work. I.O., the proverb-quoting Snopes, is more a comical scoundrel than an incarnation of the repulsiveness Snopesism generally conveys. The idiot, Ike, is too much a victim of fate to arouse any feeling but pity: "the mowing and bobbing head, the eyes which at some instant, some second once, had opened upon, been vouchsafed a glimpse of, the Gorgon-face of that primal injustice which man was not intended to look at face to face and had been blasted empty and clean forever of any thought, the slobbering mouth in its mist of soft gold hair." (87)* Even the murderer Mink, whose grotesque attempts to hide the body of his victim in a hollow tree by jumping up and down on it are horrifying, displays a certain pride and integrity. The other mature Snopes in *The Hamlet*, Lump, who never reappears in the trilogy, is obviously Flem's alter ego, introduced to replace Flem temporarily while he is in Texas.

The clue to the genesis of Snopesism is provided by the honorable and moral Ratliff. As soon as the Snopes tribe begins its invasion of Frenchman's Bend, Ratliff becomes a defender of the community. But why, one wonders, does Ratliff, the friend, confidant, and even admirer of Will Varner, consider the Snopeses so baleful a menace? Why is the upstart Flem so dangerous to a community that has been subjected for years to the unscrupulousness of Will Varner?

This reaction by the tolerant Ratliff makes little sense until it is recognized as the reaction of a member of the in-group to the invasion of the out-group. In many ways, this anti-Snopesism reflects a feeling that is identical with the feeling every new immigrant group in the United States has engendered in the entrenched social group. Before individuals have emerged, the new group is collectively considered immoral, unsanitary, excessively

* Vintage Edition.

prolific, socially obnoxious, and economically unscrupulous and pushing—in short, a menace to the community. These are the very characteristics of Snopesism.

Snopesism has been equated by many critics with evil. Undeniably, the clan does perpetrate in Frenchman's Bend and Jefferson a good deal of skulduggery, but the aura of evil that Faulkner creates about the group is far in excess of the evil it actually does. For one thing, any reader of the Yoknapatawpha County fiction has witnessed more cantankerousness, stupidity, malice, selfishness, cold-bloodedness, viciousness, immorality, and crime of all kinds in Jefferson among the Sartorises and Compsons, as well as among the lesser citizens, than the entire Snopes clan could possibly commit. Though Faulkner sustains throughout the three novels an aura of Snopesian evil, he detaches so many Snopeses from the group by presenting them as individual personalities that in the second volume, the intense anti-Snopes feeling of Ratliff and Gavin Stevens, and their enthusiastic anti-Snopes campaign, strike the reader as too much ado about too little.

Actually, Snopesism merges into Flemism, an abstraction which is sustained far longer, but only because Flem is not presented as an individual human being until the end of *The Town*. Flem is the only Snopes guilty of the worst crime in the Faulkner canon—a lack of humanity, a complete failure to recognize and respect the integrity, the needs, and the feelings of other human beings. Every crime is, in some way, a violation of another's rights as a human being. Faulkner is tolerant of the man guilty of a crime of passion: he can view Mink, the murderer, with compassion; Montgomery Ward, he treats with much sympathy; but the money-maker who violates no law but is empty of feeling, he makes into an incarnation of evil.

Flem has often been described by critics as Faulkner's image of Americans whose sole ambition is wealth and whose values are symbolized by the dollar. There is some validity in this interpretation of Flem's character and role, and yet it is not really his pursuit of money that makes Flem evil so much as his lack of response to other people. Flem's relative, Wall Street Snopes, for instance, receives the approbation and admiration of the Jefferson community. Wall is industrious and clever and honest, but his ambition is identical with Flem's. Ratliff and Stevens do not disapprove of Wall because he is determined to make money; in fact, they invest money in his wholesale grocery business. If Flem were a symbol of the American money-seeker, then Wall's story could hardly have been incorporated into the trilogy. The American experience has proved that men like Wall who devote so much time and energy to money-making have little chance of developing into much more than human cash registers. But the approval with which Wall is presented indicates that the evil Flem represents is not the dehumanizing influence of the American rags-to-riches dream. Flem's uncanny, cold rapacity makes him evil. Like Snopesism, however, Flemism also dissolves when Faulkner finally approaches Flem as a human being. The abstract idea of the Snopeses as a polluting menace, which seems to reflect an in-group prejudice against an out-group, diminishes gradually in the trilogy, as it does in society, when individuals become detached from the group.

The presentation of Flem as an emotional zero is the controlling principle in the structure of *The Hamlet*. Each character and incident in the novel serves as a moral or emotional contrast to Flem. The most dramatic and effective contrast is the character of Eula Varner. The marriage of Flem and Eula unites the epitome of human frigidity with the epitome of human passion. Eula is the fertility goddess, the symbol of that passion in the human being that fixes him in the continuum of nature. She is "the supreme primal uterus." (114) At eight years, just by walking down the aisle, she can transform the one-room school into "a grove of Venus and fetch every male in the room . . . springing into embattled rivalry, importunate each for precedence in immolation." (115) She is the queen, the matrix, "tranquilly abrogating the whole long sum of human thinking and suffering which is called knowledge, education, wisdom, at once supremely unchaste and inviolable. . . ." (116)

Eula symbolizes the passion that gave birth to the enduring symbols (in a male world and a male literature) of Lilith and Eve and Semiramis and Helen. Though man refines the passion, incorporating in its symbol his ideals of beauty and truth and goodness (as tradition does with Helen, and as Gavin Stevens does with Eula, in *The Town*), fundamentally, the passion is sex. Faulkner devotes two of his longest sections in *The Hamlet* to two sexual symbols—Eula and the cow. In the descriptions of Eula, her bovine qualities are emphasized; and in the Swinburnian descriptions of the cow, the distinction between female animal and human female is difficult to discern. In both sections, the allusions to classical fertility images abound, and the idiot's pursuit of the cow symbolizes the human being's unity with nature. The idiot is the lowest common denominator of humanity, as close to the animal as to the human species, united to both by the passion of sex. With its glowing rhetoric, the Ike Snopes section is a remarkable achievement. The idiot's perversion is transformed into a powerful and moving evocation of human love. By investing irresistible love in perversion, Faulkner points out dramatically the sexual basis of this human passion. And as basic as love is, the passion is unknown to Flem. As Labove foresees, Venus (Eula) will be owned by a crippled Vulcan "who would not possess her but merely own her by the single strength which power gave, the dead power of money . . . as he might own . . . a field, say. He saw it: the fine land rich and fecund and foul and eternal and impervious to him who claimed title to it, oblivious, drawing to itself tenfold the quantity of living seed its owner's whole life could have secreted and compounded, producing a thousandfold the harvest he could ever hope to gather and save." (119)

The history of Labove complements the love story of Ike Snopes. Labove's is the same passion on a higher level. Driven by an ambition not unlike Flem's, Labove struggles and sacrifices to become a lawyer. He gets through his years of study by playing football for the college and by teaching in the Frenchman's Bend school forty miles from the campus. When he finally earns his law degree, he realizes that he cannot leave the hamlet where each school day he can be in the same room with the thirteen-year-old Eula. Labove becomes "the virile anchorite of old time," living an abstemious life in his cold, small lean-to room, paying no attention to food, living for the moment when he can return to the school and see her. (118) "And he did not want her as a wife, he just wanted her one time as a man with a gangrened hand or foot thirsts after the axe-stroke which will leave him comparatively whole again." (119) Eula sits in his class, bovine and unresponsive, and Labove acknowledges to himself that he is mad. He is so obsessed, however, that he must kneel after school beside her empty chair and put his face on the seat still warm from her body. When he finally does attack her and is repulsed, he awaits with a feeling approaching pleasure the blows that her brother Jody, of the same flesh and blood at least, will rain upon him. And when he realizes that Eula has not even bothered to tell her brother, he leaves the hamlet.

Labove offers a close-up view of the passion that Eula will arouse in all the men from nine to ninety who come into her orbit, except the man she marries—Flem. As she advances through adolescence, Eula seems to exist in a torpor, as if all her energy were being absorbed by the development of her physical being. She comes to life, at last, on the night she helps Hoake McCarron fight off the local wooers. In that scrimmage, which is a village replica of the Trojan conflict, Hoake (with the aid of Eula) beats off the attackers. He suffers a broken arm, which is set by the local veterinarian, Eula's father. Later that night, Eula gives herself to Hoake, supporting his broken arm which, despite her efforts, comes unset. Symbolically Eula is Helen, but Hoake is obviously no Paris. As soon as he learns that she is pregnant, he flees. And this village goddess, who sets aflame so many men, becomes the property of the passionless Flem.

Altogether, there are five stories of irresistible passion in the two middle sections (entitled "Eula," and "The Long Summer"), which are enclosed by two sections which deal more directly with Flem's manipulation of others for profit. Houston's story is one of tragic love. He is a "victim of a useless and elaborate practical joke at the hands of the prime maniacal Risibility." (191) For fourteen years, Houston resists his irresistible love for the quiet girl five years his junior, whom he meets in school. At sixteen, two years after he meets her, he flees from his future and remains away twelve years, living for seven years in reciprocal fidelity with a former whore. He does not sell the property he inherits from his father, not quite understanding why he does not until the night he returns to Frenchman's Bend. Three months after he marries the girl whom he has resisted so long, she is killed by his stallion.

Until he is murdered four years later, Houston grieves. It is his cow that the idiot loves, and despite his revulsion, Houston cannot help sympathizing with the idiot's passion, and he gives him the cow. Houston's grief for his dead bride provokes his murder. He cuts himself off from his fellow men with his cold, bitter arrogance. His enforcement of the pound fee law, after Mink has worked off his debt for letting Houston winter his cow, is to Mink the ultimate joke of that "maniacal Risibility" which has dogged the existence of both men.

Mink's story is more than a love tale, though love plays an important role in it. Mink carries the cognomen Snopes, but he represents the poor, defeated, exacerbated, earth-bound tenant farmers who populate Frenchman's Bend. The son of sharecroppers, Mink tries to escape the fate of his people. He sets out to go to sea, but en route he falls in love. In spite of his un-Snopesian desire for a virgin bride, and his sensitivity to the shades of previous lovers, Mink cannot resist the loggerman's nymphomaniac daughter. He falls in love and marries her. Their love persists through years of degrading poverty: when Mink kills Houston, his wife sells herself to Will Varner for ten dollars to help her husband escape. Mink refuses to touch the money.

Mink became a neighbor of Houston through Flem, who came into possession of a portion of Houston's land when Houston sold it to buy furniture for his bride. Mink is a tenant farmer, and his fate is the defeating, degrading, unrewarding struggle of the sharecropper against absolute poverty. In his simple, childish, stupid way, Mink is fighting that primal injustice reflected in his idiot cousin's face which ordains some men to an inescapable existence of toil and poverty and others to a life of comparative ease. His decision to let his strayed cow remain with Houston's herd is not prompted so much by personal greed as it is by a need to assert himself against cosmic injustice. It is the same need that drives him to murder. He does not kill Houston as the man who pushes him too far, but Houston as the agent of a force beyond man which violates basic human rights and dignity. Just as the story of Ike and his cow pulsates with love, so the story of Mink and his cow pulsates with seething fury, a fury that boils up frequently in Faulkner's fiction when he presents downtrodden farmers. The old man, for example, from whom Ike Snopes is taking food for his cow, reacts to the discovery of the missing feed with a murderous, relentless fury that drives him to forsake his work and his sleep to pursue the thief. It is as if these people have known and suffered all the blows that outrageous fortune can heap upon them, accepted their fate as inevitable, and accepted a status quo arrangement in which they contain their anger so long as no further injustice is inflicted upon them. Then any occurrence, no matter how minor in comparison to their standard afflictions, is enough to upset the balance and trigger their pent-up fury. Overwhelmed by rage, they move close to madness.

Henry Armstid actually goes mad. His truce with "primal injustice" has apparently long since been abrogated; he exists in a constant state of fury. Armstid provides the serious note in the wonderfully comic horse-auction episode, and the tragic note in the buried-treasure tale, as he insanely digs and digs for nonexistent treasure. Armstid is thrust over the border of sanity by Flem's rapacity.

The final section of the book continues to highlight Flem's immunity to passion with tales of men caught in the grip of forces as irresistible as love. The hamlet's male population is stripped of its senses by the dream of a horse bargain. Everyone knows that the ponies are wild and that the untrustworthy Flem is engineering the auction. The men make jokes about it; they all expect to be cheated, but they are as helpless as was Labove in the grip of their passion. Flem utilizes their passion. The Texan trader's refusal to take Armstid's money dramatizes Flem's implacable inhumanity, his isolation from his fellow men.

Ratliff, a shrewd trader by nature and profession, does not participate in the auction; but even Ratliff, a confirmed bachelor (who responds to Eula while calmly acknowledging that she is not for him), has his weakness. He cannot resist the lure, ancient and honorable, of buried treasure. Actually, that Ratliff should become a victim of one of the oldest tricks in the trading game is hardly credible. Some commentators have described Ratliff's walking into Flem's trap as proof of Flem's superior shrewdness. Planting coins, however, is hardly shrewd or imaginative, and Ratliff, who can usually see two or three steps beyond educated, sensitive men like

Gavin Stevens and who has had so much experience already with Flem, should not become a Snopes pawn. But in the plan of the novel, Ratliff must succumb. If he is not bested by Flem, he too will remain beyond the pale of emotional fallibility in which everyone except Flem is gathered. Flem is isolated by his lack of emotional response. His heart is a dollar sign; his goal is the accumulation of money, and his tools are human beings whose emotions he does not share and can therefore manipulate for his financial profit.

The first rung on Flem's ladder is Jody Varner's fear. And once he is in charge of the Varner store, his progress is certain because he has no interest to detract him from making money. All the energy which other men devote to family or pleasure—to the satisfaction of their emotional needs—Flem can devote to money-making. Unhampered by moral or humane considerations, he needs only opportunity, and opportunity his neighbors, slaves to their emotions, provide him. Ratliff, who thinks in terms of normal human beings, imagines Flem taking sexual advantage of a hungry Negro girl who comes into the store. Of such an act, a man like Varner would be capable. As unscrupulous as Flem in matters of money, Varner has other than economic appetites. Ratliff comes close to the truth about Flem when he indulges in his fantasy of Flem confronting the Prince of Hell to reclaim his bartered soul. Flem's soul, which " 'wasn't no big one to begin with nohow,' " has dried up to a tiny smear, and the rulers of hell are at a loss to redeem the pledge. (151) They have offered him the gratifications and the vanities without success. The Prince of Hell, himself, offers Flem every temptation man is subject to. Nothing interests Flem but fulfilling the bargain to the letter, and the fantasy ends with the devil scrabbling hysterically across the floor to escape the new incumbent of the throne.

It is not Flem's shrewdness in barter that defeats men and the devil; it is his immunity to feeling. As a trader, Ratliff is his equal, even beating him in their initial encounter, the goat trade. But Ratliff sacrifices ten of his fourteen dollars profit to redeem and destroy the idiot's note so that Flem cannot use it again. Ratliff and Flem are, of course, direct opposites in their response to people. Even the clothes they wear indicates this difference. Ratliff's immaculately clean, homemade blue shirt aligns him with the poor farmers from whom he sprang. Flem, a sharecropper's son, begins to wear an unclean white shirt and a machine-made black bow tie as soon as he begins to make money. The sewing machine agent prefers to travel about selling three machines a year rather than remain in Jefferson to operate the restaurant that he partly owns. He is far more interested in people than he is in running a business. Ratliff is an intelligent, kindly observer of the human comedy, whose compassion and sense of human dignity provide him a moral code that is firm but not rigid. Though some of the residents of Frenchman's Bend, such as Bookwright, are moved to moral antipathy by Flem's rapacity, only Ratliff, who merely visits the community, actively opposes Flem. It is therefore ironic that it is he who provides Flem the chance to begin his career in Jefferson.

The diverse stories of irresistible passion in *The Hamlet* reach a climax in the final scene in which the passionless Flem, with his Venus bride beside him, stops for a moment to watch Armstid insanely digging for nonexistent treasure, and then spits over the wagon wheel before he moves on to Jefferson. The varied tones and styles of these stories—the poetic mock heroic of the idiot's tale, the grotesque horror of Mink's struggle to hide Houston's body and ward off Lump's attempt to take money from the dead man's pocket, the wild humor of the horse auction—all serve to isolate Flem in a black nimbus of cold horror. Even the setting in the tiny hamlet, with the men lounging on the store gallery, helplessly watching the rise of Flem and trembling in the clutch of his increasing power, helps to characterize Flem. The whole atmosphere and tone of the village, its poverty, its lazy pace of existence, which Faulkner captures so well, serve to emphasize the ruthless purposiveness of the man.

Basically, *The Hamlet* is thematically unified by the moral conflict between the community, which is a mixture of human weakness and sinfulness, and Flem, who is single-minded in his rapacity. Faulkner's sympathy permits no simple moral judgment of human beings: Mink is a murderer, but he is also a victim, and he has pride and dignity and integrity. At this stage of his career, however, Faulkner can still create in Flem an archetype of evil. In the succeeding volumes of the trilogy, his compassion scales down the archetype to human proportions, and the thematic unity of the trilogy is impaired.

The Town

Faulkner's basic plan in *The Town* seems to be to show the impact upon Jefferson of the two archetypes he created in *The Hamlet*—the essence of passion and the essence of cold inhumanity. Such a description of the novel is obviously vague and general, but a more precise one would not cover a novel that moves in several thematic directions and that develops on several story levels simultaneously. The overall result is a confused novel. The source of the confusion is probably the attempt to retain a design conceived in the 1920's that is much too simple for the author's moral vision in the 1950's. As we have seen, *The Hamlet* and many of Faulkner's other novels are groups of stories unified by theme. *The Town* is a failure because its stories are not thematically unified.

The original design, the invasion of Jefferson by Flem and the Snopes clan, requires clearly defined moral opposites: pernicious Snopeses versus relatively moral Jeffersonians. But Faulkner's interest in the complexity of the human character had evidently become so intense by the time he returned to his trilogy that he was far less interested in the distinction between good and bad than in the mixture of the two. The result in *The Town* is that Flem's advancement to bank president and proprietor of an ante-bellum mansion provides the structural framework of the novel, but the thematic significance of that rise becomes obscured as the novel progresses. The theme shifts from a concern with the encroachment of an immoral new social class upon an established moral but weakened order, to an interest in the complex moral forces in the human being and in the human community.

For purposes of analysis, it might be useful to begin by unwinding some of the strands in this complicated novel and isolating them sufficiently to make the various story levels and their thematic significance clear. One of the strands is the social and moral impact on the genteel Jefferson society of the upstart Flem and of his wife. Another is the influence that a small community like Jefferson has upon the character and actions of its members. The novel also analyzes in depth the character and moral development of Gavin Stevens and describes, at the same time, the education of Gavin's nephew, Charles Mallison. And, finally, as I noted, it is a study of the complexity of the human character.

Narrative technique is an important tool in Faulkner's attempt to achieve these various ends, and as in earlier books, the multiple-narrator technique is used to reveal the complexity of personality and to point up the difficulty of making moral judgments.[6] *The Town* is narrated by three of its major characters: V. K. Ratliff, Gavin Stevens, and Charles Mallison. None of these narrators can be designated as the spokesman of the author. The knowledge that each has about the events he describes is limited. Much of what each records is hearsay, much is pure speculation; and, invariably, his own personality and emotional biases color his descriptions of events and analyses of character and motive. Of the three narrators, Ratliff is probably the most objective. His guesses, at least, are proved by events to be the most accurate. His knowledge, however, is often limited, and Ratliff tends to tell a story as he thinks it should have occurred. In *The Mansion*, for example, when he reviews Eula's affair with Hoake McCarron, he keeps repeating that if it did not happen exactly the way he describes it, then that is the way it should have happened.

By means of this narrative technique, Faulkner reveals how difficult it is for the human mind to approach truth and how isolated one individual is from his fellow men. The mind sees what it is prepared to see. Gavin Stevens provides a good example. Before he ever comes into direct contact with any of the Snopeses, Gavin is prejudiced against them. His friend Ratliff has told him about Flem's activities in Frenchman's Bend. Ratliff's account of these activities is, of course, colored by his personality and moral attitudes. And Gavin's background—his family's social position in Jefferson, his community loyalty, and his moral idealism—provides a perfect soil for the seed that Ratliff plants to blossom into prejudice. As a result, when Gavin first hears of Wall Street Snopes's activities, he decides that they must be morally questionable. Only when the evidence that Wall is honest is unmistakable, does Gavin change his mind.

Gavin's nephew, Charles, who narrates most of the chapters, also reveals how the mind is separated from truth by its training. At the end of *The Town*, Charles is about thirteen. The events that he narrates cover about eighteen years. Though a principal character, Charles is not even alive when many events in the novel occur. He is retelling stories which have been told to him by his cousin Gowan Stevens, by his uncle, and by Ratliff. The very stories that he is retelling have helped to mold his own attitudes, ideas, and feelings. Derived as these stories are from a number of sources, they appropriately reflect, when Charles tells them, the filtered reactions of the entire community. As Charles indicates, when he says "I," he means Jefferson. The community in which he is born and raised helps to mold the personality of Charles; its attitudes and its reactions to past events are part of his heritage. The way Charles's mind works and what it does with facts reflect the influence of the community upon its development.

Faulkner structures his narrative around a few central incidents. The narrators continually mull over such events as Stevens's decision to withdraw his suit against DeSpain, Flem's ascendancy to vice-presidency and then presidency of the bank, and Eula's suicide. They speculate about motive, try to trace the pattern of events that led to these incidents. Because they are attempting to understand human motives, they can never be certain that they have discovered the truth. The motives that each narrator attributes to Flem or to Eula are motives which reflect more about the narrator's personality and background than about the personality of Flem or Eula. Without an authorial voice to depend upon, the reader also becomes involved in this process of seeking truth. And all he can do is to add his own speculations, which reflect his own personality and background.

The great achievement of Faulkner's multiple-narrator technique is that it mirrors perfectly the frustrations involved in determining absolute truth—particularly truth about other human beings. Our understanding of others is achieved by an identical process of speculating over scraps of information. The quality of our minds, our personalities, and our emotional biases influence these speculations, and even if we hit upon the exact motivation for another's acts, we can never be certain of our conclusions. The ultimate effect of being subjected to Faulkner's narrative technique in *The Town* is to intensify our awareness of the complexity of interpersonal relations. In the course of the novel, we are permitted to see many facets of Gavin's personality through the eyes of the other narrators. As a result, we come to know so much about him that it is difficult to see him objectively. He is admirable, yet at the same time frequently silly; he is obviously sensitive and perceptive, yet very often prejudiced and obtuse; he can be interesting and entertaining, but he can be a bore. He is, in other words, as complicated a person and as difficult to judge, as any real person whom we come to know well.*

The artistic effect of Faulkner's narrative technique is probably the most interesting thing about *The Town*, but the technique does pose a difficult problem for the critic. Should the excessive sentimentality of the episodes involving Gavin and Eula and DeSpain, for example, be credited to Faulkner or to his narrators? The presentation of the vestigial ante-bellum traditions in Jefferson society creates the sentimentality. The Stevens family represents the old order—the tradition of social elegance and moral integrity. To convey the character of this society, Faulkner (through Charles) resorts to overemphasis upon manners and rituals: when Judge Stevens leaves the dinner table, for example, everyone rises, the youngest member of the family runs to hold the door, and the Judge invariably says thank you to his daughter-in-law. The same adherence to form produces the run on Mrs. Rouncewell's flower

---

* The only weakness apparent in Faulkner's use of the multiple-narrator technique in this novel is his failure to integrate it into the structure of the story. In *Absalom, Absalom!*, when Miss Rosa narrates, she provides information that only she possesses. In contrast, the choice of Ratliff rather than Charles as narrator of a particular incident seems arbitrary. Only the Stevens chapters have to be narrated by Stevens. In *Absalom*, also, the narrators talk to one another. In *The Town* the narrators have no reason for telling their stories, and their audience is obviously the reader.

Though *The Town* and the other later novels are not artistically comparable to the great works of the early period, they do reveal that Faulkner continued to develop his techniques of narration to expand the boundaries of the novel.

shop before the Christmas dance. If one man sends a corsage to his partner, every man must. These episodes—in the original design of the novel—are obviously intended to suggest the kind of society that Flem will invade. One could argue that the sentimental image which Charles has of this society was created for him by the adults who, in describing days gone by, conveyed its character by exaggerating its adherence to form. Whoever is responsible for the sentimentality, it is excessive, and fortunately, by the end of the episode, when Gavin leaves for Heidelberg, the old order, as far as the novel is concerned, has vanished. Its rituals, its atmosphere, its codes are never invoked again, even indirectly. Gavin, who, at the beginning of the novel, represents the old order, emerges at the end as too much of an individual to represent anything but Gavin Stevens.

Gavin is a moral idealist, and though his opposition to the Snopes clan begins as a social struggle, it turns quickly into a struggle against evil. And even that struggle becomes quickly inconsequential as the theme of the novel alters. At one point, Gavin tries to decide why he is so concerned with the Snopeses, and the only answer he can come up with is that his obsession with Eula has made the family she married into his natural concern. In Gavin's soliloquy on this subject Faulkner reveals that the great to-do that Gavin and Ratliff make about the Snopes invasion is really unwarranted. Flem, himself, has taken over the task of ridding Jefferson of his relatives. Early in the novel, Snopesism, as a major theme, becomes to a considerable extent meaningless, though Faulkner does sustain the atmosphere of Snopesian pollution throughout the book. Individually, the episodes devoted to the skulduggery of the Snopes clan are excellent stories, but, like the Byron Snopes Indians episode, a superb example of the grotesque, with which the novel closes, their thematic significance is not clear.

Snopesism is, in fact, replaced by Flemism. Flem Snopes remains the money-making machine that he was in Frenchman's Bend. His total lack of response to people, and his brilliant use of other people's emotional weaknesses for his own material and social ends guarantee his success. Throughout the novel, Flem is terrifying in his ability to turn any situation that arises into personal profit. The secret of his evil power is simplicity. He has one aim: to make money. His eyes never waver from his goal. He has no other desires, no other interests. Against so single-minded a person, the ordinary mortal can offer little resistance. In fact, the ordinary mortal cannot even conceive of such single-mindedness. Stevens, trying to puzzle out how and why Flem ousts DeSpain from the bank presidency, attributes to him a desire to revenge himself for DeSpain's years of adultery with Eula. But this is a motive that the passionless Flem could not possibly know. Even after many years of watching Flem, Gavin and Ratliff continue to be shocked by each indication of his rapacity because they cannot escape the limitations of their own humanity. Even Flem's relatives, as corrupt as they are, boggle at his coldness; they expect that he will respond, at least, to blood ties. Mink is certain that Flem will assist him; Montgomery expects his relative to save him from prosecution; and I.O. is horrified to learn that the fifty percent of Mrs. Hait's insurance, which he unjustly insists belongs to him, has been appropriated by Flem.

In *The Hamlet*, Flem's inhumanity is underscored by contrast to the violent passions of his fellow men. In *The Town* his single-minded rapacity is dramatized by contrast to the complexity of those around him. The adultery of Eula and Manfred DeSpain, with which the novel opens, triggers a series of complex responses and complex moral issues.

The effect of Venus upon the male population of Jefferson in *The Town* is as explosive as her effect in Frenchman's Bend in *The Hamlet*. When DeSpain becomes Eula's lover—or at least the town is sure he is, though no one has any unequivocal evidence—the entire community, despite its rigid Baptist morality, participates vicariously in the adultery. DeSpain becomes the symbol of the town's male response to the presence of a sex goddess. Eula, herself, seems to be beyond the dictates of morality. A Helen has to be: when Helen and Paris meet, ordinary moral codes lose their significance. So effective is Faulkner's evocation of Eula's grandeur that not only the community but the reader champions adultery. And yet, DeSpain's deliberate creation of the superintendent's position in the power plant to placate what should be an outraged husband is a callous breach of decency and a violation

of public ethics. We know, of course, that Flem is using his wife.
for his own advancement, but we also know that no one in Jefferson possesses that information. The complexity of the moral issue can best be illustrated by examining DeSpain's action more
closely. Because of it, one could make a very good case in defense
of Flem's career in Jefferson, a career which begins with the power
plant incident. DeSpain, as a member of the best Jefferson society,
a descendant of one of its first families, and as the elected mayor
of the town, should be above, not adultery with Venus perhaps,
but certainly the callous immorality of creating a publicly-paid position to mollify the husband of Venus. The acquiescence of the
town, including such families as Gavin's, in so immoral a misuse
of public funds simply because DeSpain is one of them and because they are enraptured by Eula is a manifestation of hypocrisy
so rank that it would seem to say plainly that hypocrisy provides
the key to success in Jefferson. All Flem needs to succeed, by this
standard, is the facade of respectability, such as a gravestone com-
memorating a virtuous wife and an ante-bellum mansion. Faulkner
does not make an issue of DeSpain's misuse of public office, but he
is apparently not unaware of its moral implications. Ratliff, many
years later, says that he was not on DeSpain's side, but he admits
he was not against him either: And when eighteen years later
Eula commits suicide, the community reacts to its own guilt. The
nail in the tree, to use Charles Mallison's image, is crusted over,
but it is still there. On the morning after the suicide, the hypocritical
facade must be maintained. DeSpain has to follow routine, appear
at the bank, because eighteen years of fidelity to Eula give him no
right to mourn publicly.

Gavin's reaction to Eula also introduces a complex moral issue.
Gavin falls uncontrollably in love with Flem's wife. When she offers herself to him, his conscience does not restrain him; his romanticism does. For a romantic idealist, sex must be garbed in the
white mantle of pure love. No consideration of her married state,
no question of morality concerns Gavin. If Eula had come to him
bearing the semblance of love, Gavin Stevens would have become
another of Eula's lovers.

To describe these manifestations of corruption in the old order
as evidence of a deterioration of its moral fiber, as some critics have,

is to ignore the passionate *ambiance* that Faulkner creates about Eula. Faulkner's imagery, his effervescent description of Eula, his obvious approval of her visit to Stevens, clearly place him on the side of love. The irresistible passion that Eula stimulates in Gavin and DeSpain is a rare, almost mystical experience that cannot be dismissed as a simple, carnal temptation to the weak. As Faulkner makes clear, in fact, Eula is so great that only a great man deserves her. Gavin and Manfred are not of her stature, but they can, at least, approach it enough to warrant her regard. Gavin and Manfred respond, as men always respond, to the passion of love. The response brings them into conflict with moral standards, but the fierce pull of passion is a human experience, honorable and fine, even if it does conflict with morality. Gavin's recognition that he did not have it in him to be Paris to Helen is a traumatic experience, and his lifelong devotion to Eula and to her daughter, Linda, is rooted in the love she inspires. Gavin is a moral man, but he is also capable of falling in love, which Flem, of course, is not.

As do so many of Faulkner's other novels, *The Town* depicts the emergence of a young man from adolescence. Gavin's loss of Eula marks his first step toward maturity. Though Gavin's passion for Eula and his adolescent idealism are successfully conveyed in the episodes describing his contest with DeSpain, the episodes are perhaps too contrived and more adolescent than they need be. Why DeSpain, for instance, mayor of the town and already Eula's lover, should indulge in schoolboy pranks with Gavin is never satisfactorily explained. Gavin's idealism is essential to the rest of the novel, and despite all the silliness of these episodes, they do dramatize it effectively. Gavin's response to Eula is like the response of every other man in Frenchman's Bend or Jefferson—it is sexual. But naked sex is not for idealists. And, for idealists, woman cannot simply be woman. Sex must be elevated to glorious, eternal love, and woman must be the shining citadel of chastity and purity, beauty and honor. Gavin's reading at Harvard has, apparently, been restricted to the lady novelists of the nineteenth century and to chivalric tales of the Middle Ages. For him, even an earth goddess, a fertility symbol, a living poem to sex must be transformed into a Guinevere, whom Lancelot can defend and adore for her purity. Gavin knows, as everyone in town knows, that Eula is De-

Spain's mistress. The knowledge tarnishes the image of Guinevere, and so he imposes his ideal image upon the entire town. His sister, abetting him, forces the Jefferson women to receive Eula socially and thus publicly to declare her a moral woman. No one in Jefferson society could possibly entertain an adulteress; hence Eula is not an adulteress. At the Christmas dance, however, the public display of sexual grandeur by Eula is too much for the idealist to bear. Manfred's response to Eula's dancing expresses what every man in the room feels. Gavin will not, cannot accept the reality. He must ignore Eula's sensuality and label DeSpain's response an aggressive, lewd insult to a maiden fair. Gavin's attempt to deny reality reaches its climax when he sues DeSpain. What he hopes to accomplish is not clear even to him, but he must strike out against the living proof that his dream is false.

Eula's visit to Gavin to offer herself to him is a devastating experience for the young man. He is forced to face the truth about himself: he is not great enough or simple enough to be above morality as Eula is. Not for a conventional, romantic idealist is so simple a code as hers: " 'Dont expect. You just are, and you need, and you must, and so you do.' " (94)* Eula suffers from no illusions; she accepts Gavin's passion as essentially sexual. The convention-trapped Gavin restrains an impulse to turn off the light when he sees her coming to his office only because he decides it would be more suspicious off than on. Then as she enters, he thinks, *"For God's sake take off your shoes or at least tiptoe."* (89) Hoping desperately that love has brought her to him, though he knows it has not, Gavin quizzes Venus. Is she trying to save Manfred or Flem by coming to him? He does not yet know that she is trying to preserve a home for her daughter, but he does realize that it is pity, not love, which she feels for him. Faulkner's rendering of this scene creates superb comedy. Unlike the preceding episodes, its humor arises from character rather than an exaggeration of form. Gavin's backing away from his pursuing maiden fair, gasping, " 'Don't touch me,' " is like a scene by Cervantes. (94)

Gavin never regrets that he did not take Eula that evening. At the same time, he can never forget that he was not man enough to meet her on her own terms. The scene, which climaxes the open-

* Vintage Edition.

ing section of the novel, explodes with conflicting values. Passion is set above morality. Eula's realistic attitude is made to seem admirable; Gavin's romanticism and conventionality appear to belong to a lower order of human reaction. Dramatized effectively is the intricate web of conflicting forces in the human being. Gavin is intelligent, quixotic, conventional, moral, and passionate. All these qualities, frequently at odds and pulling him in opposite directions, influence his actions and reactions. When Gavin, a normal, complicated person, comes into contact with an incarnation of a single aspect of the human experience, such as sex in Eula or single-minded greed in Flem, he is set to whirling. Flem's inhumanity does for Gavin's moral sense what Eula's sensuality does for his romanticism: they make him an obsessed crusader against Snopesian immorality, and a lifelong vassal of Eula and her daughter. Gavin's idealism is unquestionably his dominant character trait; it makes him the admirable man that he is, but it also retards his recognition that absolutes are not applicable to human beings. Gavin will be nearly sixty before he is ready to share Faulkner's vision of moral complexity.

Gavin's devotion to Eula's daughter involves him in a repetition of his adventures with DeSpain. The automobile, the symbol of young love in modern American life, once more tears past the Stevens home with its cut-out open, and Gavin sheds blood a second time for a Snopes woman. Though Matt, Linda's wooer, and the entire community, including Gavin's family, assume that he is in love with the girl half his age, Gavin is not. He wants to develop Linda's mind and save her soul from contamination by the man she considers her father. He campaigns to get her to enroll in an out-of-state college. His efforts bring him, for the first time, into direct conflict with Flem, who refuses to let his daughter leave Jefferson because he is afraid that she will get married. If Linda marries, Eula will no longer have to preserve the facade of a respectable family. She can leave Flem and marry DeSpain. If Eula leaves, Flem will lose his opportunity to control the money that she will inherit from Will Varner.

Eula has her own little campaign working: she wants Stevens to marry Linda. She tries subtlety; it fails. So, without subterfuge, she proposes to Stevens that he marry Linda. Being an idealist, however, Stevens can marry only for love. Flem keeps Linda at home, deliberately frustrating her desire to go to college long enough to make her so grateful when he finally gives his permission—though only for the state university in Oxford—that she is impelled to express her appreciation. On her own initiative, she signs over to Flem the money she will inherit from her mother. This act, which is crucial to the plot, is contrived and implausible, but it is typical of the plot and character breakdowns in *The Town*. A lapse of inventiveness, rare for Faulkner, is concealed to some extent by the indirection with which the events leading to Eula's death are narrated. The speculations of Gavin and Ratliff serve to obscure the implausibility of what occurs, but implausible it is.

Linda's independent, uncoerced decision to reward Flem with money that she will inherit from her thirty-eight-year-old mother, who has not yet inherited it from Will Varner, requires that Linda know so much about Flem that she could only hate him, not reward him. Will Varner's role in the crisis is difficult to accept, also. In *The Hamlet*, he is a likeable character despite his immoral financial and sexual activities. He is certainly no moralist. Jody is outraged when Eula announces that she is pregnant, but Will is calm: " 'Hell and damnation, all this hallubaloo and uproar because one confounded running bitch finally foxed herself.' " (H, 145) In *The Town*, we are hardly prepared for Will's role as moralist by Gavin's repetition of information he received from Ratliff: that Will had three mulatto concubines "By whom he now had grandchildren." Gavin's conclusion about Will is that he is "anything in the world but unmoral since his were the strictest of simple moral standards: that whatever Will Varner decided to do was right, and anybody in the way had damned well better beware." (276)

It is this man who, a few pages later, we are asked to believe is so horrified and shocked to discover that his daughter has been living in adulterous fidelity for eighteen years that he will rush into town at four in the morning and demand that his daughter, her husband, and her lover leave Jefferson at once. Then, we are further asked to believe that the morally outraged father has no objections to the husband's solution to the problem: Flem will buy DeSpain's bank stock and Eula and DeSpain can go off together.

The entire imbroglio is, of course, the work of Flem. He foresees that Linda will be grateful and give him a notarized control of her inheritance, and he estimates correctly how Will Varner will react when he brings him Linda's document. Will's furious reaction to the idea that Flem will get control of his money is in character, and I suspect that Faulkner intended to have Will act out of fury rather than an outraged moral sense. But apparently, Faulkner realized or discovered that Linda's document would not stand legal challenge, and he had to compound the original implausibility of the document with Will's pseudo-outraged morality. Flem, at least, remains consistent as the cold, calculating manipulator of others' emotions for his financial gain.

Among these plot and character breakdowns, Eula's sacrificial maternity, her perceptiveness, and her sensitivity appear almost credible. Yet Faulkner was so successful in creating her as an archetype that the reader has difficulty adjusting to the very human Eula who visits Stevens before she kills herself. It is true that her maternal concern has characterized her existence for eighteen years, but throughout *The Hamlet* and most of *The Town*, Eula is Helen and Semiramis and Lilith. She is not presented realistically, and when she is suddenly scaled down to human proportions in her creator's imagination, the reader is not sufficiently prepared to accept the downscaling. Certainly the woman who could say, at the beginning of this novel, " 'Dont expect. You just are, and you need, and you must, and so you do,' " has altered her philosophy by the time she pays Gavin a second visit. (94) In reality, her suicide is submission to public opinion. She prefers, for her daughter's sake, to be branded suicide rather than whore. But if Eula was so far beyond public opinion as she seemed to be, and as it is necessary to believe she was if we are going to accept Ratliff's conclusion that she was bored, that she was too great for Jefferson, how could she be finally so conventional? Why did Eula not leave Jefferson, with or without DeSpain, when Linda was still a child, if she was really too great for the small town? Eula bored by Jefferson fits in with the original image of her as Helen, but not with the image of Eula as convention-conscious mother.

Eula's second visit to Gavin is as important to his moral development—which has become the main story of the novel—as was her first. She exacts from him three promises. He agrees to marry

Linda if marriage will be warranted by circumstances after Eula has left town, and if Linda wants to marry him. His other promises are not to use information that she gives to him. He promises not to reveal Ratliff's great secret—what his initials V.K. stand for. Eula's possession of this secret shocks Stevens, and it is certainly disturbing to the reader. Stevens knows jealousy, suspecting that his friend has succeeded where he failed. The reader has been given no hint in all of Ratliff's long discourses on Eula of any intimacy between them. As a result, the reader is left with the feeling that Eula's possession of this secret is simply an authorial decision to reveal, finally, Ratliff's full name. Surely, the long historical account of Ratliff's heritage by a woman on the verge of suicide stretches credulity. If the incident can be justified at all, it is only on the grounds that it contributes to our recognition of how mysterious and complicated people really are.

Gavin's third promise concerns Flem. Eula reveals that her husband is impotent. Eula's words must be considered carefully because they hold the clue to the theme of *The Mansion*. She tells Stevens:

"He's . . . impotent. He's always been. Maybe that's why, one of the reasons. You see? You've got to be careful or you'll have to pity him. You'll have to."

Up to this point in her speech, it is possible to interpret Eula's words in the way that Warren Beck does, as a warning to Gavin that pity might lead him to mitigate the inhumanity of Flem's character, to invest in him more humanity that he possesses.[7] Her next statement, however, makes absolutely clear her own sensitivity to Flem's humanity:

"He couldn't bear that, and it's no use to hurt people if you dont get anything for it. Because he couldn't bear being pitied. It's like V.K.'s Vladimir. Ratliff can live with Ratliff's Vladimir, and you can live with Ratliff's Vladimir. But you mustn't ever have the chance to, the right to, the choice to. Like he can live with his impotence, but you mustn't have the chance to help him with pity." (331)

Eula, obviously, is not telling Gavin that her husband is too horrible to deserve pity. She is arguing that he is too vulnerable to be subjected to pity. Gavin is not yet ready to deal morally with this information. He will not be until the end of *The Mansion* when he can say, " 'The poor sons of bitches that have to cause all the grief and anguish they have to cause.' "

Eula's words also point up the central cause of the novel's failure. The design of a Snopesian invasion of Jefferson, of a new, vigorous, but socially and morally obnoxious group replacing the fine, moral, but weakened old order is too simple and too abstract a concept to withstand the deepening sympathy with which Faulkner has come to view human beings. The archetypes that he created have become multi-dimensional under the close-up lens, and in the same scene in which Faulkner scales Eula down to human proportions, he welcomes Flem into the family of man. Impotence has been a symbol of Flem's separation from his fellow man; it now becomes a symbol of his union with all mankind. He too is a victim of a primal injustice, a "maniacal Risibility."

Faulkner does not explore in this novel the significance of this revelation about Flem; he reserves that for *The Mansion*. But the revelation climaxes the many scenes in the novel that explore the depth and breadth, the complexity of the human personality, the intricacy of human relations, and the difficulty of making moral judgments. This exploration of personality is an impressive achievement, but it does not sufficiently offset the artistic failure of the novel. There are many reasons, as I have indicated, why *The Town* is one of Faulkner's weakest novels, but all these reasons are rooted in a central cause: Faulkner's emotional detachment from his material. This detachment has nothing to do with the multiple-narrator technique. *Absalom, Absalom!*, in which the same technique is used, is charged with a powerful emotional undercurrent generated by the author's involvement in his story. Faulkner's masterpieces are great artistic creations because they create an overwhelming emotional current—despair, or pity, or outrage, or incredulity, or indignation, or horror—that tears the reader from his familiar moorings and sweeps him into a world created, shaped, and illuminated by Faulkner's personal vision of life. This emotional undercurrent, which the other books of the trilogy have, *The Town* lacks. Faulkner seems to be detached, objectively look-

ing down upon the complicated pattern of human existence, as he
has Gavin, toward the end of the novel, look down upon Jefferson:

And you stand suzerain and solitary above the whole sum of your life
beneath that incessant ephemeral spangling. First is Jefferson, the center, radiating weakly its puny glow into space; beyond it, enclosing it,
spreads the County, tied by the diverging roads to that center as is the
rim to the hub by its spokes, yourself detached as God Himself for this
moment above the cradle of your nativity and of the men and women
who made you, the record and chronicle of your native land proffered
for your perusal in ring by concentric ring like the ripples on living water above the dreamless slumber of your past; you to preside unanguished and immune above this miniature of man's passions and hopes
and disasters—ambition and fear and lust and courage and abnegation
and pity and honor and sin and pride—all bound, precarious and ramshackle, held together by the web, the iron-thin warp and woof of his
rapacity but withal yet dedicated to his dreams. (315-6)

Faulkner does seem, in *The Town*, to preside "unanguished
and immune," with deep sympathy for what he views, but without
sufficient personal involvement to give artistic unity to his panorama of life.

The Mansion

The climax of *The Mansion*—a muted and sober climax—occurs
when Ratliff and Gavin Stevens gain the moral vision of their creator and can say with him about people, the good and the bad, the
rich and the poor, the irascible and the gentle, "the poor sons of
bitches."

The moral indignation that created the role of the Snopes tribe
is gone, replaced by a compassion so all-encompassing that no
moral code is flexible enough to reflect it. All the Snopeses, the
murderers, the usurers, the purveyors of pornography, have been

embraced and welcomed into the human family because not just they, but all men, are trapped in the iron web of life. Gavin's pronouncement is no moral judgment of others. He has just gone through the ultimate experience for a moral idealist—condoning a murder. His pronouncement sums up human existence.

The framework of the novel is simple. Mink Snopes is sustained through thirty-eight years of prison by one thought: he must kill his cousin Flem for failing to aid him at his murder trial. The simple moral fact is that Mink is a murderer; he has taken a human life and he intends to take another one. Between a man who has killed and the community whose laws have been violated, a moral as well as an iron bar is erected. The man is labeled murderer for having broken the strongest taboo of the community. In this novel, Faulkner removes that moral bar, brings us into the mind of a murderer and engages our sympathies for him. The more we learn about Mink, the more willing are we to be placed in the difficult moral position of not only condoning Mink's murder of Jack Houston, but also of championing his determination to kill his cousin.

Faulkner's technique in achieving this upheaval of values is simple. He presents Mink as a man who epitomizes human pride in a struggle against the cosmic forces that buffet all men. By murdering Houston, Mink strikes back at the forces which he personifies in his thoughts as *"They."* *They* have created the condition of Mink's existence: the dehumanizing poverty of a tenant farmer. No matter how hard he works, how much he endures, his energy makes someone else richer. All Mink can look forward to in life is producing children who will suffer the same hardships and privations and degradations. As Mink works it out, there is a "simple fundamental justice and equity in human affairs, or else a man might just as well quit; the *they, them, it,* call them what you like, which simply would not, could not harass and harry a man forever without some day, at some moment, letting him get his own just and equal licks back in return." (6)*

Mink's ability to endure the harassment and the worry is a test of his manhood. *Their* acceptance of his right to get his just licks back is proof of simple justice in human affairs. He could take everything that *They* handed out to him, but the moment

* Random House, 1959.

would come "when they would have to prove to him that They were as much a man as he had proved to Them that he was; when he not only would have to depend on Them but had won the right to depend on Them and find Them faithful. . . ." (6) When that moment comes for Mink, and he finds *Them* faithless, he kills. Houston's arrogance is part of their harassment of Mink. Grief has made Houston bitter, but he, at least, is rich enough to shoot the horse that kills his wife and then buy another one to ride along the road that Mink must walk. Mink knows that he has no right to let his cow winter at Houston's expense, and he knows that Frenchman's Bend is too small a place to do it with impunity. He therefore prepares an elaborate story of having sold his cow to a man who returned it in the spring, demanding his money back because the cow ran off right after he bought it. Mink is so poor that the eight dollars which he must pay Houston for wintering his cow represents not only all his savings, but the luxuries that could have provided a bit of Christmas for himself and his family—a jug of liquor and a few trinkets. What hurts Mink most is that he must pay the desperately needed eight dollars to a man who is served by a Negro and who does not miss the feed that wintering Mink's cow cost him. Mink's outrage is not directed against Houston but against the very conditions that fate has imposed upon him.

He accepts Varner's judgment as a challenge to his integrity and manhood, and he works out his debt to the last penny. On the evening of the day that he finishes digging the post holes, he sits in his cabin waiting for Houston's Negro—or perhaps even Houston himself—to return the cow. He indulges in the fantasy of refusing to accept the cow until dawn, fulfilling Varner's judgment of a certain number of work days to the letter. Mink has gone without sleep to fulfill his obligation, drawing upon the spiritual strength that his years of drudgery have brought him. He "knew the trick of it. He had learned that the hard way; himself taught that to himself through simple necessity: that a man can bear anything by simply and calmly refusing to accept it, be reconciled to it, give up to it." (21) He had learned endurance, and he had learned patience; and patience "was his pride too: never to be reconciled since by this means he could beat Them; They might be stronger for a moment than he but nobody, no man, no nothing could wait longer than he could wait when nothing else but waiting would do, would work, would serve him." (22)

When Mink has proved his manhood to himself and to *Them*, *They* fail him. He does not ask Varner to force Houston to retract his demand of a pound fee, and he will not accept the money from Varner. Mink is not interested in the two days of extra work that he will have to put in. He merely wants to be certain that the law exists and is applicable to him. Its existence symbolizes to him *Their* injustice. The simple justice that he believed in does not exist, and his integrity is at stake. He faithfully worked out his debt, accepted all the harassment *They* heaped upon him, fulfilled his obligation. To accept this final outrage would be to deny his manhood.

Our sympathies are not only engaged by Mink's pride and patience, but also by our recognition that the forces he pits himself against are the universal conditions of life—the accidents of blind chance that decree one person the child of a sharecropper and another the child of a rich man, one man whole and another defective, one man talented and another stupid, one man lucky and another dogged by misfortune. The outrage and indignation at the human condition in Faulkner's early works and the writer's steadfast admiration of man's ability to accept and endure these impossible conditions suffuse the portrait of Mink and give to the whole novel the emotional unity that *The Town* lacks.

Faulkner's task of engaging reader sympathy for Mink as the murderer of his cousin Flem is more complicated because Mink's motive for this second murder is simply personal revenge. Moreover, we are not even certain that Flem could have helped Mink. At the time of the trial, Flem has become an important man in Frenchman's Bend, but in Jefferson, he is unknown. We believe with Mink, of course, that Flem, for his own reasons, does not want to help his kinsman, but there is no evidence offered to indicate that Flem could have helped even if he had tried. When Flem schemes to get Mink's sentence doubled, however, and is successful, our sympathy for Mink's desire to get vengeance increases. The degree to which Faulkner succeeds in involving the reader's sympathy for the murderer becomes obvious toward the end of the novel when Gavin and Ratliff try frantically to subvert Mink's goal. Gavin's cautionary concern for Flem's safety strikes the reader as perhaps excessive, and his active intervention seems unwarranted. Such reader empathy for a character with a mono-maniacal determination that lasts thirty-eight years is achieved also by implying that Mink is to some extent an instrument of divine justice.

During his years in prison, Mink's faith is reawakened. He belongs to none of the religious groups in the prison, but, as he explains to the Warden, his loss of faith was temporary—an aspect of growing up, of feeling his manhood and independence and strength. When he stymies a prison break and is in danger of being killed by the one convict who escapes, and is therefore kept in prison for his own safety, Mink realizes that he is too weak to do without God, and he puts his trust in Him. His trust is justified. An abandoned church, which the convict has taken over for some kind of illicit dealing, suddenly collapses. The convict is killed. The church, the Warden tells his prisoner, " 'fell down. They don't know why: it just fell down all of a sudden.' " Filled with awe, the Warden, who has come to admire Mink, adds, " 'Tell me again about that church you said you used to go to before Houston made you kill him.' " (101)

After his release, Mink's meeting with the Marine sergeant serves also to arouse sympathy for the convict. The Marine's prayer, " 'Save us, Christ, the poor sons of bitches,' " iterates the theme of the novel. (271) Goodyhay's conversion is not unlike Mink's. As the sergeant's experience illustrates, war intensifies and concentrates the horrors and terrors of normal existence. Fear, pain, anguish, and death are the unalterable realities of war, and man has nothing to rely upon but his own willingness and ability to endure. Goodyhay suffered and endured. He even sacrificed himself to help another man during a battle. But then he could stand no more and he capitulated and knew the peace of quitting the struggle to endure. According to him, as he tells the story, Jesus appeared to him and gave him three chances to say, "I cant." And Goodyhay realized that he need not give up the struggle. Jesus told him: " 'What we want are folks that believe they cant, and then do it.' " (280) Converted from that moment on, the Marine devotes his life to awakening in all the other "poor sons of bitches" —the weak, the sinful, the pitiful, black or white, who suffer—the faith in Jesus that will help them to endure.

Mink does not ostensibly respond to Goodyhay's preaching, but the two men have undergone, in different ways, the test of their manhood and have discovered that even the strongest men cannot endure without faith. More and more as his goal comes closer, Mink finds comfort in his faith that " 'Old Moster dont play jokes.' " (414) For a second when he finally faces Flem and the hammer pin strikes the rim of the cartridge cap instead of the cap, Mink doubts: "that faint something out of the past nudged, prodded: not a warning nor even really a repetition: just faint and familiar and unimportant still since, whatever it had been, even before it had not been strong enough to alter anything nor even remarkable enough to be remembered; in the same second he had dismissed it. *Hit's all right* he thought *Hit'll go this time: Old Moster dont play jokes. . . .*" (415-6)

The role of chance in the fulfillment of Mink's revenge—the theft of his money, the generosity of Goodyhay, the functioning of the worthless pistol, the timing of his arrival at Flem's house during the short period that Biglin is not on guard, the futility of Gavin's efforts to intercept him, and Flem's failure to resist his terrified murderer—create an aura of divine retribution about the mission.

And when we, as readers, have acceded, through sympathy, to this murder, the experience gives us no alternative but to join Faulkner and Gavin and Ratliff in their summation of the human plight. What Faulkner suggests in his prefatory note that he has learned in thirty-four years about "the human heart and its dilemma," is what Gavin and the reader learn in the course of the novel.

The process of preparing us for that knowledge consists of engaging our sympathies for Mink. For this reason, Faulkner uses the omniscient-author technique in the first and the last section of the novel. The multiple-narrator technique of the middle section would have been fatal to his design because reader involvement in the narrators' search for truth tends to make attitudes equivocal. Faulkner could not permit Mink to be viewed through

eyes that the reader could not completely trust; the slightest doubt
that our sympathies for Mink are justified would be fatal to the
work. Mink's thoughts, his feelings, his adventures after his release
from prison, and the action at the time of the murder must be accepted as fact if we are to understand Gavin's pronouncement.

Gavin's relationship to Linda provides the catalyst for his own
insight. Idealism continues to be the dominant characteristic in
his personality. His nephew, Charles Mallison, a college student
when Linda returns from Spain, cannot conceive of so close a relationship between a man and a woman without a sexual basis.
Despite the strong sexual overtones in the portrayal of the relationship, sexual attraction has little role in it. Gavin's involvement
with Linda begins with his devotion to her mother, but it is nurtured by Linda herself when she returns to Jefferson, a deaf widow
in her thirties. For Gavin, Linda's undying love for her dead
husband is the realization of an ideal. She is living proof to him
of fidelity and love. To love one man so completely that her love
will flame until she herself is dead is Linda's fate and her doom.
The sexual overtones in the presentation of the friendship serve,
perhaps, to dramatize by ironic contrast the purity of the love
between the couple, but the excessive emphasis upon sex weakens
and cheapens the novel and tends to obscure the real significance
of the kind of love that Linda and Gavin share. (Faulkner did occasionally use sex in his novels for sensational purposes and sometimes, as here, for its titillative effects.)

Linda offers herself to Gavin when he asks her to tear up her
Communist card and leave Jefferson. He refuses her as he had
refused her mother. The F.B.I. agent's visit has made Gavin afraid
that Linda will be harassed if she remains in town. Gavin knew
long before that Linda was a card-carrying Communist, but he
never questioned her right to believe as she wished. He considers
her affiliation with the party a manifestation of the same quality
she shares with her mother:

. . . needing, fated to need, to find something competent enough,
strong enough (in her case, this case, not tough enough because Kohl
was tough enough: he happened to be mere flesh and bones and so
wasn't durable enough) to take what she had to give; and at the same

time doomed to fail, in this, her case, not because Barton failed her but because he also had doom in his horoscope. So if the Communist party, having already proved itself immune to bullets and therefore immortal, had replaced him, not again to bereave her. . . . (233)

Some years before, Gavin sanctioned Linda's decision to live with Bart Kohl seven years before she married him, and now he does not question her right to be a member of the Communist party. When he suggests that she leave Jefferson, Linda asks him to marry her. She has not yet recovered from the shock of losing her husband and her hearing, and she needs the security that Stevens's fidelity provides. But he refuses. He can see in her eyes her abiding love for Kohl. Then, in her too-loud, quacking duck's voice, she bluntly—using the four-letter word—offers herself to Stevens. Shocked, Gavin says it is not necessary; he tests her by asking if she wants to. She does not answer, and as she repeats, " 'Gavin, Gavin, Gavin,' " he again reads in her eyes, "the immeasurable loss, the appeaseless grief, the fidelity and the enduring. . . ." (239)

Linda completes her recovery while she is in Pascagoula, working in a wartime shipyard. In a note, she asks Gavin to come to see her; she has something to ask him. He goes, reluctantly, afraid that Linda has fallen in love again and that his ideal has been shattered:

. . . you have heard of love and loss and grief and fidelity and enduring and you have seen love and loss and maybe you have even seen love and loss and grief but not all five of them—or four of them since the fidelity and enduring I am speaking of were inextricable: one. . . . (248)

The beauty of Linda's love and fidelity means so much to Gavin that he thinks, it "must be so at least once in your lifetime, no matter who suffers." (248) His ideal is not shattered. Linda exacts from him a promise that he will marry, find someone whom he can love as she has loved Bart Kohl. Gavin keeps his promise. We are provided no information about Gavin's relationship with Melissa, and it almost appears as if Gavin has once again proved his devotion to a Snopes woman by keeping his promise to marry.

We do ultimately learn, however, that Gavin is happily married, and we can therefore conclude that perhaps Linda's undying love for Bart provided the impetus that a bachelor-idealist required to marry.

Though Linda's enduring love and fidelity are archetypical, Faulkner does not present her, as he does Eula, as an archetype. She is very much a complex human being, cut off from the world by her deafness, requiring her weekly supply of liquor, capable of making what Gavin and Faulkner's Negro spokesman consider a serious mistake by attempting to help the Negro. But most significantly, this strange, fascinating woman is capable of being an active accomplice in the murder of the man most people in Jefferson (including Charles Mallison) consider her father. She can order a new car months in advance, and wait cold-bloodedly in the same house with her victim until the man, whom she has helped to get released from prison, arrives to kill Flem. Though deaf, she can appear as soon as Flem is dead, and she can calmly pick up the pistol of the terrified murderer, return it to him and help him to escape.

It is hardly surprising that Gavin, who loves Linda, in part, because of the purity of her love for Bart, undergoes the most rending moral experience of his life when he discovers that she has been an accomplice in the murder of Flem. Gavin, the elected prosecutor of the County, the champion of justice, the humanist who would try to protect even a man like Flem Snopes, now also, in a sense, becomes an accomplice in the murder. His decision— if decision it can be called—to abet Linda by ignoring her guilt and by carrying the money she gives him to Mink, forces him into an act that is morally and legally wrong—an act that he can no more help doing than breathing.

Gavin reveals the effect of this traumatic moral experience when he tells Ratliff—for the first time—that Flem was impotent and says about him: " 'The poor sons of bitches that have to cause all the grief and anguish they have to cause.' " (430) A sinner among sinners, a man driven into wrong by his own idealism and love, Gavin knows at last the full burden of the human dilemma. Flem, guilty of so much wrong, of such incredible inhumanity, so much "a son of a bitch," *has* to cause the grief he causes. Whether his cold rapacity was an expression of defiance against the brutal fate that made him incapable of loving, or whether it was an attempt to compensate for his difference from other men by dominating them despite his lack of manhood, we do not know. But the victimizer has become the victim. Perhaps, as Ratliff suggests, when Flem faced Mink's pistol, he did not defend himself because he recognized simple justice, he had had his licks and now it was Mink's turn. Or perhaps, Flem had had enough, had struggled to endure his impotence and discovered that the struggle was meaningless. He had gained power and become rich, risen from sharecropper's son to be president of a bank and owner of a mansion, but all he could do was sit in his mansion with his feet on the fireplace and chew on air, evening after evening, while other men loved and lived.

Gavin's pronouncement includes himself, includes all men. The human being is at once a victim of fate and a cause of misery to others; he is so incredibly complicated a mixture of good and bad, strength and weakness, selfishness and altruism that he is almost beyond moral judgment—at least by his fellow men. It is possible to brand Linda a murderess and forget her great capacity for fidelity; to condemn Gavin for abetting a murder and to ignore his idealism, his sense of justice, his decency and honesty; to condemn Ratliff for abetting a murder and to forget his sixty years of honesty and integrity and compassion. Faulkner, it would seem, is not denying that certain acts are wrong; he is simply recognizing the complexity of the human heart and embracing all men—the "poor sons of bitches"—with sympathy.

Faulkner's overall vision of life, as I have pointed out before, and as we shall see in his final novel, *The Reivers,* is not optimisic. The all-embracing compassion expressed, especially, in the works of his final period, stems from his vision of man as a victim—of himself and of a maniacal Risibility. His admiration for the human being and his assurance that man can and will endure is a defiant response and hope. His compassion does not excuse wrongdoing. Despite Stevens's declaration, " 'There aren't any morals . . . People just do the best they can,' " Faulkner clearly presents the murder of Flem as a wrong, and Linda's role in it as immoral. (429) Flem's inhumanity, too, is a crime, no matter what its source. As Temple learns in *Requiem for a Nun*, a man is responsible for his acts, and he has a moral responsibility to himself and to those around him. He is sinned against but still a sinner—that is the dilemma of the human heart. In the final scene of the novel, Faulkner evokes the feeling of peace and quiescence which comes about when the living man escapes from the paradoxes of existence, through death. Flowing back into the earth, he becomes part of nature again.

Despite the profundity of Faulkner's theme in this novel and the masterful way in which it is handled and developed, *The Mansion* has too many weaknesses to rank among Faulkner's great works. For one thing, it shares *The Town*'s weakness in being too obviously a finale to the County novels. Too much effort is devoted to tying up loose ends, to retelling stories that are not essential to the theme and development of the novel. Charles Mallison, prompted by Linda's return from Spain, recalls, for example, stories of other returning Jefferson veterans. These tales are part of Charles's and Linda's heritage and do, perhaps, help to portray the atmosphere of the small town to which Linda is returning, but there is a failure of proportion. The series of stories occupies far too much space and attention for their minor and tangential relationship to plot and theme. The same criticism can be made of the final Snopes story involving Meadowfield and a new Snopes in Jefferson. The story itself is not a particularly good one: plot dominates character, and neither through tone nor theme does it add anything to the novel. In the first place, the truly obnoxious character in the tale is Meadowfield, not Res Snopes, and the idea that evil is a continuing problem in human existence hardly requires so elaborate an illustration. Secondly, a resurrection of the Snopesian invasion theme, which it obviously is, at this stage of the trilogy is incongruous. We have viewed too many Snopeses sympathetically not to realize by now that Res may be a scoundrel, but if we knew him better, we would discover some fine (or at least human) qualities in him. We have had to alter our image of Mink as an "out-and-out" mean Snopes, and we have learned that the purveyor of pornography, Montgomery Ward, has a sensitive conscience. We have even recognized that Montgomery's impotence or whatever it is that makes women unattractive to him, has given him the insight that Gavin Stevens acquires only eighteen years later. Montgomery and Miss Reba, the whorehouse madam, are the first in the novel to embrace sinners with their compassionate, "the poor sons of bitches."

One of Faulkner's most interesting achievements in *The Mansion* undermines the novel's structural unity—his dramatization of the end of the small town as an isolated unit in American life. In the first book of the trilogy, no breath of the outside world penetrates the hamlet. A few years later, in *The Town*, some of Jefferson's sons go to foreign countries, and soon national and international events begin to affect the lives of the inhabitants. By 1946, Charles Mallison is as much a product of national and world events as he is of Jefferson. His realistic attitude reflects the attitude of his World War II generation, just as Gavin's romantic idealism is of World War I vintage, and Linda's social idealism a symbol of the 1930's. By making Barton Kohl a Jew and Linda a Communist and patron of the Negro, Faulkner reveals the effects on Jefferson society of complex issues. The portrait of Clarence Snopes reflects, of course, the political demagoguery that has plagued Mississippi. And the emphasis upon Ratliff's Russian heritage tarnishes the American image of the Russians as the enemy. By embracing so much in his novel, however, Faulkner sacrifices unity. Ratliff's story—his response to Kohl's modern sculpture, his meeting with Allanova, who is noted for her seventy-five-dollar ties, and his journey to the spot where the first Vladimir Kyrilytch in the United States was found by Nelly Ratcliffe—is a sentimental indulgence by Faulkner of his fondness for Ratliff that is artistically unjustified.

There are other artistic lapses. Charles Mallison's attitude toward the relationship of Linda and his uncle when she first returns to Jefferson is understandable. He is not jealous of his uncle because of Linda, but jealous of Linda because she absorbs his uncle's interest. Even his prurient concentration on the possibility of sex between the couple is justifiable and amusing—at first. But when Charles returns from the war, and from months of imprisonment in a German stalag, his continued adolescent speculations about the possible sexual activities of his uncle (who is nearing sixty) and Linda border on obscenity. The scene in which he asks his uncle if there would be any objections if he tried to seduce Linda violates good taste.

Thus, structurally and thematically, *The Mansion* is marred by diffusion. When Faulkner deals with his theme of moral complexity, he is the master artist. When he diffuses his vision and attempts to incorporate in his novels his views on social issues, such as the Negro problem or Southern demagoguery, he sacrifices the role of artist to the role of sage. Certainly, he ties these issues to his plot, but the connections are contrived and the issues essentially extraneous.

Considering the trilogy as a whole, one might argue that the three novels are unified by a progressive demonstration of moral complexity, beginning with the simple archetypes of Flem and Eula and the sharp opposition of the moral Ratliff to the immoral Flem in *The Hamlet,* and ending with the dissolution of the archetypes and the deliberate blurring of the clear demarcation between good and evil in the final volume. But, as I have tried to show, the confused second volume indicates clearly that an alteration of design and theme occurred. During the many years separating the first volume from the second, Faulkner's view of life became more comprehensive and comprehending. The trilogy as a whole, therefore, suffers from the alteration of design, and though it is an imposing achievement, it lacks the unity which might have made it a monumental work of art.

The Reivers

In *The Reivers* (1962), a thematic progression which we have observed in Faulkner's successive novels reaches its conclusion: a sensitive and intelligent young man learns to accept the polarities of life—the good and the bad, the brutal and the gentle—as the unchanging condition of existence. To dramatize this philosophy of acceptance by an elite male character, Faulkner had to write a didactic fairy tale, ignore reality and create a sentimental, make-believe world. *The Reivers* is a light-hearted rendering of the initiation into manhood that serves as the basic pattern of so many of the novels.[1] Lucius Priest, who is basically a carbon copy of the other elite young heroes, is fortunate.* He has none of the problems that afflict his predecessors. He is not psychologically insecure as is Quentin Compson; he is not burdened as is Ike McCaslin with a guilt-laden past; he is not troubled by racial problems as is Chick Mallison. And most important, the adult world which Lucius discovers is a fairy-tale world. It contains evil characters and terrors, but it is essentially a pleasant world in which the good triumph. For these reasons, Lucius Priest can quickly acquire that quality of non-resistance which only the primitive characters and some of the elite women possess in the earlier novels. In *The Reivers*, Faulkner calls attention to that quality by attributing it to women. At the beginning of the novel, for example, the young hero's maternal grandfather dies. Regarding his mother's conduct in this crisis, the boy muses: "It's not men who cope with death; they resist, try to fight back and get their brains trampled out in consequence; where women just flank it, envelop it in one soft and instantaneous confederation of unresistance like cotton batting or cobwebs. . . ." (46-7)† (The sentence is a succinct summation of much of Faulkner's fiction.) Lucius's instinct is to resist, to fight back as do his predecessors, but because his creator is using him to point a moral, Lucius quickly gains the wisdom of women who "can bear anything because they are wise enough to know that all you have to do with grief and trouble is just go on through them and come out on the other side." (111)

The plot of *The Reivers* is simple. The title is an archaic word meaning "the plunderers." Lucius Priest, a boy of eleven, Boon Hogganbeck, who has the mentality of a child, and a Negro, who gives his full name as Ned William McCaslin Jefferson Missippi,

---

* See the McCaslin Genealogy, p. 231.
† Random House, 1962.

go off to Memphis in the car of Grandfather Priest.* Boon wants to visit a prostitute, Corrie, who works in Miss Reba's sporting house. In Memphis, Boon and Lucius stay at Miss Reba's. On their first evening there, Ned comes to tell them that he has exchanged the automobile for a race horse. To get the car back, the reivers must race the horse and win. They get plenty of cooperation because all the world loves a horse race. Eventually, with Lucius riding and Ned masterminding the race and the horse, they get their car back and return to Jefferson. Corrie is so impressed by the manners and innocence of the curtsying Lucius that she forsakes her profession to marry Boon. Over an extended weekend, Lucius learns more about life than an eleven-year-old can readily absorb. But Lucius comes through his adventure a mature and wise young man: he has learned to accept life.

The plot, despite its devious twists and turns, is about the simplest that Faulkner ever devised for a full-length work. Fairy tales seldom have complicated plots. The world of the novel is a never-never land where parents are all they should be, prostitutes are reformed by the innocence of a boy, the bad people are thoroughgoing bogey men, and the rest of the inhabitants may have a few vices, but they are really warm, good-hearted people.

The Reivers, in fact, is a natural for Hollywood. Faulkner probably never turned out so tailor-made a script when he was actually writing for the movies. With the elimination of a few curse words and an episode here and there, the novel could be transferred to the screen to provide popular sentimental comedy in the tradition of Clarence Day's *Life With Father*. A few scenes will illustrate the point. Grandfather Priest buys one of the first automobiles in Jefferson, but he refuses, at first, to ride in it. Then Grandmother Priest becomes addicted to the lure of motion and speed. With the entire family clad in dusters and veils and goggles, a daily drive becomes a ritual. Grandfather sits beside the driver; Grandmother, daughter-in-law, and children are piled in the back seat of the open car. Tobacco-chewing Grandfather suddenly turns and spurts a

---

* Ned's character and family connections identify him unmistakably as the same character who is called Lucas Beauchamp in *Go Down, Moses*, and *Intruder in the Dust*. Ned, Miss Reba, Minnie, and Boon, all of whom are earlier creations, are the most deftly drawn characters in the novel.

mouthful of tobacco juice into the wind. Grandmother stiffens with horror and shock. She is a lady. She cannot, will not, believe that any gentleman, let alone her own husband, would spit in a lady's face. In the next scene, Grandmother is missing. Daughter-in-law holds a fan-like shield that she raises each time Grandfather's head begins to turn. The first half of the novel is filled with such comic scenes.

It is also rich in sentimentality; in one such sentimental episode, Corrie sits beside the pallet on which Lucius lies in the attic of Miss Reba's. The boy has been slightly hurt defending her honor. The prostitute, sobbing, promises that she will reform. Later on in the novel, on the day of the final race, Grandfather Priest arrives. He is a friend of the two gentlemen who own the horses, and we are provided some wonderful shots of a Southern mansion with the three Southern gentlemen, all looking like retired Confederate colonels, drinking toddies before dinner. They too love horse racing, so they are gentle with the reivers. In the finale of the novel, Lucius, of course, must be punished. The action is embarrassingly familiar. The camera (which we feel to be shooting the scene) follows the boy climbing the stairs behind his father to the bathroom for the razor strop, then back down the stairs, focusing for a moment on the face of the troubled but silent mother as father and son march past her and down the cellar steps. In the storage room lined with home-made preserves, it takes a close-up of Father's face. Father must do his duty, but his heart is not in it. Then Grandfather enters and gratefully Father exits with strop. A gentle admonitory speech from Grandfather, and Lucius's boyhood ebbs away on a tide of tears. Few novels provide a suitable ending for this type of Hollywood movie, but *The Reivers* has the perfect scene. The reformed prostitute, now Mrs. Boon Hogganbeck, shows her baby to Lucius and announces she has named it Lucius Priest Hogganbeck.

Most of the characters in the novel are vintage products of the nineteenth-century sentimental novel. Butch, the villain, is so clearly hateful that it is an unmitigated pleasure to see him get the thrashing he deserves. The foil for this bad law officer is Poleymus, the constable who administers the law with understanding and justice when he is not caring for his invalided wife. The foil for the good, naïve Lucius is the fifteen-year-old Otis, who is nasty through and through. Uncle Parsham is a stereotype of the dignified old Negro; Colonel Linscomb, of the old-time Southern gentleman. Life as depicted in *The Reivers* is the romantic image we have come to associate with the sentimental novel, television, and Hollywood. There may be problems, but fundamentally all is right with the world. Some white people mistreat Negroes, of course, but the Negroes are really satisfied with the hierarchy of Southern society, and relations between the races are gentlemanly and agreeable. Some women may be prostitutes, but prostitutes are really good souls. They can, after all, be redeemed by mere exposure to innocence.

Such a viscous immersion in the trite and the sentimental may not be artistically justifiable, but it is, at least, comprehensible once one recognizes that Faulkner chose to ignore reality in order to dramatize a sensitive young man adopting the philosophy of acceptance. The tragic vision that informs Faulkner's novels has not, as a number of passages throughout *The Reivers* clearly indicate, suddenly become radiantly optimistic. In one of a number of quasi-philosophical digressions, for instance, the storyteller rates animals according to intelligence, which he defines as "the ability to cope with environment: which means to accept environment yet still retain at least something of personal liberty." (121) He tells a fable about cats. In one period of the earth's history, he says,

. . . the dominant creatures were cats: who after ages of trying to cope with the anguishes of mortality—famine, plague, war, injustice, folly, greed—in a word, civilised government—convened a congress of the wisest cat philosophers to see if anything could be done: who after long deliberation agreed that the dilemma, the problems themselves were insoluble and the only practical solution was to give it up, relinquish, abdicate, by selecting from among the lesser creatures a species, race optimistic enough to believe that the mortal predicament could be solved and ignorant enough never to learn better. (122)

The passage is amusing, but the mortal predicament is not. Also, underneath the sugar coating that Faulkner liberally applies, the experiences of Lucius are brutal. In Memphis, the boy encounters pimps and tough-talking prostitutes; he witnesses naked carnality and ugly cruelty. He learns the facts of life from the foul mouth of Otis, an adolescent version of Popeye, the impotent voyeur of *Sanctuary*. Lucius, like a number of his adolescent predecessors in the novels, reacts violently to the discovery of sex. And, on the following day, when he has to witness Butch mauling Corrie and insulting Negroes, Lucius is ashamed, ". . . hating all of us for being the poor frail victims of being alive, having to be alive . . , hating that such not only was, but must be, had to be if living was to continue and mankind be a part of it." (174) At first, Lucius longs to run away, return home and obliterate from his memory everything he has seen and learned, but he does not. The boy may hate the way life is, but he understands that the bad and the ugly are part of living; they always have been and they always will be.

The moral of this fairy tale is the same one that Faulkner incorporated in many of his novels—but most often in the character of simple-minded people like Nancy in *Requiem for a Nun*. To make the same point with one of his intelligent young protagonists, he had to create a never-never land that was apparently so foreign to him that he had to fall back on sentimental stereotypes. Fundamentally, *The Reivers* is like Mark Twain's *The Adventures of Huckleberry Finn*. The auto replaces the raft, and Ned serves as Jim. The major difference between Twain's masterpiece and Faulkner's minor work is that Huck Finn encounters reality, while Lucius Priest remains in a fantasy world.

A minor aspect of this didactic tale is interesting. The novel begins: "Grandfather said." The writer of that line is Lucius Priest III, who is setting down a story told to him in 1961 by his grandfather Lucius Priest II. The grandfather is recounting an adventure that occurred fifty-six years earlier, in 1905 when he was eleven years old. The storyteller's own grandfather, Lucius Priest I, who was a young man during the Civil War, plays an important role in Lucius's adventures. The five generations of the Priest family presented in the novel extend over a period of more than a hundred years. Faulkner subtitles the novel "A Reminiscence." Now, we know that throughout the fiction, storytelling about the past has a major influence on the lives of Faulkner's young protagonists.[3] Their characters are molded and their attitudes and values are established by the stories they hear during their childhood. We also know that the family storytellers create legends about the past, and that these legends bear only tangential relation to reality. In effect, what Faulkner is doing in this novel is creating a legend about the world of 1905 just as the storytellers of an earlier generation created legends about the ante-bellum South.

We also know that Faulkner himself grew up on legends about the old South. In *The Reivers*, there are certain similarities between Faulkner's own boyhood and that of Lucius which are too obvious and too obtrusive to be ignored. Though Faulkner was five years younger than Lucius in 1905, his father Murray Falkner ran, for a time, a livery stable, as does Maury Priest, the father of Lucius. For all the effect the fact has upon the novel, Lucius could have been an only child, but like Faulkner, he is the eldest in a family of four boys. The grandfather of Lucius is president of a bank as was Faulkner's own grandfather, and even the location of grandfather's house across the street from his son's is autobiographical fact. The name of the Negro Mammy in this novel suggests the Caroline Barr to whom Faulkner dedicated *Go Down, Moses*, and to whom he paid warm tribute in his dedication for giving "to my childhood an immeasurable devotion and love." It may be that Faulkner enjoyed the irony, as he wrote this final novel, of seeing himself as a grandfather recasting reality, reminiscing about a world that never existed, could never have existed, just as the storytellers of his own youth had created legends of the past.

Though a minor work, *The Reivers* may be of major importance in future studies of Faulkner. In no other novel does Faulkner identify himself so clearly with his young hero, who is so much like the other young heroes of the novels. And as we learn more and more about Faulkner's personal life, we may be able to see more clearly the extent to which the works of this great American writer constitute, in effect, a spiritual autobiography.

Appendix, Notes and Bibliography

The Sound and the Fury

» » Section I: Chronology of scenes

SCENE	DATE *	BENJY'S ATTENDANT
Damuddy's Death	1898	Versh
Benjy's Name Changed	1900 (Nov.)	
Dec. 23: Delivery of Message		
End of Uncle Maury-Patterson Affair		
Caddy Uses Perfume	1905-6	T.P.
Caddy in the Swing	1906-7	
Benjy, 13, Must Sleep Alone	1908	
Caddy's Loss of Virginity	1909 (Late Summer)	
Caddy's Wedding	1910 (April 24)	
Benjy at the Gate	1910 (May)	
Quentin's Suicide	1910 (June 2)	
Benjy Attacks the Burgess Girl and is Castrated		
Death of Mr. Compson	1912	
Trip to Cemetery		
Death of Roskus		Luster
The Present	1928 (April 7)	

* No dates are given for those scenes which, from the evidence in the novel, cannot be assigned to a specific year. They are, however, set in their chronological order. The double date assigned to two scenes indicates that the year was established according to Caddy's age. Without knowing the month of her birth, we cannot be certain which of the dates is correct.

Because Sections III and IV are relatively easy to follow, I have provided no chronologies for these sections.

» » Section I: Fragments of scenes unified and set into chronological sequence

Most of the scenes listed above in the *Chronology of scenes* appear in the book as Benjy's fragmented and separated recollections. Below, all of the fragments of each scene have been collected and set into chronological sequence. (The "Clues" are words or phrases that will assist the reader to identify the scene that Benjy is remembering.)

Damuddy's death

CLUES: "Damuddy"—Roskus calls children for supper—lights in the windows —Caddy in the tree—Dirty muddy drawers

The Compson children, Quentin, Caddy, Jason, and Benjy, and Benjy's attendant, Versh, are wading in the creek. Caddy, who had squatted and wet her dress, takes it off with Versh's help, despite Quentin's insistence that she leave it on. When Quentin slaps her, Caddy slips and gets her drawers muddy. She retaliates by splashing Quentin, and both children are wet. Farther down the branch, Jason plays by himself. Roskus arrives and calls everyone to supper. Versh buttons Caddy's dress as Jason threatens to tell that Quentin and Caddy had splashed each other. Quentin sulks and follows as the others go up the hill toward the house. There, they are greeted by Mr. Compson, to whom Jason immediately blurts the story of the splashing. Caddy receives permission from their father to be in charge as they all go into the kitchen to eat supper. The sound of Mrs. Compson's crying penetrates to the kitchen. After supper, Dilsey tells the children to go upstairs to bed, but Caddy leads them into the yard toward the Negro cabin. Frony and T.P. are playing with lightning bugs. The talk between Frony and Caddy turns to funerals with Caddy recalling the death of the mare, Nancy. (The horse fell into a ditch and was shot by Roskus.) Led by Caddy, the group of children go toward the front of the house, passing a snake on their way. There are lights in many windows of the house and Caddy decides that the adults are having a party. She climbs into a tree to get a view of the inside of the house. As she climbs, the children below can see her muddy drawers. Quentin, who has not joined the group, remains by himself, first sitting on the back stairs of the house and then going off to the barn. Dilsey, arriving from the kitchen, lifts Caddy out of the tree, sends Frony and T.P. to their cabin, dispatches Versh after Quentin, and leads the others into the kitchen. Caddy pleads for permission to carry Benjy upstairs, but Dilsey insists upon doing it herself. Mr. Compson, in his shirt sleeves, awaits them at the top of the stairs to caution them to be quiet because their mother is ill. Dilsey brings Caddy and Jason and Benjy into a spare bedroom which is usually used only when one of the children is sick. As they get into their night clothes, Versh brings in Quentin who is crying. Quentin gets into one of the beds with Jason and turns his face to the wall. Dilsey discovers Caddy's muddy drawers and scrubs her clean. Caddy and Benjy sleep in the same bed.

Benjy's name changed

CLUES: fire—mirror—rain—the cushion. Scene takes place in the library (with several units in Mrs. Compson's room).

On a rainy November day in 1900, Caddy, Benjy, and Mrs. Compson are in the library. Caddy tells Benjy that his name is no longer Maury; he is now Benjy. Mrs. Compson, reclining in a chair with red and yellow cushions, asks Caddy to bring Benjy to her. Sitting before the fire, Benjy howls when Caddy tries to lift him by the arms. The mother tells her daughter not to lift the child; he can come to her by himself. Benjy wants to remain near the fire, and Caddy says that when he is finished looking at the fire then Mrs. Compson can tell him that his name has been changed. But his mother insists that Benjy come to her. Caddy picks up her brother and staggers toward her mother's chair. She tries to put Benjy in her mother's lap. Mrs. Compson, however, demands that Benjy stand in front of her. Benjy howls. Ignoring her mother's objections, Caddy gives Benjy a cushion to hold. Arguing that Caddy babies the boy too much, Mrs. Compson insists that the cushion be removed. Caddy does as her mother wishes, but when Benjy howls, she goes behind her mother's chair and holds the cushion so Benjy can see it. Mrs. Compson complains that she is developing a headache, and Caddy offers to get Dilsey for her. She and Benjy go into the kitchen where Dilsey admonishes her for making her mother nervous. Caddy explains to Dilsey that Benjy was being told his new name. Dilsey brings Mrs. Compson upstairs as Benjy and Caddy return to the library. Benjy sits before the fire. Caddy, putting her head on the lap of her idiot brother, cries. Dilsey enters and says it will be her turn next to cry on Maury's lap. When Caddy reminds her that his name is now Benjy, Dilsey denounces the name change.

Mr. Compson, smelling of rain, enters and picks up Benjy. In his father's arms, Benjy can see reflected in the mirror Caddy attacking Jason for cutting up Benjy's paper dolls. Mr. Compson breaks up the fight. He has difficulty holding Caddy, who is so furious she kicks at Jason. As Mr. Compson whips Jason, Caddy promises Benjy to make some more paper dolls for him and she hands him his cushion.

Quentin enters, also smelling of rain, and wants to know what Jason has done. Caddy notices that her brother has been in a fight. When Mr. Compson asks about it, Quentin explains that some boy had tried to put a frog in Caddy's desk. Mr. Compson tells Jason, who is out in the hall still crying, to come into the library and stop the crying or he will get another licking. Dilsey announces that supper is ready.

Versh, smelling of rain, enters and sits beside Benjy in front of the fire, nudging the child out of the way so he can dry his legs. He tells Benjy that he is going to be a bluegum because his name has been changed. Caddy wants to feed Benjy, so she brings him into the kitchen. Roskus sits in front of the stove. As Caddy feeds Benjy, Roskus comments on the rain and Dilsey complains that her hip hurts her from climbing up and down the stairs caring for Mrs. Compson. After supper, Versh carries Benjy up the stairs, and Caddy brings the child into her mother's bedroom to say goodnight. Mr. Compson is sitting with his wife. It is only ten minutes to seven, too early for Benjy's bedtime, so the father leads the children downstairs to the library, admonishing them to be quiet because Quentin is studying. Caddy gives Benjy the cushion and he sits before the fire. In a corner, Jason is sulking. When his father calls him over, Jason throws his spitball into the fire and joins Caddy on Mr. Compson's lap. Benjy comes to the chair and Caddy holds him.

Dec. 23: Caddy and Benjy deliver Uncle Maury's message to Mrs. Patterson

CLUES: the cold—hands in pocket—"Patterson"

Benjy is crying: he wants to go outdoors to meet Caddy. Versh complains that it is too cold to go outside, and Mrs. Compson agrees. Uncle Maury, her brother, urges her to send the child out. After much complaining about her burdens, the mother permits Versh to dress Benjy and bring him outdoors. Benjy hurries to the gate. Versh warns him not to put his hands on the cold gate. Caddy, returning from school, sees Benjy waiting for her and breaks into a run. Benjy tries to communicate that he is happy to see her. They run to the house and go into the room where Mrs. Compson and Uncle Maury are. The uncle calls Caddy aside while Versh takes off Benjy's coat and overshoes. Caddy tells Versh to wait, asking her mother if she can take Benjy outdoors again. Mrs. Compson once more laments her fate and finally consents. Caddy brings Benjy into the hall, where she buttons his coat and embraces him. Outside she warns him to keep his hands in his pockets. They go around the barn and look toward the branch where a pig is being slaughtered. Caddy promises Benjy that they can come back that way. They cross the creek and go up the hill to the Patterson place. Caddy climbs over the fence and delivers Uncle Maury's note to Mrs. Patterson. On the way home, the children crawl through a fence and Benjy gets snagged on a nail. They go by the pig pen and Caddy says the pigs are snorting because one of them was killed.

The end of Uncle Maury's affair with Mrs. Patterson

CLUE: Uncle Maury's black eye

It is early spring. Uncle Maury has apparently taken to sending Benjy with messages to Mrs. Patterson. When Benjy arrives, Mr. Patterson is hoeing in the garden. His wife runs toward Benjy to get the message, but Mr. Patterson is quicker and more successful in getting over the fence. As Benjy races down the hill, Mrs. Patterson remains caught on the fence. Uncle Maury's eye is blackened by Mr. Patterson. Versh carries a tray up to him in his bedroom, as, downstairs, Mr. Compson taunts his wife about her brother. Mrs. Compson tells Versh to tell Dilsey to put Benjy to bed.

Caddy at fourteen uses perfume

CLUE: "She put her arms around me again, but I went away."

Benjy cries when he sees his sister all dressed up. Jason sasses her about acting all grown up with her prissy dress. Caddy walks away from him, and Benjy follows her up the stairs. She does not understand why he is crying. In their mother's room, Benjy is given a box (probably a jewel case) to play with. When Caddy tries to leave the room, Benjy howls. He ignores his mother and follows his sister. Mr. Compson, at the foot of the stairs, shouts for T.P. to bring Benjy downstairs. But Benjy refuses to move away from the bathroom door. When Caddy comes out of the bathroom, they go into her room. Benjy again cries when Caddy sits at her dressing table. Picking up the perfume bottle, she invites him to smell it. He continues to cry, and as soon as she is dressed, Caddy leads him downstairs where she makes Dilsey a present of her bottle of perfume.

Caddy in the swing

CLUES: evening—the moon shining—the dog Dan with Benjy—Caddy and Charlie

Benjy is looking for Caddy. The kitchen is in darkness and he goes into the yard, where the dog Dan begins to follow him. T.P. is searching for Benjy, who is now heading out of the moonlight into the cedar grove where the swing is located. When he sees Caddy in the swing with Charlie, Benjy cries. Caddy rushes to her brother and embraces him. Angrily, Charlie tells Caddy to send Benjy away. He tries to kiss her. Benjy howls and Caddy fights off Charlie. She brings Benjy to the house, and on the porch she kneels to embrace him, promising she " 'won't any more, ever.' " They go into the house where Caddy washes her mouth.

Benjy at thirteen must sleep alone

CLUE: " 'Come on now,' Dilsey said, 'You too big to sleep with folks.' "

Dilsey tells Benjy that he must sleep by himself in Uncle Maury's room. The mention of Uncle Maury's room sets off Benjy's recollection of the time Uncle Maury was ill with the black eye and the scene between his mother and father which ended with Mrs. Compson's telling Dilsey to put Benjy to bed. When he is put to bed alone, Benjy cries. So Dilsey brings Caddy, who, in her bathrobe, gets on the bed with her brother. He is under the covers and Dilsey spreads a blanket over Caddy, telling her that she can leave as soon as Benjy goes to sleep.

Caddy's loss of virginity

CLUES: "We could hear Caddy walking fast."—"We were in the hall."

Caddy walks quickly down the hall. Mrs. Compson tells her to come into the room. Benjy looks at his sister and begins to howl. Crying, Caddy shrinks against the wall. Benjy pulls at her dress, urging her to go upstairs to the bathroom to wash. They go into the hall, where Caddy stares at her brother. Both are crying. They climb the stairs, and Caddy again shrinks against the wall. She tries to go into her bedroom, but Benjy pulls at her dress to get her into the bathroom to wash.

Caddy's wedding

CLUES: Sasprilluh—Cellar—T.P.'s "Whooey"—Caddie's veil—Cows jumping —Quentin beating T.P.

Caddy's wedding reception apparently takes place in the evening. T.P. and Benjy watch the car lights coming up the drive; then, T.P., after checking to see if Dilsey is occupied in the kitchen, goes into the cellar and gets a bottle of champagne. They drink the bottle and then another. T.P. laughs drunkenly and rolls in the grass. He drags a box close to the parlor window and tells Benjy to get on it. Benjy climbs on the box and, when through the window he sees Caddy in her wedding veil, he begins to cry. T.P. brings him back to the cellar to drink more champagne. Now unsteady on their feet, they both fall and then struggle up the cellar stairs into the moonlight. Benjy tries to climb back on the box; it slips from under him and hits him on the back of the head. His howls bring Quentin and Caddy rushing out of the house. Caddy embraces Benjy, and Quentin chases T.P. around the yard until he catches him and kicks him into the pig trough. With Benjy and the unsteady T.P., Quentin heads toward the barn. To Benjy, everything seems to move up and down the hill. He passes out momentarily. In the barn he is sick. Quentin, thumping T.P. against the wall to sober him up, tells him to stay in the barn until he returns. Benjy is slumped on the floor as Versh comes in and asks T.P. where he got the liquor. Quentin returns with something hot for Benjy to drink. The idiot passes out as they lay him in the barn crib.

Benjy at the gate

CLUE: " 'You cant do no good looking through the gate,' T.P. said."

Benjy stands at the gate crying. T.P. tells him that it will do no good because Caddy has gone a long way off. The scene shifts to the house. Benjy is crying and Mrs. Compson asks T.P. what is wrong. T.P. explains that Benjy wants to go to the gate to wait for Caddy. The mother tells him to play with Benjy and keep him quiet. It is raining and they cannot go outside. T.P. tells Mrs. Compson that nothing will keep Benjy quiet. She replies, " 'Nonsense.' " As they talk, Benjy slips out of the house, runs to the gate and follows the school girls along the fence. They are frightened and cross the street. T.P. runs out and gets Benjy.

Quentin's death

CLUES: Dilsey singing—Roskus talking about bad luck—Dan howling

T.P. dresses Benjy and they go into the kitchen to eat. Dilsey is moaning and Benjy begins to cry. Dilsey tells T.P. to keep him away from the house and they go down to the creek to play. Later they return to the house. Apparently Quentin's body has arrived because T.P. keeps Benjy from going around to the front of the house. From the kitchen, they go to the barn where Roskus is milking with one hand; his other is crippled by rheumatism. T.P. takes over the milking and advises his father to see a doctor. Roskus declares it will do no good because there is no luck on the place. On the evening of the same day, in the Negro cabin, Dilsey puts Benjy to bed with T.P. Roskus again talks about bad luck, referring to Benjy and to the deaths of the grandmother and Quentin. He is certain that there will be another death. Dilsey tells him that he should not complain about his luck because Versh is working, Frony is married, and T.P. is old enough to help with the chores. Besides, she declares, there will be a lot more deaths than just one: everyone dies.

Benjy assaults the Burgess girl and is castrated

CLUE: " 'How did he get out,' Father said."

Mr. Compson asks Jason if he had left the gate open. Jason denies it, saying the family is bad enough without this kind of thing happening. He tells his father that now he will have to send Benjy to Jackson, that is, if Mr. Burgess does not shoot the idiot first.

The next scene, beginning "It was open when I touched it" presents Benjy's recollection of the incident. The school girls know that the gate is always locked, and they stop to watch Benjy. When the idiot touches the gate, it opens. They run, but he catches one of them.

This memory merges into the castration operation: ". . . and she screamed and I was trying to say and trying and the bright shapes began to stop and I tried to get out. I tried to get it off my face." He is fighting the anesthesia mask, but he breathes in and goes off to sleep.

Mr. Compson's death and funeral

CLUES: I could smell it—Dan howling—Father sick—Luster and Quentin playing with spools—Funeral carriages

Benjy awakens from sleep howling; he hears his mother crying. T.P. unpins his bedclothes and dresses him quickly to bring him to the Negro cabin. They go into the hall. Someone tells T.P. to take Benjy out of the house. Dilsey comes up the stairs and tells T.P. that Frony is fixing a bed for Benjy. Someone opens the father's bedroom door and advises T.P. to keep Benjy at the Negro cabin. They go downstairs and out the door into the moonlight. Dan is howling in the yard. Benjy continues to howl and T.P. leads him across the yard along a brick wall, past the pigpen and the barn and down to the branch. Benjy slips and gets his leg wet. Dan is still howling. They reach the ditch in the pasture where Roskus shot the mare, and T.P. tells Benjy he has twenty acres and the whole night to bellow in. T.P. lies down in the ditch and Benjy sits staring at the horse's bones, recalling the buzzards eating Nancy.

The evening or so following, after supper, Dilsey tells T.P. to take the child Quentin (Caddy's daughter whom Mr. Compson had brought home two months previously) and Benjy to the Negro cabin where Frony can watch them and they can play with Luster. The two babies and Benjy play with spools and fight over them. Frony brings them to the barn where T.P. is milking under the supervision of his father, who sits on a box. T.P. and Benjy then go to the house where they hear Dilsey singing (moaning). Benjy wants to go around the front, but T.P. lures him away by bringing him back to the cabin where Luster and Quentin are playing. A fire burns in the hearth and Roskus sits before it talking about the bad luck he had known was coming two years earlier when Quentin died. Frony enters and Roskus denounces raising a child—Quentin, Caddy's daughter—not to know her own mother's name. (Mrs. Compson has forbidden anyone to mention Caddy's name.) Dilsey puts Benjy to bed with Luster. When Frony objects, Dilsey puts a board between Benjy and Frony's child. On the day of the funeral, T.P. holds Benjy back until the carriages leave the drive; then carrying the baby Quentin, he runs with Benjy to the corner to watch the funeral coach go by.

Carriage drive to the cemetery

Dilsey puts Benjy into the carriage. Mrs. Compson, wearing a veil and carrying flowers, comes out of the house. She objects that Roskus cannot drive and she must go with T.P. Dilsey warns her eighteen-year-old son to drive carefully, and she tells Mrs. Compson to let Benjy hold a flower. The mother objects; Dilsey takes a flower from the bunch and gives it to him. As soon as they leave the drive, Mrs. Compson orders T.P. to turn around; then she is afraid to have him turn the carriage, so they go on to town, past the Civil War memorial and up to the store where Jason works. Jason refuses his mother's invitation to accompany her to the cemetery. T.P. drives Mrs. Compson and Benjy to the cemetery.

The death of Roskus

CLUES: "They moaned at Dilsey's house."—"Dilsey moaned."

The year of this event is uncertain. Though Roskus is ailing when Mr. Compson dies and is unable to drive the carriage for the trip Mrs. Compson and Benjy take to the cemetery, his death seems to have taken place long enough after the death of Mr. Compson to allow Luster to reach an age when he could take over the care of Benjy. The dog Dan who howled at Mr. Compson's funeral has been replaced by Blue.

Benjy and Luster are near the Compson house, but they can hear Dilsey moaning in the cabin. Blue is howling under the kitchen steps. Frony, taking her mother's place in the Compson kitchen, tells Luster to bring Benjy and Quentin down to the barn. Luster refuses, saying he saw his grandfather waving his hands there the night before.

The present: April 7, 1928

CLUES: the golf course—the presence of Luster

The opening scene is in the Compson yard, now separated by a fence from the golf course that had once been the Compson pasture. Benjy watches the players on the green, then follows them along the fence, howling when they call for their caddies. It is Benjy's thirty-third birthday. Luster, preoccupied by his search for the quarter he has lost, leads Benjy across the garden toward the creek. As they crawl through a hole in the fence, Benjy gets snagged on a nail. He moans because they are now out of sight of the players on the golf course. To keep him quiet, Luster gives him a jimson weed. Benjy continues to moan as they pass the carriage house and then go through the dilapidated barn. Benjy wants to go back toward the golf course, but Luster leads him toward the creek. At the branch, Negroes are washing clothes. Luster gets Benjy, who is still moaning about the golf course, to sit on the bank and play with the jimson weed. Luster asks the children if they have seen his quarter. As he talks to them about the show he hopes to see, he gets them to help him look for the quarter. A golf ball drops into the water. Luster grabs it and, slipping it into his pocket, waits for the players to come for it. They arrive and their caddie accuses Luster of taking the ball. Luster removes Benjy's shoes so he can wade in the creek. As he reacts to his memories, the idiot continues to moan. Benjy wants the golf ball that Luster has pocketed. As they move away from the creek, Luster keeps searching for his quarter, and Benjy keeps moving in the direction of the golf course. Luster, suddenly remembering where he might have lost the coin, tells Benjy to wait. Luster runs off and Benjy heads toward the grove of cedars, where the swing is located. Luster returns and tries to keep Benjy from going toward the swing. They come upon Miss Quentin and the showman in the red tie who pull hurriedly out of an embrace. Quentin accuses Luster of allowing Benjy to follow her around. The pitchman puts a match in his mouth and asks Benjy if he wants to try the trick. Quentin curses him and runs off. Luster asks the man in the red tie for a quarter, then he offers to sell him the golf ball. As he and Benjy move off toward the golf course, Luster spots a shiny tin box in the grass and hands it to Benjy to play with. The pitchman recognizes the box as a condom container and asks Luster who had come to see Quentin the night before. Luster replies that Quentin climbs out of her window and slides down the tree at night.

He and Benjy go to the fence along the golf course. Benjy moans because there are no players visible and he moves along the fence to the gate. Players appear on the green and Luster offers to sell them the golf ball. One of them takes it from him and keeps it without paying. Benjy moans when the man shouts for his caddie. Discarding his jimson weed, he follows the players along the fence until he can go no farther. Luster gives him another weed to hold. Benjy moves off toward the cedar grove where his play graveyard is. There is a weed in the bottle and he puts in the one he is carrying. Luster, irritated because he cannot find his quarter, taunts Benjy by knocking over the bottle and whispering "Caddy" into his ear. Benjy howls and Dilsey calls. Luster quickly puts the weeds back into the bottle and brings Benjy to the house. In the kitchen, Dilsey opens the stove door and sets Benjy before the fire to quiet him. She lights the candles on Benjy's birthday cake. Luster's concern over the lost quarter and the show he had hoped to get into with the money explodes into a minor rebellion with Benjy its target. Luster blows out the candles and cuts the cake when Dilsey leaves the room. While Benjy eats a piece of cake staring at the fire, Luster, standing behind him, closes the stove door with a long piece of wire. Benjy's howl brings Dilsey, who threatens Luster with telling his father if he does not behave.* Behind her back, Luster again closes the stove door and earns a good shaking from his grandmother. Benjy puts his hand on the stove and burns himself. He screams, and Dilsey cuffs Luster and then applies soda to the burn. She wraps the injured hand in cloth and opens the fire door to soothe the crying Benjy. Mrs. Compson enters, complaining that she is being disturbed. Dilsey brings her back upstairs and when she returns, hands Benjy a slipper and sends him and Luster into the library. Benjy heads for the place on the wall where the mirror used to hang. Luster lights the fire and Benjy sits before it, continuing to cry. His brother Jason enters, objects to the moaning of the idiot and reads his newspaper. Dilsey, announcing supper, calls Quentin, who enters the library and plumps herself on a chair. Jason refuses Luster's request for a quarter and tells Quentin that he will not tolerate her going around with the showman. Dilsey calls them to supper. Jason tells Luster to stop bothering Benjy, who continues to moan. Quentin declares that her idiot uncle should be in Jackson. When Jason tells her to get out if she does not like it, she says that she will do just that. She also complains about having to sit at the table with Benjy and his dirty slipper. Dilsey tells her that Benjy will not bother her any more, but Quentin insists that he has been spying on her. She again threatens to run away; Jason tells her to go. She rises angrily. Dilsey goes to her, but the girl pushes her away and picks up a glass of water, raising it to hurl at Jason. Dilsey thwarts her aim. The glass

---

* Dilsey first says she will tell Versh and then speaks of telling Luster's father. It is not clear if Versh is the name of Luster's father or if the Versh mentioned is the same Negro who took care of Benjy when he was young. In the Appendix, Faulkner sets Luster's age at 14 in 1928, which contradicts the evidence in the novel if Luster is the son of Frony. At the father's funeral, Luster is about the same age as Miss Quentin who, in 1928, is 18. Either Faulkner's statement in the Appendix is incorrect or there are two Lusters, one, the son of Frony, would be about 18, and the other, the one caring for Benjy, would be the son of Versh. It is more probable that there is only one Luster, and Faulkner became a bit confused in the novel and made an error in the Appendix.

shatters on the table and Quentin runs out shouting " 'goddamn you.' " The other diners return to the library.

Later, Benjy squats in an empty room. Luster finds him and leads him into his own bedroom. Mrs. Compson locks Quentin's bedroom door, then comes in to bid Benjy goodnight, telling Luster to ask Dilsey to bring her a hot water bottle. Benjy undresses and moans at the sight of his loss. Luster, who has put a nightgown on Benjy, hears something at the window. He and Benjy watch Quentin climb down the tree and go across the lawn.

» » Section I: Guide to the scene shifts

Page numbers quoted first are for the Modern Library and the Vintage Book editions, which have the same pagination. The second provides the pages for the New American Library Signet edition. An (X) indicates new scenes that are not designated in the text by a change in type face.

ML	NAL	First Words of Scene	
23	17	Through the fence	Present
24	18	*Caddy uncaught me*	Dec. 23
25	19	It's too cold out there	Dec. 23
26	20	*What are you moaning about*	Present
26	20	What is it. Caddy said	Dec. 23
28	21	*Cant you shut up that moaning*	Present
29	21	Git in, now, and set still	Drive to Cemetery
32	24	*Cry baby, Luster said*	Present
32	24	Keep your hands in your pockets	Dec. 23
33	24	*Mr Patterson was chopping*	End of Patterson Affair
33	25	They aint nothing over yonder	Present
37	27	*and Roskus came and said*	Damuddy's Death
39	28	*What is the matter with you*	Present
39	28	Roskus came and said	Damuddy's Death
40	29	*See you all at the show*	Present
40	29	"If we go slow,	Damuddy's Death
40	29	*The cows came jumping*	Caddy's Wedding
42	30	*At the top of the hill Versh*	Damuddy's Death
47	34	*There was a fire in it*	Death of Quentin
48	34	Taint no luck on this place	Death of Quentin
49	35	*Take him and Quentin down to*	Death of Mr. Compson
51	36	*You cant go yet. T.P. said.*	Funeral of Mr. Compson
51	37	*Come on, Luster said, I going*	Present
51	37	Frony and T.P. were playing	Damuddy's Death
52	37	*They moaned at Dilsey's house*	Death of Roskus
52	37	Oh, Caddy said	Damuddy's Death
52	37	*Dilsey moaned*	Death of Roskus
52	37	I like to know why not, Frony	Damuddy's Death
53	37	(X) The bones rounded out	Death of Mr. Compson
54	39	*I had it when we*	Present
55	39	Do you think buzzards	Damuddy's Death

56	40	*When we looked around the corner*	Caddy's Wedding
56	40	A snake crawled out	Damuddy's Death
56	40	*You aint got to start*	Caddy's Wedding
57	40	We stopped under the tree	Damuddy's Death
57	40	*They getting ready to start*	Caddy's Wedding
57	41	(X) They haven't started	Damuddy's Death
58	41	*I saw them. Then I saw*	Caddy's Wedding
59	42	*Benjy, Caddy said*	Caddy Uses Perfume
62	43	Come on, now, Dilsey said,	Benjy Must Sleep Alone
62	44	(X) Uncle Maury was sick	End of Patterson Affair
63	44	(X) "You a big boy."	Benjy Must Sleep Alone
63	45	*Caddy smelled like trees*	Damuddy's Death
65	46	*Where you want to go*	Present
65	46	The kitchen was dark	Caddy in the Swing
65	46	*Luster came back*	Present
65	46	It was dark under the trees.	Caddy in the Swing
65	46	*Come away from there, Benjy*	Present
65	46	It was two now, and then one	Caddy in the Swing
67	47	*I kept a telling you*	Present
70	49	*You cant do no good*	Benjy at the Gate
71	50	*How did he get out*	Benjy Attacks Girl
71	50	It was open	Benjy Attacks Girl
72	50	(X) . . . and the bright shapes	Castration Operation
72	50	*Here Loony, Luster said*	Present
75	52	*What you want to get*	Name Change
75	52	"Aint you shamed of yourself,"	Present
76	53	*I could hear the clock*	Name Change
76	53	I ate some cake	Present
77	53	*That's right, Dilsey said.*	Name Change
77	54	The long wire	Present
80	55	*Your name is Benjy.*	Name Change
80	56	Caddy said. "Let me carry	Damuddy's Death
80	56	*Versh set me down*	Name Change
81	56	Mother's sick, Father said	Damuddy's Death
81	56	*We could hear the roof*	Name Change
84	58	*Jason came in*	Present
85	59	*You can look*	Name Change
85	59	Dilsey said, "You come, Jason."	Present
85	59	*We could hear the roof*	Name Change
85	59	Quentin said, "Didn't Dilsey	Present
86	60	*I could hear the roof*	Name Change
87	60	*Dilsey said, All right*	Present
87	60	*Versh smelled like rain.*	Name Change
87	60	We could hear Caddy	Caddy's Loss of Virginity
87	60	*Versh said, Your name*	Name Change
88	61	We were in the hall	Loss of Virginity
88	61	*What are you doing*	Present
88	61	Versh said, "You move back	Name Change
89	61	*Has he got to keep*	Present
89	61	Steam came off	Name Change
89	62	*Now, now, Dilsey said*	Present

89	62	It got down below	Name Change
89	62	*Yes he will*	Present
90	62	Roskus said, It going	Name Change
90	62	*You've been running*	Present
90	62	Then I dont know	Name Change
90	62	*Oh, I wouldn't be*	Present
90	62	She sulling again, is she	Name Change
90	62	*Quentin pushed*	Present
90	62	"Mother's sick again	Name Change
90	62	*Goddamn you, Quentin said*	Present
90	62	Caddy gave me	Name Change
91	63	*She smelled like trees*	Present
91	63	We didn't go	Damuddy's Death
92	63	*Quentin, Mother said*	Present
92	63	Quentin and Versh	Damuddy's Death
92	64	*I got undressed*	Present
93	64	There were two	Damuddy's Death

» » Section II: Chronology of scenes

SCENE	DATE
Damuddy's Death and Benjy's Name Changed	1898, 1900
Natalie Scene	— —
Caddy Kisses a Boy	1906-7
Caddy's Loss of Virginity	1909 (Late Summer)
The Wedding Announcement	1910
Quentin Meets Herbert	1910 (April 22)
The Eve of the Wedding	1910 (April 23)
The Wedding	1910 (April 24)
The Present (Quentin's Suicide)	1910 (June 2)

» » Section II: Fragments of scenes unified and set into chronological sequence

Damuddy's death and Benjy's name changed

Quentin's recollection of the day Damuddy died centers upon the fight he had with Caddy because she took off her dress at the creek. Caddy, irritated with Quentin, says she is going to run away. But when Benjy begins to cry, Caddy puts her arms around him and assures him that she will not run away. Quentin associates this memory with Dilsey's denunciation of the change of Benjy's name.

Allusions to Benjy's power to sense death and tragedy are frequent in Quentin's thoughts. Benjy's power is attributed to his sense of smell. "He smell it. He smell it." The repeated "by the nose seen" is synesthesia: Benjy knows immediately that Caddy has lost her virginity.

Natalie scene

On a rainy day, Caddy and Natalie, playing in the barn, quarrel. Caddy runs off and Quentin comes to Natalie, asking where Caddy had hurt her. He offers to carry her. When he touches her he is sexually aroused. They embrace and apparently play at the movements of intercourse to the accompaniment of Quentin's sigh: Oh Oh Oh. Then Quentin sees his sister standing in the barn door with her hands on her hips watching them. Natalie accuses Caddy of pushing her, telling her to keep her hands off her, but Caddy insists that she is only trying to brush off Natalie's dress.

Caddy leaves and Quentin runs out into the rain after her. He watches Natalie going home through the garden, thinking: "Get wet I hope you catch pneumonia go on home Cowface." Then he jumps into the hog wallow. He goes toward Caddy, who turns her back on him. He taunts her and smears the the mud from his body on hers. She slaps at him. He pushes her down, smearing mud on her. She scratches at his face. They lie back on the grass. Quentin, panting, says "do you care now, do you care now." Caddy says she is sorry that she scratched his face and suggests going to the creek. They sit in the water watching the mud from their bodies float to the surface.

Caddy kisses a boy

The remembered scene beginning "What did you let him for kiss kiss" may be the same incident described in Benjy's section as the scene with Charlie in the swing, and in Jason's section as the occasion that Mrs. Compson discovers Caddy has kissed a boy and dresses herself in black. Jason places Caddy's age at the time as fifteen. In the scene Quentin recalls, Caddy is also fifteen. Quentin's references to his sister's dates—the pimple-faced boy whom she meets at the fair and the boy at whom he throws coal when he is confined to bed with a broken leg—do not make clear if it is always the same boy or several.

In the scene, Caddy taunts Quentin by saying that she made the boy kiss her. Quentin slaps her face. (He remembers his father's detecting his agitation at the dinner table: "You swallow as if you had a fishbone in your throat what's the matter with you.") Quentin throws Caddy on the ground, rubs her head in the grass and tells her to say "calf rope." Caddy retorts, "I didn't kiss a dirty girl like Natalie anyway."

Caddy's loss of virginity

Caddy begins to meet Dalton Ames, a stranger in town who wears khaki shirts. Quentin sees him, but at first pays no attention to him. Mrs. Compson, becoming aware that Caddy is going out with someone, sets Jason to spy on her. Quentin talks to his sister about going out with a stranger, and she tells him not to meddle with her, to leave that to their mother and Jason. Mr.

Compson is furious when he learns that his wife has Caddy spied upon and declares that he will not tolerate it. Mrs. Compson indulges in a spree of self-pity: "What have I done to have been given children like these." She says she is paying for the sins of the Compson family. She does not, at this time, know that Caddy has given herself to Dalton, but she laments that Caddy is befouling herself by slipping out to meet this man who is unknown to the family.

That evening, from the porch of the Compson home, where Quentin can see the street lamps extending down the hill into town, Quentin tells his father that he has not spied on Caddy, as his mother had implied. Mr. Compson apologizes for speaking sharply to him, explaining that his mother had said that because women just did things that way. He tells his son, who is apparently protesting against his mother's accusations against Caddy, that his mother acts that way because she loves Caddy. Quentin replies that as far as his mother is concerned, Caddy has already sinned: "Done in Mother's mind though." His father says that he is confusing sin and morality. It is morality that his mother is worried about. In this same conversation Quentin wonders aloud if his mother's attitude toward the children has anything to do with her family being less distinguished than the Compsons. He also voices the thought that it is strange that Caddy will not bring the man to the house. The father says that Caddy is also a woman and has a woman's reasons.

Late one afternoon, the family is sitting together. Caddy walks rapidly by the open door. Mrs. Compson calls to her, and when Caddy comes into the door frame, Benjy immediately begins to howl. "One minute she was standing in the door the next minute he was pulling at her dress." Benjy is trying to get her to the bathroom to wash. Smelling her alteration, he wants her to wash it away as she had the perfume. Caddy shrinks against the wall as Benjy looks into her eyes and howls. They go into the hall and up the stairs to the bathroom door. Benjy pushes at Caddy, trying to shove her into the washroom.

Downstairs, Mrs. Compson lies back in a chair with a camphor-scented handkerchief to her nose. Father sits beside her and holds her hand. Quentin leaves the room and sits on the outside steps. He muses that Caddy would have told him if it were true. He hears his sister's door closing and her steady weeping. He decides that she will have to come down for supper and then he will face her.

When Caddy does come down, T.P. is feeding Benjy. As soon as his sister enters, the idiot begins to whimper, and when she touches him, he howls. Caddy runs out and Quentin follows her down to the creek where she sits in the water. He tells her to get out of the water. She talks to him about Dalton and in response to his question, "do you love him," she has him put his hand against her chest to feel her heart beat. Quentin asks if Dalton made her do it, swearing he will kill him. Then, with his matriculation money, he and Caddy can run away and no one need ever know. She asks him if he has ever done "that." Quentin begins to cry, and he asks if she remembers the day Damuddy died and she dirtied her drawers. He draws out his knife and suggests that he kill her and then commit suicide. She agrees but wants to know if he can do it to himself. He puts the knife to her throat and insists that she touch her hand to it also. She refuses to do so. He drops the knife and fumbles for it.

They leave the creek. Caddy tells her brother to go home because she is on her way to meet Dalton. They walk by the ditch in which the mare Nancy's bones had lain. Quentin tries to prevent his sister from going to her meeting, but she insists that he go back to the house. He refuses to go, and together they meet Dalton, who lifts Caddy and kisses her, and then shakes hands with Quentin. As her brother leaves, Caddy tells him to wait for her at the branch. He walks to the creek and throws himself down on the bank. When Caddy arrives, she offers herself to her brother if he wants her. Quentin shakes her hard and tells her to shut up.

They leave the creek and walk home. As they approach the steps of the house, Quentin asks his sister again if she loves Dalton. She apparently does not answer and he asks her what she is thinking about. Her reply may have been to offer herself again to her brother, because Quentin says "you shut up you shut up you shut up."

Several days later, Quentin meets Dalton in front of the barber shop and Dalton agrees to meet him at one o'clock by the bridge over the creek. Caddie overhears her brother tell T.P. to saddle his horse Prince. He calls her "whore, whore." He does not take the horse but walks to the bridge where Dalton awaits him. He tells his sister's lover to get out of town, threatening to kill him if he does not leave. Dalton is calm and tells Quentin not to take it so hard because it had to be someone. Quentin replies, "did you ever have a sister did you." And Dalton says, "no but they're all bitches." Quentin tries to slap him, but Dalton catches both his hands. Tearing off a piece of bark from a tree, Dalton throws it into the stream. He lets it float downstream and then shoots at it. He then offers the pistol to Quentin, who, trying to strike Dalton, faints. When he recovers consciousness, he asks Dalton, "did you hit me." Dalton generously says yes, and he offers Quentin his horse. When Quentin refuses, Dalton leaves.

Quentin sits with his back against a tree. Caddy, who followed her brother on Prince, heard the pistol shot and rushed toward the bridge. She met Dalton and told him never to speak to her again. She hurries toward her brother thinking that he has been hurt. Once more Quentin asks his sister if she loves Dalton, and again she tells him to feel the blood pounding in her throat.

Mrs. Compson now knows about Caddy, and she tells her husband that she wants to go away and take Jason with her. Mr. Compson replies, "nonsense," and suggests that she might take Caddy to French Lick for a while to give Caddy a chance to forget Dalton. Mrs. Compson decides that at French Lick she might be able to get Caddy a husband. When the trunks are being brought down from the attic, Quentin thinks they sound like coffins.

Quentin, talking to his father, tells him that it was not Dalton but he who had possessed Caddy; they had committed incest. Mr. Compson declares that his son is obviously a virgin, adding that virginity means less to women. Quentin says, "If we could have just done something so dreadful." To which his father replies that the sad thing is that nothing is so dreadful that it will be remembered tomorrow. He tells his son that man "must just stay awake and see evil done for a little while." And Quentin, announcing that he is contemplating suicide, declares, "it doesn't have to be even that long for a man of courage." His father asks him if he considers that courage, and he adds, "I think you are too serious to give me any cause for alarm." Mr. Compson tells Quentin that he confessed to incest because "you wanted to sublimate a piece of natural human folly into a horror and then exorcise it with truth." In other words, Quentin tried to put something into words that he wanted to be true, and he is doing the same thing, says Mr. Compson, with his talk of suicide. He is not thinking of death but of a transmogrification of a temporary state of mind into a permanent one, because he is trying to escape the thought that this feeling will pass. Quentin keeps expressing shock at the idea of his feeling about Caddy being temporary. His father declares that he will kill himself only when he believes that Caddy was not worth the despair. He suggests that Quentin leave for Harvard early and spend a month in Maine.

The wedding announcement

Quentin, at Harvard, receives the formal announcement of his sister's coming marriage to Herbert Head. Quentin lets the announcement sit on his table, envisioning it as a bier, for three days. He quarrels with his roommate Shreve about it: Shreve jokes with him about his not opening it, and Quentin is tempted to hit his roommate.

Quentin meets Herbert

Two days before the wedding, Quentin arrives in Jefferson. He meets his sister's fiancé in the car that Herbert has bought for Caddy. It may be that they meet him at the station. Caddy drives as Mrs. Compson talks, telling her son that she wants Herbert to be his older brother. She is overwhelmed by Herbert's gift of a car to his bride, and she delights in the thought that Caddy is the first woman to be driving in the town. Mrs. Compson is also delighted by Herbert's flattery and his promise to give Jason a job in the bank.

At the house, Herbert follows Quentin into the living room or library. Quentin is hostile to him, telling him that he knows all about his cribbing and cheating at cards during his stay at Harvard. Herbert tries to bribe Quentin. Caddy comes in and, sending Herbert from the room, tells her brother not to meddle, reminding him that he had meddled enough last summer. Quentin protests that Herbert is a blackguard, that he had cheated at cards.

The eve of the wedding

Quentin and Caddy are in Caddy's bedroom. Outside the open window, through which the spring breeze blows, stands an apple tree. Quentin is aware of a gabble of voices from the first floor as house guests arrive for the wedding. Above the gabble, he can hear the voice of Herbert.

Caddy asks him to look after their father and Benjy, and to make sure that Benjy is not sent to Jackson. She asks him to promise because she is sick. Quentin accuses her of causing all the trouble. Quentin promises he will take care of Father and Benjy, and he tries to embrace her. She tells him not to touch her.

They hear the car leave for the station to pick up the guests arriving on the 8:10 train. Quentin kneels with his head on the arm of the chair, listening to the car go down the hill. He argues that if Caddy is sick, then how can she marry. She replies that she has to marry someone, confessing that she is pregnant. He wants to know if there have been many. She replies that there have been too many and asks him again to promise to look after Benjy and their father. He keeps asking why she must marry someone and she answers, "Do you want me to say it do you think that if I say it it wont be." He tells her to say it to Father. Quentin asks her to go away with him. She tells him that he must finish school, and she expresses her feeling of responsibility for their father's heavy drinking.

The wedding

Quentin's recollections of the wedding center on Benjy's bellowing and Caddy's running out of the house to him, followed by her brother and father.

The present (Quentin's final day)

Ca. 7:45 A.M. Quentin awakens, hears Shreve get out of bed. He gets up to turn over his watch. Shreve comes in to warn him that it is two minutes to the bell and runs off to chapel. Quentin goes to the dormitory window and watches the students running for chapel. He sees the slow-moving Spoade, who is famous for not getting his socks on until about ten and his tie and shirt on until about noon.

8:00 Quentin listens to the chimes as he stands at the window staring at a sparrow. He breaks his watch, paints his cut finger with iodine, and packs his trunk, leaving out a complete change for himself and another which he is leaving for Deacon.

8:15 Quentin bathes and shaves, packs his handbag, puts the key of his trunk into an envelope addressed to his father, writes two notes, stamps them and leaves the room. At the doorway of the dormitory he pauses, waiting until the sun has moved enough to put his shadow behind him. He meets Shreve returning from Chapel.

8.30   He goes to the post office and mails a letter, then looks around for Deacon, the Negro factotum. He gets on a streetcar and goes to Boston to have breakfast at Parker's.

9:00   He finishes his breakfast and buys a fifty-cent cigar. As he walks down the street, he passes a jeweler's shop. At the corner he gives two bootblacks his cigar and a nickel, then turns back to the jeweler's shop and enters it.

9:20   When he learns from the jeweler that none of the clocks in the window is correct, he goes outside to look at them. He focuses his attention upon one with its hands extended slightly off the horizontal. (He has probably chosen the time of his death: 2:49 or 9:17). He enters a hardware store and purchases two six-pound flat irons. Wrapped, they look like shoes. He gets on a streetcar that is headed back to Cambridge. Quentin sits beside a Negro. The car is stopped by an open drawbridge over the Charles River. He gets out of the car to watch a sailing boat passing through. Then, when the bridge is down, he crosses it and stands looking at the Harvard boathouse as Gerald Bland emerges with his shell. He watches Gerald row on the river. He boards a streetcar headed for the campus.

11:00   He continues to look for Deacon and notes that Spoade has his shirt on.

11:15   He finds Deacon, and he gives him a note which is to be given to Shreve the next day. The note instructs Shreve to give Deacon the clothes he has left for him.

11:30   Quentin returns to the post office. He meets his roommate, who tells him that there is a note for him from Gerald Bland's mother.

11:45   He boards a streetcar heading for Alston. To go out to the country, he must shift to an interurban car. At the interurban platform, he discovers a car just left. To escape the noon whistles, he takes another streetcar.

12:00   When he feels certain that noon has passed, Quentin leaves the streetcar, and he boards another going in the opposite direction which will take him back to the interurban platform. There he gets on a waiting interurban and seats himself next to a window. The car passes the river and heads inland. Quentin, getting hungry, leaves the car at a platform which has a wooden marquee. He notes a man eating his lunch. He sees a smokestack, and then walks down the road, which crosses the interurban tracks, toward the river. He reaches a stone bridge, and, apparently deciding this is the place he will drown himself, he hides the flatirons under the end of the bridge. He stares down into the water and watches a large trout.

Ca. 1:00   Three boys with fishing poles approach the bridge and they all watch the trout. Quentin heads for the town, above which rises the steeple of a Unitarian church. He goes up a hill and sits in the grass just too far away from the town to see the clock on the steeple. The three boys come over the hill, and Quentin walks along with them until they reach an orchard. At the entrance to a lane, two of the boys go off to swim at the mill, and the other continues along the road. Quentin tries to make conversation with him, but the boy remains silent. When they reach a settled area, the boy goes over a fence and crosses a lawn to a tree which he climbs to sit quietly in a fork. Quentin walks on and can now see the face of the clock. (As Quentin becomes more absorbed in his memories his awareness of passing time diminishes.)

He enters a bakery shop to buy two buns and meets the little girl he will call sister. He defends the child against the accusations of the woman in the shop and buys her another bun. By way of apology, the shopkeeper gives the girl a cake. They leave the store and Quentin buys some ice cream for himself and the child. He tries to send her home, but she continues to follow him. He therefore returns to the center of the town and asks two men standing in front of a store what he is to do with the girl. They advise him to find the marshal Anse. He tries and fails. He is then advised to bring the girl to the community across the tracks. He leads the child to this group of rundown houses along the river. At the first house, the woman he approaches speaks no English. The girl will not tell him in which house she lives, and finally at the end of the row of houses, Quentin leaves the child and tries to escape her by running along a path behind the houses. When he climbs over a wall, the girl is waiting for him.

They walk on together and reach the river where boys are swimming. The little girl's brother, Julio, accompanied by Anse, now bears down on Quentin and jumps on him. When Anse tells Quentin that Julio wants to charge him with assault, Quentin laughs hysterically. They all go into town to the justice. In front of the drugstore is Mrs. Bland's car. Spoade and Shreve accompany Quentin as he is brought before the justice. He pays the six dollar fine and gives Julio a dollar. The three students return to the car where Mrs. Bland, Gerald, and two girls, Miss Dangerfield and Miss Holmes are waiting. They all get into the car, and Mrs. Bland begins to talk. As they pass the row of houses, Quentin sees the little girl standing in front of one of the houses and he waves to her. The child does not return his wave.

They reach the picnic area and they all leave the car. Quentin attacks Gerald who blackens his eye and bloodies his nose. Shreve and Spoade get him to a farmhouse, where they get water to clean him up and a damp cloth for his eye. He refuses to return to the picnic with them and insists that Shreve not accompany him back to Cambridge. Quentin walks up the hill by himself, sees Shreve watching him and waves. He arrives at a trolley stop with a wooden marquee, gets on a car and sits on the left side to keep his black eye hidden from the passengers. It is now dusk and the lights in the car are lit. Quentin can see his reflection in the window merged with the broken feather on the hat of a woman sitting across the aisle. He notes that they pass the interurban platform where he had left the car in the early afternoon.

Quentin leaves the interurban and takes a trolley to Cambridge, remaining at the rear of the car because there are no vacant seats on the left side. He leaves the trolley near the post office and goes to his dormitory room. He is worried that Shreve will come after him, but then he remembers that after six o'clock the Interurban runs only on the hour. He changes his collar, shirt, and tie, and cleans his vest with gasoline. While the vest dries, he stands at the window, then goes to the corridor bathroom for a drink. He forgets to bring his glass and has to cup his hands to drink. He returns to his room and again stands at the window. The quarter-to-the-hour chimes sound as he puts on his vest. He checks the address on the letter he leaves for Shreve and puts his watch into his roommate's dresser drawer. He remembers to brush his teeth and then remembers to wear his hat. He brushes the hat before putting it on.

» » Section II: Guide to the scene shifts

Quentin's thought association is rapid, and many of his memories are fused. I have attempted in the following listing to identify references to major scenes, such as "She ran right out of the mirror," a reference to Caddy's Wedding. Many of Quentin's thoughts, however, are not associated with remembered scenes. These thoughts, such as "Jason furnished the flour," I have identified as thoughts about someone or something. A (?) indicates identifications that are questionable.

ML	NAL	First Words of Scene	
95	65	When the shadow of the sash	Present
96	66	*She ran right out of the mirror*	Caddy's Wedding
96	66	*Mr. and Mrs. . . . Compson announce*	Wedding Announcement
96	66	I said I have committed incest	Caddy's Loss of Virginity
97	66	Shreve stood in the door	Present
97	67	Calling Shreve my husband	Quarrel with Spoade
97	67	Because it means less to women	Loss of Virginity
98	67	and Shreve said	Quarrel with Spoade
98	67	Did you ever have a sister	Loss of Virginity
98	67	Spoade was in the middle of them	Present
98	67	*I have committed incest*	Loss of Virginity
99	68	And I will look down and see	Death by Drowning
99	68	Dalton Ames. Dalton Ames	Loss of Virginity
99	68	I went to the dresser	Present
100	69	*Only she was running*	Caddy's Wedding
101	69	Shreve said, "Well, you didn't	Present
105	72	But I thought at first that I ought	Christmas Vacation, 1909
107	73	I wouldn't begin counting until	A Day in Grammar School
107	73	*Moving sitting still*	Natalie Scene
107	73	*One minute she was standing*	Loss of Virginity
108	73	*I'm going to run away*	Damuddy's Death
108	73	*Dilsey. ([He smell what you tell him*	Name Change
108	73	The street car stopped	Present
109	74	Benjy knew it when Damuddy died	Damuddy's Death
109	74	The tug came back downstream	Present
111	75	*Did you ever have a sister*	Loss of Virginity

111	76	And after a while I had been hearing	Present
111	76	*Harvard my Harvard*	Meets Herbert
111	76	That pimple-faced infant she met	Caddy Kisses a Boy
112	76	*He was lying beside the box*	Caddy's Wedding
112	76	that could drive up in a limousine	Meets Herbert
112	76	Mr. and Mrs. Compson . . . announce	Wedding Announcement
113	77	Country people poor things	Meets Herbert
113	77	*Jason furnished the flour*	Jason, the Business Man
113	77	There was no nigger in this street car	Present
113	77	Going to Harvard	Mr. Compson Sells Pasture
113	77	*He lay on the ground*	Caddy's Wedding
113	77	*We have sold*	Mr. Compson Sells Pasture
114	77	You should have a car	Meets Herbert
114	77	*Father I have committed*	Loss of Virginity
114	77	Dont ask Quentin he and Mr Compson	Meets Herbert
114	77	*My little sister had no*	Loss of Virginity
114	77	Unless I do what I am tempted	Meets Herbert
114	77	*A face reproachful*	Loss of Virginity
114	78	Hats not unbleached	Present
115	78	I wouldn't have done it	Loss of Virginity
115	78	Trampling my shadow's bones into	Present
115	78	*I will not have my daughter spied*	Loss of Virginity
115	78	The chimes began	Present
115	78	*think I would have*	Loss of Virginity
115	78	I walked upon the belly of my shadow	Present
115	78	*feeling Father behind*	Loss of Virginity
116	78	He was coming along	Present
119	81	*Lying on the ground*	Caddy's Wedding
119	81	He took one look at her	Loss of Virginity
119	81	*the street lamps*	Loss of Virginity
119	81	The chimes ceased	Present
119	81	*go down the hill*	Loss of Virginity
120	81	Uncle Maury straddling his legs	Uncle Maury and Jason
120	81	*Whyn't you keep them hands outen*	Damuddy's Death—Jason
120	81	Rolling his head in the cradle	Uncle Maury and Jason
120	81	Shreve was coming	Present
120	82	*The street lamps*	Loss of Virginity
121	82	The car came up	Present
121	82	*your mother's dream for*	Mr. Compson Sells Pasture
121	82	what have I done to have been given	Loss of Virginity
123	83	It that was the three quarters	Present
123	84	*Who would play*	Death Image
123	84	Eating the business of eating	Present
124	84	*Dalton Ames oh asbestos*	Loss of Virginity
124	84	background. Something with girls	Present (Mrs. Bland)
124	84	*always his voice above the gabble*	Eve of Wedding
124	84	that breathed an affinity	Present (Mrs. Bland)
124	84	*Quentin has shot Herbert he shot*	Eve of Wedding
124	84	tone of smug approbation	Present (Mrs. Bland)
124	84	*the curtains leaning in on the*	Eve of Wedding

124	84	*the voice that breathed o'er eden*	Caddy's Wedding (Benjy's howl)
125	84	*clothes upon the bed*	Eve of Wedding
125	84	*by the nose seen*	Loss of Virginity
125	84	what he said?	Present (Mrs. Bland)
125	84	*Are you going to look after*	Eve of Wedding
125	85	wondered who invented that joke	Present (Mrs. Bland)
126	85	*shot him through the*	Eve of Wedding
126	85	I saw you come in here so I	Meets Herbert
130	88	*You're sick how are you sick*	Eve of Wedding
130	88	Not that blackguard Caddy	Meets Herbert
130	88	Now and then the river glinted	Present
130	88	*that blackguard, Caddy*	Meets Herbert
130	88	The river glinted away	Present
130	88	*I'm sick you'll have to promise*	Eve of Wedding
131	88	The car stopped	Present
131	89	*There was something terrible in me*	Eve of Wedding
131	89	I could still see the smoke stack	Present
132	89	*The street lamps go down the hill*	Eve of Wedding
132	89	*Then they told me the bone*	Quentin's Broken Leg
132	89	At last I couldn't see	Present
132	89	*told me the bone*	Quentin's Broken Leg
133	90	Even sound seemed to fail	Present
133	90	Niggers. Louis Hatcher	Hatcher and the Flood
134	91	*Got to marry somebody*	Eve of Wedding
134	91	I began to feel the water	Present
134	91	*Caddy that*	Eve of Wedding
134	91	Versh told me	Castration Image
135	91	And Father said it's because you	Loss of Virginity
135	91	Where the shadow of the bridge fell	Present
135	91	*If it could just be a hell*	Clean Flame Image
135	92	The arrow increased without	Present
140	94	Caddy that blackguard	Meets Herbert
140	94	Their voices came over the hill	Present
141	95	*Why must you marry somebody*	Eve of Wedding
141	95	Let's go up to the mill	Present
141	95	*Say it to Father will you*	Eve of Wedding
141	95	"Ah, come on," the boy said	Present
142	96	*it is because there is nothing else*	Loss of Virginity (?)
142	96	He paid me no attention	Present
142	96	*that blackguard*	Meets Herbert
142	96	Do you like fishing better	Present
142	96	*Caddy that blackguard*	Eve of Wedding
142	96	The boy turned from the street	Present
142	96	*Else have I thought*	Eve of Wedding
142	96	Some days in late August	Present
143	96	*But now I know I'm dead*	Eve of Wedding
143	96	The buggy was drawn	Present
143	96	On what on your school money	Eve of Wedding
143	96	His white shirt	Present
143	97	*Sold the pasture*	Eve of Wedding

143	97	*one minute she was standing*	Loss of Virginity
143	97	When you opened the door	Present
147	99	*Seen the doctor yet*	Eve of Wedding
147	99	Because women so delicate	Loss of Virginity
147	99	You'd better take your bread	Present
148	99	*getting the odour of honeysuckle*	Loss of Virginity
148	100	We reached the corner	Present
152	102	getting honeysuckle all mixed	Loss of Virginity
152	102	*What did you let him for kiss kiss*	Caddy kisses a Boy
153	103	The wall went into shadow	Present
153	103	*not a dirty girl like Natalie*	Caddy kisses a Boy
153	103	*It was raining we could hear*	Natalie Scene
153	103	She walked just under my elbow	Present
153	103	*I bet I can lift you up*	Natalie Scene
154	103	We went on in the thin dust	Present
154	103	*It's like dancing sitting down*	Natalie Scene
154	104	The road went on	Present
155	104	*I hold to use like this*	Natalie Scene
155	104	We began to hear the shouts	Present
155	104	*Stay mad. My shirt was getting*	Natalie Scene
155	104	"Hear them in swimming	Present
155	105	*mud was warmer*	Natalie Scene
156	105	They saw us from the water	Present
157	105	*We lay in the wet grass panting*	Natalie Scene
157	106	There's town again, sister	Present
157	106	*and the water building*	Natalie Scene
157	106	Then we heard the running	Present
166	111	*ever do that Have you*	Loss of Virginity
166	112	They do, when they can get it	Present
166	112	*her knees her face*	Loss of Virginity
166	112	"Beer, too," Shreve said.	Present
166	112	*like a thin wash of lilac*	Loss of Virginity
166	112	"You're not a gentleman,"	Present
166	112	*him between us*	Loss of Virginity
166	112	"No, I'm Canadian,"	Present
166	112	*talking about him*	Gerald Identified with Ames
167	112	"I adore Canada,"	Present
167	112	*with one hand he could lift*	Loss of Virginity
167	112	"no," Shreve said	Present
167	112	*running the beast*	Sex image
167	112	*how many Caddy*	Eve of Wedding
167	112	"Neither did I," Spoade said	Present
167	112	*I dont know too many*	Eve of Wedding
167	112	*Father I have committed*	Loss of Virginity
167	112	"and Gerald's grandfather	Present
167	112	*we did how can you not know*	Loss of Virginity
167	112	"never be got to drink wine	Present
168	112	*did you love them Caddy*	Eve of Wedding
168	113	one minute she was standing	Loss of Virginity
182	122	It kept on running for a long time,	Present

As I Lay Dying

» » Chronology of events

First day

Cora Tull and two of her five daughters, Kate and Eula, sit beside the bed of the dying Addie Bundren. Dewey Dell, Addie's only daughter, moves a fan back and forth over the face of her mother. Directly outside the bedroom window, the eldest son, Cash, is building Addie's coffin. In the yard, Vernon Tull sits with Addie's husband, Anse. The youngest child, Vardaman, comes into the yard carrying in his extended arms a large fish. When he throws it on the ground, his father tells him to cut it up so Dewey can cook it. Up the hill, on the top of which the Bundren house sits, come two other sons, Darl and Jewel. After Jewel goes to the barn to feed his horse, they come into the yard to discuss with Anse the advisability of leaving on a lumber-hauling job. Anse is hesitant because Addie is so near death, but Darl points out that they will need the three dollars for the burial trip to Jefferson. Jewel, who denies that his mother is at the point of death, objects to the presence of Tull and his family. Finally Anse agrees that they should go, and Darl enters the house to stand for a moment at the door of Addie's room. He and Jewel take the wagon and leave, and the Tulls depart for their home.

In late afternoon, Dr. Lucius Peabody, a heavy man of seventy years, arrives. The wind is blowing and rain is threatening as he reaches the base of the hill which he cannot drive up with his buggy. A rope is thrown down to him. He fastens it around himself and is hauled up the hill by Anse and Vardaman. After he examines Addie, he calls Anse into the room. The dying woman indicates with her eyes that she does not want the doctor with her. When he leaves, Addie sits up in her bed and calls to Cash, who shows her the board on which he is working. Addie lies back and with her eyes on Vardaman, dies.

Vardaman, unable to deal with the reality of death, hysterically relates his mother's death to the presence of Dr. Peabody. He runs to the barn, gets a stick, and rushes down the hill to beat the doctor's horses until they run off wildly. Vardaman returns to the barn where he enters a stall to cry. Dewey Dell, who has come looking for him in the gathering dusk, finds him and gives him a good shaking for having overheard her say aloud the name of her lover, Lafe, about whom she has been thinking. The doctor is the target of Dewey's venom also. Pregnant and unmarried, she thinks of the doctor as someone who could help her if he only knew her predicament, though she has no intention of telling him.

The family and the doctor eat the supper of cold greens that Dewey sets before them. Cash continues to work on the coffin and as the evening progresses, the rain begins to fall. Vardaman, who has begun to identify his mother with the fish he cut up, is either sent to fetch the Tulls or wanders there in a state of near-hysteria. He knocks on their door about midnight. He is not coherent, but Cora understands that Addie must have died. She and Vernon, with the child between them, drive in the heavy rain to the Bundren house. All through the night, working by lamplight, Vernon helps Cash to finish the coffin. Twice during the night Vardaman opens the window of his mother's room to let in air. It is nearly dawn when the coffin is completed and the men carry it into the room and place the body in it. When he is alone, Vardaman bores holes in the coffin lid. Later it is discovered that the auger had bored twice into the face of the dead woman. Tull returns to his house and goes to bed, but Cora remains. In the meantime, Darl and Jewel load the wood and set off to deliver it. But the rains have made the road bad, and the wagon tilts into a ditch. Jewel attempts to raise it but he cannot. The tilted wagon with the broken wheel remains in the ditch and Darl and Jewel get quarters for the night.

Second day

About ten, Tull returns to the Bundren house with Dr. Peabody's team hitched to the back of the wagon. The doctor's buckboard has already been returned by the neighbors who found it. People from the Frenchman's Bend community—including Armstid, Houston, Littlejohn, Quick, and Uncle Billy (probably Will Varner) have gathered for the funeral service and await the arrival of the preacher, Whitfield. The women have dressed Addie in her wedding dress and placed her, despite Cash's objections, in the coffin backwards to provide room for the flared skirt. Over Addie's face has been placed a veil to hide the auger holes. Cash has repaired the coffin lid with carved plugs.

Anse had promised his wife that he would bury her in her own family's burial plot in Jefferson, forty miles away. The men sit around the yard discussing the heavy rains and the difficulty Anse will have getting to Jefferson with some bridges down and others impassable. As a group, the men enter the house to view the body. They then return to the yard. When Whitfield arrives and the service begins, the men gather around the steps of the house with their hats in their hands.

On their way home, the Tulls pass Vardaman about a mile from his house. He is sitting on the edge of a slough with a fishing pole across his knees.

Third day

No events can be specifically assigned to this day. But either sometime on the second or the third day, Darl and Jewel come back to get a wheel for the wagon and then return to deliver the wood. There is some discrepancy about the day that the Bundrens set out on their journey. Tull says, "On the third day they got back and they loaded her into the wagon." (404) However, Samson, who sees the Bundrens on the first day of their journey says that Quick had "been to the funeral three days ago." (416) Other evidence indicates that the first day of the journey is the fourth day after the death, and it may be that Tull meant on the third day after the funeral.

Fourth day (first of the journey)

Addie's coffin is carried down the hill. Jewel, in front, moves so quickly that Cash, whose leg had once been broken, cannot keep up and is left behind. As Darl and Jewel place the coffin in the wagon, down the hill come Anse and Dewey Dell. She carries a parcel which she tells her father contains Cora Tull's cakes but which actually contains clothes. Though Anse protests, Jewel insists upon bringing his horse and goes up to the barn as the wagon, with Anse driving, starts off. After a short time, Jewel, on his horse, joins them and keeps pace with the wagon.

They pass Tull's farm and then have to make a detour because Tull's bridge is impassable. The detour takes them eight miles to Samson's bridge. On the way they pass the road leading to New Hope where the Bundrens usually bury their dead. Darl and Cash silently consider the possibility of going there, but the wagon moves on until it reaches a store run by Samson who sends someone to inform the travelers that the bridge is down. He invites them to spend the night at his farm. The coffin is placed in the barn, and, though the Bundrens accept supper, they refuse Samson's invitation to sleep in the house. Anse insists that he will sit all night by the coffin. The odor of the decomposing body horrifies Samson and his wife. The next morning, the Bundrens leave before breakfast.

Fifth day (second of the journey)

The wagon retraces the route of the preceding day and again passes the sign indicating the road to New Hope. Tull is plowing in his field and he comes to the bank of the river to help them try fording. Anse, Dewey, Vardaman, and Vernon Tull walk over the nearly submerged bridge. The older sons locate the ford and with Jewel ahead on his horse to guide the wagon with a rope, and Cash and Darl riding on the wagon, they move into the swift-moving, debris-filled water. They are making good progress until a log rears up out of the water. The team shies and the wagon hangs for a moment on the edge of the ford. Darl jumps free and lets the current carry him downstream to the bank. Cash is thrown out of the wagon and breaks a leg. The mules lose their footing and are drowned. Cash is pulled out of the water, and Jewel rescues the coffin and the wagon. With the help of Darl and Tull, he also manages to retrieve all of Cash's carpentering tools.

Jewel rides to Armstid's and returns with two mules. Tull returns across the river to his farm, and the Bundrens move on to Armstid's farm where they spend the night. Dr. Peabody has left the area and Will Varner is called to set Cash's leg. Anse refuses the loan of Armstid's team for the trip to Jefferson and decides to do some trading with Snopes.

Sixth day (third of the journey)

Early in the morning, Anse rides off on Jewel's horse to find Snopes. As the day progresses, the smell from the coffin becomes so bad that Armstid finally approaches Jewel and suggests that he borrow a mule to go after his father. Jewel understands Armstid's motive and angrily insists that they will move the wagon. Darl refuses to help him, and Jewel pushes the wagon himself. When Anse finally returns, he announces that he has made a trade. One item in the trade is Jewel's horse. Furious, Jewel jumps on his horse and rides off. With Armstid's mules, Anse drives the wagon about a mile down the road. The Bundrens refuse Armstid's offer to keep Cash at the house, and they place him on top of the coffin. That evening, the family, insulted by Armstid's reaction to the odor, will not accept his offer of supper. Nevertheless, Armstid brings food to them. The family spends the night with the wagon.

Seventh day (fourth of the journey)

In the morning, Eustace Grimm, to the surprise of everyone, brings a span of mules. Jewel, he says, brought the horse and went off. Armstid is certain that the boy is on his way to Texas. The new mules are attached to the wagon and the journey is resumed, with the buzzards circling overhead.

Eight day (fifth of the journey)

The Bundren wagon is parked in front of a hardware store in the center of Mottson. Dewey Dell enters Moseley's drug store and tries to buy some medicine with the ten dollars that Lafe gave her. Moseley refuses to sell her anything. Darl is buying ten cents worth of cement to put on Cash's leg. The horrified townspeople with handkerchiefs covering their noses stare at the Bundrens. The marshal tells Anse that he cannot stay in the town, and Anse insists that he has a right to park his wagon on a public street. When Darl returns, they drive out of town and then stop near a farmhouse to mix the cement and put in on Cash's leg. As they resume their journey, Jewel rejoins them.

That night the family stays at the Gillespie farm. Cash's foot has turned black, and he is put to bed. The coffin is placed beneath an apple tree in the yard. Vardaman, who has been chasing away the buzzards, decides to find out what they do at night. During the evening, the wind shifts and the coffin is carried into the barn. Vardaman, watching the buzzards, sees Darl set fire to the barn. He tells Dewey Dell, but she warns him not to tell anyone else.

Followed by Anse, Gillespie, and Mack, Jewel rushes out of the house and runs toward the flaming barn. When he goes toward the coffin, Darl insists that he save the animals first. Jewel gets a terrified horse out of the flames by putting his shirt over the horse's head. When the other animals are safe, Jewel rushes into the burning building and pulls the coffin off the sawhorses and, turning it end over end, as the sparks shower down on his exposed back, he gets the coffin out of the flames. The coffin is once again placed under the apple tree. Jewel's back is treated, and the cement is broken away from Cash's leg. Outside, Darl lies on the coffin, sobbing.

Ninth day (sixth of the journey)

As the wagon approaches the outskirts of Jefferson, the family becomes more and more aware of the outraged faces coming to the doors along the route to stare at them. Walking toward the wagon are three Negroes and about ten feet behind them a white man. Shocked by the odor, one of the Negroes makes a comment and Jewel curses and whirls on them, but by this time the white man is beside Jewel and becomes the boy's target. Darl tries to restrain Jewel. The man draws his knife. With the help of Anse and Dewey, Jewel is pushed away, and Darl explains to the man that his brother had been burned in a fire the night before. Jewel finally apologizes, and the wagon enters Jefferson.

Anse goes into a house from which can be heard the music of a gramophone and returns with two spades. Addie is finally buried, and just beyond the gates of the cemetery, two men from the Jackson insane asylum await the family. Dewey Dell and Jewel pounce furiously upon Darl. Handcuffed, Darl is led away.

The rest of the family drives to the center of town and Anse returns the spades. He remains in the house for some time; finally, Cash is brought to Peabody who cares for the leg and informs Cash that he will limp for the rest of his life. Dewey Dell, who had that morning forced her father to stop the wagon so that she could go into the woods and change her clothes, enters a drugstore. It is lunch time and the drug clerk, Skeet MacGowan, tells the girl that he is the doctor and that he can help her but it will cost her more than money. He gives her something that tastes like turpentine and tells her to return for the payment and the rest of the medicine that evening at ten.

Sometime during the day, Anse discovers that his daughter has ten dollars and takes it from her to get himself some teeth. That evening, with his hair slicked down, Anse goes courting, and Dewey Dell and Vardaman go to the drugstore. While Dewey is with Skeet in the cellar, Vardaman sits outside the store thinking of the train that is no longer in the show-window as Dewey promised it would be, and of his brother Darl being taken away. When Dewey comes out, she knows that she has been tricked and that the medicine will do no good.

Tenth day

Early in the morning Anse leaves his family and then returns to tell them to hitch up and get ready to leave as soon as he gets back. On the train, Darl with his keepers is heading for Jackson as his brothers and sister sit placidly in the wagon waiting for their father. With his new set of teeth plainly visible, Anse approaches the wagon. Behind him is a duck-shaped woman carrying a "gramaphone." Anse introduces her to his children as Mrs. Bundren.

Sanctuary

» » Chronology of events

The year: 1930*

May 2 (Thursday) Little Belle returns from school with a boy she met on the train. Horace Benbow, her stepfather, chastises her.

May 3 (Friday) Horace returns from his weekly trip to the railroad station for his wife's shrimp and decides, suddenly, to leave his wife and his home in Kinston. He heads toward his hometown of Jefferson, hitching rides.

May 7 (Tuesday) Horace stops for a drink at a spring and discovers a small dark man in a black suit covering him with a pistol. For two hours, the man, Popeye, holds Horace at the spring and then leads him to the house, which is known as the Old Frenchman place. This house is located in Frenchman's Bend, about two miles from Vernon Tull's farm. Horace talks to the uncomprehending audience about his troubles. His group of listeners is composed of the feeble-minded Tommy, Goodwin, Ruby, and Popeye. In the background is an old deaf and blind man. Late at night, Horace is escorted by Tommy to a waiting truck, which is, apparently, heading for Jefferson with a load of bootleg whiskey.

May 8 (Wednesday) On his arrival in Jefferson, Horace goes out to the Sartoris house, two miles from Jefferson, where his sister Narcissa and his ten-year old nephew live with Aunt Jenny. Visiting Narcissa is a suitor, Gowan Stevens, who is leaving for Oxford to attend a Friday night dance. Horace remains for the night.

May 9 (Thursday) Horace returns to the Jefferson house he inherited from his parents. During the ten years of his marriage to Belle, he has kept the unoccupied house. He opens the house and tries to clean it.

May 10 (Friday) Gowan Stevens escorts Temple Drake to the college dance. After he has brought Temple back to her dormitory, Gowan picks up three town boys and they get some moonshine liquor. Attempting to demonstrate

* Bory Sartoris, born in June 1920, is ten years old.

his university-learned ability to drink, Gowan gulps several glasses of whiskey and passes out in a public toilet of the railroad station in Oxford.

May 11 (Saturday)   Gowan regains consciousness about six in the morning. Scheduled to meet Temple at Taylor, he rushes to get there before the 6:30 Special for the baseball game leaves. He arrives just as the train is leaving, and Temple jumps off the observation platform to join him. He drives to Dumfries and gets more liquor; then when that runs out, heads toward the Old Frenchman place. Drunkenly arguing with Temple because he has discovered that she dates town boys, Gowan does not see the tree that Popeye has placed across the road. He drives right into it, and the car turns over on its side. Tommy leads the couple to the farmhouse. Temple is terrified by the gangsters in the hideout. Throughout the night she is the target of a series of attempts by the men to assault her. Ruby helps her, and finally Temple gets some sleep in a corn crib in the barn.

May 12 (Sunday)   Temple awakens about nine o'clock. During the morning, Ruby leaves the farmhouse to protest Goodwin's intention of raping Temple. Hiding in the crib with Tommy, who also wants to make love to her, Temple watches Popeye approach. Tommy is shot and Temple raped with a corncob. When Popeye drives off with Temple, Ruby goes to Tull's to telephone for the sheriff. Temple and Popeye arrive about five in the afternoon at Miss Reba's in Memphis. About ten-thirty, Temple eats the first food she has had in days.

May 13 (Monday)   Tommy's body has been brought to town and is viewed by the townspeople. Goodwin is in the Jefferson jail house, charged with the murder of Tommy.

May 13-18   Sometime during the week, Horace undertakes to defend Goodwin. He brings Ruby to his house. When he informs his sister that the woman is staying there, Narcissa protests so vehemently that Horace decides to take Ruby to a hotel.

May 19 (Sunday)   Horace visits Aunt Jenny and reads Gowan's letter to Narcissa.

May 21 (Wednesday)   Accompanied by Ruby and the baby, Horace visits Goodwin in the jail cell. He tries to persuade Goodwin to let him mention at the trial the presence of Popeye at the scene of the murder. Goodwin turns down his plea and asks to speak to Ruby alone. Horace realizes that something happened at the Old Frenchman place about which he is ignorant.

May 24* (Friday)   Horace is awakened at six-thirty by a messenger from

* Faulkner's chronology begins to get confused at this point. The events which I have listed for Friday actually occur on a Saturday, the day on which the Negro murderer is hanged. The evening before, Horace is depressed, thinking of the Negro singing at the window "since this would be his last night." (159) He goes to bed late, and tosses till daylight. At six-thirty he is awakened

Ruby. He rushes to the hotel, where he discovers that the baby has been very sick throughout the night. Ruby tells him that Temple and Gowan were at the Old Frenchman place. That same evening, Horace drives out to his sister's house and tells Aunt Jenny that Gowan was at the hideout. Aunt Jenny informs him that Gowan had proposed to Narcissa during his visit before that weekend and been told by Narcissa that she already had one child to take care of. Horace returns to Jefferson and stares at the picture of Little Belle. Late that night he takes a train for Oxford.

May 25 (Saturday)   Horace makes inquiries at the University and discovers that Temple left school about two weeks earlier. He returns to the railroad station and sees on the washroom wall Temple's name. On the return trip he meets Clarence Snopes. Both men get off the train at Holly Springs to wait for the Jefferson train. Horace sees Clarence meet his nephew Virgil Snopes and a friend Fonzo who are on their way to Memphis. Horace gets on the Jefferson train and avoids sitting with Snopes. At the railroad station, he takes a cab and arrives in the town square at 8:20 P.M. The cab driver informs him that Ruby has been put out of the hotel and been taken in by Mrs. Walker, the jailer's wife.

May 26 (Sunday)   Horace visits his sister who is adamant in her refusal to permit Horace to bring Ruby back to their Jefferson house. She begs her brother to give up Goodwin's case. Horace remains at the Sartoris place for the night.

May 27 (Monday)   At breakfast, Narcissa asks who will be Horace's opponent in the trial and learns from him that it will be the District Attorney.

May 29 (?)   Horace finds shelter for Ruby in the shack of a demented old woman.

May 30 (?)   Horace installs a phone in his house.

May 31—June 16*   Sometime during this period, Clarence Snopes arrives

---

by Ruby's messenger. Apparently, the confusion occurs because when he revised, Faulkner added the fact that the hanging was to take place on Saturday and did not adjust the chronology. I set the events on Friday because it is obviously not a Sunday when Horace goes to Oxford.

*   Until June 17, the chronology is so confused that it seems pointless to attempt a day-by-day listing. (Cleanth Brooks makes a valiant attempt at a chronology for this period in his article "Faulkner's *Sanctuary*: The Discovery of Evil," *The Sewanee Review*, LXXI (Winter, 1963), pp. 1-24. The chronology he offers is logical but somewhat arbitrary. His defense of it hinges upon the discovery by Clarence that Temple is at Miss Reba's long before Clarence discovers that his nephew and Fonzo are there. Clarence, according to Miss Reba, made his appearance for the first time when he was searching for the two boys. However, it seems arbitrary to me to assume, as does Professor Brooks, that Clarence did not find out the boys were there on those visits but that he did discover what Miss Reba would certainly want to conceal:

at Miss Reba's looking for Virgil and Fonzo and discovers Temple's presence there. He is caught peeping through the keyhole of her room and burned on the neck by Popeye. Clarence calls Horace and sells him the information for a hundred dollars. Horace visits Temple at Miss Reba's and learns what happened at the Old Frenchman place. He returns to Jefferson completely disillusioned. When Clarence tried to reach Horace, he first called him at his sister's. Narcissa answered the phone, and several days later she goes to the office of Eustace Graham, the District Attorney, and tells him about the call her brother received from Snopes. Graham also pays Clarence for the information about Temple. About a week before the trial opens on June 20, Horace calls Miss Reba and learns that Temple is still in the house. Sometime during the latter part of this period, Popeye brings Red to Temple on four separate occasions.

June 17 (Monday) Temple bribes Minnie and leaves Miss Reba's to call Red from a public phone. She returns to her room and at nine o'clock leaves to meet Red at the Grotto. She was under surveillance, and Popeye awaits her outside. He forces her into the car and they drive to the Grotto. There, Temple dances and drinks heavily. Red enters, and a short while later, Temple eludes her guards and enters a private room where she is joined by Red. She throws herself on him, but Red pulls away from her. When she leaves the room, Temple sees Red at one of the gaming tables. She is escorted out of the building by some of Popeye's henchmen and put into a car. As she is driven away, she sees Popeye sitting in his car waiting for Red. That night Red is murdered.

June 18 (Tuesday) Clarence Snopes sells information to Popeye's lawyer and angrily mutters about the Jew Lawyer who gave him only a tenth of what the other lawyers paid.

June 19 (Wednesday) Horace calls Miss Reba and discovers that Temple Drake is no longer in the house.

June 20 (Thursday) Goodwin's trial opens. That evening, Horace stays with his client and Ruby, preparing Ruby for her appearance on the witness stand the following day.

June 21 (Friday) Temple Drake testifies that Goodwin raped her with a corncob and killed Tommy. About midnight a mob takes Goodwin from the prison cell. Around 12:30 Horace runs to the square and sees the fire, in the center of which is the dying Goodwin.

---

that Temple was present. Another error in Faulkner's chronology which cannot be glided over is the time lapse between the installation of the phone by Horace (May 30) and Clarence's phone call one week (June 13) before the trial. Obviously, something is wrong, because we are told later by Faulkner that a week before the trial, Horace phoned Miss Reba's to find out if Temple was still there. Horace goes to Memphis to see Temple a day or two after Clarence's call, so he had to have made his visit before the 13th.

August   Popeye is arrested in Birmingham for the murder of a policeman in a small Alabama town on June 17. He makes no defense at his trial, is found guilty and hanged.

Absalom, Absalom!

» » Chronology of events

In this chronology, which is much more detailed than Faulkner's, I have attempted to sift fact from speculation and list all the essential facts about the life of Henry Sutpen and the people involved in his history.

1807   In a mountain community of the territory to become West Virginia, Thomas Sutpen is born. His father is a shiftless man, his mother a Scotch mountain woman who never learned to speak English well.   **1817**   Thomas's mother dies and the Sutpen family begins a slow journey down the mountain. They settle as tenants on a plantation in the lowlands around the James River. Thomas is ten at the beginning of this journey that introduces him to a society in which the color of one's skin and the value of one's possessions determine human worth.   **1818**   Ellen Coldfield, the future wife of Thomas Sutpen, is born in Tennessee.   **1823**   Thomas Sutpen, about fifteen, is sent by his father to deliver a message to the plantation owner. Innocently, he walks to the front door of the plantation house. He is told by a Negro servant to go to the back door, and that night he conceives his grand design.   **1827**   Sutpen quells a Negro uprising on a Haitian sugar plantation where he has become overseer. Since his arrival on the island he has learned both the patois of the Negroes and the French of the white men. At the outbreak of the insurrection he is barricaded in the plantation house with the planter, a man of French descent, the daughter of the planter, and two half-breed servants. He marries the planter's daughter, Eulalia Bon.   **1828**   Goodhue Coldfield moves from Tennessee to Jefferson, Mississippi, with his mother, sister, wife, and daughter Ellen.   **1829**   Charles Bon is born to Eulalia Bon and Thomas Sutpen. **1831**   Sutpen discovers that his wife has Negro blood. He repudiates her and his son, turning over to them all the possessions deeded to him at his marriage and all that he has earned, retaining only twenty Negro slaves whom he brings back to the United States.

1833   On a Sunday morning in June, Sutpen rides into Jefferson. He takes a room at the Holston House, but he does not fraternize with the other guests.

He spends his days away from the village. One day he files a deed with the County Recorder for a hundred miles of land located twelve miles from Jefferson. He derived the land, somehow, from the Indian chief Ikkemotubbe. Sutpen leaves Jefferson for two months, then returns in a covered wagon with twenty Negro slaves—two of whom are women—and a French architect. Working naked with his slaves, he begins to build a mansion on the property that becomes known as Sutpen's Hundred.

1834   Clytemnestra (Clyde) is born to one of the slave women. Sutpen is the father. (A previous child of one of these slaves is mentioned by Mr. Compson as Sutpen's also. But there is no other reference to this child in the novel.)

1835   The foundation of the Sutpen mansion is completed, and all the timber for the house cut, when the French architect tries to escape. Sutpen takes a day off from his labor, invites some acquaintances from Jefferson, including Compson, to join him on his manhunt. During the course of the pursuit, Sutpen reveals to Compson the facts of his childhood and tells him about his ambitions. The manhunt is successful; the architect is permitted to leave only after the house is completed and the promenades and the outlines of the formal gardens laid out. For three years, Sutpen lives alone in the mansion that still has no windows, fixtures, or furnishings. For diversion he invites his Jefferson acquaintances to gambling, drinking and hunting parties. Compson offers to lend him money so that he can furnish the house. Sutpen refuses, but he does accept a loan of cotton seed.

1838   Dressed in the clothes he wore when he arrived in Jefferson five years before, Sutpen attends the Methodist church in the village, where he sees Ellen Coldfield. The gambling and hunting parties stop because Sutpen is spending his time in Jefferson. He enters into some kind of shady financial speculation with Goodhue Coldfield who eventually withdraws from the venture and refuses his share of the profits. For the second time, Sutpen goes off on a trip. A few weeks later, he returns with four large oxen-drawn wagons loaded with furniture and fixtures for his mansion. The townspeople suspect Sutpen of getting these furnishings illegally, and on the day that he rides into town to propose to Ellen, he is accosted by a deputation. He defies them. The deputation grows into a mob as he changes his clothes in the Holston House. Coldly and calmly, he walks through the mob carrying a bunch of flowers in his hand. Ellen consents to become his wife.

Against the wishes of Goodhue, Ellen and her aunt make plans for a big June wedding. A hundred invitations are sent out, but antipathy toward Sutpen is strong, and the aunt has to make personal appeals to the invited to attend. At the evening weeding, only a few people are present. Riffraff, assembled outside the Methodist church, pelt Sutpen and his bride. The couple takes up residence at Sutpen's Hundred, and Sutpen entertains himself and his friends with bloody fighting matches between his Negro slaves and often between himself and a slave.

March, 1839   A son, Henry, is born to Thomas and Ellen Sutpen.

Oct. 3, 1841   A daughter, Judith, is born to Thomas and Ellen Sutpen.

1845   Rosa Coldfield, the child of her parents' middle age, is born. Her sister Ellen is twenty-seven and has been married for seven years. Rosa Coldfield's nephew is six, her niece four, when she is born. Her mother dies in childbirth, and Rosa is cared for by her aunt and her father.

1848   Racing his carriage wildly into town, Sutpen brings his family to the Methodist church for Sunday services. The minister admonishes Sutpen about racing the carriage right up to the church steps, and Sutpen immediately gives up church-going.

1849   Ellen Sutpen fears that her husband's wildness will have a bad influence on her children.

1850   The shiftless Wash Jones, destined to murder Thomas Sutpen within twenty years, and his daughter Melicent move into an abandoned fishing camp on Sutpen's land.

1853   Milly Jones is born to Melicent. The father is unknown.

1855   The aunt of ten-year-old Rosa Coldfield slips out of a window and elopes with a horse trader. At Sutpen's Hundred, Ellen discovers her children watching their father fighting one of the Negro slaves.

1859   Charles Etienne De Saint-Velery* Bon is born, the legitimate son of an octoroon and Sutpen's Haitian-born son, Charles Bon.

Sept., 1859   Henry Sutpen (age 20) enrolls at the University of Mississippi in Oxford, forty miles from Jefferson. He meets Charles Bon, who is nine years his senior.

Dec., 1859   Henry brings his friend Charles Bon home for the Christmas holidays. Charles and Judith meet.

June, 1860   Henry returns from Oxford, accompanied by Charles Bon. Thomas Sutpen is away from the plantation on a journey to New Orleans. Bon remains for two days. Ellen Sutpen, who decided six months earlier that Charles should be Judith's husband, begins to enjoy the role of a rich planter's wife as she prepares an elaborate trousseau for Judith.

Nov., 1860   Abraham Lincoln is elected President of the United States.

Dec. 20, 1860   South Carolina secedes from the Union.

Dec. 24, 1860   Henry and Charles are again at Sutpen's Hundred for the Christmas holidays. Thomas Sutpen forbids the marriage of his daughter to Charles. The following day, Ellen Sutpen takes to her bed.

Jan. 9, 1861   Mississippi secedes from the Union.

* Spelled Valery and Velery in the text.

Spring, 1861   John Sartoris and Henry Sutpen form a regiment—the 23rd Mississippi Infantry. Sartoris is elected its Colonel and Sutpen is chosen as second in command. Henry and Charles join the University Greys, a company in Compson's regiment. Goodhue Coldfield nails himself into his attic; and that same night, his daughter Rosa writes her first ode to Southern soldiers.

April, 1862   Charles Bon is wounded in the shoulder, and General Compson loses his right arm at the battle of Shiloh (Pittsburg Landing).

Summer, 1862   The 23rd Mississippi Regiment votes John Sartoris out of command and elects Thomas Sutpen its colonel.

1862-3   Ellen Coldfield Sutpen, ill since December, 1860, dies. (The date on Ellen's tombstone assigns January 23, 1863 as the date of her death. In his chronology, Faulkner sets her death in 1862.)

1864   Goodhue Coldfield's three-year self-incarceration ends with his death. In late fall of this year, Thomas Sutpen returns to Jefferson on a one-day leave, bringing with him two tombstones which he ordered from Italy. He sets one on Ellen's grave; the other, on which is carved his own name, rank, and regiment, he leaves in the hall of his mansion. He visits the recuperating General Compson in his Jefferson law office and explains to him that his design is threatened by Charles Bon. He tells the General that his choice is to do something to make sure that Charles does not marry Judith or to let them marry. If they marry, his grand design will appear successful, but to himself it will be a meaningless and hollow success.

1865   Charles Bon writes to Judith and tells her that they have waited long enough. She begins to prepare a wedding gown. General Robert E. Lee sends reinforcements—including the 23rd Mississippi Regiment—to General Johnston under whose command is the Compson regiment in which Henry and Charles are serving. Henry requests and receives permission to talk with his father.

May 3, 1865   Charles Bon, age 33 years and five months, is shot and killed at the gate of Sutpen's Hundred by Henry Sutpen. Wash Jones informs Rosa Coldfield of the murder and she rushes out to the plantation. Clytie prevents her from running up the stairs to see the dead man. Finally Judith permits her to ascend the stairs. In front of the closed door of the bedroom in which the body lies, stands Judith. Her face is cold, her eyes tearless; in her hand she holds a metal frame containing the picture of an octoroon and a child. Rosa does not see Henry or the body of Charles. Wash Jones and a helper build a coffin, and, with the help of the three women, the coffin is carried down the stairs. Judith has Charles Bon buried in the family graveyard, beside the body of her mother. To General Compson's wife, Judith brings Bon's letter. Rosa remains with her niece and Clytie in the deteriorating plantation house.

Dec., 1865   Seven months after the death of Charles Bon, Colonel Sutpen (cited personally by General Lee) returns to his plantation. Judith tells him that Henry has murdered Charles and has disappeared. Sutpen (age 59) sets to work to rebuild his plantation.

March, 1866 A deputation from Jefferson demands that Sutpen join the group organized to rid the area of carpetbaggers. Sutpen refuses. He proposes marriage to Rosa Coldfield.

April, 1866 Sutpen realizes that he can save no more than one mile of his land from taxes and waste. He suggests that Rosa prove herself capable of bearing him a son before they marry. Rosa leaves Sutpen's and returns to her father's house in Jefferson where she subsists on charity and grubbing. In this same year, Sutpen establishes a crossroads store and takes up with Wash Jones's adolescent granddaughter, Milly Jones.

Aug. 12, 1869 On this Sunday morning, Sutpen arises at dawn to tend Penelope, his mare, who gives birth to a stallion. He goes to the cabin of Wash Jones where Milly has been delivered of Sutpen's child. In the presence of Jones and a Negro midwife, Sutpen walks into the cabin, discovers that the child is female, and tells Milly: "Well, Milly, too bad you're not a mare like Penelope. Then I could give you a decent stall in the stable." He leaves, followed by Jones. In front of the cabin, Jones kills Sutpen with a scythe. All that day Wash awaits the arrival of the sheriff's party. When it arrives, he slashes the throats of his granddaughter and his great-granddaughter, rushes out of the cabin, picks up the scythe and charges at the group led by DeSpain. He is shot down.

Judith (age 30) arranges for Sutpen's funeral service in the church where he married Ellen. On the way to the church, the wagon, drawn by borrowed mules, overturns. The body of Thomas Sutpen, arrayed in full regimentals, is thrown into the ditch. Judith replaces the body in the coffin, has the wagon turned around and goes directly to the Sutpen burial ground. She reads the burial service herself.

1870 Mrs. Charles Bon and her eleven-year-old son, Charles Etienne, arrive from New Orleans to visit the grave of Charles.

Dec., 1871 Clytie goes to New Orleans to get Charles Etienne Bon. Judith entrusts to General Compson one hundred dollars (derived from the sale of her father's store) to be used for Charles Etienne's gravestone in the Sutpen burial plot when he dies. Clytie returns with the twelve-year-old boy, who speaks no English. He sleeps in Judith's room on a trundle bed, between Judith in the bed and Clytie on the floor.

1879 Charles Etienne (age 20) is arrested and brought into court before Judge Jim Hamblett. He is charged with starting a fight at a social gathering held in a Negro cabin not far from Sutpen's Hundred. General Compson, in response to Judith's appeal, gets the indictment quashed, gives the boy some money and sends him away from Jefferson.

1881 Charles Etienne returns to Jefferson with his wife, an anthropoid-looking black woman who is well advanced in pregnancy. He rents a cabin from Judith and farms the land. He lives apart from everyone, appearing in town occasionally to get drunk in a Negro store on Depot Street.

1882   A son is born to Charles Etienne and his Negro wife. Named Jim, the idiot child becomes known as Jim Bond. He lives on the Sutpen place for twenty-six years and then disappears.

Feb. 12, 1884   Judith Sutpen (age 42) dies of yellow fever (in Faulkner's chronological account—small pox) contracted while nursing Charles Etienne. Judith's tombstone is ordered by Rosa Coldfield. Charles Etienne Saint-Velery Bon dies shortly after Judith. He is buried in the Sutpen plot.

1890   Shreve McCannon is born in Edmonton, Canada.

1891   Quentin Compson is born in Jefferson, Mississippi.

Sept., 1909   Rosa Coldfield sends for Quentin Compson. He goes to her house and she tells him the story of Thomas Sutpen. She asks him to accompany her to the Sutpen house that evening. While waiting to pick up Rosa, Quentin sits on the porch of the Compson house with his father, who gives him his version of Sutpen's history and shows him the letter from Bon that Judith gave to Quentin's grandmother. Quentin and Rosa go out to Sutpen's Hundred. The front door is locked; Quentin pries open a window and opens the front door for Rosa, who rushes in, knocks over Clytie, and runs up the stairs. Clytie begs Quentin to prevent Rosa from going up. When Rosa descends, Quentin goes up to the bedroom where Henry Sutpen, seventy years old, is lying. Quentin Compson leaves Jefferson to go to Harvard.

Dec., 1909   Around Christmas, Rosa Coldfield drives with a deputy sheriff and an ambulance to Sutpen's. Before they reach the house, it bursts into flames. Rosa has to be restrained from rushing up the staircase to the second floor. The idiot, Jim Bond, howls as the house burns to the ground. Rosa Coldfield collapses and rides back to Jefferson in the ambulance.

Jan. 8, 1910   After remaining in a coma for almost two weeks, Rosa Coldfield dies. She is buried on January 9.

Jan., 1910   On the day Quentin Compson receives a letter dated Mississippi, January 10, 1910 from his father, he and his roommate Shreve MacCannon try to piece together the story of Thomas Sutpen.

Go Down, Moses

» » Chronology of important dates

1772 Lucius Quintus Carothers McCaslin is born in Carolina.

1779 Thucydus, the son of Negro slaves, Roskus and Fibby, is born.

1799 Twin sons Theophilus and Amodeus (later called Uncle Buck and Uncle Buddy) are born to Lucius Q. C. McCaslin and his wife.

1807 About this time, McCaslin migrates to Mississippi. In 1807 he travels to New Orleans and purchases a Negro slave, Eunice.

1809 Thucydus and Eunice are married.

1810 Tomasina, fathered by Lucius Q. C. McCaslin, is born to Eunice.

1832 On Christmas day, Eunice drowns herself in the creek.

1833 Tomasina gives birth to a son, Terrel (called Tomey's Turl) and dies in childbirth. The father is Lucius Q. C. McCaslin.

1837 (*June 27*) Lucius Q. C. McCaslin dies. On the same day his twin sons free Roskus and Fibby, who refuse to leave the plantation.

(*June 28*) Buck and Buddy read their father's will, which assigns ten acres of land to Thucydus. The legacy is refused, and the twins offer Thucydus two hundred dollars and freedom. He insists upon earning his freedom by working off the $200.00. The will also provides a $1,000 legacy for Tomey's Turl, to be turned over to him when he is twenty-one. At that time, he refuses the legacy and the twins increase it to $3,000 to be divided among the three surviving children of Tomey's Turl.

Right after their father's death, the twins move out of the large plantation house and put the Negroes in it, each evening latching the front door, though the windows and other doors are open.

(*1838*)* At Warwick, a plantation twenty-two miles away from the McCaslin land, owned by Hubert and Sophonsiba Beauchamp, a Negro child, Tennie, is born.

---

* Parentheses around a year indicate the date is approximate.

1841 (*January 12*)   Roskus, the freed McCaslin Negro, dies.

  (*November 3*)   Thucydus is given the $200.00 he earned, and he sets up a blacksmith shop.

1849   Fibby, the wife of Roskus, dies.

(*1850*)   Carothers Edmonds, later known as Cass, the great-nephew of Buck and Buddy, is born.

1854 (*February 17*)   Thucydus, the son of Roskus and Fibby, dies.

1856 (*March 3*)   Uncle Buck purchases Percavil Brownly from N. B. Forest for $265.00.

1859   Uncle Buddy wins Tennie Beauchamp from Hubert Beauchamp in a poker game. The Negro girl is brought to the McCaslin plantation and marries Tomey's Turl. A son, named Amodeus, is born to the couple and dies at birth.

1862   A daughter, named Callina (probably after the twins' sister), is born to Tennie and Turl and dies at birth. Percavil Brownly, freed and sent away from the plantation, returns to live for a while, undetected by the twins. He spends his time preaching and leading revival meetings.

1863   A third child, unnamed, born to Tennie and Turl dies at birth.

1864 (*December 29*)   James Thucydus Beauchamp, son of Tennie and Turl, is born and survives.

1866   Uncle Buck sees Percavil Brownly riding in the entourage of an army paymaster. Percavil looks into Uncle Buck's eyes and flees.

1867   Isaac, the son of Theophilus McCaslin (Uncle Buck) and Sophonsiba Beauchamp, is born. Uncle Buck is sixty-eight years old. Hubert Beauchamp gives his nephew a silver cup containing fifty gold pieces. In the presence of the family the cup is wrapped in burlap and sealed, to be opened by Isaac on his twenty-first birthday. Within six months, Hubert substitutes an IOU for five of the gold coins.

1869   Sophonsiba ("Fonsiba"), the daughter of Tennie and Turl, is born.

1873 (*January*)   Uncle Hubert Beauchamp substitutes an IOU for twenty-five gold pieces.

1874 (*March 17*)   Lucas Quintus Carothers McCaslin Beauchamp, the last child of Tennie and Turl, is born. About this time Zachary Edmonds, the son of Cass, is also born.

1876   Jobaker, the last surviving full-blooded Chickasaw Indian in the area dies, and Sam Fathers, who has lived as a Negro on the McCaslin plantation, goes to live in the woods.

1877   Ike (10 years old) joins the semi-annual hunting party for the first time. On this trip he catches his first glimpse of Old Ben, the bear.

1878   Ike (11) receives his first rifle from his cousin Cass. On the hunting trip, he seeks Old Ben. Ridding himself of his rifle and compass, he sees the bear.

1879   Uncle Buddy dies, and within twelve months Ike's father, Uncle Buck, also dies.
Ike (12) shoots his first deer and Sam Fathers daubs his face with the blood of the slain animal. Uncle Ash, jealous of the boy, demands the right to hunt. Followed by Ike, the Negro cook sets out on a futile expedition.

1880   Sam Fathers captures Lion. Boon becomes Lion's caretaker.

1881   Hunting Old Ben with a fyce, Ike is close enough to the bear to shoot, but holds his fire.

1882   Lion corners Old Ben, but the bear escapes as Boon shoots five times and misses five times.

1883   Ike is sixteen. He, Sam Fathers, and Boon are present at the death of Old Ben. Lion is killed in the fight and is buried with the paw of Old Ben. Sam Fathers dies and is buried. Ike reads the ledgers in the plantation commissary and learns that his grandfather had fathered a child upon his own half-breed daughter.

1885   Major DeSpain sells the hunting lodge and camp, reserving from the sale only the small area in which Sam Fathers is buried. Ike asks and receives permission to visit the camp once more. Except for Ash and Boon, he is alone on this trip. He visits the grave of Sam Fathers.
(*December* 29)   On his twenty-first birthday, James Thucydus Beauchamp, Ike's cousin, leaves the plantation.

1886 (*January*)   Ike traces James to Tennessee and then loses his trail. He returns the $1,000 legacy to the bank.
Ike learns that Percavil Brownly is the prosperous proprietor of a New Orleans brothel.
In the fall, Fonsiba Beauchamp, Ike's cousin, marries a Negro preacher who brings her to Arkansas. On Dec. 11, Ike goes to Midnight, where the preacher's farm is located, to give Fonsiba her $1,000 legacy. After talking with her husband, he decides to put the money in the local bank with instructions to give Fonsiba three dollars a month.

1888   On Ike's twenty-first birthday, the legacy from Uncle Hubert is opened. In the presence of Cass, Ike finds in the burlap-wrapped package, a coffee pot instead of the silver cup for which (among all the other IOUs and the copper coins) there is another IOU.
In the plantation commissary, on an October evening of this year, Ike relinquishes his heritage of the McCaslin plantation and explains to his cousin Cass his reasons for doing so. The following day Ike moves to a rooming house in Jefferson.

1895 (*March* 17) On his twenty-first birthday, Lucas Beauchamp travels the seventeen miles from the plantation to Jefferson to see his cousin Ike, who is now married. Lucas asks for his legacy and requests not only his thousand dollars but that of his brother James. At the bank the full amount is transferred to Lucas's account. Not too long after this incident, Lucas marries Molly Worsham. Cass Edmonds gives to Lucas some acreage and a house that will be his as long as he elects to remain on the plantation.

1898 Carothers (Roth) Edmonds is born, the son of Zachary and Louisa Edmonds. Louisa dies in childbirth and Molly is brought to the plantation house to care for the infant. For six months Lucas lives alone and then tells Zack to send his wife to her own home. On the night that she returns, Lucas decides he must kill Zack. In the confrontation, Lucas wrests Zack's pistol from him and fires it. A misfire saves Zack and satisfies Lucas's need to assert his manhood. In this same year Molly bears Lucas's son Henry.

(1914) A daughter of Lucas and Molly bears a son, Samuel Worsham Beauchamp.

(1920) Zachary Edmonds dies and his son Roth inherits the McCaslin plantation.

(1940) Lucas gets a divining machine to search for buried gold and nearly loses his wife Molly, who institutes divorce proceedings.
On the annual hunting trip Ike now makes with Roth Edmonds and some of the younger men, Ike, in his seventies, meets the granddaughter of his long-lost cousin James Beauchamp. He gives to her new-born son, the illegitimate child of Roth Edmonds, the silver-trimmed hunting horn which General Compson left to Ike in his will.
Samuel Worsham Beauchamp is executed for murder. At the request of the boy's grandmother, Molly, Gavin Stevens arranges to have his body returned to Jefferson.

A Fable

» » Chronology of events

TIME: A week in May, 1918.
PLACE: France: The Western Front, Chaulnesmont, Paris.
Inclusive pages for each event are listed at the left. Only two long passages in

the novel—the story of the horse and the English groom, and the supreme general's history—do not properly belong to the day under which Faulkner presents them. The horse story is told under the heading "Tuesday," Chapter VI, pp. 140-207. The supreme general's history is inserted in the events listed under "Wednesday Night," Chapter VII, pp. 234-271.

MONDAY

(20-55)   At noon, Charles Gragnon, forty-seven-year-old French Division Commander, orders a regiment of his division to attack. Except for a few noncommissioned officers, none of the enlisted men leaves the trenches. The Germans do not launch a counterattack. Gragnon, certain that he is faced with a mutiny, goes at once to the headquarters of Lallemont, the corps commander. These two generals pick up Henri, the army commander, and drive to the headquarters of Bidet, the group commander. Gragnon demands that the entire regiment of three thousand men be executed for mutiny. Bidet orders him to return to his headquarters. There, Gragnon is notified by telegram that he is to meet with the supreme general at 3 P.M. on Wednesday at Chaulnesmont. After long meditation, Gragnon decides to resign his commission. Late Monday night, he goes to Bidet's headquarters. Bidet refuses to accept his resignation.

(86-98)   Within three hours after the French regiment disobeys the order to attack, the entire western front is quiet. An eighteen-year-old pilot, Levine, on his first combat mission, is flagged down. The pilot refuses to believe that the war has ended and he has been denied an opportunity for glory. In a state of shock, he wanders that evening toward the hangars and discovers that though some planes are being worked over, armed guards prevent him from entering the hangars to see what is being done. (We learn later that the planes are being loaded with dummy ammunition.)

TUESDAY

(99-101)   Levine remains in a state of shock throughout the day.

(121-6)   The regiment that disobeys Gragnon's order was recruited from the district around Chaulnesmont, and when rumor of the mutiny spreads throughout the countryside, the relatives of the soldiers in the regiment flock into the city. Among those who arrive is a former prostitute from Marseille. She is the wife of the corporal who inspired the mutiny.

(56-85)   An English message runner, returning from a mission, gets a ride in a lorry which is part of a convoy heading for the front lines. The runner, a recent convert of the corporal's, discovers that the convoy is loaded with blank anti-aircraft ammunition. He surmises that the dummy ammunition is part of a plot by the military hierarchy to efface the effects of the mutiny that stopped the war. The runner goes into the front-line trenches to speak to an

English sentry, Harry, who has a mysterious power over the men in his regiment. The runner pleads with Harry to lead the regiment into no man's land to prove to the military commanders that the corporal's efforts were not in vain and that the enlisted men of all the nations want peace. Harry is viciously uncooperative, and finally he beats the runner, knocking him unconscious. The sentry is placed under arrest.

WEDNESDAY

(3-19) At dawn, the relatives of the mutinying regiment's soldiers are gathered on the boulevard leading to the *Hôtel de Ville*. A troop of infantry, led by a light tank, clears the boulevard, and the soldiers line up along the curb with locked bayonets to keep back the volatile mob. The wife of the corporal faints, and a man gives her a piece of bread. Down the boulevard, a staff car approaches, bearing three generals, an American, an Englishman, and a Frenchman who is the supreme general of the Allied forces. At the *Hôtel*, the generals stand on the steps and watch the caravan of trucks loaded with the mutineers pass. In the last truck are only thirteen men—the corporal and his twelve disciples.

(127-39) Throughout the day, the mob of relatives mills around the chateau or watches the wire compound being erected for the prisoners. At the gates of the city, the corporal's wife awaits the arrival of his sisters. In the afternoon, the crowd watches the arrival of General Gragnon, who, it is noted, no longer wears his saber. The relatives know that he has come to demand the execution of the prisoners.

(102-20) During the afternoon, three airplanes take off from the English airfield, the first combat planes to leave the ground since Monday afternoon. One of the planes is piloted by Levine. Over the front lines, the planes meet and attack a German plane. Levine maneuvers the enemy plane into his cross sights and fires. He is certain that his aim is perfect, but the plane continues on its path, undamaged. Unable to believe that he missed and suspecting something has been done to his machine guns, Levine dives straight down at one of the Allied anti-aircraft emplacements, shooting at the men around the gun. Watching Levine's performance from the ground is the English runner who gets hit in the leg by one of the blank bullets. Levine turns his plane for home and lands at the air field behind the German plane. From the enemy plane, a German general steps. He pulls a pistol from its holster and shoots the German pilot. Levine brings his plane to the edge of the field and sets it on its nose so that the machine guns face toward the ground. He begs a fellow pilot, Bridesman, to fire the guns. Levine stands in direct line of fire, and a blank tracer sets his Sidicott to smoldering slowly.

(208-11) After the English runner watches Levine spatter the AA battery with blanks, he leaves for Paris to get help from a Negro, the Reverend Sutterfield, who knew the sentry, Harry, in the United States several years before. In Paris, Sutterfield heads an organization called **Les Amis Myriades et Anonymes à la France de Tout le Monde.**

WEDNESDAY NIGHT

(212-22) During the evening, the corporal's two sisters, Marthe and Marya, arrive at the city gates and are met by the corporal's wife. They join the crowds of relatives who are camping in the city. Marya carries a basket containing bread, and Marthe offers one woman stirring something in a cooking pot, bread in exchange for the use of her fire. The woman hysterically denounces them as the corporal's whores and flings a spoon at them. The spoon disappears. In the fracas, Marya's basket is overturned and the bread is lost. Incited by the cries of the woman, a mob surrounds the three women. They are rescued by a provost's patrol, and they wander about until they find shelter in a stone stable. They sit on the straw, and out of the empty basket, the witless sister, Marya, takes bread which they eat.

(223-27) They are aroused by the cries of the people who watch the prisoners being sent out of the barracks and into the newly constructed compound. All the prisoners, except the corporal and his disciples, are pushed out of the barracks. Marthe decides to go to the mayor of the city, and the three women leave their stone niche.

(228-34) At the supreme general's headquarters, General Gragnon is ushered into the presence of the Allied commander. He repeats his demand that the entire regiment of three thousand men be executed.

(272-4) The supreme general has dinner and then meets with the mayor, who presents the complaint of the woman who lost her spoon. The general orders a party of soldiers to search for the spoon.

(274-82) The corporal and his disciples are brought before the general. An Englishman, Colonel Beale, a Frenchman, Major Blum, and an American, Captain Middleton, identify the corporal as three men whom they have witnessed die.

(283-301) The supreme general meets Marthe and is identified by her as the father of the corporal.

(301-09) The generals of the Allied armies meet with the German general to make plans for concealing the mutiny.

THURSDAY

(310-21) The English runner arrives at the headquarters of the Reverend Sutterfield. The Negro, dressed in a French corporal's uniform, returns to the front lines with the runner. At gun point, the sentry, Harry, is persuaded to go over the top of the trenches. The men in the regiment follow, and from the enemy trenches unarmed soldiers rush to meet them. An artillery barrage of

Allied and German guns concentrates on the two groups of soldiers. Harry, Sutterfield, and his son are killed. Only the English runner, horribly maimed, survives the bombardment.

(3ɒɒ 6)   The young aviator, Levine, commits suicide.

(326-33)   The quartermaster general visits the supreme general and offers his resignation.

(333-40)   In their prison cell, the corporal and his twelve disciples are served supper. One of the men, Polchek, who informed the military commanders of the planned mutiny, is very nervous. Another man, called Pierre, denies, when a guard calls the roll, that he is a member of the corporal's group. The corporal is led from the cell to visit the supreme general.

(340-56)   The supreme general brings his son, the corporal, to a hill overlooking the city and offers him freedom and wealth if he will forsake the men who followed him. The corporal refuses, and he is returned to prison.

(357-61)   In the cell in which the corporal is placed are two men, also scheduled to be executed—Lapin, and Casse-tête, also known as Horse.

(361-70)   The corporal is brought to a room in which a priest has prepared the utensils for the Last Sacrament. The priest, serving as agent for the supreme general, tries again to get the corporal to betray his men and refuse martyrdom. The corporal cannot be persuaded. Later, the priest borrows a bayonet from a soldier and kills himself.

(370-81)   General Gragnon is executed by three American soldiers.

FRIDAY

(382-94)   In the afternoon, the corporal and the two other men, one on each side of him, are executed by a firing squad. The corporal's sisters, Marthe and Marya, arrive with a cart and place the body of the corporal in it. They have received permission from the supreme general to bury the body on the farm of Marthe and her husband. At Châlons, a detachment of soldiers places the body in a plain coffin and informs Marthe that arrangements have been made for rail passage to St. Mihiel, where her husband will meet her.

SATURDAY

(394-99)   At St. Mihiel, Marthe's husband meets them, and they bring the body to the farm. They dig a grave in a land bank and place the coffin into it.

SUNDAY

(400-01)   In the early hours, an artillery bombardment tears up the farm. When Marthe searches for the grave of her brother, she discovers that the body of the corporal has disappeared.

TOMORROW

(402-25)   A detachment of soldiers is sent to get a body for the tomb of the unknown soldier in Paris. The body that it returns with is from the area around Marthe's farm.

(425-33)   Marthe is visited by Polchek and the English runner.

(433-37)   The supreme general is buried with full military honors.

Snopes Trilogy

» » Chronology of significant events*

1889   Eula Varner is born.

1896   Labove begins teaching school in Frenchman's Bend.

1897   Eula, eight years old, attends school. Labove falls in love with her.

1902   Flem Snopes arrives in Frenchman's Bend.

1903   Jack Houston marries. Three months later his wife is killed.
Labove, frustrated wooer of Eula, leaves the village.
Eck Snopes marries a local belle.
By September of this year, Jody Varner is relegated to keeping the store and Flem is handling the Varner acounts. He moves into the Varner household.

1907   Eula becomes pregnant by Hoake McCarron, who flees the county. Flem becomes the owner of Varner's Old Frenchman place and marries Eula. They go off to Texas.
Mink Snopes murders Jack Houston and is brought to the Jefferson jail house.

1908   Linda Snopes is born.
Mink is tried for murder and is sent to the state prison at Parchman.

1909   By tricking V. K. Ratliff into buying the Old Frenchman place, Flem gains an entry into Jefferson and arrives with his wife and her child.

1910-11   DeSpain courts Eula, and Flem becomes superintendent of the Jefferson power plant.

*   A number of these dates are established by working with the ages of the various characters. They are therefore only approximately correct.

1913   Gavin Stevens vies with DeSpain over Eula. Gavin leaves Jefferson to study in Heidelberg.

1918   Judge Stevens, Gavin's father, dies.

1919   Gavin visits his home town.

1922   Gavin returns to live in Jefferson. Linda is fourteen.
Flem Snopes becomes vice-president of the bank.

1923   Montgomery Ward's atelier is closed with the cooperation of Flem Snopes. Montgomery Snopes is sentenced to a term in Parchman. Carrying out Flem's orders, he persuades Mink to try a prison break. Mink is caught, and his original sentence is doubled.

1927   Flem permits Linda to go to the University in Oxford, Miss.
He becomes president of the bank.
Eula Varner commits suicide.
Linda Snopes leaves for New York where she falls in love with Bart Kohl and lives with him.

1936   Linda meets her father Hoake McCarron. Her marriage to Bart Kohl is witnessed by Gavin Stevens and V. K. Ratliff who have come to New York. Linda and Bart leave for Spain to fight in the Spanish Civil War. Bart is killed within a few months.

1937   Linda returns to Jefferson, a deaf widow.

1940   An F.B.I. agent investigating Linda's affiliation with the Communist party calls on Gavin Stevens. Afterwards, Gavin visits Linda to suggest that she leave town; in the course of the interview he refuses her offer of marriage.

1941   Linda goes to Pascagoula to work in a shipyard. Gavin visits her there and she asks him to find someone he can love and marry.

1942   Gavin marries Melisandre Backus. His nephew, Chick Mallison, goes to war.

1943   Flem Snopes acquires the Compson land.

1945   Chick Mallison returns to Jefferson.
Ratliff eliminates Clarence Snopes as a candidate for the U.S. Congress.

1946   Mink Snopes is released from prison, comes to Jefferson and murders his kinsman, Flem Snopes.

As one might expect, there are a number of inconsistencies in the trilogy. Ratliff, for example, is at least in his thirties when he appears in *The Hamlet*. (Around 1902, he says that he has not seen Ab Snopes in twenty-five years.) But in the rest of the trilogy he is Gavin's age, which would place his birth date around 1886-7. Gavin Stevens, too, floats a few years in age, being, at one point, a year younger than Eula, but to fit into other events of the story, he would necessarily have to be older than birth in 1890 would make him. Will Varner is sixty in 1902 when *The Hamlet* opens, but when Ratliff, in *The Mansion*, reviews the events recorded in *The Hamlet*, Varner's age is altered to forty.

Notes

PART ONE: INTRODUCTION

1. Information about Faulkner's life and career was drawn from the articles and books by Robert Cantwell, Carvel Collins, Robert Coughlan, and William Van O'Connor that are listed in the bibliography under "Life and Career."

2. *Faulkner at Nagano*, Robert A. Jelliffe, ed. (Tokyo, 1956), p. 108.

3. Quoted by Robert Cantwell in "The Faulkners: Recollections of a Gifted Family," *Three Decades of Criticism*, Frederick J. Hoffman, and Olga W. Vickery, eds. (East Lansing, 1960), pp. 65-6.

4. Carvel Collins, "About the Sketches," *William Faulkner: New Orleans Sketches* (New York, 1961), pp. 9-34, states that during the period in 1925 that Faulkner was in New Orleans and contributing sketches to the *Picayune*, he "was hard at work on his novel, *Soldiers' Pay*" (p. 30). Frederick L. Gwynn, "Faulkner's Raskolnikov," *Modern Fiction Studies*, IV (Summer, 1958), 169-72, in his footnote listing of dates of composition for the early novels, assigns 1924 as the year in which this first novel was written. Professor Gwynn also states that between *Soldiers' Pay* and *Mosquitoes*, Faulkner wrote a novel which he destroyed.

5. See Melvin Backman, "Sickness and Primitivism: A Dominant Pattern in William Faulkner's Work," *Accent*, XIV (Winter, 1954), 61-73.

6. In a seminar paper, Miss Toni Cade drew my attention to the similarity between Faulkner's novels and the *Bildungsroman*.

7. The quotations from the novels in Part I are from the following editions: *As I Lay Dying* (Modern Library); *Go Down, Moses* (Modern Library); *Soldiers' Pay* (Signet); *Light in August* (Modern Library); *Absalom, Absalom!* (Modern Library); *Intruder in the Dust* (Random House, 1948); *Requiem for a Nun* (Signet); *The Hamlet* (Vintage); *Sartoris* (Signet); *Collected Stories* (Random House, 1950); *The Town* (Vintage); *The Reivers* (Random House, 1962).

8. Malcolm Cowley, "Introduction," *The Portable Faulkner* (New York, 1946), makes a similar observation: "He is not primarily a novelist: that is, his stories do not occur to him in book-length units of 70,000 to 150,000 words" (p. 18). Leslie Fiedler, "William Faulkner: An American Dickens," *Com-*

mentary, X (October, 1950), 384-7, also expresses the view that Faulkner is essentially a short story writer.

9. *Intruder in the Dust* (New York, 1948), p. 194. For a discussion of time in Faulkner's fiction, see Frederick J. Hoffmann, "Introduction: Time and Space," in his *William Faulkner* (New York, 1961), pp. 17-39; and Olga W. Vickery, "The Contours of Time," in her *The Novels of William Faulkner* (Baton Rouge, 1959), pp. 226-36.

10. Faulkner's technique of withholding information was probably adapted from the detective story, a genre with which Faulkner was fascinated and which he practiced. *Knight's Gambit* is a collection of detective stories. Francis Blazer O'Brien, "Faulkner and Wright, Alias S. S. Van Dine," *Mississippi Quarterly* XIV (Spring, 1961), 101-07, writes that Faulkner was quoted in a local newspaper acknowledging the influence of S. S. Van Dine.

11. "Mirrors of Chartres Street," *New Orleans Sketches*, p. 54.

12. Alfred Kazin, *On Native Grounds* (New York, 1942), p. 462.

13. Arthur L. Scott, "The Faulknerian Sentence," *Prairie Schooner*, XXVII (Spring, 1953), 94.

14. *Faulkner at Nagano*, p. 37.

PART TWO: THE NOVELS

Sartoris

1. Olga W. Vickery, *The Novels of William Faulkner: A Critical Interpretation* (Baton Rouge, 1959), suggests Bayard's fear of dying when she notes that Bayard is grimly determined to "prove himself a Sartoris, but his own nature interferes. There is a tenseness each time he takes a chance and risks his life that is foreign to Johnny's casualness" (p. 20). Melvin Backman, "Faulkner's Sick Heroes: Bayard Sartoris and Quentin Compson," *Modern Fiction Studies*, II (Autumn, 1956), 95-108, interprets Bayard's "inner conflict" as a "welling upward of a dark suicidal force." Backman also couples, as I have, the figures of Bayard and Horace, though he sees them, as I do not, as "twin symbols of the antipodal forces of self-destruction." (Pp. 97, 100.)

The Unvanquished

1. Irving Howe writes: ". . . *The Unvanquished* is the least serious of the Yoknapatawpha novels." *William Faulkner*, p. 42. Olga Vickery omits consideration of the book in her analyses of the novels, and Peter Swiggart describes the book as a collection of stories with "little thematic unity." *The Art of Faulkner's Novels*, p. 36. Hyatt Waggoner believes, as I do, that *The Unvanquished* is a serious work and a novel. His judgment of it as a work of "power and beauty," however, seems to me excessive for a book with so many weaknesses and so much slick sentimentality. *William Faulkner: From Jefferson to the World* (Lexington, 1959), p. 180.

2. George Marion O'Donnell, "Faulkner's Mythology," *Kenyon Review*, I (Summer, 1939), 285-99. Reprinted in *Three Decades*, pp. 82-93.

The Sound and the Fury

1. Jean-Paul Sartre, "Time in Faulkner: *The Sound and the Fury*," *Three Decades*, p. 226.

2. Lawrance Thompson, *William Faulkner: An Introduction and Interpretation* (New York, 1963), and Hyatt Waggoner, *William Faulkner*, have also noted the influence of T. S. Eliot. Waggoner sees the greatest influence in Faulkner's conception of Quentin.

3. Freudian critics view the first three sections of the novel as representations of the id, the ego, and the super-ego. The idea is interesting and appealing, but describing Jason as a representative of the super-ego seems to me a distortion for the sake of a thesis. As I show in my analysis, Jason is alienated from his entire society and he is governed by irrational forces.

4. For an interesting analysis of Quentin's emotional problem, consult Melvin Backman's "Faulkner's Sick Heroes: Bayard Sartoris and Quentin Compson," *Modern Fiction Studies*, II (Autumn, 1956), 95-108.

5. Cleanth Brooks, "Primitivism in *The Sound and the Fury*," *English Institute Essays*, 1952 (New York, 1954), pp. 5-28, reaches the same conclusion: Quentin . . . commits suicide for fear that his father may be right. . . ." (P. 16.)

6. Lawrence E. Bowling, "Faulkner and the Theme of Innocence," *Kenyon Review*, XX (Summer, 1958), 466-87, interprets the novel as "an exploration of the idea of innocence," and he sees Quentin's fastidiousness about the state of his clothing as a manifestation of his puritanism (p. 466).

7. Vickery describes Jason as a man without any "illusions about his family or himself," and attributes far more stature to him than I would when she ascribes to him a conscious attempt to order his existence by means of his calculating approach to life. *William Faulkner*, p. 42. See also the analysis of Jason's character by John Lewis Longley, Jr., *The Tragic Mask* (Chapel Hill, 1963), pp. 144-50.

As I Lay Dying

1. Rabi, "Faulkner and the Exiled Generation," *William Faulkner: Two Decades of Criticism*, Hoffman and Vickery, eds. (East Lansing, 1951), pp. 118-38, was one of the first critics to see *As I Lay Dying* as an expression of life's absurdity: "In Faulkner's world the struggle is intrinsically absurd, because the universe itself is absurd: always the same tale, told by an idiot signifying nothing" (p. 134). William Rossky, whose essay, "*As I Lay Dying*: The Insane World," *Texas Studies in Literature and Language*, IV (Spring, 1962), 87-97, is one of the few that come to grips with the problems of the novel, also views the novel as a reflection of "the universal and terrible incongruities of existence" (p. 91). Walter J. Slatoff's illuminating thesis of suspension created by opposing and irreconcilable forces as the dominant pattern in Faulkner's fiction leads him to a similar conclusion: "Life, Faulkner seems to be saying, is nothing more than a grim and horrible joke . . . a joke which might well be regarded with amusement." *Quest for Failure: A Study of William Faulkner* (Ithaca, 1960), p. 172.

2. Olga W. Vickery, "The Dimensions of Consciousness: *As I Lay Dying*," *William Faulkner*, pp. 50-65. Reprinted in *Three Decades*, pp. 232-47.

Sanctuary

1. French criticism preceded the American in recognizing the literary merit of *Sanctuary*, probably because, as André Malraux indicates, "A Preface for Faulkner's *Sanctuary*," *Yale French Studies*, No. 10 (Fall, 1952), 92-4, the novel seemed to fit so readily into the tradition of Edgar Allen Poe. For many years, George Marion O'Donnell's interpretation of the novel (*op. cit.*), as an allegorical rendering of the struggle between traditional morality and evil modernism dominated criticism. But most of the recent criticism recognizes the importance of Horace's role in the novel. William Van O'Connor, *The Tangled Fire*, limits the nature of the evil in the story to a flaw in human nature and to modernism; but Hyatt Waggoner, *William Faulkner*, though he emphasizes the evil of modernism, declares that what ". . . we find when we look at *Sanctuary* itself, without keeping *Requiem* in mind, is an 'outrage' for which there is no real solution, moral or otherwise" (pp. 96-7). Frederick Hoffman conjectures that "Perhaps what distressed readers of *Sanctuary* more than its ingenious obscenities was the grinding helplessness of Benbow's good will." (*William Faulkner*, p. 68.) Olga Vickery attributes Horace's failure, as I do, to his idealism. Lawrance Thompson interprets *Sanctuary* in terms of the ideas that Faulkner developed many years later in *Requiem*: ". . . Faulkner's view would seem to be that just as soon as any individual comes to realize there is a logical pattern to evil, that individual discovers his duty to assert his own moral responsibility to others and to himself by going into action against that logical pattern, regardless of the possible consequences of such a struggle. By contrast, Faulkner implies, the individual who submits to Horace's sense of impotence might just as well be dead." (*William Faulkner*, p. 108.) Thompson limits the pattern of evil to human acts and interprets the "savage indignation" expressed in the novel as directed against the sins of man (p. 115).

2. Cleanth Brooks, "Faulkner's Sanctuary: The Discovery of Evil," *Sewanee Review*, LXXI (Winter, 1963), 1-24, writes: "Horace is the sentimental idealist, the man of academic mind, who finds out that the world is not a place of justice and moral tidiness. He discovers, with increasing horror, that evil is rooted in the very nature of things" (p. 1).

3. See Vickery, *William Faulkner*, p. 106.

Light in August

1. Among the many good interpretations, I have found most illuminating Ilse Dusoir Lind's "The Calvinistic Burden of *Light in August*," *The New England Quarterly*, XXX (September, 1957), 307-29; C. Hugh Holman's "The Unity of Faulkner's *Light in August*," *PMLA*, LXXIII (June, 1958), 155-66; and Olga W. Vickery's "The Shadow and the Mirror: *Light in August*," *William Faulkner*, pp. 66-83.

2. C. Hugh Holman, *op. cit.*, p. 161.

3. For a different view of Joe Christmas's dilemma, see Alfred Kazin,

"The Stillness of *Light in August*," *Partisan Review*, XXIV (Fall, 1957), 519-38. Reprinted in *Three Decades*, pp. 247-65.

4. For an interesting discussion of Lena Grove and Keats's Ode, see Norman H. Pearson, "Lena Grove," *Shenandoah*, III (Spring, 1952), 3-7.

5. For a detailed exploration of the Christian parallels, consult Beekman W. Cottrell, "Christian Symbols in 'Light in August,'" *Modern Fiction Studies*, II (Winter, 1956-1957), 207-13.

Pylon

1. Hyatt Waggoner offers a more extensive comparison of Eliot's poetry and *Pylon*. *William Faulkner*, pp. 122-32.

2. *Faulkner in the University*, p. 36.

3. For an opposing interpretation of the Reporter's quest, see Olga W. Vickery, "A New World Folklore: *Pylon*," *William Faulkner*, pp. 145-55.

4. John R. Marvin, "'Pylon': The Definition of Sacrifice," *Faulkner Studies*, I (Summer, 1952), 20-23; and Donald T. Torchiana, "Faulkner's 'Pylon' and the Structure of Modernity," *Modern Fiction Studies*, III (Winter, 1957-1958), 291-308. Walter J. Slatoff details the ambiguities of the novel in *Quest for Failure*, pp. 211-15.

Absalom, Absalom!

1. See, for example, Clifton Fadiman's review, "Faulkner, Extra-Special, Double-Distilled," *The New Yorker*, XII (October 31, 1936), 62-64.
Arthur L. Scott, "The Myriad Perspectives of *Absalom, Absalom!*" *American Quarterly*, VI (Fall, 1954), 210-20, provides an interesting discussion of Faulkner's form and its relation to modern art.
Walter Sullivan, "The Tragic Design of *Absalom, Absalom!*," *The South Atlantic Quarterly*, L (October, 1951), 552-66, discusses the novel's relation to the form of tragedy.

2. Many of the critics who have undertaken extensive analyses of *Absalom, Absalom!* have focused attention upon Sutpen's "innocence," with varying conclusions about its meaning and significance. John Lewis Longley, Jr., *The Tragic Mask*, pp. 206-18, comes to a conclusion similar to mine concerning the traumatic experience Sutpen undergoes at the plantation door, but does not expand the rejection theme to include the other characters. Cleanth Brooks, "*Absalom, Absalom!*: The Definition of Innocence," *The Sewanee Review*, LIX (Autumn, 1951), 543-58, sees Sutpen's innocence as representative of the innocence of Faulkner's male characters, which "comes down finally to a trust in rationality—an overweening confidence that plans work out—that life is simpler than it is" (p. 556). The most comprehensive and most perceptive analysis of the novel is provided by Ilse Dusoir Lind, "The Design and Meaning of *Absalom, Absalom!*," *PMLA*, LXX (December, 1955), 887-912. Reprinted in *Three Decades*, pp. 278-304.

3. *Faulkner in the University*, p. 98.

The Wild Palms

1. Most interpreters of the novel do not view the love story as satire. Joseph J. Moldenhauer, "Unity of Theme and Structure in *The Wild Palms*," *Three Decades*, pp. 305-22, for instance, takes the love of the couple seriously and interprets the story as a tragedy produced by Harry's inability to give himself to love because of his puritanism. Peter Swiggart, *The Art of Faulkner's Novels*, sees the novel as a "successful *tour de force* in which puritan minds are placed in conflict with natural forces that they seek to suppress or control" (p. 52). Olga W. Vickery, *William Faulkner*, pp. 156-66, also views the love of the couple seriously. Hyatt Waggoner, *William Faulkner*, pp. 132-47, points up the exaggerations of the love, but he does not see it as satiric in intent. Irving Howe, *William Faulkner*, pp. 233-42, is very much disturbed by the exaggerations in the love but does not pursue the implications. William Van O'Connor in *The Tangled Fire* says, "The story can be read as the tragedy of love in the modern world, but it probably should be read primarily as the tragedy of love in the physical world, in nature" (p. 109). Only much later did O'Connor pursue the implications of this idea. "Faulkner's One-Sided 'Dialogue' with Hemingway," *College English*, XXIV (December, 1962), 208-15.

2. H. Edward Richardson in his "The 'Hemingwaves' in Faulkner's 'Wild Palms,'" *Modern Fiction Studies*, IV (Winter, 1958-1959), 357-60, has noted a number of these parallels, though occasionally with an excess of zeal. Hyatt Waggoner, *op. cit.*, also makes comparisons with *A Farewell to Arms*. See also W. R. Moses, "Water, Water Everywhere: 'Old Man' and 'A Farewell to Arms,'" *Modern Fiction Studies*, V (Summer, 1959), 172-4.

Go Down, Moses

1. There are very few critical essays devoted to *Go Down, Moses* as a novel. Most critics have focused attention upon "The Bear," treating it as an integral short novel. As a result, many perceptive studies of that story are limited in usefulness, it seems to me, by failing to see it as a section of a novel dealing with inherited guilt and the racial problem. R. W. B. Lewis, for instance, in his very fine study, "The Hero in the New World: William Faulkner's *The Bear*," *Kenyon Review*, XIII (Autumn, 1951), 641-60, argues that Ike undergoes a moral regeneration, but he carefully avoids treating the ineffectiveness of Ike after his regeneration. Kenneth LaBudde, "Cultural Primitivism in William Faulkner's 'The Bear,'" *American Quarterly*, II (Winter, 1950), 322-28, is restricted to discussing the validity of the primitive rituals in the story; he does not touch upon their significance. W. R. Moses, "Where History Crosses Myth: Another Reading of 'The Bear,'" *Accent*, XIII (Winter, 1953), 21-33, ignores the racial issue and sees the story as a mythical dramatization of a struggle between mechanized society and the wilderness. Unlike Lewis, Moses does attempt to deal with Ike's failure, but sees it only as a childish attempt by Ike to remain within a mythical world because he is afraid to face society. Among the few essays which treat *Go Down, Moses* as a novel, the most helpful are Walter F. Taylor Jr.'s "Let my People Go: The White Man's Heritage in *Go Down, Moses*," *The South Atlantic Quarterly*, XVIII (Winter, 1959), 20-32, and Olga W. Vickery's "Initiation and

Identity: *Go Down, Moses* and *Intruder in the Dust*," *William Faulkner*, pp. 134-44.

2. Ike may also take too much of Old Carothers's pride and that rigidity which makes Ike's counterparts in other novels incapable of adapting to the complexities of adult life. See Herbert A. Perluck's very fine analysis of Ike's failure in " 'The Heart's Driving Complexity': An Unromantic Reading of Faulkner's 'The Bear,' " *Accent*, XX (Winter, 1960), 23-46.

Intruder in the Dust

1. See Hyatt Waggoner's discussion of the meaning of Faulkner's title in *William Faulkner*, pp. 214-15. Illuminating discussions of this novel are provided by Andrew Lytle, "Regeneration for the Man," *The Sewanee Review*, LVII (Winter, 1949), 120-7; and Elizabeth Hardwick, "Faulkner and the South Today," *Partisan Review*, XV (October, 1948), 1130-35.

2. James Baldwin offers a counter to Faulkner's argument in "Faulkner and Desegregation," *Partisan Review*, XXIII (Fall, 1956), 568-73.

A Fable

1. *William Faulkner*, p. 231. See also, Roma A. King Jr., "Everyman's Warfare: A Study of Faulkner's 'Fable.' " *Modern Fiction Studies*, II (Autumn, 1956), 132-8, and Irving Howe, *William Faulkner*, pp. 268-81.

2. In a very fine review-essay of *A Fable*, Andrew Lytle, "The Son of Man: He Will Prevail," *The Sewanee Review*, LXIII (Winter, 1955), 114-37, writes: "The insistence on endurance as the measure of immortality in mortal man is a stoical attitude that appears in late stages of civilization. Whatever virtues it lends to behavior it remains a naturalistic interpretation of man's predicament. Jesus is either divine or he stands for an archetypical performance, the essence of which remains in man's consciousness to be repeated again, say in the Twentieth Century at the time of a false spring armistice in a world war." (P. 125.)

3. *Faulkner at Nagano*, p. 186.

4. Most reviewers and interpreters of *A Fable* have either ignored the horse-groom story or struggled vainly to see its connection to the novel. This is mainly, I think, because so many have approached the novel as a Christian allegory. However, the story of the horse and the story of Christ have, obviously, little in common. Even Heinrich Straumann, "An American Interpretation of Existence: Faulkner's *A Fable*," *Three Decades*, pp. 349-72, whose essay is the best analysis of the novel yet published, offers a weak explanation of the link between this story and the novel. Straumann, who considers *A Fable* a masterpiece, and "a milestone in the history of American literature," interprets the dualism in the novel not as a reflection of man's dual nature, as I do, but as a dualism of the whole tragic "world order," tragic "because it is shown in successive pairs of opposites each of which is absolutely irresolvable, and hence the whole allows room neither for the idea of completion nor for reconciliation." (P. 351.)

5. This incident has a number of parallel scenes throughout the book in

which the cry of birds symbolizes man's need for hope. See Andrew Lytle's discussion of the hanged man and the bird theme (*op. cit.*).

6. See James Hafley's discussion of the political implications of the novel in "Faulkner's 'Fable': Dream and Transfiguration." *Accent*, XVI (Winter, 1956), 3-14.

The Snopes Trilogy

1. *Faulkner in the University*, p. 90.

2. Warren Beck, who considers the Snopes trilogy the "very crown of Faulkner's creativity," has made the only full scale study of the three novels as a trilogy: *Man in Motion: Faulkner's Trilogy* (Madison, 1961), p. 5.

3. *The Hamlet* is composed of revised stories and parts of stories that were published previously: "Spotted Horses" (1931), "The Hound" (1931), "Lizards in Jamshyd's Courtyard" (1932), "Fool about a Horse" (1936), and "Afternoon of a Cow," first printed in a French translation by Maurice Edgar Coindreau in 1943. Peter Lisca, "The Hamlet: Genesis and Revisions," *Faulkner Studies*, III (Spring, 1954), 5-13, discusses the revisions that Faulkner made in these stories to achieve unity in the novel. Robert Penn Warren, "The Snopes World," *Kenyon Review*, III (Spring, 1941), 253-57, was one of the few reviewers to recognize the book as a unified novel, noting the intricate patterning of contrasts that make up the book's structure, though he does describe the effect of the organization as "loose and casual." Florence Leaver, "The Structure of *The Hamlet*," *Twentieth Century Literature*, I (July, 1955), 77-84, describes the book as structured upon a hierarchy of minds set in resistance to Flem. Viola Hopkins, "William Faulkner's 'The Hamlet': A Study in Meaning and Form," *Accent*, XV (Spring, 1955), 125-44, points out the close relationship between the stories; and T. Y. Greet, "The Theme and Structure of Faulkner's *The Hamlet*," *PMLA*, LXII (September, 1957), 775-90, details the tonal contrasts that thematically unify the stories into a novel.

4. There is no criticism that can be cited to support this view of Snopesism. The O'Donnell thesis remains pervasive, and Snopesism is usually described as a symbol of evil, sometimes just social evil, sometimes cosmic.

5. The British edition of *The Hamlet* (Chatto and Windus: London, 1957) does not contain the final section of this chapter: the scenes in which Ratliff discovers Lump's peep show enterprise and arranges for the Snopes clan to purchase the cow to stop the sodomy. The chapter in the British version ends with Houston's statement, " 'God damn it, keep them both away from my place. Do you hear?" on page 199 of the Vintage edition.

6. Consult Lawrance Thompson's analysis of the multiple narrator technique in this novel. *William Faulkner*, pp. 148-58.

7. *Man in Motion*, p. 85.

The Reivers

1. *The Reivers* calls attention to the theme of adolescent recognition in Faulkner's novels. The experience of Lucius is basically the same as that of

the other young protagonists. His violent reaction to the discovery of sex, for instance, is a variant of the experience Joe Christmas undergoes in *Light in August*. In this novel, as the following passage makes clear, Faulkner is retelling the initiation story for a didactic purpose: to show how an adolescent should accept reality.

> I was just eleven, remember. There are things, circumstances, conditions in the world which should not be there but are, and you cant escape them and indeed, you would not escape them even if you had the choice, since they too are a part of Motion, of participating in life, being alive. But they should arrive with grace, decency. I was having to learn too much too fast, unassisted; I had nowhere to put it, no receptacle, pigeonhole prepared yet to accept it without pain and lacerations. (155)

Bibliography

» » Works by Faulkner

The Marble Faun [Poems]. Boston: The Four Seas Co., 1924.
Soldiers' Pay [Novel]. New York: Boni and Liveright, 1926.
Mosquitoes [Novel]. New York: Boni and Liveright, 1927.
Sartoris [Novel]. New York: Harcourt, Brace and Co., 1929.
The Sound and the Fury [Novel]. New York: Cape and Smith, 1929.
As I Lay Dying [Novel]. New York: Cape and Smith, 1930.
Sanctuary [Novel]. New York: Cape and Smith, 1931.
These 13 [Stories]. New York: Cape and Smith, 1931.
Light in August [Novel]. New York: Smith and Haas, 1932.
A Green Bough [Poems]. New York: Smith and Haas, 1933.
Doctor Martino and Other Stories [Stories]. New York: Smith and Haas, 1934.
Pylon [Novel]. New York: Smith and Haas, 1935.
Absalom, Absalom! [Novel]. New York: Random House, 1936.
The Unvanquished [Novel]. New York: Random House, 1938.
The Wild Palms [Novel]. New York: Random House, 1939.
The Hamlet [Novel]. New York: Random House, 1940.
Go Down, Moses and Other Stories [Novel]. New York: Random House, 1942. Reissued in a Modern Library Edition in 1955 as *Go Down, Moses.*
Intruder in the Dust [Novel]. New York: Random House, 1948.
Knight's Gambit [Stories]. New York: Random House, 1949.
Collected Stories of William Faulkner [Stories]. New York: Random House, 1950.
Requiem for a Nun [Novel]. New York: Random House, 1951.
A Fable [Novel]. New York: Random House, 1954.
Big Woods [Stories]. New York: Random House, 1955.
The Town [Novel]. New York: Random House, 1957.
The Mansion [Novel]. New York: Random House, 1959.
The Reivers [Novel]. New York: Random House, 1962.

Collections of works and interviews

The Portable Faulkner. Malcolm Cowley, ed. New York: The Viking Press, 1946.
The Faulkner Reader. Saxe Commins, ed. New York: Random House, 1954.
Faulkner at Nagano. Robert A. Jelliffe, ed. Tokyo: The Kenkyusha Press, 1956.

William Faulkner: New Orleans Sketches. Carvel Collins, ed. New Brunswick:
   Rutgers University Press, 1958. Evergreen Edition, New York: Grove
   Press, 1961.
Faulkner in the University. Frederick L. Gwynn and Joseph L. Blotner, eds.
   Charlottesville: The University of Virginia Press, 1959.
William Faulkner: Early Prose and Poetry. Carvel Collins, ed. Boston: Little,
   Brown and Co., 1962.

Bibliographies of Faulkner's works

Daniel, Robert W. *A Catalogue of the Writings of William Faulkner*. New
   Haven: Yale University Library, 1942. Published twenty years before
   Faulkner's death, the bibliography has only a limited value.
Meriwether, James B. "William Faulkner: A Check List," *The Princeton
   University Library Chronicle*, XVIII (Spring, 1957), 136-58. This listing
   of Faulkner's books, stories, and miscellaneous publications is the most
   useful bibliography yet compiled.
————. *The Literary Career of William Faulkner: A Bibliographical Study*.
   Princeton: Princeton University Library, 1961. Of value chiefly to Faulkner scholars, this bibliography catalogues the Faulkner exhibition of 1957
   in the Princeton University Library. It includes a section listing the man-
   uscripts in that collection, and sections devoted to the English editions,
   the translations, the motion pictures and television shows which Faulkner
   did, and a final section which reproduces and annotates the schedule
   Faulkner kept on the stories he submitted to magazines.

» » The criticism

Bibliographies of Faulkner criticism

Vickery, Olga W. "A Selective Bibliography," *William Faulkner: Three Decades of Criticism*. East Lansing: The Michigan State University Press,
   1960, pp. 393-428. Compiled by a scholar who knows the Faulkner
   criticism thoroughly, this selection is the most accurate and useful bibliography to date.
Sleeth, Irene Lynn. "William Faulkner: A Bibliography of Criticism," *Twentieth Century Literature*, VIII (April, 1962) 18-43. The most complete
   listing of Faulkner criticism through 1961, this bibliography is marred
   by the compiler's failure to include essential bibliographical information—
   the issue of the magazine in which articles appeared—for many entries.

Critical books and reminiscences*

* Beck, Warren. *Man in Motion: Faulkner's Trilogy*. Madison: The University
   of Wisconsin Press, 1961.
* Brooks, Cleanth. *William Faulkner: The Yoknapatawpha Country*. New
   Haven: Yale University Press, 1963.
*   An asterisk before an entry in this section indicates that the books contain
analyses of individual novels. Chapters of these books which were originally
published in magazines are not listed in the *Articles* section of this bibliography.

Campbell, Harry Modean, and Foster, Ruel E. *William Faulkner: A Critical Appraisal.* Norman: University of Oklahoma Press, 1951.

Coughlan, Robert. *The Private World of William Faulkner.* New York: Harper & Bros., 1954.

Cullen, John B. in collaboration with Watkins, Floyd C. *Old Times in the Faulkner Country.* Chapel Hill: The University of North Carolina Press, 1961.

Faulkner, John. *my brother Bill: An Affectionate Reminiscence.* New York: Trident Press, 1963.

Hoffman, Frederick J. *William Faulkner.* New York: Twayne Publishers, Inc., 1961.

Hoffman, Frederick J. and Vickery, Olga W. eds. *William Faulkner: Two Decades of Criticism.* East Lansing: Michigan State University Press, 1951.

———. *William Faulkner: Three Decades of Criticism.* East Lansing: Michigan State University Press, 1960.

* Howe, Irving. *William Faulkner: A Critical Study.* New York: Random House, 1952. Second Edition, revised and expanded, Vintage Books, 1962.

Longley, John Lewis, Jr. *The Tragic Mask: A Study of Faulkner's Heroes.* Chapel Hill: The University of North Carolina Press, 1963.

Malin, Irving. *William Faulkner: An Interpretation.* Stanford: Stanford University Press, 1957.

* Millgate, Michael. *William Faulkner.* New York: Grove Press, 1961.

Miner, Ward L. *The World of William Faulkner.* Durham: Duke University Press, 1952.

Nilon, Charles H. *Faulkner and the Negro.* (University of Colorado Studies: Series in Language and Literature, No. 8.) Boulder: University of Colorado Press, September, 1962.

* O'Connor, William Van. *The Tangled Fire of William Faulkner.* Minneapolis: University of Minnesota Press, 1954.

———. *William Faulkner.* (Pamphlets on American Writers, No. 3), Minneapolis: University of Minnesota Press, 1959.

Robb, Mary Cooper. *William Faulkner: An Estimate of his Contribution to the American Novel.* Pittsburgh: University of Pittsburgh Press, 1957.

Slatoff, Walter J. *Quest for Failure: A Study of William Faulkner.* Ithaca: Cornell University Press, 1960.

* Swiggart, Peter. *The Art of Faulkner's Novels.* Austin: University of Texas Press, 1962.

* Thompson, Lawrence. *William Faulkner: An Introduction and Interpretation.* New York: Barnes & Noble, Inc., 1963.

* Vickery, Olga W. *The Novels of William Faulkner: A Critical Interpretation.* Baton Rouge: Louisiana State University Press, 1959.

* Waggoner, Hyatt H. *William Faulkner: From Jefferson to the World.* Lexington: University of Kentucky Press, 1959.

» » Articles

The following listing of articles is highly selective. Space requirements forced the exclusion of many articles that added to my knowledge and indirectly contributed to this book. Included are only those works referred to in the text or chapter notes and a few others which are intended to provide a student or general reader a limited but useful list of general background articles and studies of the individual novels.

Career and life

Cantwell, Robert. "The Faulkners: Recollections of a Gifted Family," *New World Writing*, No. 2 (November, 1952), 300-15. (*Three Decades*, pp. 51-66.) *

Collins, Carvel. "About the Sketches," *William Faulkner: New Orleans Sketches*. New Brunswick: Rutgers University Press, 1958, pp. 9-34.

———. "Faulkner at the University of Mississippi," *William Faulkner: Early Prose and Poetry*. Boston: Little, Brown and Company, 1962, pp. 3-33.

Coughlan, Robert. *The Private World of William Faulkner*. New York: Harper & Bros., 1954.

Grenier, Cynthia. "The Art of Fiction: An Interview with William Faulkner—September, 1955," *Accent*, XVI (Summer, 1956), 167-77.

O'Connor, William Van. *The Tangled Fire of William Faulkner*. Minneapolis: University of Minnesota Press, 1954.

Stein, Jean. "William Faulkner: An Interview," *Paris Review*, IV. (Spring, 1956), 28-52. Reprinted in *Writers at Work*, Malcolm Cowley, ed. New York: Viking Press, 1958, pp. 119-41. (*Three Decades*, pp. 67-82.)

General studies

Arthos, John. "Ritual and Humor in the Writing of William Faulkner," *Accent*, IX (Autumn, 1948), 17-30. (*Two Decades of Criticism*, Hoffman and Vickery eds, pp. 101-18.)

Backman, Melvin. "Sickness and Primitivism: A Dominant Pattern in William Faulkner's Work," *Accent*, XIV (Winter, 1954), 61-73.

Baldwin, James. "Faulkner and Desegregation," *Partisan Review*, XXIII (Fall, 1956), 568-73.

Brumm, Ursula. "Wilderness and Civilization: A Note on William Faulkner," *Partisan Review*, XXII (Summer, 1955), 340-50. (*Three Decades*, pp. 125-34.)

Cowley, Malcolm. "Introduction," *The Portable Faulkner*. New York: Viking Press, 1946, pp. 1-24. (*Three Decades*, pp. 94-109.)

Fiedler, Leslie A. "William Faulkner: Highbrow's Lowbrow," *No, In Thunder!* Boston: Beacon Press, 1960, pp. 111-18.

Frohock, W. M. "William Faulkner: The Private Versus the Public Vision," *Southwest Review*, XXXIV (Summer, 1949), 281-94. Reprinted in *The Novel of Violence in America*. Dallas: Southern Methodist University Press, 1950, pp. 101-24.

Hoffman, Frederick J. "William Faulkner: Part One: The Growth of a Reputation; Part Two: The Nobel Prize and the Achievement of Status," *William Faulkner: Three Decades of Criticism*. East Lansing: Michigan State University Press, 1960, pp. 1-50.

*   In this bibliography, *Three Decades* or *Two Decades* indicates the article is reprinted in the collections of Hoffman and Vickery.

Hopper, Vincent F. "Faulkner's Paradise Lost," *Virginia Quarterly Review*, XXIII (Summer, 1947), 405-20.

Kazin, Alfred. "Faulkner: The Rhetoric and the Agony," *Virginia Quarterly Review*, XVIII (Summer, 1942), 389-402. Reprinted in *On Native Grounds*. New York: Reynal & Hitchcock, 1942, pp. 453-70.

———. "Faulkner in His Fury," *The Inmost Leaf*. New York: Harcourt Brace, 1955, pp. 257-73.

O'Brien, Francis Blazer. "Faulkner and Wright, Alias S. S. Van Dine," *The Mississippi Quarterly*, XIV (Spring, 1961), 101-7.

O'Donnell, George Marion. "Faulkner's Mythology," *Kenyon Review*, I (Summer, 1939), 285-99. (*Three Decades*, pp. 82-93.)

Rabi. "Faulkner and the Exiled Generation," *William Faulkner: Two Decades of Criticism*, pp. 118-38.

Schwartz, Delmore. "The Fiction of William Faulkner," *The Southern Review*, VII (Summer, 1941), 145-60.

Swiggart, Peter. "Time in Faulkner's Novels," *Modern Fiction Studies*, I (May, 1955), 25-9.

Tritschler, Donald. "The Unity of Faulkner's Shaping Vision," *Modern Fiction Studies*, V (Winter, 1959-1960), 337-43.

Warren, Robert Penn. "Cowley's Faulkner," *The New Republic*, CXV (August 12, 1946), 176-80; continued (August 26, 1946), 234-7. (*Three Decades*, pp. 109-24.)

Narrative techniques and style

Aiken, Conrad. "William Faulkner: The Novel as Form," *The Atlantic Monthly*, CLXIV (November, 1939), 650-54. (*Three Decades*, pp. 135-142.)

Beck, Warren. "William Faulkner's Style," *American Prefaces*, VI (Spring, 1941), 195-211. (*Three Decades*, pp. 142-56.)

Campbell, Harry M. "Structural Devices in the Works of Faulkner," *Perspective*, III (Autumn, 1950), 209-26.

Leaver, Florence. "Faulkner: The Word as Principle and Power," *South Atlantic Quarterly*, LVII (Autumn, 1958), 464-76. (*Three Decades*, pp. 199-209.)

Riedel, F. C. "Faulkner as Stylist," *South Altantic Quarterly*, LVI (Autumn, 1957), 462-79.

Scott, Arthur L. "The Faulknerian Sentence," *Prairie Schooner*, XXVII (Spring, 1953), 91-8.

Slatoff, Walter J. "The Edge of Order: The Pattern of Faulkner's Rhetoric," *Twentieth Century Literature*, III (October, 1957), 107-27. (*Three Decades*, pp. 173-98.)

Zink, Karl E. "William Faulkner: Form as Experience," *South Atlantic Quarterly*, LIII (July, 1954), 384-403.

Studies of individual novels

Absalom, Absalom!

Brooks, Cleanth. "*Absalom, Absalom!*: The Definition of Innocence," *The Sewanee Review*, LIX (Autumn, 1951), 543-58.

Hoffman, A. C. "Point of View in *Absalom, Absalom!*" *University of Kansas City Review*, XIX (Summer, 1953), 233-9.

Lind, Ilse Dusoir. "The Design and Meaning of *Absalom, Absalom!*" *PMLA*, LXX (December, 1955), 887-912.

Poirer, William R. " 'Strange Gods' in Jefferson, Mississippi: Analysis of *Absalom, Absalom!*" (*Two Decades*, pp. 217-43).

Scott, Arthur L. "The Myriad Perspectives of *Absalom, Absalom!*" *American Quarterly*, VI (Fall, 1954), 210-20.

Seiden, Melvin. "Faulkner's Ambiguous Negro," *Massachusetts Review*, IV (Summer, 1963), 675-90.

Sullivan, Walter. "The Tragic Design of *Absalom, Absalom!*" *South Atlantic Quarterly*, L (October, 1951), 552-66.

Zoellner, Robert H. "Faulkner's Prose Style in *Absalom, Absalom!*" *American Literature*, XXX (January, 1959), 486-502.

As I Lay Dying

Allen, Charles A. "William Faulkner: Comedy and the Purpose of Humor," *Arizona Quarterly*, XVI (Spring, 1960), 59-69.

Goellner, Jack. "A Closer Look at 'As I Lay Dying,' " *Perspective*, VII (Spring, 1954), 42-54.

Handy, William J. "*As I Lay Dying*: Faulkner's Inner Reporter," *The Kenyon Review*, XXI (Summer, 1959), 437-51.

Roberts, J. L. "The Individual and the Family: Faulkner's *As I Lay Dying*," *Arizona Quarterly*, XVI (Spring, 1960), 26-38.

Rossky, William. "*As I Lay Dying*: The Insane World." *Texas Studies in Literature and Language*, IV (Spring, 1962), 87-97.

A Fable

Hafley, James. "Faulkner's 'Fable': Dream and Tranfiguration," *Accent*, XVI (Winter, 1956), 3-14.

Lytle, Andrew Nelson. "The Son of Man: He Will Prevail," *The Sewanee Review*, LXII (Winter, 1955), 114-37.

Pritchett, V. S. "Time Frozen," *Partisan Review*, XXI (September-October, 1954), 557-61.

Rice, Philip Blair. "Faulkner's Crucifixion," *Kenyon Review*, XVI (Autumn, 1954), 661-70. (*Three Decades*, pp. 373-81.)

Straumann, Heinrich, "An American Interpretation of Existence: Faulkner's *A Fable*," *Anglia*, LXXIII (Heft 4, 1956), 484-515. (*Three Decades*, pp. 349-72.)

Go Down, Moses

Sultan, Stanley. "Call Me Ishmael: The Hagiography of Isaac McCaslin," *Texas Studies in Literature and Language*, III (Spring, 1961), 50-66.

Taylor, Walter F. Jr. "Let My People Go: The White Man's Heritage in *Go Down, Moses*," *South Atlantic Quarterly*, LVIII (Winter, 1959), 20-32.

Tick, Stanley. "The Unity of *Go Down, Moses*," *Twentieth Century Literature*, VIII (July, 1962), 67-73.

Studies of "The Bear"

Backman, Melvin. "The Wilderness and the Negro in Faulkner's 'The Bear,' "
   PMLA, LXXVI (December, 1961), 595-600.
LaBudde, Kenneth. "Cultural Primitivism in William Faulkner's 'The Bear,' "
   American Quarterly, II (Winter, 1950), 322-8.
Lewis, R. W. B. "The Hero in the New World: William Faulkner's 'The
   Bear,' " *Kenyon Review*, XIII (Autumn, 1951), 641-60.
Moses, W. R. "Where History Crosses Myth: Another Reading of 'The
   Bear,' " *Accent*, XIII (Winter, 1953), 21-33.
O'Connor, William Van. "The Wilderness Theme in Faulkner's 'The Bear,' "
   Accent, XIII (Winter, 1953), 12-20. (*Three Decades*, pp. 322-30.)
Perluck, Herbert A. "The Heart's Driving Complexity: An Unromantic Read-
   ing of Faulkner's 'The Bear,' " *Accent*, XX (Winter, 1960), 23-46.

The Hamlet (See Snopes Trilogy)

Intruder in the Dust

Hardwick, Elizabeth. "Faulkner and the South Today," *Partisan Review*, XV
   (October, 1948), 1130-35. (*Two Decades*, pp. 244-50.)
Lytle, Andrew. "Regeneration for the Man," *The Sewanee Review*, LVII
   (Winter, 1949), 120-7. (*Two Decades*, pp. 251-9.)

Light in August

Benson, Carl. "Thematic Design in *Light in August*," *South Atlantic Quar-
   terly*, LIII (October, 1954), 540-55.
Chase, Richard. "The Stone and the Crucifixion: Faulkner's *Light in August*,"
   Kenyon Review, X (Autumn, 1948), 539-51. (*Two Decades*, pp. 205-17.)
Cottrell, Beekman W. "Christian Symbols in 'Light in August,' " *Modern
   Fiction Studies*, II (Winter, 1956-1957), 207-13.
Holman, C. Hugh. "The Unity of Faulkner's *Light in August*," PMLA,
   LXXIII (March, 1958), 155-66.
Kazin, Alfred. "The Stillness of 'Light in August,' " *Partisan Review*, XXIV
   (Fall, 1957), 519-38. (*Three Decades*, pp. 247-65.)
Lind, Ilse Dusoir. "The Calvinistic Burden of *Light in August*," *The New
   England Quarterly*, XXX (September, 1957), 307-29.
Longley, John L. Jr. "Joe Christmas: the Hero in the Modern World," *Vir-
   ginia Quarterly Review*, XXXIII (Spring, 1957), 233-49. (*Three Decades*,
   pp. 265-78.)
O'Connor, William Van. "Protestantism in Yoknapatawpha County," *Hop-
   kins Review*, V (Spring, 1952), 26-42.
Pearson, Norman Holmes. "Lena Grove," *Shenandoah*, III (Spring, 1952),
   3-7.

Pylon

Monteiro, George. "Bankruptcy in Time: A Reading of William Faulkner's
   'Pylon,' " *Twentieth Century Literature*, IV (April-July, 1958), 9-20.
Torchiana, Donald T. "Faulkner's 'Pylon' and the Structure of Modernity,"
   Modern Fiction Studies, III (Winter, 1957-1958), 291-308.

Sanctuary

Beck, Warren. "Faulkner: A Preface and a Letter," *Yale Review*, LII (October, 1962), 157-60.

Brooks, Cleanth. "Faulkner's Vision of Good and Evil," *The Massachusetts Review* (Summer, 1962), 692-712. A revised version: "Faulkner's Sanctuary: The Discovery of Evil," *The Sewanee Review*, LXXI (Winter, 1963), 1-24.

Brown, James. "Shaping the world of *Sanctuary*," *University of Kansas City Review*, XXV (Winter, 1958), 137-42.

Cole, Douglas. "Faulkner's *Sanctuary*: Retreat from Responsibility," *Western Humanities Review*, XIV (Summer, 1960), 291-8.

Malraux, André. "A Preface for Faulkner's *Sanctuary*," *Yale French Studies*, No. 10 (Fall, 1962), 92-4.

Massey, Linton. "Notes on the Unrevised Galleys of Faulkner's *Sanctuary*," *Studies in Bibliography*, VIII (1956), 195-208.

Sartoris

Sartre, Jean-Paul. "*Sartoris*," *Literary and Philosophical Essays*. London: Rider, 1955, pp. 73-8.

Scholes, Robert. "Myth and Manners in *Sartoris*," *Georgia Review*, XVI (Summer, 1962), 195-201.

Snopes Trilogy

Farmer, Norman Jr. "The Love Theme: A Principal Source of Thematic Unity in Faulkner's Snopes Trilogy," *Twentieth Century Literature*, VIII (October, 1962-January, 1963), 111-23.

Kerr, Elizabeth M. "Snopes," *Wisconsin Studies in Contemporary Literature*, I (Spring-Summer, 1960), 66-84.

Leibowitz, Herbert A. "The Snopes Dilemma and the South," *University of Kansas City Review*, XXVIII (Summer, 1962), 273-84.

Levine, Paul. "Love and Money in the Snopes Trilogy," *College English*, XXIII (December, 1961), 196-203.

The Hamlet

Greet, T. Y. "The Theme and Structure of Faulkner's *The Hamlet*," *PMLA*, LXXII (September, 1957), 775-90. (*Three Decades*, pp. 330-47.)

Hopkins, Viola. "William Faulkner's *The Hamlet*: A Study in Meaning and Form," *Accent*, XV (Spring, 1955), 125-44.

Leaver, Florence. "The Structure of *The Hamlet*," *Twentieth Century Literature*, I (July, 1955), 77-84.

Warren, Robert Penn. "The Snopes World," *Kenyon Review*, III (Spring, 1947), 253-7.

The Town

Lytle, Andrew. "*The Town*: Helen's Last Stand," *The Sewanee Review*, LXV (Summer, 1957), 475-84.

Marcus, Steven, "Snopes Revisited," *Partisan Review*, XXIV (Summer, 1957), 432-41. (*Three Decades*, pp. 382-91.)

The Mansion

Beck, Warren. "Faulkner in the Mansion," *Virginia Quarterly Review*, XXXVI (Spring, 1960), 272-92.
Greene, Theodore M. "The Philosophy of Life Implicit in Faulkner's *The Mansion*," *Texas Studies in Literature and Language*, II (Winter, 1961), 401-18.
West, Anthony. "A Dying Fall," *The New Yorker*, XXXV (December 5, 1959), 236-43.

The Sound and the Fury

Adams, Robert M. "Poetry in the Novel: or, Faulkner Esemplastic," *Virginia Quarterly Review*, XXIX (Summer, 1953), 419-34.
Backman, Melvin. "Faulkner's Sick Heroes: Bayard Sartoris and Quentin Compson," *Modern Fiction Studies*, II (Autumn, 1956), 95-108.
Bowling, Lawrence Edward. "Faulkner: Technique of *The Sound and the Fury*," *Kenyon Review*, X (Autumn, 1948), 552-66. (*Two Decades*, pp. 165-79.)
———. "Faulkner and the Theme of Innocence," *Kenyon Review*, XX (Summer, 1958), 466-87.
Brooks, Cleanth. "Primitivism in *The Sound of the Fury*," *English Institute Essays 1952*, Alan S. Downer, ed. New York: Columbia University Press, 1954, pp. 5-28.
Collins, Carvel. "A Conscious Literary Use of Freud?" *Literature and Psychology*, III (June, 1953), 2-3.
———. "The Interior Monologues of *The Sound and the Fury*," *English Institute Essays 1952*, Alan S. Downer, ed. New York: Columbia University Press, 1954, pp. 29-56.
Cross, Barbara. "*The Sound and the Fury*: The Pattern of Sacrifice," *Arizona Quarterly*, XVI (Spring, 1960), 5-16.
Lowrey, Perrin. "Concepts of Time in *The Sound and the Fury*," *English Institute Essays 1952*, Alan S. Downer, ed. New York: Columbia University Press, 1954, pp. 57-82.
Sartre, Jean-Paul. "Time in Faulkners *The Sound and the Fury*," *Two Decades*, pp. 180-8; and *Three Decades*, pp. 225-32.
Stewart, George R., and Backus, Joseph M. "Each in its Ordered Place: Structure and Narrative in 'Benjy's Section' of *The Sound and the Fury*," *American Literature*, XXIX (January, 1958), 440-56.

The Wild Palms

Backman, Melvin. "Faulkner's 'The Wild Palms,'" *University of Kansas City Review*, XXVIII (Spring, 1962), 199-204.
Moldenhauer, Joseph J. "Unity of Theme and Structure in *The Wild Palms*," *Three Decades*, pp. 305-22.
Moses, W. R. "The Unity of *The Wild Palms*," *Modern Fiction Studies*, II (Autumn, 1956), 125-31.

————. "Water, Water Everywhere: 'Old Man' and 'A Farewell to Arms,' "
    Modern Fiction Studies, V (Summer, 1959), 172-4.
O'Connor, William Van. "Faulkner's One-Sided 'Dialogue' with Hemingway,"
    College English, XXIV (December, 1962), 208-15.
Richardson, H. Edward. "The 'Hemingwaves' in Faulkner's 'Wild Palms,' "
    Modern Fiction Studies, IV (Winter, 1958-1959), 357-60.

Index